THE CLASSICS OF WESTERN SPIRITUALITY

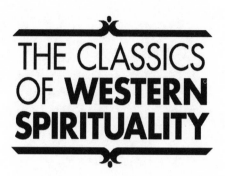

THE CLASSICS OF WESTERN SPIRITUALITY
A Library of the Great Spiritual Masters

Knowledge of God in Classical Sufism

FOUNDATIONS OF ISLAMIC MYSTICAL THEOLOGY

TRANSLATED AND INTRODUCED BY
JOHN RENARD

PREFACE BY
AHMET T. KARAMUSTAFA

PAULIST PRESS
NEW YORK • MAHWAH, NJ

Cover art: Detail courtesy of the Saint Louis Art Museum (108:29), gift of James F. Ballard. The niche of this Turkish prayer rug alludes to the Qur'ān's Verse of Light (24:35) and therefore to a central Sufi metaphor for the experiential knowledge of God.

Book design by Lynn Else
Cover and caseside design by A. Michael Velthaus

Library of Congress Cataloging-in-Publication Data

Knowledge of God in classical Sufism : foundations of Islamic mystical theology / translated and introduced by John Renard ; preface by Ahmet T. Karamustafa.
p. cm.
Includes bibliographical references and indexes.
ISBN 0-8091-4030-6 (paper); 0-8091-0536-5 (cloth)
1. God (Islam)—Worship and love. 2. Sufism—Doctrines. I. Renard, John, 1944-

BP189.65.L68K56 2004
297.4′1—dc22

2003021982

Published by Paulist Press
997 Macarthur Boulevard
Mahwah, New Jersey 07430

www.paulistpress.com

Printed and bound in the United States of America

Contents

In memory of Annemarie Schimmel (1922–2003),

Mentor and Friend to so many,

who exemplified the insight of the poet Sanā'ī:

Any knowledge that does not help you transcend

yourself is just ignorance in disguise.

Translator of This Volume

JOHN RENARD received a PhD in Islamic Studies from the Department of Near Eastern Languages and Civilizations at Harvard University in 1978. He has taught in the Department of Theological Studies at Saint Louis University since then. Among his publications are a dozen books in Islamic Studies and Comparative Religion. They include these Paulist books: *Ibn ʿAbbād of Ronda—Letters on the Ṣūfī Path* (also in this series); volumes on Islam, Buddhism, Hinduism, and Daoism, and Confucianism and Shinto in the 101 Questions series; and *Understanding the Islamic Experience*. He is currently writing *A Historical Dictionary of Sufism* for Scarecrow Press and beginning work on a thematic overview of Islamic Hagiography for the University of California Press.

Author of the Preface

AHMET T. KARAMUSTAFA (PhD, McGill University, 1987) is associate professor of History and Religious Studies at Washington University in St. Louis, where he also directs the Religious Studies Program. He is the author of *God's Unruly Friends* (Salt Lake City: University of Utah Press, 1994), a monograph on ascetic movements in medieval Islamic mysticism, and *Vahidi's Menakib-i Hvoca-i Cihan ve Netice-i Can* (929/1522): *Critical Edition and Analysis* (Cambridge, Mass.: The Department of Near Eastern Languages and Civilizations, Harvard University, 1993), a study of a sixteenth-century mystical text in Ottoman Turkish. He is also the assistant editor as well as the author of several articles in *Cartography in the Traditional Islamic and South Asian Societies* (Chicago: The University of Chicago Press, 1992). Professor Karamustafa's main area of research is premodern Islamic thought; he is currently working on two book projects, one on *Islamic Perspectives on Religion* and the other a historical survey of Sufism (under contract with Edinburgh University Press). At Washington University, Professor Karamustafa teaches courses on all aspects of Islam, Islamic history, as well as general courses in Religious Studies.

Preface

John Renard's *Knowledge of God in Classical Sufism* is a treasure chest that contains the most precious jewels of Islamic spiritual wisdom. In an earlier volume in the Classics of Western Spirituality series titled *Early Islamic Mysticism,* Michael Sells effortlessly opened numerous windows to the stunning and bewildering vistas of the landscape of spirituality spun by early Sufi masters. In the present volume, Renard takes up the opportunity to explore this landscape further by crafting an exquisite anthology, where he guides readers of the Classics of Western Spirituality series on a fascinating tour of a lush garden that is located at the very center of the spiritual terrain of classical Islamic mysticism. This is the garden of mystical knowledge of God, the garden of *ma'rifa.*

Ma'rifa, translated by Renard alternatively as "experiential, infused, intimate, or mystical knowledge," is arguably *the* quintessential Sufi concept. The term *ma'rifa* does not appear in the Qur'ān; nor does it figure prominently in the prophetic reports known as Ḥadīth. In both of these basic sources of Islam, the word *'ilm* is used for all knowledge, with no distinction made between different kinds of knowing. However, already within the second and third centuries of Islamic history specific disciplines of intellectual inquiry began to take shape, and the term *'ilm,* though it never lost its holistic sense altogether, gradually came to mean primarily "discursive, received, or acquired" knowledge of the type cultivated within the new disciplines of Qur'ān and Ḥadīth studies as well as theological, legal, and philosophical inquiry. In the meantime, spiritually inclined Muslims started to carve out an alternative approach to the question of knowledge, one that foregrounded the experiential and essentially personal, even private, dimensions of all knowing. They found validation of this approach in select Qur'ānic verses, such as (and the speaker is God), "I created the jinn and humankind just so that they might worship Me" (51:56) where, following the early Qur'ān commentator Ibn 'Abbās, they understood the words "worship Me" *(yaʿbudūni)* to mean "know Me" *(yaʿrifūni)*. A special category of Ḥadīth known as "Sacred Ḥadīth" was also pressed to service, so that God was reported to have said, "I was a hidden treasure and I desired to be known, so I created the world," and "Whoever knows himself knows his Lord." Thus characterized as nothing less than the ultimate purpose of creation, this special kind of knowledge was dubbed *maʿrifa,* perhaps for the first time by Dhu'n-Nun of Egypt (d. 860), in contradistinction to *ʿilm,* which had come to acquire undesirable connotations of intellectualism.

In a very real sense, the subsequent history of Islamic mysticism can be said to be the history of *maʿrifa*. If the central occupation of the mystic was the effort to know God experientially, then all other human activity was to be subordinated to this central goal. More properly, all specifically Sufi concepts and doctrines (e.g., the spiritual path, the primordial covenant with God, Muhammadan reality, and the hierarchy of the friends of God) as well as distinctively Sufi practices (e.g., the invocation known as *dhikr*, the forty-day seclusion, keeping the company of the initiated, and contemplation of the Divine in His creation) can be seen as so many different manifestations of the overarching attempt to attain *maʿrifa*. The mystic, in short, was the seeker of experiential knowledge of God, the *ʿārif.*

The astonishingly single-minded concentration of Sufis on the concept of *maʿrifa* and their unceasing attempts to attain such intimate knowledge of God insured that Islam evolved as a tradition with exceptionally strong spiritual dimensions. This is what prompted Carl Ernst to observe, in his preface to Michael Sells's *Early Islamic Mysticism*, "Islamic mysticism is one of the most extensive traditions of spirituality in the history of religions." The abundance, as well as the spiritual depth, of Sufi texts available in different Islamic languages is indeed staggering. Yet, the ultimate measure of the significance of Sufism lies perhaps not in its pervasiveness and sheer magnitude but in the dynamic and dialectical relationship it has with the legalistic and ethical dimensions of Islam. Throughout the history of Islam, Sufi insistence on "experiencing" God served as a powerful counterbalance on the tendency to understand worship of God primarily in a legalistic sense to mean the attempt to live in accordance with God's will. That will, commonly known as the *sharīʿa,* was enshrined in the Qur'ān and the example of the Prophet Muhammad, and many learned Muslims spent their lives distilling God's will from the divine sources of Islam into a normative framework for the conduct of human life on Earth. The result was a majestic and spacious mansion of moral, legal, and theological precepts, advice, and at times sheer speculation that dazzled the eyes. This mansion of many rooms, the culminating achievement of the ethical/legalistic dimension of Islam, was, however, built almost solely out of *ʿilm,* of discursive, acquired, received knowledge, and it carried within itself the very real pitfalls of unbridled intellectualism, scholarly arrogance, and scholastic desiccation. The only antidote was *maʿrifa.* The normative needed to be leavened by the spiritual to achieve full rigor and vitality and to gain true meaning, just as the spiritual could only grow on the island of security provided by the normative. The mansion of the *sharīʿa* achieved its full beauty only when adorned by the surrounding gardens of spiritual delight and nourished by the deep wellsprings of spiritual wisdom dug out by mystics.

Maʿrifa, therefore, is a key Islamic concept. It is the core ingredient of Islamic spirituality and the flip side of normative Islam. When, after the initial formative phase of pioneering mystical speculation during the ninth and tenth centuries, some literary minded Sufis began to take stock and reflect on the achievements of their forebears in a series of comprehensive, encyclopedic manuals of mystical knowledge and lore, they were keenly cognizant of the centrality of the concept of *maʿrifa* and included whole sections on it in their surveys. These works, starting with Sarrāj's *Book of Flashes,* Kalābādhī's *Explorations of Sufi Teachings,* and Makkī's *Sustenance of Hearts,* all composed during the tenth century, to Hujwīrī's *Revelation of the Veiled* and Qushayrī's masterful summation simply known as the *Treatise* of the following century, set the pattern for all later manuals. At the end of the eleventh century, Ghazālī based the mystical sections of his sprawling *Revitalization of the Religious Disciplines* in large part on Makkī's *Sustenance,* and more than a century later, Suhrawardī harnessed the teachings found in the early manuals to the cause of spiritual training in his *Benefits of Intimate Knowledge,* which is sometimes seen as the last ring in this long chain of Sufi manuals in Arabic (of the works listed only Hujwīrī's *Revelation of the Veiled* is in Persian).

It is regrettable that of these seminal surveys of Islamic mysticism, only the works of Hujwīrī and Kalābādhī as well as large portions of Qushayrī's treatise are available in usable English translation. The significance of the present volume comes into full view when Renard's project is seen in this light. This anthology is the first of its kind in English that brings together the writings of nine eminent Sufi theorists on the concept of experiential knowledge of God. Fully five of these selections are translated into English here for the first time, while all of the other four have been thoroughly "refreshed" for inclusion in this volume. Practically all of the texts excerpted are difficult and dense in their original Arabic and Persian (the impenetrable style of Makkī in particular is legendary), and they present unique challenges to the modern translator. In a remarkable feat of adaptation, however, John Renard meets these challenges with erudition, dexterity, and verve, producing extremely smooth and fresh translations that capture the meaning of the original texts without making any major sacrifices along the way. The result is a rich compilation of Sufi theoretical writings on the most fundamental concept of Islamic mysticism that is now readily available to a broad readership. The publication of this volume marks a major advance in the scholarship on Islamic mysticism in the English language, and John Renard and Paulist Press are to be congratulated for this accomplishment.

Ahmet T. Karamustafa

Foreword

Islam and the Classics of Western Spirituality

Over the past quarter of a century, the Paulist Press Classics of Western Spirituality series has published nine volumes representing selections from over a dozen important sources of the Islamic mystical tradition, commonly called Sufism. They span nearly eight centuries and provide an overview of many important themes and literary forms through which Muslim authors have articulated their convictions about the interior life. The present volume is meant to complement Michael Sells's *Early Islamic Mysticism* (1996), which describes the origins and growth of the mystical tradition, beginning with the Qur'ān and Ḥadīth and proceeding through foundational issues in a number of classical and early medieval texts. Both volumes are mini-anthologies whose texts were selected from across several centuries for the purpose of making available primary sources on classic themes in Islamic spirituality. In addition to presenting some material that overlaps chronologically with *Early Islamic Mysticism*, the present volume traces a central theme in Islamic mystical theology from several late classical and early medieval Sufi manuals into the twelfth and early thirteenth centuries, including excerpts from several Persian texts.

The other Islamic volumes in the series offer complete texts from various major authors. Taken together, they cover a wide expanse of space and time and are packed with primary source samples of the most important literary genres produced by Sufi authors in Arabic and Persian. A tiny gem of personal prayer by the eleventh century Khwāja ʿAbd Allāh Anṣārī (d. 1089) called *Intimate Conversations* (W. Thackston, 1978, included in the first Islamic volume published in the series, along with *The Book of Wisdom* mentioned below) is a fine sample of the heartfelt expression of a still-popular Persian-writing Sufi. Four volumes are dedicated to individual major thirteenth-century

Sufis. Poems from the work of Cairene Ibn al-Fāriḍ (d. 1235), one of the greatest mystical poets of the Arabic tongue, are collected in *ʿUmar Ibn al-Fāriḍ: Sufi Verse, Saintly Life* (Th. Emil Homerin, 2001). An unusual work of mystical prophetology, *The Bezels of Wisdom* (R. W. J. Austin, 1980) of the Spanish-born Ibn al-ʿArabī (d. 1240) gives readers a useful introduction to the thought of one of Islam's most prolific and influential mystical theologians. Fakhr ad-Dīn ʿIrāqī's (d. 1289) *Divine Flashes* (W. Chittick and P. Wilson, 1982) put the reader in contact with one of Islam's most eloquent poets of mystical love.

Ibn ʿAṭā' Allāh of Alexandria (d. 1309) belonged to one of North Africa's largest and most important Sufi confraternities, the Shādhilī Order. His aphoristic *Book of Wisdom* (V. Danner, 1978) became a favorite of Sufis all across the western Mediterranean during the fourteenth century and many centuries thereafter. A fellow Shādhilī, the Iberian-born Ibn ʿAbbād of Ronda (d. 1390), wrote a major commentary on the *Book of Wisdom* but is perhaps best known for his letters of spiritual direction. The Classics volume *Letters on the Sufi Path* (J. Renard, 1986) translates a collection of sixteen of those letters and gives insight into the ordinary spiritual concerns of Ibn ʿAbbād and his Moroccan and Iberian correspondents. From the same time period, but halfway around the world, *The Hundred Letters* (P. Jackson, 1980) of Sharāf ad-Dīn Manērī (d. 1381) represents part of the large output of an Indian Sufi master of the Firdawsī Order. Manērī wrote in Persian, as did his contemporary from another Order, Niẓām ad-Dīn Awliyā' (d. 1325). The latter's Persian-language *Morals for the Heart* (B. Lawrence, 1992) represents still another distinct literary genre made popular by Sufi authors, the "conversational utterances" attributed to a great teacher, largely in prose but peppered with poetic verse, as edited and published later by his dedicated disciples.

Choice of Theme and Texts in the Present Volume

There has been a great deal published in recent years on Islamic spirituality, including newly available primary sources in translation.

Much of that material has focused on Sufi psychology, epistolography, hagiography, and the "historiography" of the tradition. But relatively few offerings have focused on a theme of fundamental importance to a broader systematic appreciation of the theoretical underpinnings of Islamic mystical theology. The present volume grew out of a twofold desire: to make accessible selections of major works by highly influential authors still relatively little known outside Islamic Studies circles; and to assemble a substantial selection of texts on a theme that represents a foundational development in Islamic theology, namely, the concept of experiential knowledge and its relationship to other modes of knowing. It has become customary to speak of Islamic theology as restricted to a relatively narrow vein of the greater tradition, a vein known as *kalām,* speculative or systematic theology. But the Sufi tradition of "manuals" or compendia represents an equally important, even if not always so clearly "systematic," lode of credibly theological significance. Hence the subtitle of this volume.

Of the nine principal text selections translated here, four include excerpts from larger works previously translated into English either in their entirety (Kalābādhī, Hujwīrī, and Ibn al-ʿArīf) or in large part (Qushayrī). Kalābādhī's *Kitāb at-taʿarruf* has long been well-represented in A. J. Arberry's venerable translation (1935), but the sections on knowledge needed a refresher to demonstrate more crisply Kalābādhī's contribution to the theme. R. A. Nicholson's equally venerable rendering of Hujwīrī's Persian *Kashf al-maḥjūb* (1911) required a new look for the same reason, but also because Nicholson was often quite selective in his translation, at least of the explicitly epistemological sections. Barbara von Schlegell's fine rendering of sections on several dozen central Sufi concepts from Qushayrī's *Risāla* (1990) is quite useful and available, but I decided for the sake of completeness to include a version of the brief section on *maʿrifa*. Ibn al-ʿArīf's unusual treatise *Maḥāsin al-majālis* represents an interpretation of the theme by an author who lived and wrote at the western end of the Mediterranean. French (1933) and English (1980) translations have appeared, but, like the translations of the other three works, they hewed to the tradition of characterizing the core of Sufi epistemology as "gnosis." I have sought to recast that interpretation in these new translations of excerpts from all four of those works.

None of the other five selections presented here has appeared in full English translation. Key works by two tenth-century authors, Abū Naṣr as-Sarrāj and Abū Tālib al-Makkī, have been translated in their entirety only in German. That of Sarrāj has appeared in substantial English excerpts only in Sells, *Early Islamic Mysticism*, in this series, while Makkī's very large work has not yet been rendered into English at all, except perhaps in small, far-flung bits. Relevant selections are provided here from two works of ʿAbd Allāh Anṣārī. Sections on *ʿilm* and *maʿrifa* from his Persian *The Hundred Fields* are juxtaposed with those in his Arabic *Resting Places of the Wayfarers*. To the best of my knowledge, these are the first full English renderings of those excerpts. Various selections of Abū Ḥāmid al-Ghazālī's works with epistemological implications have merited English versions, including the first "book" of his masterpiece, *Revitalization of the Religious Disciplines,* on acquired or traditional knowledge (see bibliography). Perhaps Ghazālī's single most important focus on the core of Sufi epistemology, that of the twenty-first section of that same larger work, is called "The Analysis of the Marvels of the Heart." A partial German translation, now virtually inaccessible, is well over a half-century old in any case; and a long-promised reissuing of an equally old English rendering has not materialized. Selections of the work are readily available in Richard McCarthy's *Freedom and Fulfillment* (1981), and I have translated here only the sections not included in that volume.

Strictly speaking, Suhrawardī's work does not fit neatly in the category of "classical Sufism," but, since his was arguably the last of the great "manuals" of Sufi spirituality, there is sufficient warrant for including its first three chapters here. No worthwhile English rendering of this work has yet become available, but a complete German translation appeared twenty-five years ago.

Priorities and Practicalities

Several concerns have determined the shape and presentation of this volume. My first priority was to make as much of this marvelous material accessible as possible, given space limitations. Second, I wanted to make the material pedagogically useful, while presenting it in a way that would engage a broader readership as well. I have generally steered away from a purely literal translation in favor of readability. A third purpose was to make this volume useful as a companion to Michael Sells's 1996 Classics volume, *Early Islamic Mysticism*. These three concerns led to a series of practical decisions.

First, Sells opted to retain throughout an English rendering of the complete traditional "epithets" usually attached to the names of God, Muḥammad, the most important early Muslims, significant "Friends of God" of all generations, and finally, to all Muslims (as, for example, in the instance of someone deceased). I have retained those epithets in the first selection only, deleting them thereafter, partly in the interest of smoothing out the reading, and partly in the interest of space. Therefore, let the reader keep in mind throughout that traditional Islamic literary and conversational etiquette require that virtually whenever one mentions the name of God, it is followed by "exalted and glorified," "most high," "praised be He," or "may His majesty be magnified." After the name of Muḥammad, the words "God's blessing and peace upon him" typically follow; other prophets' names usually have "upon whom be peace" attached. The names of important Muslim leaders merit such devout wishes as "God be pleased with..." while ʿAlī often merits uniquely "May God ennoble his person (literally, countenance)." The most common phrase for all deceased Muslims is "God be compassionate to..."

I have retained full chains of transmitters *(isnād)*—lists of the names of individuals credited with passing along Ḥadīths (So-and-so told such-and-such a person that he heard so-and-so say that the Prophet said...)—in the text of the first selection only (Sarrāj). My purpose was to provide the reader one example of text that retains the full range of formalities a reader would encounter in the original language. Thereafter, I have generally put into endnotes those chains of transmitters that include two or more names, leaving that historical information readily available, while attempting to leave the flow of the text unimpeded by data not essential to its immediate meaning.

I have included both the traditional Islamic, or Hijrī, dates and the more familiar "Western" solar dates, for example, 1/622, when providing such information as death dates.

I have deleted the initial Arabic definite article (al-) from single-word names, such as Ḥallāj, Junayd, but retained the article when the individual's second name is included, as in Ḥasan al-Baṣrī.

Philological and text-critical notes I have slighted (for reasons of space) in favor of historical data on as many individuals mentioned in the texts as possible. My hope is that adding this kind of information will facilitate the reader's appreciation of historical contexts. In the historical notes I have ordinarily not listed sources for the identifications; the bibliography lists all the sources on which I have relied for such information. I have also often dispensed with parentheses around English words implied in the original languages. Similarly, I have opted in general to minimize inclusion of Arabic or Persian equivalents in parentheses within the text.

Attempts at a balanced approached to gender-inclusive language in texts like these are difficult at best, and I confess that I was unable to provide a satisfactory solution. I have left all pronominal references to God/Allāh in the masculine, but, to set them apart as out of the ordinary, I have made them upper case. And I ask that the reader recognize that the use of the masculine pronoun to mean both male and female best reflects the original writings, although it conflicts with current inclusive-language practices. Except where the original language refers explicitly to males, of course, it was not my intent, nor the intent of the original writers, to use it in anything but an inclusive sense.

Parentheses ( ) serve four purposes: Qur'ānic citations (Sūra #: verse #); my interpolated text, including occasional additional topic headings; full or alternate names of individuals; and dates of individuals on whom I found insufficient other information to warrant an endnote. *Italics* are used, as in Sells's *EIM*, to set off introductory and unincluded-text summary sections in the translations.

Brackets [ ] serve two purposes: bracketed translated text represents significant variant material; bracketed numbers indicate the page of the principal text from which I translated. I have generally deleted the term *Section (faṣl)*, which appears occasionally in the original languages, but have retained fuller headings given in the original text.

Following Sells's various specific implementations of the principle of "familiarization," I have on occasion left common Arabic terms in the text. That is particularly the case in respect to four epistemologically significant terms and cognates:

ʿilm, rendered variously as "discursive knowledge," "acquired knowledge," or "traditional knowledge";

maʿrifa, variously translated as "experiential knowledge," "infused knowledge," "intimate knowledge," or "mystical knowledge" (though the Persian use of this term is usually transliterated as *maʿrifat,* I have generally used the term without the final "t");

fiqh, a term now most widely recognized as "jurisprudence" or "positive law," but used in these texts more often to refer to a level of penetrating, insightful knowledge beyond the ordinary, here generally rendered "deeper understanding"; and its cognate *faqīh,* referring to the individual endowed with such understanding;

fahm, a term generally rendered here as "comprehension," or "profound comprehension." Since these texts often attempt to define and give scope to these technical concepts, I ask the reader's indulgence in this effort to "enrich the target language";

To minimize parenthetical insertion of key Arabic technical terms in the text, here are some additional common terms and the English equivalents I have used most often:

ahl, "people," I have generally translated "proponents" or "practitioners," except where it means "worthy."
ʿaql = intellect, rational thought, discursive knowledge
fatwā = legal opinion or advisory; *muftī* = one who issues a *fatwā*
fu'ād, qalb = heart
ḥāl, pl. *aḥwāl* = spiritual state
insān = person, individual
khāṭir, pl. *khawāṭir* = passing inclination, impulse
maqām, pl. *maqāmāt* = spiritual station
muḥāsaba = self-assessment, self-scrutiny
murāqaba = introspection
mukāshafa = disclosure
mushāhada = contemplation, experience
nafs = ego-self, ego-soul
ṣadr = center of one's being, which God "amplifies" or "expands" *(sharaḥa)*
sharīʿa = Revealed Law

sunna = prophetic example
umma = (global) community (of Muslims)
wajd = "being found," ecstasy, mystical experience
wara' = spiritual reticence

As for transliteration, I have employed the same conventions for diacritical marks used in Sells, except that I have included them throughout the book rather than on first appearance only.

Acknowledgments

First of all, this work owes a great deal to the meticulous scholarship and prodigious erudition of the German Jesuit Islamicist Richard Gramlich. His are still the only complete European language translations of the texts of Sarrāj, Qushayrī, Makkī, and Suhrawardī excerpted here. More important, Gramlich's text-critical annotation provides the virtual equivalent of critical editions of the major works of these four sources. I have often followed his suggestions concerning variant readings. In addition, Gramlich's commentary on the content of the works, along with his massively detailed indexes, provide a wealth of information unavailable elsewhere so concisely.

Next, I wish to thank a number of friends and colleagues who kindly read portions of various drafts and offered invaluable suggestions: Fatemeh Keshavarz and Nargis Virani, of Washington University in St. Louis; Hayrettin Yucesoy of Saint Louis University; Peter Heath, provost of the American University in Beirut; Aron Zysow, of the Harvard Islamic Law program; and Mashhad al-Allaf of St. Louis. I am particularly indebted to Kenneth Honerkamp, of the University of Georgia, for his detailed commentary on extensive portions of the text; to Michael Sells, of Haverford College, for careful reading of, and suggestions on, portions of each of the major Arabic texts; and to Ahmet Karamustafa, of Washington University, for graciously agreeing to write the Preface. I am grateful to series editor Bernard McGinn, of the University of Chicago, for deeming this project appropriate for the Classics series; and to Paulist editor Chris Bellitto for his responsiveness and support throughout the project, as well as to Lynn Else of Paulist Press, for her attentiveness to the added complexities of putting this text into print. My thanks also to Juliet Mousseau and Inta Ivanovska, of Saint Louis University, for their able research and editorial assistance at various stages of the project. I am indebted to Saint Louis University for supporting this work in the form of a Graduate School Summer Research Award, a Mellon Summer Stipend, and a SLU 2000 Faculty Research Leave. To my spouse, Mary Pat, I express my deepest gratitude for her patience, encouragement, and good humor across the long haul.

Finally, coming to terms with material of such antiquity and complexity is an often humbling experience, and I ask the reader's indulgence with the shortcomings of this attempt to make these marvelous texts more accessible.

Introduction

Between the tenth and thirteenth centuries a number of important Muslim authors penned substantial prose works, both in Arabic and Persian, that supply much of what we know about the evolution of Islamic mystical thought. Their compendia offer a vast array of information, from the anecdotal to the more theoretical. These manualists have addressed the problem of experiential knowledge from various points of view. The concept of *maʿrifa*, traditionally—and inadequately—translated as "gnosis," does imply privileged connection between certain human beings and the divine. But it also suggests much more than mere intellectual knowing. It means access to the divine presence, perhaps even an invasion or being overcome by the reality of God. It includes both the experiential dimension and knowing in a way that "gnosis" cannot quite convey. Aquinas's *cognitio experimentalis* more closely approximates the meaning of *maʿrifa* as the Sufis developed it.

As an entrée to understanding the distinction among the rational, discursive, acquired, or traditional knowledge expressed by the term *ʿilm*, and the experiential, infused, or mystical/apophatic modes of knowing expressed by the term *maʿrifa*, an anecdote attributed to the philosopher Ludwig Wittgenstein may be useful here. He remarked that one would find it surprising if an individual who knew the elevation of Mont Blanc were unable to articulate that knowledge verbally. It would, however, not be surprising if an individual who knew the sound of a clarinet were unable to put that knowledge into words.[1]

I have divided this introduction into two major sections. In the first, by way of background, I discuss the evolution of fundamental concepts of knowledge in relation to the faith tradition called Islam. That will supply the broader context within which to situate later developments in Sufi epistemology. After a brief historical survey of key terms for, and notions of, knowledge in early Islamic times as evidenced especially in the Qur'ān and Ḥadīth (the primary record of

Muḥammad's own words and deeds), I provide a summary of the various subdisciplines within the larger category of Islamic religious epistemology.

The second section addresses specifically the material translated here, discussing the structure, major themes, and significance of the manuals or compendia of Sufi spirituality that remain such an essential source of our understanding of the Islamic mystical tradition. In that section I discuss the major works from which I have selected the principal texts on knowledge. In addition, I summarize the relevant concerns of several other authors of similar works that a single volume like this cannot accommodate. Not all of those major figures have penned manuals of spirituality as such, but they nonetheless deserve mention because of their broad influence in the development and communication of Sufi modes of knowing. In the instance of several authors who wrote manual-like works but whose specific analyses of the relevant epistemological themes were less sustained or systematic, I have included short excerpts in translation within the Introduction. Finally, I very briefly allude to some major postclassical, postmedieval Sufi sources on our theme. If not for considerations of space, dozens of other influential figures would have had a place in a fuller survey.

Part One: Foundational Sources and the Islamic Religious Disciplines

Franz Rosenthal's *Knowledge Triumphant: The Concept of Knowledge in Medieval Islam* presents a comprehensive overview of many of the major elements necessary to establish the broader context of our topic. Here in brief follow the main outlines of the earliest developments in the pre-Islamic understanding of what and how human beings know, and what would become distinctively Islamic approaches to the issue, beginning with the Qur'ān and Ḥadīth and evolving into the formative religious disciplines.[2]

Early Conceptions of Knowledge: Pre-Islamic Poetry, Qur'ān, Ḥadīth

The most commonly used Arabic term for knowledge, *ʿilm*, seems to derive from a root from which also grow words for "marker, sign, indicator" (*ʿalam* and *ʿalāma*) and "world, universe" *(ʿālam).*[3] "Knowledge" in pre-Islamic times, as evidenced especially by the highly evolved poetry of the age known to Muslims as the *Jāhilīya*, may have been intimately bound up with the practical acumen needed to survive and find one's way in an often unforgiving physical environment. Knowing meant navigating, negotiating a landscape that to the untutored eye must have appeared bewilderingly undifferentiated. By contrast, the word now commonly translated "ignorance" *(jahl)* may have been associated with a root *(j-w-l)* that meant to wander aimlessly in circles, unable to discern the markers necessary to make for a hospitable destination. In addition, an early Arabic word for poetry *(shiʿr)* was related to a verbal root *(sh-ʿ-r)*, which meant "to know" in the more specialized sense of being able to express complex and subtle feelings and understandings.

Early Muslims called the time before Islam *al-Jāhilīya,* the age before genuine knowledge, because the new *ʿilm* that the Qur'ān brought rendered banal all ways of knowing previously considered important. According to the Qur'ān, when Muḥammad's critics wanted to damn the Prophet with faint praise, they dismissed him as a (mere) poet *(shāʿir)* (for example, 21:5, 52:30, 69:41). Still, the Qur'ān often uses verbs from the root *sh-ʿ-r,* meaning "to realize, be aware, perceive," usually referring to people's *failure* to grasp some fundamental truth such as mortality, final accountability, or their own self-destructive tendencies (see, for example, 2:9, 6:26, 7:95, 16:26). Terms derived from this root are virtually nonexistent in the epistemological vocabulary of the texts translated here.

The Qur'ān frequently juxtaposes God's *ʿilm* with humankind's lack thereof, often suggesting that "knowledge" means familiarity with events of sacred history, as in 3:65–66: "You People of the Book—why do you argue about Abraham when the Torah and Injīl were not sent down until after his time? Do you not understand? You are the ones who argued with each other (even) about things of which you possessed (some) *ʿilm.* Why do you argue about things of which you have no *ʿilm*? It is God who possesses *ʿilm* (of those things), while you do not." One of the most frequently used Qur'ānic names of God is *al-ʿālim,* the all-knowing. On the whole, the consistent implication of Muḥammad's preaching was that *ʿilm* was represented as an advanced form of knowing, one that did not come naturally to humankind and whose content was the substance of divine revelation. One who did not attain this knowledge during his or her earthly life would in any case do so, though too late, at the judgment: "(When all the signs of the end are evident)…then will the individual attain *ʿilm* as to the implications of his deeds" (81:[1–]14). The Qur'ān uses words based on the root *ʿ-l-m* with reference to some aspect of knowledge approximately 750 times, accounting for just under 1 percent of the scripture's seventy-eight thousand words and making this one of its most frequently expressed clusters of meaning. Surprisingly, perhaps, the root's frequency is somewhat greater than that of words associated with "faith, belief."[4]

Far less often used (fewer than seventy occurrences), but of equal significance for present purposes, are words from the root *ʿ-r-f,* including most prominently *maʿrifa.* As several Sufi authors point out, it is proper to characterize God as possessing, or being the source of, *ʿilm,* but one does not speak of God that way in relation to *maʿrifa.* In many instances this root has to do with "recognition," sometimes with a seemingly ordinary sense of identifying (as in 12:58, where Joseph recognizes his brothers). Most important, it is used when people recognize the truth of divine signs and revelation, as in the oft-cited "You will see their eyes overflow with tears as they listen to what is revealed to the Messenger, for they recognize *(ʿarafū)* the truth…" (5:86). Or, again, "Those to whom We have given the scripture recognize this *(yaʿrifūnahu)* (prophetic revelation) as intimately as they know *(yaʿrifūna)* their own sons" (6:20).

Two other terms of importance for the present study are those derived from the roots *f-q-h* (nineteen occurrences), and *ḥ-k-m* (just over two hundred). Verbs related to the root *f-q-h* typically refer to an "understanding" (or lack thereof) of the deeper significance of divine signs (for example, 4:78, 6:65, 98). The most common noun derived from that root, *fiqh,* long ago came to be identified with religious law or jurisprudence, but it does not occur in the Qur'ān. Sufi texts often use *fiqh* and its cognates not as a technical term referring to law as such, but in its more fundamental meaning of "penetrating, deeper understanding." Permutations of the root *ḥ-k-m* in the Qur'ān are generally associated with wise judgment in the "practical" implementation of what one knows. When our Sufi authors use related terms, such as "statutes," they often do so in reference to the objects of outward knowledge relating to religious law. Finally, a number of important passages pair the concept of faith with key terms for knowledge; for example, with words rooted in *ʿ-l-m* (e.g., 2:26, 30:56, 58:11) and *f-q-h* (6:98). As we will see, this identification of faith with knowledge became an important theme for several Sufi authors.

Virtually every major collection of Ḥadīth, sayings attributed to Muḥammad, includes a section dedicated to "knowledge" *(ʿilm)*.[5] The Muwaṭṭā' of Mālik Ibn Anas (c. 91/710–179/795) is perhaps the most notable exception, in that his solitary Ḥadīth (which in any case concerns the Sage Luqmān and not the Prophet Muḥammad) relating to knowledge is virtually lost in a "book of miscellaneous sayings" at the very end of his collection. Rosenthal suggests that in this early scholar's time, "*ʿilm* apparently had not achieved the state of a problem in traditionist religious thought and scholarly methodology."[6]

In some later collections of Ḥadīth, it appears that the provision of a section in which to place sayings on the subject was largely a formality, since several collectors seem to have come up with only a few relevant Ḥadīths. Such is the case, for example, with the Ṣaḥīḥ of Muslim (c. 202/817–261/875), including only a small handful of sayings. He locates the section tellingly just after the "Book of Predestination" *(qadr)*, thus underscoring that what God has in mind for the individual is far more important than what one attains by way of knowledge. Bukhārī (194/810–256/870) locates a much more substantial "Book of Knowledge" very close to the beginning, just after chapters on revelation and faith, thus, evidently, initiating a pattern evidenced in several of the major Sufi works presented in translation here.

The popular eleventh-century anthology of Ḥadīth called *Mishkāt al-maṣābīḥ* also locates its section on knowledge toward the front, immediately after the one on faith.[7] Whatever the scope and placement of chapters on knowledge, they include material with four common concerns frequently expressed in the Sufi manuals: a warning against speculation and disputation concerning the meaning of the sacred scripture; the importance—indeed, the religious duty—of seeking knowledge; the superiority of the individual who possesses genuine knowledge over the person who is devout but ignorant; and the danger of allowing genuine knowledge to be corrupted by entrusting it to those unworthy of it (that is, those who use knowledge only for worldly gain).

Evolution of the Islamic Religious Disciplines

Early in Islamic history, scholars specialized in several aspects of religious study that soon came to be referred to as "disciplines" or "sciences." These included, for example, the *ʿilms* of the Ḥadīth, of Qur'ānic exegesis *(tafsīr)*, of the grammatical erudition needed to support exegesis, and of religious jurisprudence (generally called *fiqh*). Not surprisingly, the discipline or *ʿilm* of Ḥadīth includes a great deal more than merely Ḥadīths about *ʿilm*. In addition to the Ḥadīth collections that organized their material thematically (as discussed above), a number of specialists opted for other organizational principles as well. A thematic approach (called *muṣannaf*, from a root that means "to categorize") gave priority to the content or the text *(matn)* of each Ḥadīth. Another approach, used especially in the earlier collections, gave priority to evaluating the integrity of the chains of transmission (*isnād*, "supports").

A collection that arranged Ḥadīths by grouping together those traced back to one of Muḥammad's Companions was called a *musnad*. Works of this type, however, were generally far less useful than the thematic works. Six of the latter, now accorded virtually universal authority, appeared during the ninth century. Very early on, an essential ingredient in the discipline of Ḥadīth study was the careful scrutiny of individuals mentioned in *isnād*, evaluating each one's veracity and credibility. This made it possible to judge more precisely the relative reliability of the Ḥadīth itself. Scholars then devised a spectrum of reliability and a set of technical terms with which they labeled every Ḥadīth, providing specialists in other religious disciplines with a convenient standard against which to decide how much weight to give to a particular saying as they elaborated specific issues that arose in the course of their exegetical or legal work. Several of our Sufi authors make specific and extended references to the discipline of Ḥadīth studies, Sarrāj and Makkī offering the most detailed descriptions.

Exegesis, like Ḥadīth studies, covers much more than merely Qur'ānic texts about knowledge. A sacred text about *ʿilm* will be instructive in describing the function of knowledge of the sacred text. A Qur'ānic verse that bears on both the bedrock principles of exegetical theory and the centrality of religious *ʿilm* is Qur'ān 3:7:

> It is He who has revealed the scripture to you (Muḥammad), containing verses of certain meaning. They are the "mother of the book," while others are susceptible to broader (or: metaphorical) interpretation. There are some whose perversity of heart causes them to pursue those verses that may be more broadly interpreted, in the desire to foment discord and eagerness to derive esoteric meanings from the text. None, however, is endowed with *ʿilm* of its esoteric interpretation *(ta'wīl)* but Allāh. While those firmly rooted in *ʿilm* say, "We put our faith in (the scripture), all of which is the work of our Lord." Only those who possess understanding *(ūlū 'l-albāb)* will master it.

This translation already implies important hermeneutical judgments. One of them involves a matter of punctuation that may appear, on the surface at least, quite minor. If in the verse that begins "None, however,..." one should change the period after Allāh to a comma, and then change "While..." to "and...," the sense of the passage would take a dramatic turn: "None, however, is endowed with *ʿilm* of its esoteric interpretation *(ta'wīl)* but Allāh and those firmly rooted in *ʿilm*. They say, 'We put our faith in (the scripture)....'" No longer are those scriptural texts whose ambiguity leaves their interpretation fraught with the potential danger of serious misunderstanding subject to God's judgment alone. Now the sacred text itself sanctions flexible exegesis, provided the interpreters are "those firmly rooted in *ʿilm*." Suddenly it is a question of determining who those people are and how one recognizes them as such. It is on questions such as this that the relationship of Sufi exegesis to the broader Muslim exegetical tradition hinged, and in those issues all of our authors were keenly interested. In this, as in many other texts, exegetes would naturally have recourse to Ḥadīths on the subject of knowledge, in search of extra-scriptural commentary with the weight of prophetic authority to support one or another slant in their interpretation of challenging texts.[8]

A more general connection of our theme with the science of exegesis is the early distinction between exegesis on the basis of traditional knowledge (*tafsīr bi 'l-ʿilm,* also known as *tafsīr bi 'l-ma'thūr,* that which is "attested by tradition)" and that based on individual judgment or opinion (*tafsīr bi 'r-ra'y,* or *bi 'l-hawā,* "on the basis of whim"). Some religious authorities, particularly during the second Islamic century (c. 720–820), opposed any form of exegesis on the grounds that all such interpretation suggested the inappropriate appeal to personal judgment. However, the majority of scholars gave their approval to exegesis based on *ʿilm,* by which the more conservative scholars meant interpretation based on the Qur'ān itself, the Ḥadīth, sayings attributed to the Companions and Followers, and Jewish and Christian sources. In other words, the most reliable interpretation is one that cites earlier authorities rather than venture a "new" reading.[9]

Religious law, including both the study of the principles of jurisprudence (*uṣūl* or "roots" of *fiqh*) and the elaboration of specific injunctions (*furūʿ,* "branches"), has been a critical Islamic discipline since the early Muslim generations. An issue with legal implications that elicited considerable attention from our Sufi authors was the one raised by a Ḥadīth (found only in Ibn Mājah[10] among the six authoritative collections) in which Muḥammad said that the "quest for *ʿilm* is a duty for all Muslims." Brief as the Ḥadīth is, legal scholars, as well as the Sufis whose works are excerpted here, have found a great deal in it that needs interpretation. Three obvious issues have to do with the scope of the term *ʿilm*; the legal weight of the word "duty" and its relationship to other religious obligations; and the significance of the phrase "for all Muslims." On the face of it, one might be inclined to assume that *ʿilm* in this Ḥadīth simply refers to the "traditional" knowledge that is the object of these three religious disciplines. However, that is not how everyone has interpreted the matter. Although the Sufi compendia rarely engaged directly in the kind of thinking that was the stock-in-trade of legal scholars, they did talk a great deal about religious duties and included numerous narratives whose protagonists are *muftīs* (scholars authorized to issue legal advisories or *fatwās*) and judges.

As is abundantly clear from the great handbooks of spirituality, these three religious disciplines (exegesis, Ḥadīth, and religious law), whose *ʿilm* constitutes a vast body of "traditional" knowledge, were very much the backdrop against which their authors took up the task of defining Sufism as a credible branch of Islamic learning, a valid and necessary religious discipline *(ʿilm)* in its own right. As Rosenthal observes, "Sufism attempted to add something of its own, some new twist as it were, to the generally accepted concept of *ʿilm*. It was therefore unable and unwilling to identify itself with it without reservation."[11]

Part Two: Experiential Knowledge of God in Classical and Medieval Sufi Texts

Several of the major Sufi theorists go to some lengths to distinguish between ordinary, traditional, discursive, acquired or "scientific" knowledge *(ʿilm)* and more intimate, infused, experiential or "mystical" knowing *(maʿrifa)*, explaining how the latter both presupposes the former and transcends it.[12] In terms of overall method, the larger treatises fall into two general groups. First, four of the sources, of which excerpts are presented here in translation (Sarrāj, Hujwīrī, Ghazālī, and Suhrawardī), establish as their first order of business that Sufi modes of knowing have a credible place in the larger context of religious knowledge. These same authors eventually move on to consider higher forms of knowledge specifically, developing *maʿrifa* as a distinctively mystical mode of knowing. Second, three of the major authors excerpted here (Kalābādhī, Makkī, and Qushayrī), as well as those who wrote less extensively on the topic (Anṣārī and Ibn al-ʿArīf), locate experiential knowledge within their treatments of spiritual development but do not make knowledge function as a structural basis for their overall approaches to the spiritual life. Here I introduce these authors and their principal works in more or less chronological order, inserting in several places brief summaries of how some other important authors have understood and developed epistemologically significant concepts. I have placed in bold type the names of authors selections of whose works are translated here.

Ninth Century: Dhū 'n-Nūn, Muḥāsibī, Kharrāz, Tirmidhī, Ḥallāj

Dhū 'n-Nūn al-Miṣrī

Thawbān ibn Ibrāhīm, better known as Dhū 'n-Nūn of Egypt (c. 180/796–245/860), is traditionally acknowledged as the first Sufi to make a significant distinction between *ʿilm* and *maʿrifa* with respect to their specific functions in the spiritual quest. He identified the individual endowed with *maʿrifa* as the person whose entire being has been taken over by the divine presence, as in the famous Sacred Ḥadīth of Supererogatory Devotions. According to that tradition, God says that when a servant loves God he or she does not cease to perform deeds of devotion, so that God loves that person to such a degree that God becomes the person's ears, eyes, tongue, and hand.[13]

Muḥāsibī

It was Abū ʿAbd Allāh al-Ḥārith al-Muḥāsibī (c. 165/781–243/857) who produced the earliest in-depth systematic analyses of the various permutations of knowledge in relation to the Sufi path. Muḥāsibī was born in the southern Iraqi city of Basra and spent much of his adult life in Baghdad, where he died. He became a specialist in religious law according to the Shafiʿi school. Like Dhū 'n-Nūn, Muḥāsibī got himself into trouble in connection with the mid-ninth-century debates over the Muʿtazilī doctrine of the createdness of the Qur'ān.[14] Ironically, however, Muḥāsibī ran afoul of the traditionists for daring to use the dialectical method of the Muʿtazila against them—a sort of guilt by association, perhaps—whereas Dhū 'n-Nūn had been imprisoned by the Muʿtazila themselves for denying the createdness of the Qur'ān. In his most influential work, *The Book on the Observance of the Rights of God (Kitāb ar-riʿāya li ḥuqūq Allāh),* Muḥāsibī organizes the steps in his method for rooting out all forms of ego-centeredness. Here, in this manual for the discernment of spirits, as well as in several of his other works, Muḥāsibī emphasizes the importance of a depth of genuine *maʿrifa,* which alone can establish the foundation for right action. He regards action based on *maʿrifa* as a blend of pure divine gift and the judicious application of rational understanding *(ʿaql).*[15]

In a treatise called *The Analysis of maʿrifa and the Giving of Advice (Sharḥ al-maʿrifa wa badhl an-naṣīḥa),* Muḥāsibī elaborates on the four fundamental types of knowledge: of God through contemplation; of the devil through spiritual discernment; of the ego-soul through self-scrutiny; and of God's action through examining the power underlying all that happens. Muḥāsibī took a slightly different tack in another work widely attributed to him, *The Book of Knowledge (Kitāb al-ʿilm).* There he argues that the three fundamental forms of knowledge have as their respective goals the outward understanding of things lawful and unlawful in this life; the inward understanding of matters pertaining to the next life; and a still higher level of awareness of God *(maʿrifa)* and His plans for all of creation. As will shortly become clear, a number of later authors developed the distinction between those who are knowledgeable about this world only and those who are endowed with knowledge of the next life. One can acquire Muḥāsibī's first two forms of knowledge both through acceptance of traditional learning handed down from reliable sources and through careful use of intelligent, rational reflection *(tafakkur),* without which one cannot be truly aware of the quality of one's deeds of service to God. For the third, however, one relies entirely on God and the kinds of intimate experience possible only through a personal relationship with God.

Muḥāsibī was inclined to believe that the potential for such knowledge is inherent in every person, but he cautioned that lack of clarity in the heart prevents most from advancing to that stage. Only those who are willing to undergo the discipline of polishing the mirror of the heart have hope of attaining *maʿrifa* as they await God's good pleasure in granting it. Ultimately it is the ethical implications of knowledge that are of the greatest concern to Muḥāsibī. Like Makkī and other later Sufi authors, Muḥāsibī emphasizes "useful" knowledge; unlike many of those who came after him, Muḥāsibī reserved a high place for the role of intellectual understanding in the acquisition and implementation of the lower levels of knowledge. He did, however, make a critical distinction between rational understanding *(ʿaql)* and *ʿilm,* on the grounds that what one knows rationally is not always convertible into moral action, and because (as other Sufi authors teach) genuine understanding demands a certain kind of attentiveness. He also distinguishes between faith and *maʿrifa.* What is most important for present purposes is that Muḥāsibī's work represents perhaps the earliest major systematic effort to establish the foundations of Sufi thought as a legitimate religious discipline that could respectably take its place alongside of the other traditional "sciences" of the faith.[16]

Abū Saʿīd al-Kharrāz

Abū Saʿīd al-Kharrāz (d. 277/890 or 286/899) of Baghdad's one major surviving work, *The Book of Spiritual Authenticity (Kitāb aṣ-ṣidq),* is among the earliest extant instructional texts.[17] Its intent was to lay out one version of the spiritual path by articulating sixteen aspects of spiritual experience variously referred to as stations or stopping places along the path. Kharrāz does not elaborate on the nature of *maʿrifa* as such in the course of his development, but he does describe three essential features of its praxis in aspects four, five, and twelve of the sixteen he discusses, concerning intimate knowledge of the ego-soul *(maʿrifat an-nafs),* of the "enemy" called Iblīs, and of God's graces, respectively.[18] Kharrāz is echoing here the views of Muḥāsibī. In the latter section Kharrāz cites a story in which Moses acknowledged in prayer that his very ability to be grateful to God was itself a grace, and to which God responded that Moses was thereby demonstrating that he had attained the most fundamental form of knowledge *(ʿilm).*

Kharrāz is not concerned with the theoretical dimensions of *maʿrifa,* but only with the absolute need for anyone who is intent on spiritual progress to seek a level of knowledge, both tactical and strategic in its requirements and implications, that transcends the traditional and more ordinary learning called *ʿilm.* Here Kharrāz offers an early Muslim analogy to what Christian tradition has called "discernment of spirits," a practical knowledge of the often subtle forces at work upon and within the psyche. Knowledge therefore fits into Kharrāz's scheme of spiritual development as one element among many. Not until his "epilogue"—after he has examined in turn the implications of authenticity in sincerity, patience, repentance, knowledge of the ego-soul and the devil, spiritual reticence *(wara^c),* using only what is religiously acceptable, renunciation/asceticism, trust in God, fear of God, shame, knowledge of and gratitude for divine favors, love, spiritual contentment, desire, and intimacy—does Kharrāz comment more pointedly on the nature of knowledge as an essential element in spiritual pedagogy. Here one finds the beginnings of a theme that later authors would develop in much greater detail, namely, the superiority of *ma^crifa* over *^cilm.*[19] He emphasizes the ethical and affective dimensions of this higher level of knowledge, but Kharrāz's observations reflect the kind of ambivalence and apparent imprecision in the use of terminology evident in Qur'ān and Ḥadīth, an ambiguity that later Sufis would seek to address. Three brief excerpts will summarize Kharrāz's views on the subject:

> According to a non-canonical Ḥadīth: "God says, 'When a person of acquired knowledge relies on this world, the most immediate (or possibly: the least) effect I bring about in him is to extract from his inmost being the sweetness of intimate conversation with Me and leave him in confusion in this world.' Another tradition has it that when the godservant relies on this world once he has attained *^cilm* and *ma^crifa* along with spiritual insight, God says to Gabriel, 'Strip his inmost being of the sweetness of intimate conversation with Me, leaving him with this world's scraps so that he can distract himself from Me with them.'"[20]

> I will call to mind for you another station, so direct your attention to it, along with that of any other person you notice adverting to *ma^crifa* and *^cilm* and resting in God. If you have imbibed from the cup of *ma^crifa* of God, so that God has caused pure certainty to dawn on you as to what has been set aside for you eternally in God's presence—for He wanted you before you ever wanted Him, and was fully informed about you before you sought to know Him inti-

mately, and remembered you before ever you brought Him to mind, and loved you before you ever loved Him—then as a result you will now swell with thankfulness for His gifts and your heart will be moved with love of Him for those benefits.[21]

Bestir your mind now and focus your intent. Do not attend to *ʿilm*, for your profound comprehension *(fahm)* has turned aside from what that knowledge presents to you. You therefore have no excuse now, once you have *ʿilm* and exposition, for the proof has been impressed upon you. Act therefore with sincerity toward God, and perhaps you will be rescued and rejoice in the *maʿrifa* of Him in this temporary dwelling place that precedes eternity. Yes, then your sadness will be unending and your distress intensified, and each spiritual state in which you find yourself will be doubled over what you had experienced prior to *maʿrifa* and (mystical) attainment (lit. arrival). God's Book and the Sunna of His Messenger provide proof of that. God said, "Among God's servants those who possess *ʿilm* fear Him" (Q 35:28). Said the Prophet, "I am endowed with greater *ʿilm* of God than you (pl.), and I fear Him the most intensely." He said, as well, "If you possessed the kind of *ʿilm* with which I am endowed, you would laugh little and weep profusely, and you would set out risking all on the highroads toward God." This is the Prophet's approach, and the one who has *maʿrifa* of God lives accordingly: unlike others, such a person even in the midst of worldly things finds support in every spiritual state he experiences.[22]

Ḥakīm at-Tirmidhī

To the east, in Central Asia (on the northern border of Afghanistan), a major ninth-century Sufi author called Muḥammad ibn ʿAlī Al-Ḥakīm at-Tirmidhī (d.c. 295/908) further developed the differentiation of modes of knowing begun by the likes of Muḥāsibī.[23] Tirmidhī was a well-known traditionist as well as a legal specialist educated in the

Ḥanafī school of jurisprudence. In a short work called *The Book of the Elucidation of Knowledge (Kitāb bayān al-ʿilm)*, Tirmidhī responded to the criticism of scholars who identified *ʿilm* solely with *fiqh,* a term whose root connotes "deep understanding" but which had come to be widely associated with jurisprudence. Tirmidhī argued that *ʿilm* is much broader in scope and encompasses three objects of knowledge, which, he explains, are rooted in the Ḥadīth, "Knowledge consists of three things: a clear verse (of the Qur'ān), a well-established *sunna,* and a fair religious duty."[24] The first, which Tirmidhī elsewhere calls simply *ʿilm* or traditional learning, has as its object familiarity with the outward dimensions of religious command and prohibition in this world; the second, which he elsewhere calls *ḥikma* (wisdom), encompasses inward familiarity of matters pertaining to the next world—what later Sufi authors would detail as the various stations and states; and the third, which Tirmidhī characterizes as *maʿrifa*, refers to experiential knowledge of God and divine action in the world.

Unlike Muḥāsibī, Tirmidhī considered faith and *maʿrifa* virtually inseparable. As Sarrāj and others would develop further later on, those who attain the third level have, a fortiori, mastered the first and second as well. Tirmidhī associated *maʿrifa* intimately with God-mindfulness *(dhikr),* calling *dhikr* the "sustenance" of *maʿrifa*, which is "sweet and agreeable" and whose vessel is the heart. "*Maʿrifa* has various branches: one (God's) sublimity, another His grandeur, the third His compassion, the next intimacy, still another (divine) magnificence, followed by might, and finally the (divine) beauty. The root of these branches is (divine) omnipotence, and they branch off from omnipotence."[25]

Ḥallāj

Ḥusayn ibn Manṣūr al-Ḥallāj (d. 309/922) was among the most influential of the early Sufis, and is most famous as Sufism's first martyr-mystic. He was executed ostensibly for blasphemous utterances in which he seemed to arrogate divinity unto himself (especially "I am the Truth"). His views on knowledge took a different turn from those of his contemporaries—especially his mentors, Sahl at-Tustarī (d. 283/896) and Junayd (d.c. 297/910), and predecessors, especially

Ḥasan al-Baṣrī (d. 110/728)—in that Ḥallāj insisted on the superiority of *ma'rifa* over *'ilm*, whereas Junayd, for example, ceded priority to *'ilm*. As Massignon notes, Ḥallāj believed the purpose of knowledge was "to find Reality itself and to partake of it forever by distinguishing it from what is fleeting, from tangible and possible things, conceivable things, and by conforming our intentions from within to the divine Command." *'Ilm* means self-scrutiny that transcends simple assent to religious custom—it is the "science of hearts." But, Massignon continues, "it excludes neither the use of rational dialectics to conduct discussion nor recourse to traditional authority to define its limits; but it subjects both to a test of interior experimentation in order to check their data and the conclusiveness of evidence by results."[26]

In Ḥallāj's view, faith is the bedrock of deeper understanding *(fiqh)* of God's providential gifts, and the memory of those gifts constitutes the substance of one's *'ilm*.[27] Ḥallāj's brief enigmatic text *The Book of Ṭā-Sīns (Kitāb aṭ-ṭawāsīn)* further clarifies his epistemology in chapters 2, "The *Ṭa-Sīn* of *Fahm*," and 11, "The Orchard of *Ma'rifa*." The former distinguishes between "*'ilm* of ultimate reality" and (the realization of) "the ultimate reality of ultimate reality." Using the metaphor of the moth's self-destructive attraction to the candle's flame, he likens general knowledge to seeing the light from a candle, and its full realization to feeling the heat in the process of being consumed in the fire. In the latter section Ḥallāj describes *'irfān*, knowledge of the object of *ma'rifa* (God), as full awareness of one's total ignorance. Just as the moth cannot return to describe to its mates the ultimate encounter with the flame, neither can the human being claim communicable knowledge of God. The "how" and "where" of God are now irrelevant. *Ma'rifa* transcends all fact, boundaries, consciousness, and tradition. Ḥallāj then goes on to respond to nearly a dozen theological views of various of his contemporaries, refuting their claims to "possessing" something known when all is said and done. *Ma'rifa* remains a realm beyond all claims to knowing.[28]

Tenth Century: Niffarī, **Sarrāj, Kalābādhī, Makkī**

Niffarī

The Iraqi ʿAbd al-Jabbār an-Niffarī's (d. 354/965) *Book of Standings (Kitāb al-mawāqif)* is surely one of most important contributions to Islamic mystical thought.[29] Niffarī's highly allusive and consistently theological approach to the topic of knowledge is in many ways quite congenial with that of Ḥallāj. Niffarī's language is relentlessly elusive, and his "standings" are couched in the form of clustered aphorisms rather than that of short treatises. In the "Standing of standing" he comes as close as he ever gets to a description of what happens when God "stands" or positions the individual in a particular aspect of spiritual experience, and his interpretation of *ʿilm* and *maʿrifa* are crucial.

"Standing" is the source of *ʿilm*, so that apart from standing, one's knowledge rests outside of the self. On the other hand, if one has *maʿrifa* of the experience of standing itself, *maʿrifa* is no longer a possibility—presumably because the individual is enthralled with the experience itself rather than with the One who alone is the object of intimate knowledge. Standing obliterates both *ʿilm* and its opposite, *jahl;* and while inherent in every standing there is a vantage point *(muṭṭalaʿ)*[30] over *ʿilm*, *ʿilm* has no vantage point over the experience of standing, which is as close to true *maʿrifa* of God as a human being can get. This "vantage point," or "mystical perception" in Arberry's rendering, introduces a range of light imagery because the term *(muṭṭalaʿ)* derives from a root associated with the rising of the sun. Gain an enlightened vantage point on both *ʿilm* and *maʿrifa*, says Niffarī, and you see each in the other. Failing that, you can be sure that neither is genuine. One needs to set up a barrier of *ʿilm* as a protection against ignorance, but one also needs a barrier of *maʿrifa* as defense against *ʿilm*. *ʿIlm* may be the door to God, but *maʿrifa* is the doorkeeper.

Paradoxically, however, standing is the spirit of *maʿrifa*, but *maʿrifa* is the spirit of *ʿilm*, which in turn is the spirit of life itself. Similarly, standing upholds *maʿrifa* as *maʿrifa* upholds *ʿilm*; as *maʿrifa* devours *ʿilm*, so standing devours *maʿrifa*. And while every stander is endowed with *maʿrifa*, the converse is not necessarily true, for the one endowed with *maʿrifa* sees the limits of his *ʿilm*, whereas the stander transcends all limits. People who possess *ʿilm* talk about it; those endowed with *maʿrifa* dwell on it; one who stands talks about God. As *ʿilm* is a veil before God, *maʿrifa* is how God speaks, and standing is God's very presence.

Niffarī's pithy paradoxes are like a thousand facets of a gem, each revealing subtle variations in color and brilliance. Each removes one of countless gossamer veils over what Niffarī understands to be the ineffable experience of knowing, which transcends all the boundaries of both *ʿilm* and *maʿrifa*. Getting beyond the basic terms with their limitations, he plunges into the *maʿrifa* of *maʿrifa*s *(maʿrifat al-maʿārif)*, which he defines as the "ignorance of all things through" God, in which one makes *ʿilm* a beast of burden on the journey to enjoying God's own hospitality. To entrust one's very unknowing to God is to enter into God's friendship, but to present oneself to God as one possessed of *ʿilm*—and proud of it—is all loss. The problem with *ʿilm* is that it masquerades as a straight, unobstructed trajectory, whereas in fact there are false exits and detours all along it. Only by letting go of conventional meanings can one arrive at *maʿrifa*.

Spiritual progress is something like a continual cycling from ignorance to *ʿilm* to *maʿrifa*, only at each successive level the three aspects of knowing and unknowing take the wayfarer into new territory. Beyond all the standings lies ignorance, but to flee that ignorance is to abandon knowledge. Perhaps by way of veiled reference to the axiom that things are known by their opposites, Niffarī observes that *maʿrifa* devoid of ignorance goes unmanifest. One who possesses a knowledge with no opposite belongs to neither heaven nor earth. The dilemma of one endowed with *maʿrifa*, however, is that one who goes on inquiring about *maʿrifa* of God truly has no experiential knowledge of God, but one who is content with status-quo *ʿilm* does not belong to God.

Niffarī's intensely allusive and imaginative work sets him apart from other major tenth-century Sufi prose authors. Sarrāj and his fellow manualists spoke, more directly and pedagogically, to a very different audience.

Sarrāj: *The Book of Flashes*

Abū Naṣr as-Sarrāj (d. 378/988) was born in Tus, in the northeastern Iranian province of Khurasan. Few details about the course of his life are well established. Judging from his references to a number of major cities in the central Middle East, including Baghdad, Basra, Damascus, and Cairo, he traveled widely. Traditional accounts suggest that several major teachers influenced Sarrāj's thought. Sarrāj often mentions Jaʿfar al-Khuldī (d. 348/959), who had been a disciple of various important Sufis, including Junayd (d. 297/910), Ruwaym of Baghdad (d. 303/915), Ibrāhīm al-Khawwāṣ (d. 291/904), to whom a lost work called *The Book of the Maʿrifa of Maʿrifa* is attributed, and Samnūn al-Muḥibb ("The Lover," d.c. 298/910). During an extended visit to Damascus, Sarrāj came to know Abū Bakr ad-Duqqī (d.c. 366/977), a companion of the famed Abū ʿAlī ar-Rūdhbārī (d. 322/934). And Abū 'l-Ḥasan ibn Sālim of Basra (d. 356/967) was the son of a disciple of Sahl at-Tustarī, whose Qur'ānic hermeneutics I will discuss briefly below. Though Sarrāj is celebrated for only one written work, his fellow Sufis regarded him highly enough to dub him the "Peacock of the Spiritually Poor."

In his *Kitāb al-Lumaʿ (The Book of Flashes),* Sarrāj leads off with a series of short chapters designed to situate Sufi modes of knowing squarely within the context of Islamic religious disciplines generally. He argues that a complete understanding of religious sciences must include Sufi approaches along with those of the traditionists and jurists. In this respect he sets an example later followed most notably (among the authors translated here) by Hujwīrī, Ghazālī, and Suhrawardī; all four begin with expositions of acquired or traditional knowledge *(ʿilm)* as a religious duty for all Muslims.

Sarrāj dedicates most of the first twelve chapters (out of 152 chapters in all) to setting up Sufi knowledge as a fulfillment of this foundational religious vocation, with chapter 9 arguing for Sufi knowledge as a "special religious discipline." His argument turns on the principle that just as one would not seek advice from a non-jurist concerning a matter of law, so one ought not have recourse to a person unfamiliar with the life of the spirit concerning questions of inner experience. After examining in turn the domains of Ḥadīth specialists and jurists as discrete sciences, he builds a case for understanding the uniquely Sufi approaches to knowledge and action as a necessary and respectable science, refuting along the way complaints that the Sufis are a know-nothing rabble. As Suhrawardī did much later, Sarrāj argues (chapter 8) that the Sufis are the real *fuqahā',* for theirs is the authentic *fiqh,* "profound comprehension," of religious matters. His opening foundational discussion culminates in chapter 12, where he explains that competence in the inward aspects of religious *ʿilm* is the responsibility of the Sufis.

After laying the groundwork for his case that Sufis have a legitimate claim to expertise in the inward aspects of religious *ʿilm*, Sarrāj addresses the specific nature of Sufi knowing as *maʿrifa.* Chapters 16 through 18 offer a generous sampling of citations of famous Sufis' definitions of experiential knowledge. Sarrāj adds his own glosses more extensively than, for example, Qushayrī seems inclined to do. Perhaps his most important gloss expands on Nūrī's reference to a "direct encounter" *(bi 'l-mubāshara)* with God, which he says "refers to the heart's unmediated experience of certitude and witnessing of the realities of faith in the realm of mystery" [38]. Unlike the ordinary believer who sees by the light of God, the mystic sees directly through God.

As background necessary for a deeper understanding of *maʿrifa,* Sarrāj then details seven mystical stations *(maqāmāt).*[31] He indicates that there are three levels in each station, the third being that of the person endowed with *maʿrifa* (that is, the *ʿārif*). A series of chapters on ten conditions, eight of which he explicitly calls "spiritual states," is followed by two chapters on the Sufi understanding of the Prophet's embodiment of these spiritual values. Two more substantive chapters (51 and 52) describe how, because of their experiential knowledge, Sufis can arrive at "deeper interpretations" *(mustanbaṭāt)* of Qur'ān and Ḥadīth. Sarrāj explains how their disparity of views in this respect is actually an advantage rather than a problem, given the immense variety of people waiting to benefit from their findings.

In a section (chapter 88) dealing with the diversity of concepts held by various Sufis, Sarrāj notes that, when asked about ultimate spiritual reality, ʿAbd Allāh ibn Ṭāhir al-Abharī responded, "Spiritual reality is altogether *ʿilm.*" When someone proceeded to ask him about *ʿilm,* he answered that it was "entirely the ultimate spiritual reality."

Shiblī, however, made an intriguing distinction, saying, "There are three modes of speaking: the tongue of *ʿilm*, the tongue of ultimate spiritual reality *(ḥaqīqa)*, and the tongue of truth *(al-ḥaqq)*. The tongue of *ʿilm* is that which communicates to us in mediated fashion; the tongue of *ḥaqīqa* is that by which God gives access to mysteries without use of an intermediary; but there is no path to the tongue of the truth" [216]. Later, Sarrāj explains an aspect of the use of the term "tongue" as part of a larger section devoted to idiosyncratic Sufi terminology. There he gives a slight variation on Shiblī's saying and comments, "When he uses (the term) 'tongue' he means the elucidation of the *ʿilm* of Him and disclosure about Him through (means of) expression" [354].

Finally, after devoting the bulk of the remainder of the book to countless specific hagiographical examples of lives based on such knowledge, and on definitions of hundreds of key terms, Sarrāj returns to the subject of *maʿrifa*. Chapter 122 acknowledges that the communication of Sufi knowledge is dicey. The Qur'ānic Sūrat al-kahf's (Sūra 18) story of Khiḍr provides the paradigm of *ʿilm min ladunn* (knowledge from the divine presence). Here Sarrāj makes an important distinction: Muḥammad was commissioned to communicate what had been sent down to him, but not that which he knew experientially—that is, the private knowledge that, according to the famous Ḥadīth, is cause for weeping rather than laughter. Upon this foundation Sarrāj builds his defense of ecstatic utterance *(shaṭḥ)*. *Maʿrifa* thus stands above all the other religious sciences without in any way abrogating them.

Kalābādhī: *The Exploration of Sufi Teachings*

Abū Bakr al-Kalābādhī came, as his full name indicates, from the Kalābādh quarter of the city of Bukhara, in present-day Uzbekistan. His birth date is unknown, but it appears that he died around 384/994–95,[32] and he is known to have been buried in Bukhara. Virtually all that is known of his education and professional background is that he studied Islamic law with a Ḥanafī jurist named Muḥammad ibn Faḍl (d. 319/931). As a Sufi, Kalābādhī was a student of a man named Fāris ibn ʿIsā (d.c. 340/951), a staunch ally of Sufism's most celebrated martyr, Ḥallāj.

Kalābādhī is best known for his *Book of the Exploration of the Teachings of Those Who Subscribe to Sufism (Kitāb at-taʿarruf li madhhab ahl at-taṣawwuf),* hereafter referred to as the *Exploration.* Kalābādhī remarks that the dual purpose of his relatively brief Arabic treatise is both to defend Sufis against unjustifiable censure and to preserve the kernel of Sufi teaching during a time in which, he believed, it was at risk of being diluted and, perhaps, even irrevocably lost. In support of his first purpose, Kalābādhī follows virtually point for point an early Muslim creed, known as *Fiqh Akbar II,* demonstrating in each instance how the Sufis hew scrupulously to mainstream Islamic belief and practice. Far from being heretical, he insists, the Sufis are in fact the very paragons of strict conformity to every element of the creed.[33]

Kalābādhī's *Exploration* contains seventy-five concise chapters arranged in five sections: general background on Sufism, including several lists of authors and famous Sufis (proemium and chapters 1–4); some two dozen chapters on the various doctrinal or creedal elements (5–30); analysis of principal features of the Sufi pedagogy of spiritual experience and progress (31–51); discussions of around a dozen distinctively Sufi technical terms (52–63); and finally, a set of praxis-oriented chapters detailing evidence of Sufi teaching in action (64–75).[34]

The work is not structured primarily around the concept of knowledge and is thus less systematic epistemologically than Sarrāj, for example. Kalābādhī is more interested in providing a broad overview of Sufi doctrines, and, although his catalogue of what other writers call stations and states seems to suggest a progress, he does not connect knowledge explicitly to that development. Instead, he inserts two of his four chapters on experiential knowledge—chapter 21: On *Maʿrifa,* and chapter 22: Differences of Opinion on *Maʿrifa*—in the midst of an otherwise rather meandering listing of "doctrines" of the Sufis. In the first of those two chapters Kalābādhī emphasizes the insufficiency of the intellect and the need of God as the only guide to God. Against that background, he follows Junayd's distinction between two levels of experiential knowledge of God. The higher results from divine self-disclosure *(taʿarruf),* such as that which God granted Abraham when He showed him the *malakūt* (realms) of the heavens and earth (Q 6:75–79), and the lower from divine instruction or tutelage *(taʿrīf),* whereby all believers arrive at *maʿrifa* through their awareness of the "signs on the horizons and in their selves." Kalābādhī is evidently unique in this respect among the theorists. A brief follow-up chapter lists a series of opinions and definitions of *maʿrifa*.

When Kalābādhī revisits the subject nearly forty chapters later (chapter 60: On the Realities of *Maʿrifa*), he leads off with another interesting distinction between two types of *maʿrifa*: that of a truth, which involves affirming God's transcendent unity; and that of an ultimate spiritual reality *(ḥaqīqa)*, which involves the realization that such a knowledge is pure gift and cannot be achieved through effort of intellect (a distinction reminiscent of that which Sarrāj had attributed to Shiblī, cited above). Finally, chapter 62 discusses "Descriptions of the One Endowed with *Maʿrifa*," emphasizing the quality of bewilderment and the insufficiency of the intellect, but it does not express any preference for one or another description.[35]

Abū Ṭālib al-Makkī: *The Sustenance of Hearts*

Abū Ṭālib al-Makkī (d. 386/996) was one of the most influential early medieval Muslim spiritual writers. Throughout the Middle East and from Spain to India his monumental treatise *The Sustenance of Hearts [in One's Conduct toward the Beloved, and the Description of the Path of the Seeker toward Divine Unity] (Qūt al-qulūb [fī muʿāmalāt al-maḥbūb wa waṣf ṭarīq al-murīd ilā maqām at-tawḥīd])* was widely read and recommended for many centuries. Arabic publishing houses have continued printing the work right down to our time, though a critical edition has yet to appear. Surprisingly little is known about so important a figure in the history of Islamic spirituality.[36]

Precisely when Abū Ṭālib was born is not certain, but he grew up in early tenth-century Mecca in a family that originated in the Jibal region, a mountainous area along southeastern Iraq's border with present-day Iran. Medieval sources suggest that Abū Ṭālib studied under three prominent Meccan scholars, each of whom Abū Ṭālib himself called "our shaykh": Abū Saʿīd ibn al-ʿArabī (d. 341/952), ʿAbīd ash-Shaṭṭ al-Muẓaffar ibn Sahl, and Abū ʿAlī al-Kirmānī. The first of these had been a student of the prominent Baghdadi "sober" mystic Junayd, and it is likely that Makkī learned principles of Junaydi Sufism through Abū Saʿīd.

During his Meccan educational career, Makkī also studied at some depth subjects other than Sufism. Under the tutelage of scholars from both Shāfiʿī and Ḥanbalī schools of law, he steeped himself in Ḥadīth studies and earned the right to relate traditions from at least three authoritative scholars. In addition, Makkī reports that his wariness of using personal judgment *(ra'y)* and analogical reasoning *(qiyās)* in the absence of "sound" Ḥadīths on which to base interpretations of sacred texts led him to accord greater than usual credence to "weak" Ḥadīths (that is, those narrated by little-known individuals or having defective chains of transmission). He supported his view by appealing to no less an authority than Ibn Ḥanbal himself, who argued in favor of accepting a weak Ḥadīth so long as it does not contradict Qur'ān, Sunna, or the consensus of believers and scholars. He held that if a tradition is certainly not a forgery, it is better to put one's trust in the saying's survival in the community than risk having recourse to methods of reasoning that might inappropriately reflect one's personal biases.

Probably between 330/942 and 356/967 (and more likely toward the latter part of that period), Abū Ṭālib traveled north to Basra, an Iraqi city that had grown up around a mid-seventh-century military encampment established during the early years of Islamic expansion into the central Middle East from the Arabian peninsula. By Abū Ṭālib's time, Basra had long been known as a center of important developments in Islamic spirituality. It had been home to Ḥasan al-Baṣrī (d. 110/728), a man known to this day for his rigorous asceticism, and to a woman often hailed as the first authentically mystical Muslim, Rābiʿa al-ʿAdawīya (d. 185/801). In Basra, Abū Ṭālib became associated with the circle of Abū 'l-Ḥasan Aḥmad ibn Muḥammad Sālim (d.c. 356/967), who was said to have been the last living disciple of Sahl at-Tustarī and after whose father, Abū ʿAbd Allāh Muḥammad ibn Sālim (d. 297/909), an early school of thought called the Sālimīya took its name.

A group of mystically inclined speculative theologians (called *mutakallimūn*) linked with the Mālikī school of religious law, the Sālimīya was actually founded by Sahl at-Tustarī himself. Since much of the information extant on the Sālimīya was written by Ḥanbalī authors, including Hujwīrī, ʿAbd al-Qādir al-Jīlānī (d. 561/1166), and Ibn al-Jawzī (d. 597/1200), who were decidedly critical of the school, an unbiased picture of their teachings is difficult to reconstruct. Still, Sahl's impact on Abū Ṭālib is evident in the approximately two hundred citations of Sahl in Makkī's work. Abū Ṭālib claims to have met the younger Ibn Sālim personally, and certain statements in *The Sustenance of Hearts* suggest that he was intimately familiar with the beliefs and practices of the Sālimīya.

Abū 'l-Ḥasan Aḥmad ibn Sālim was noted for his ascetical bent, after the example of the earlier paragon of Basran asceticism Ḥasan al-Baṣrī, whom Abū Ṭālib al-Makkī lauds as his "imām" in spiritual discipline. For Makkī, Ḥasan represented an essential link to the Prophet, since Ḥasan had "seen" Muḥammad's Companions ʿUthmān and ʿAlī. During his sojourn in Basra, and under the influence of Ibn Sālim, Abū Ṭālib engaged in a strict regimen of ascetical practice, particularly with regard to his eating habits. A preference for meager intake seems to have been a significant ascetical theme in his life. It is reported that he ate nothing but grass or herbs for such a time that his skin assumed a verdant hue. And he was particularly wary of eating foods whose status in religious law was ambiguous. As his masterwork's title suggests, Makkī was far more interested in the need for inner nourishment.

At an uncertain date Abū Ṭālib traveled further north to Baghdad, already long a center of Sufism. Very little is know about his years there, but credible reports suggest that he ran afoul of religious authorities, as had a number of Sufis before his time, for statements judged to be theologically unacceptable. He is believed to have had a son, ʿUmar ibn Muḥammad ibn ʿAlī (d. 444/1053), and to have lived most of his remaining days in solitude. Abū Ṭālib died in Baghdad in 386/996 and was buried there.

Before describing Abū Ṭālib's mystical epistemology in general and his specific approach to experiential knowledge, a summary characterization of his intellectual stance will be helpful. His background in religious studies familiarized him with the fundamentals of three of the four principal Sunnī schools of jurisprudence (Shāfiʿī, Mālikī, and Ḥanbalī), with their distinctive views on the uses of evidence from Qur'ān and Ḥadīth. His underlying concern was to give the Prophetic Sunna precedence over both customary values and cultural traditions on the one hand, and doctrinal innovation *(bidʿa)* on the other. Abū Ṭālib was especially adamant about the dangers inherent in the rationalist methods of various groups of speculative theologians.[37] At the same time, he did not exempt from criticism those Sufis whose practices he judged incompatible with the Prophetic example and the Revealed Law. On the latter account Makkī took a somewhat inconsistent position concerning the ecstatic utterances (*shaṭaḥāt,* pl. of *shaṭḥ*) for which Sufis such as Ḥallāj and Bāyezīd al-Bisṭāmī are most famous. On the one hand, he condemns such behavior as extremist, while, on the other, he excludes the two most celebrated ecstatics from his criticism on the grounds that Ḥallāj and Bisṭāmī had attained a level of spiritual development that put them beyond reproach in this matter.

Surely one of the great classics of world spirituality, *The Sustenance of Hearts* offers a comprehensive view of virtually all the issues of major concern to one important segment of tenth-century Muslim society in the central Middle East. Makkī is far more concerned about praxis than theory. In keeping with that orientation, he plunges immediately into detailed discussion of the spiritual seeker's practices of prayer and fasting in every conceivable circumstance, emphasizing the need for proper inner disposition. Subsequently, he moves into a closer consideration of specific aspects of self-scrutiny, "witnessing/vision," and of the more refined facets of spiritual discernment *(tafṣīl al-khawāṭir).*

Makkī proceeds to an analysis of the "stations of certitude and the states of those endowed with certitude," including patience, gratitude, hope, fear, self-discipline, trust (a fairly lengthy section), spiritual contentment, and love. Then comes a treatise that many readers will be accustomed to seeing as the very first item in treatments of the Islamic faith, namely, the so-called five pillars. Placing them here, Makkī makes it clear that he regards a full engagement in these "basics" as in no way merely presumed, but rather as the result of considerable progress on the spiritual path. After discussing in detail and from various angles the confession of faith, ritual prayer and its attendant duties, almsgiving, fasting, and pilgrimage, Makkī burrows into the inner dimensions of these actions as "devotional deeds of the heart." First he examines the various conditions requisite for engaging in them according to Revealed Law, along with the telltale and often subtle signs of unbelief that can manifest themselves in one's religious practice. He then returns to the fundamental issues of sincerity and right intention before introducing more advanced ascetical practices relating to hunger and spiritual poverty. The latter sections deal with a variety of social issues, including travel, marriage, companionship, commerce, and a final discussion of the importance of spiritual reticence and care in attending to the differences between forbidden and permitted practices.

Makkī's *Book of Knowledge:* Knowledge plays a central role in Makkī's thought, as the goal of the spiritual life, but his approach to knowledge is one that will likely strike the reader as unconventional. The only knowledge worth seeking is knowledge of God based on hearing rather than on seeing. Abū Ṭālib entitles the whole of Part 31, one of the largest single sections in *The Sustenance of Hearts,* "The Book of *ʿilm.*" In the course of that segment, he situates *maʿrifa* within the larger context of seeking knowledge, but he does not make epistemological concerns the overall foundation of his work, as, for example, his contemporary Sarrāj did.

Makkī's treatment is certainly one of the more difficult of its kind, since he is generally concerned with exploring the subtlest details of the interior life and motivation and somewhat less with reporting on the range of opinions expressed by famous Sufis. He is an extraordinarily shrewd observer of the human condition, and his analysis is often dense and convoluted. Like several other authors, Makkī begins with the Ḥadīth on the duty of seeking knowledge, but then he proceeds on a track unlike any other Sufi manualist: he mentions only in passing other aspects of the Islamic quest for knowledge, arguing from the outset that the knowledge that all are duty-bound to pursue is inward knowledge. He uses *ʿilm* consistently at first, but says its object is, variously, spiritual states, mystical moment, sincerity, inner movements of spirit—in short, he calls for the subtle and sophisticated self-knowledge known as the "science of hearts" *(ʿilm al-qulūb).*

One overriding theme is that of beneficial or useful knowledge, which he defines as any knowledge that assists one in negotiating the difficult journey inward. He starts with knowledge of the five pillars as the bedrock of all knowledge, since knowledge must lead to action and the five pillars are the essential requirements for action. Makkī identifies the two sources of *maʿrifa* as hearing (by which one becomes a Muslim) and seeing (or contemplative witnessing, *mushāhada*).

Maʿrifa can occur either through demonstrative proof, consisting of various levels of instruction associated with hearing, or through more subtle signs associated with vision, which can include ecstasy.

Another theme is Makkī's tactic of identifying knowledge with faith, fear of God, and a host of other spiritual qualities. For example, he establishes the relationship between faith and knowledge by identifying the Qur'ān with knowledge and light, and faith in the Qur'ān as the bedrock of Islam. Through this and other devices Makkī seeks to democratize knowledge, thus taking a different tack than, for example, Sarrāj or Kalābādhī. He does, however, maintain that there are numerous ranks distinguishing the quality of knowledge among individuals—the many stations of certitude—and highlighting the superiority of inward knowing over outward, knowledge of the next world over mundane knowing, and the science of hearts over that of tongues. To a far greater degree than any of the other manualists, Makkī offers an elaborate "sociology of experiential knowledge," describing at length, for example, the spiritual status and social function of true scholars, their relationship to the prophets, and the comeuppance awaiting those who abuse their knowledge for worldly gain. Finally, Makkī praises spiritual reticence with respect to knowledge, a quality of which anyone who tackles *Qūt al-qulūb* is reminded often.

Eleventh Century: **Hujwīrī, Qushayrī, Anṣārī,** and **Ghazālī**

Hujwīrī: *The Revelation of Realities Veiled*

ʿAlī ibn ʿUthmān Hujwīrī (d.c. 465/1071) is widely known as the first author of a major Sufi work in Persian. Originally from Ghazna, in Afghanistan, Hujwīrī eventually settled in Lahore, in present-day Pakistan, where he is still known by the honorific Data Ganj Bakhsh and where people still make pilgrimage to his tomb. Hujwīrī's *Kashf al-Maḥjūb (The Revelation of Realities Veiled)* begins with a chapter "On

ʿIlm." It turns on the critical relationship between discursive knowledge and action, emphasizing the ethical component to a greater degree than perhaps any of the other authors discussed here. He nevertheless begins to venture into a description of a higher type of knowledge (still *ʿilm*) by making a distinction between divine knowledge and human knowledge, asserting that the link is human understanding of divine essence and oneness, of God's attributes, and of God's deeds. Hujwīrī introduces the concept of experiential knowledge toward the end of the chapter. There he situates it at the pinnacle of a triad of types of *ʿilm*: first, knowledge *from* God (including all of the Revealed Law); second, knowledge *with* God (presupposing the experience of the spiritual stations and arising to the level of God's Friends); third, knowledge *of* God, which he calls *maʿrifat* (hereafter I will use a standard Arabic transliteration, *maʿrifa*, rather than the Persian equivalent). He concludes the chapter with a warning to avoid the company of those who fall short of the highest levels of knowledge. In the end, the realization of one's very incapacity to achieve full knowledge is itself the attainment of salutary knowledge.

Hujwīrī takes up the subject of higher modes of knowing in chapter 15 of *The Revelation of Realities Veiled:* "On the First Veil, *Maʿrifa*." Among authors discussed thus far, his treatment is unusual in several respects. First, he alone situates *maʿrifa* at the beginning of a typology. He does so, however, not because he thinks of *maʿrifa* as a starting point, but because experiential knowledge is the launch pad for the upper reaches of the spiritual quest and already presupposes a great deal of spiritual acumen. Second, Hujwīrī gives great attention to the causes of experiential knowledge, ruling out the deductive inference of *istidlāl,* the form of inspiration called *ilhām,* and necessary cause, on the one hand, while spotlighting God-given perplexity, on the other. Third, he underscores the immeasurable chasm between rational and experiential knowing. Fourth, he is unique in his description of *maʿrifa* as a twofold phenomenon. Acknowledging the ambiguity one encounters occasionally in the Sufi usage of the term *maʿrifa*, Hujwīrī distinguishes between discursive or conceptual *(ʿilmī)* and spiritual or affective *(ḥālī)* types. He distinguishes the two by associating *ʿilmī maʿrifa* with religious scholars who possess sound *ʿilm* about God, and *ḥālī maʿrifa* with Sufis for whom soundness of spiritual or affective relationship with God is paramount.

Hujwīrī's principal working definition of affective *maʿrifa* is this: "Experiential knowledge is the life of the heart through God, and the innermost being's refusal to attend to anything but God."

Finally, in chapter 24, amid a list of more focused definitions of key technical terms, Hujwīrī sums up fundamental meanings of *ʿilm* and *maʿrifa* and the difference between them:

> Specialists in religious principles *(ʿulamā'-i uṣūl)* have not distinguished between *ʿilm* and *maʿrifa*, indicating that the two are synonymous. However, they assert that one can refer to God as "possessing knowledge" *(ʿālim)* whereas one ought not call God "experientially knowledgeable" *(ʿārif)* because that implies the need of divinely wrought completion.[38] On the other hand, the shaykhs of this (Sufi) Path apply the term *maʿrifa* to knowledge associated with spiritual deeds and affective states when the knower communicates his own affective state. Such a knower they call a mystic *(ʿārif)*. They call *ʿilm* any learning not inherently characterized by spiritual meaning and action, and they call one who possesses such knowledge a learned person *(ʿālim)*. In other words, they call a learned person one who possesses acquired learning that is purely intellectual and lacks spiritual depth, while they refer to a person whose knowledge is characterized by spiritual depth and reality as endowed with *maʿrifa*. As a result, when Sufis want to indicate a lesser opinion of their rivals, they call them "learned" *(dānishmand)*. Most people find this unacceptable, but their intent is not to chide someone for being learned but rather to fault such a person for disregarding deeds of piety. For the person possessed of *ʿilm* relies on himself while the one endowed with *maʿrifa* relies on his Lord. [498]

Translations presented here include full texts of Hujwīrī's chapters on *ʿilm* and *maʿrifa*.

Qushayrī: *The Treatise [on Sufism]*

Abū 'l-Qāsim al-Qushayrī was born in 375/986 in the northeastern Iranian province of Khurasan, in the town of Ustuwa. The name Qushayrī indicates that his family descended from the Arab tribe of Qushayr, which had migrated into Iran probably during the seventh century. As a young man, Qushayrī traveled to the city of Nishapur, capital of the province of Khurasan, where he studied accounting, math, and finance. It was there also that he met Abū ʿAlī ad-Daqqāq (d. 412/1021), who was to become his principal teacher in Sufism as well as his father-in-law. Qushayrī also applied himself to the study of traditional religious sciences. He became an authority on Ḥadīth and steeped himself in Shāfiʿī jurisprudence under Abū Bakr Muḥammad ibn Bakr aṭ-Ṭūsī (d. 419/1029), the chief jurist of the provincial capital. In addition, Qushayrī pursued further studies in Ḥadīth, law, and Ashʿarī systematic theology with Abū Bakr Muḥammad ibn al-Ḥasan ibn Furāk (d. 406/1015–16) and Abū Isḥāq al-Isfarā'inī (d. 418/1027).[39]

After Qushayrī's principal shaykh, Abū ʿAlī ad-Daqqāq, died, the student spent a short while under the tutelage of Abū ʿAbd ar-Raḥmān as-Sulamī (d. 412/1021), who is perhaps most famous for his hagiographical anthology *The Generations of the Sufis (Ṭabaqāt aṣ-ṣūfīya).* Qushayrī is also thought to have had some contact with the colorful and controversial Abū Saʿīd ibn Abī 'l-Khayr (d. 441/1049), who lived in Nishapur and whose penchant for extreme behavior rendered him suspect to more cautious Sufis like Qushayrī. As Ḥamīd Algar notes, some Nishapur Sufis attended the sessions of both men, but Qushayrī never mentions Abū Saʿīd in the *Treatise*.[40] During the first half of Qushayrī's life, Nishapur had been ruled by a dynasty called the Ghaznavids, named after the Afghan city of Ghazna in which they rose to power. When the newly ascendant Saljuqid dynasty supplanted the Ghaznavids, the theo-political climate turned against Qushayrī. Saljuqid Sultan Ṭughril's second-in-command, ʿAmīd al-Mulk al-Kundurī, considered himself a Ḥanafī in law and (some say) a Muʿtazilī in theological method. He had taken it upon himself to make life difficult for religious rivals, chief among whom were adherents of the Shāfiʿī legal and Ashʿarī theological persuasions. Qushayrī spoke out against the chief minister's accusations, was jailed briefly in 1054, and then made his way to Baghdad.

In Baghdad, Qushayrī took a post as religious scholar in the Caliph's palace for a few years. After the first Saljuqid sultan, Ṭughril, died (455/1063), Sultan Alp Arslān installed Niẓām al-Mulk as his prime minister. Niẓām supported the Shāfiʿī and Ashʿarī schools of law and theology, allowing Qushayrī to return to Nishapur, where he lived and worked till his death in 465/1072. *The Treatise of al-Qushayrī,* also known as *The Letter to the Sufis,* is his most famous and influential work. Like Sarrāj and Kalābādhī in the previous century, Qushayrī was concerned with establishing that the authentic teachings of Sufism were entirely consistent with the Ashʿari development of fundamental Muslim belief and practice.

Written in 437/1045, the *Treatise* begins with a bit of general background on the solidly Islamic basis of fundamental Sufi beliefs, then provides sketches of nearly seven dozen famous Sufis, including representative sayings of each. Following the hagiographical section, which occupies approximately one-sixth of the total work, the *Treatise* offers definitions of over three dozen Sufi technical terms needed to understand the Path. In the largest single segment of the work, Qushayrī analyzes just under fifty categories of spiritual experience called stations and states. He concludes, as does Kalābādhī, with issues of Sufi praxis.[41]

Although Qushayrī does not explicitly address the topic of *ʿilm* as a distinct category in the *Risāla,* he does make an instructive comment about it in a brief pedagogical work called *Provision for Travelers (Tartīb as-sulūk).* It consists of a series of reflections on various dimensions of God-recollectedness *(dhikr).* In the second of them he observes that when an individual recollects God correctly with the tongue, the experience will soon become recollectedness of the heart. If, in the course of experiencing the various enticing "states" that God sends in this process, the individual is seduced away from recollection by these alluring distractions, he will forfeit any further spiritual progress. Qushayrī continues:

> If he still persists, he is punished a second time by being returned to a condition of mere *[ʿilm]* of these states, and

> then he experiences such an abundance of knowledge that he thinks all mankind's treasures of knowledge have been revealed to him. But if he pays attention to the knowledge which comes to him, again this is an offense against proper behavior, and once more he deserves to be punished. Here his punishment consists in being returned to a state of mere understanding *[fahm]*. The difference between understanding and knowledge is that knowledge is a state of being which comes over the heart as knowledge, whereas understanding is gazing at this knowledge, as if to say knowledge that one has knowledge of the matters in question. Again if he looks at understanding, he once more offends against proper behavior, and his punishment is that he is returned to the state of religious indifference.[42]

In the *Treatise,* Qushayrī includes a single "Chapter on the *Maʿrifa* of God" as part of his discussion of some four dozen terms that refer to major experiential aspects of the Sufi Path. He locates *maʿrifa* third from last in the list, after chapters on acknowledgment of God's transcendent unity and spiritual states that accompany one's departure from this world, and ahead of those on love and longing. He describes a number of spiritual and psychological characteristics of experiential knowledge such as awe and taking leave of one's ego. Qushayrī offers a long and apparently unsystematic list of citations, almost entirely without analytical comment, of dozens of major Sufis, often overlapping with similar citations in Kalābādhī and other authors. If there is an overriding theme, it is perhaps his emphasis on the mystic's perfect attentiveness to God and complete lack of interest in anything that is not God. Finally, while his account might seem to contribute the least among the manuals to a theoretical understanding of *maʿrifa*, I would point to his strong identification of experiential knowledge with *fanā',* loss of one's ego, as a distinctive aspect of Qushayrī's discussion. As he seems to imply in the brief selection from *Provision for Travelers*, the ego's need for the flashiness of spiritual "states" can threaten even the lesser attainment of *ʿilm.*

Anṣārī: *The Hundred Fields* and *Resting Places for Wayferers*

Abū Ismāʿīl ʿAbd Allāh Anṣārī (396/1006–481/1089) of Herat, in present-day Afghanistan, received his training in Islamic law in the Ḥanbalī school. That school was sometimes at theological odds with the Ashʿarī-Shāfiʿī scholars of Central Asia—of whom Qushayrī was one. Anṣārī's much-beloved writings on the Sufi path include two of particular interest in this context. Around 448/1055–56 he dictated *The Hundred Fields (Ṣad maydān)* in Persian as a helpful handbook for a student. Some twenty-five years later the now-blind shaykh dictated the Arabic *Resting Places of the Wayfarers (Manāzil as-sā'irīn). The Hundred Fields* was, along with Hujwīrī's work, one of two important eleventh-century Persian texts of significance here. Its overall structure and content have prompted one scholar to call it a "Persian rough draft" of *Resting Places,* although the similarities are relatively superficial. Both employ standard mnemonic devices, such as a ternary structure aligned with a traditional Sufi triple distinction among the generality of believers, those more advanced in the spiritual life, and the spiritual elite. According to that distinction, seekers on the spiritual path participate in the various spiritual states in proportion to their individual capacities and levels of attainment.

Resting Places presupposes a still more advanced level of spiritual growth than does *The Hundred Fields.* Its one hundred stages are arranged in groups of ten, each cluster representing a particular aspect of spiritual development from beginnings to destinations. In addition, the later work arranges the various steps and levels in a very different order. Anṣārī's pedagogically oriented works differ from many other Sufi treatises in that they have deliberately omitted the kind of often copious citation of Sufi sayings so characteristic of many classical works. Anṣārī wanted the material as accessible and easy to recall as possible.

In a third relevant work, *Generations of the Sufis (Ṭabaqāt aṣ-ṣūfīya),* Anṣārī sets the whole topic of knowledge in the broadest possible context. Giving a brief survey of all the various credible disciplines to which Muslims have dedicated their efforts, he argues implicitly for the validity of the "discipline" of Sufism. Here he lists ten "sciences" or "forms of *ʿilm,*" first with the following general statement and then with a slightly more detailed description of each:

> The knowledge of divine transcendent unity is a (way of life); the knowledge of jurisprudence is a means of healing; the knowledge of exhortatory preaching is sustenance; the knowledge of dream interpretation is a matter of one's point of view; the science of medicine is a skill; the knowledge of astronomy is experimental; the discipline of speculative theology is a total loss; the knowledge of making a livelihood is the universal concern of all humankind; the knowledge of (divine) wisdom is a mirror; and the knowledge of ultimate reality is something to be discovered.[43]

Against that general backdrop Anṣārī situates his views on the explicitly spiritual dimensions of knowledge. Translated below are Anṣārī's short sections on *ʿilm* and *maʿrifa* in both *The Hundred Fields* and the *Resting Places for Wayfarers.*

Abū Ḥāmid al-Ghazālī: *The Revitalization of the Religious Disciplines*

Abū Ḥāmid Muḥammad al-Ghazālī (450/1058–505/1111) is among the towering figures of Islamic thought in general and of the literature of spirituality in particular. Ghazālī was above all a pastoral theologian who, like Makkī in a number of important ways, set out to provide an overall structure of religious living for spiritual seekers. He was born in Tus in the Persian province of Khurasan. In Nishapur, not far away, he studied religious law in the Shāfiʿī method, and the theology of the school of Ashʿarī as taught by the renowned Juwaynī (d. 478/1085). (Anṣārī had also been a student of Juwaynī's before transferring his intellectual allegiance to the Ḥanbalī school of law.) After Juwaynī's death, Ghazālī moved to Baghdad, where he assumed a prestigious professorship under the patronage of the Saljuqid Vizier Niẓām al-Mulk. But sometime during the ensuing ten years Ghazālī experienced a period of crisis that led him to reexamine his personal convictions and motivation. When he left his professorship in 488/1095, he departed for Mecca to make the Ḥajj, never to return to his teaching post in Baghdad. During a sparsely documented hiatus of nearly eleven years, he apparently traveled about the central Middle East, visiting

Jerusalem and Hebron (site of Abraham's tomb) and spending perhaps several years in Damascus. While in relative retirement Ghazālī composed his comprehensive masterwork, *The Revitalization of the Religious Disciplines (Iḥyā' 'ulūm ad-dīn).* In 499/1106 he went back to Nishapur and resumed teaching there at the insistence of Niẓām al-Mulk's son. After about five years of lecturing and writing, the great teacher returned to his hometown of Tus, where he lived until his death.[44]

One of the developments of Ghazālī's day that prompted him to devote considerable attention to epistemological concerns was the growing influence of a school of thought that he called the Bāṭinīya ("esotericists"). Their teaching turned on the centrality of an esoteric knowledge whose truth was subject to no other criteria but the authority of a teacher who demanded unquestioning acceptance *(taqlīd)* from his followers. Ghazālī regarded such passive learning as useless at best and hazardous to the soul at worst. Of the Sufi compendia that develop a fuller epistemology, Ghazālī's opening treatise in the *Revitalization,* "The Book of *'Ilm,*" is among the most extensive and detailed. Its seven sections include much of the kind of material Sarrāj discusses, but Ghazālī is not yet concerned with situating Sufi knowing as such in this context. He chooses rather to retain the broader contextual approach, focusing on distinguishing praiseworthy from blameworthy knowledge, with two sections dedicated to teacher-student relationships and attendant ethical responsibilities.

From the start Ghazālī makes it very clear that becoming a person of knowledge is a foundational religious calling, one that outranks even devotion and martyrdom. It goes without saying that knowledge is an infinitely worthier goal than wealth, for it is the glory of humanity and makes those authentically endowed with it "heirs to the prophets." (He does acknowledge, however, that the choice of knowledge is sometimes rewarded with wealth and power.) The quality of one's knowledge directly affects one's spiritual life, for Ghazālī is interested not in the mere acquisition of information but in deeply transformative learning. Like Makkī, to whom he is beholden for a great deal of his material on the subject, Ghazālī underscores the essential links of knowledge to faith and action. He divides the "*'ilm* of the path to the next life" into the sciences of revelation, which encompasses all prophetically mediated beliefs, and of religious practice, which embraces profound awareness of the essential states of the heart that are the bellwether of an individual's relationship with God. Ghazālī notes that while the acquisition of these two aspects of knowledge are a duty for all Muslims, the pursuit of theology itself is a duty only for a "sufficient representation" of the Muslim community who are entrusted with the task of defending the faith.

Ghazālī carefully distinguishes between praiseworthy and blameworthy varieties of knowledge. Knowledge is blameworthy when it directly harms any person, when it has limited utility but is predominantly deleterious (as with astrology), and when it encourages the pursuit of trivia for its own sake. He concludes one section of the book with the telling comment that "what is acceptable among the wise is to assume that you are alone with God in this universe while before you lie death, resurrection, judgment, Paradise and Hell. Consider then what concerns you of all these and ignore the rest."[45] He thus situates this life, as Saint Augustine put it, *"sub specie aeternitatis."* Ghazālī then details the dangers of disputation as an intellectual pastime, arguing that it can lead to a host of less than virtuous attitudes and actions, and that it is invariably a narcissistic pursuit.

Two substantial sections of Book 1 address questions related to the duties of teachers and students, and the awareness needed to discern a teacher of truth from one who peddles banalities in the guise of erudition. This finally turns on the perspective articulated in the text quoted above: If a teacher does not focus the student's attention where it belongs, namely, on the life to come, the relationship bodes no good. The authentic teacher, by contrast, models essential virtues and speaks from a depth of experience rather than about what he has heard from others. Ghazālī's final section in Book 1 sets the stage for his second major occasion for speaking of knowledge, which will come in Book 21 on the "Marvels of the Heart," with its focus on *maʿrifa*. Part seven of Book 1 describes the intellect and its strengths and functions, as a background against which he will later discuss the role of the heart as the seat of genuine knowledge. "Intellect" *(ʿaql)* can refer to the faculty that distinguishes the human from the nonhuman; understanding of axiomatic fundamentals (for example, acknowledging possibility in things that are possible); learning through experience; and finally, the intelligence by which one clearly determines the goal of any undertaking and thus gives one's understanding priority over cravings.[46]

Book 21 of Ghazālī's *Revitalization* offers arguably the most systematic and comprehensive treatment of *maʿrifa* found in any of the manuals. "The Elaboration of the Marvels of the Heart" sets forth the essentials of Ghazālī's psychology and of the epistemology that undergirds his mystical theology. Farīd Jabre has produced two critical studies of Ghazālī's epistemology. He notes that, although, like many other Sufi authors, Ghazālī regards *maʿrifa* as having both intellectual and practical dimensions, he does not identify it essentially with mystical union or illumination. In Ghazālī's view, *maʿrifa* does indeed signify a higher level of cognition, namely, an immediate experiential knowledge of God.[47]

One of Ghazālī's most important theological contributions in this context is the priority he accords to the divinely instilled human predisposition *(istiʿdād)* to *maʿrifa* of God. He highlights experiential knowledge as humankind's "beauty, perfection, and glory" in this world and the substance that will sustain human beings in the next life. It is the inherent qualities of the human heart—most notably, its desire for God, its ability to draw near to God, and its potential for affinity with and capacity of striving for God—that constitute this predisposition. In Ghazālī's view, as in those of many of his fellow theologians of the inner life, the heart is at the center of the most significant modes of human knowing. Only individuals endowed with *maʿrifa* of their own hearts can enjoy experiential knowledge of God. But, paradoxically, it is God who sometimes stands between individuals and their own hearts, thus foreclosing their ability to know Him. One has first, therefore, to acknowledge God's grace before gaining access to one's own heart, through which God then opens for the individual seeker the infinite vistas of the divine worldscape.

Most people never arrive at the fundamental stage of self-knowledge that is *maʿrifa* of the heart, and still fewer move beyond the basics of self-knowledge to intimate familiarity with God. As he begins the second half of his *Revitalization of the Religious Disciplines,* Ghazālī notes that the first half dealt with outward *ʿilm* and that he will dedicate all twenty "books" of the second half to a systematic exposition of inward *ʿilm.* Since that will consist of an analysis of all of the circumstances that occur within the heart, positive and negative alike, Ghazālī says he must begin part two with a careful investigation of the nature and qualities of the heart (Book 21) and of the arduous task of disciplining and refining the heart still further as the seat of experiential knowledge of God (Book 22).[48]

In the fifteen "clarifications" or expositions *(bayān)* of Book 21, Ghazālī begins with a broader contextual description of the principal internal or spiritual human faculties—ego-soul, spirit, intellect, and heart. Quickly focusing on the heart, he devotes sections two and three to a more detailed description of the functions of the heart as the inner battleground of the human struggle. The heart is aided by its "soldiers," the internal powers of appetite or desire (including, for example, irascibility and other aspects of motivation), the capability of acquisition or taking action on what it desires or fears, and perception *(idrāk)*. In sections four and five Ghazālī focuses still more sharply on the qualities of the heart that distinguish humans from animals: knowledge and will.[49]

Clarification 6, on the heart in relation to the sciences *(ʿulūm)*, shows the master of the extended simile at his best. He begins by examining five conditions under which the mirror of the heart cannot receive images clearly, thereby preventing *maʿrifa*. He then identifies *maʿrifa* as the "trust" from God that heaven, earth, and the mountains declined to accept at creation (33:72–73). *Maʿrifa* is the third and highest level of faith, equivalent to knowing that Zayd is in a house by actually entering and seeing him—rather than accepting someone else's assurance *(taqlīd)* or hearing Zayd's voice from outside (the *istidlāl* of the theologians). Clarification 7 discusses "the State of the Heart in relation to the varieties of knowing," arguing that the heart is home to two kinds of knowing: the rational and the divinely revealed. The rational includes both the intuitive or innate and that which is acquired through both instruction and inference. Rational knowing has to do largely with this world and is like the nourishment a sick person needs after being cured. The cure, however, requires divinely revealed knowledge concerning the next world. In Clarification 8, Ghazālī analyzes the distinction between inspiration *(ilhām)* and instruction *(taʿallum)*, and between Sufi epistemology and the acquisition of reason-based knowledge.

Clarification 9, "Explaining the difference between the two situations using an analogy with sensation," discusses how the heart is capable of receiving direct information from the Preserved Tablet. The universe began in prototype, or perhaps archetype, on the Preserved Tablet prior to God's bringing it into existence. Just as an image of the universe remains accessible to the imagination even when the individual is not actually gazing upon it, the heart remains able to access the Preserved Tablet directly when the veil between the two—namely, preoccupation with sensory input—is lifted. The heart thus has two doors: one opens to the suprasensible Realm of Lordly Dominion *(ʿālam al-malakūt)* and the Preserved Tablet, and one opens to the Realm of Earthly Sovereignty *(ʿālam al-mulk)* and sense knowledge.[50] Religious scholars are like the Greeks who painted their wall, while the Friends of God are like the Chinese who polished their wall into a mirror. In Clarification 10, "Testimonies of the revealed law concerning the soundness of the path of the Sufis with respect to the acquisition of experiential knowledge other than through instruction and the accustomed path," Ghazālī completes his discussion of *maʿrifa*. Prophets and Friends of God receive images or similitudes through angels, but spiritual struggle *(mujāhada)* can also open a door of the heart to *maʿrifa*.

Ghazālī's epistemological thinking naturally suffuses his work, so that one can hardly do justice to it by means of excerpts alone. Another important document by Ghazālī is his *Treatise Explaining the Experiential Knowledge of God (Risāla fi bayān maʿrifat Allāh)*.[51] Yet another work, whose authorship has been debated, that focuses on the theme of mystical knowledge is Ghazālī's *Treatise on (Knowledge) from God (Ar-Risālat al-ladunīya)*.[52] Readers interested in a fuller treatment may wish to consult those primary sources as well as the works by Farīd Jabre already mentioned.

Twelfth and Thirteenth Centuries: **Ibn al-ʿArīf,** ʿAyn al-Quḍāt al-Hamadhānī, Sanāʾī, ʿAṭṭār, Rūmī, Ibn al-ʿArabī, and **Abū Ḥafs ʿUmar as-Suhrawardī**

By the twelfth century, the age of the comprehensive handbooks of spirituality was all but over. But the works of several authors of manuals, all highly influential in their respective cultural contexts, deserve mention here. At the western end of the greater Mediterranean world, religious studies were a vital ingredient in the Islamic culture of the Iberian peninsula. A major contributor to one important center of Iberian Sufi spirituality was Ibn al-ʿArīf. Meanwhile, far to the east, ʿAyn al-Quḍāt al-Hamadhānī's analysis of spiritual development played a significant role particularly in Persian Sufism. The most important of the later handbooks was Suhrawardī's *The Benefits of Intimate Knowledge (ʿAwārif al-maʿārif)*, excerpts of which are translated here. In addition, this section acknowledges the contributions of three Persian poets, Sanā'ī, Farīd ad-Dīn ʿAṭṭār and Jalāl ad-Dīn Rūmī, as well as that of the enormously influential Iberian-born Ibn al-ʿArabī.

Ibn al-ʿArīf, *The Beauties of Spiritual Sessions*

Abū 'l-ʿAbbās Ibn al-ʿArīf (d. 536/1141) was a Sufi of Almeria, in Andalusia on the Iberian peninsula, and member of a group led by a shaykh from Seville named Abū 'l-Ḥakam Ibn Barrajān (d. 536/1141). Ibn al-ʿArīf's sole surviving work is *The Beauties of Spiritual Sessions (Maḥāsin al-majālis)*. This brief systematic treatise on the mystical quest discusses in order ten stages of the spiritual path on which seekers already well along in the spiritual life make their way. The ten, which he calls "dwellings" *(manāzil)* are *maʿrifa*, will, asceticism, trust in God, patience, sadness, fear, hope, gratitude, and love and desire. He later added penitence and familiarity with God. His analysis of the stages tends toward elitism, pitched as it is toward those who have already progressed through more fundamental levels and have attained *maʿrifa*. Ibn al-ʿArīf thus locates *maʿrifa* at an advanced stage of the contemplative life. This explains why his first stage is one that most other Sufi psycho-spiritual typologies situate later, or higher on the list.

Ibn al-ʿArīf's work was heavily influenced by the two short but very popular works of Shaykh ʿAbd Allāh Anṣārī. In fact, apart from the sections on knowledge translated here, Ibn al-ʿArīf apparently used nearly verbatim some of the material from Anṣārī's *Resting Places of the Wayfarers (Manāzil as-sā'irīn)*.[53] Anṣārī's work arranges one hundred "stages" of the spiritual journey in ten clusters, the last of which begins with his consideration of experiential knowledge. Ibn al-ʿArīf's work thus suggests a concentration on what Anṣārī regarded as the most highly developed aspects of the spiritual journey. The order and names of the "resting places" in Ibn al-ʿArīf's work are identical to those of Anṣārī's *The Flaws of the Spiritual Stations (ʿIlal al-maqāmāt),* except that Ibn al-ʿArīf places *maʿrifa* (absent from that work of Anṣārī) at the head of the list. At the end of his list Ibn al-ʿArīf sums up by saying that these are "*resting places* of people of the Revealed Law who are *wayfarers* toward the essence of the ultimate spiritual reality," clearly alluding to Anṣārī's formulation (as indicated by my italics here). A most instructive aspect of this relationship is not that one writer depended so heavily on another—a relatively common occurrence—but that we have here a fine example of the rapid spread of the work of a Sufi author from Central Asia all the way to the western limits of medieval Islamdom in a relatively short time.[54]

In his thirteenth and final chapter Ibn al-ʿArīf summarizes by indicating that, in the end, all the stages disappear in the seeker's union with God. He then reflects more broadly on the spiritual project in general and describes a series of forty marvels *(karāmāt),* twenty to be experienced in this life and twenty in the next, in store for the servant whose entire life has been dedicated to serving God alone. He locates *maʿrifa* of God second among the twenty marvels bestowed in the next life. He then describes what he believes are four fundamental needs of the servant of God, all related to knowledge in various forms and degrees. The selections translated here include his section on *maʿrifa* as the first of a series of stages on the advanced spiritual quest, followed by his discussion of experiential knowledge as a marvel awaiting the servant in the next life.

ʿAyn al-Quḍāt al-Hamadhānī

ʿAyn al-Quḍāt al-Hamadhānī (492/1098–526/1131) established himself professionally as a magistrate in the northwestern Iranian city of Hamadhan. He studied Ghazālī's *Revitalization,* became a disciple of Ghazālī's younger brother Aḥmad (d. 520/1126), and soon came to be known as an authoritative teacher of Sufism. His ideas were controversial enough to get him executed, but his teachings on knowledge were not among the issues for which he drew the condemnation of religious authorities. His most mature work is his *Preambles [to Sufi Mystical Theology] (Tamhīdāt)* in Persian. An earlier, less important Arabic work (written when he was only twenty-four) entitled *Cream of Spiritual Realities (Zubdat al-ḥaqā'iq)* had endeavored to reconcile Sufism with philosophy. In the *Preambles* ʿAyn al-Quḍāt offers a creative and original interpretation of the secrets, symbolism, metaphysics, and epistemology of Sufism. He divides his analysis of the Sufi path into ten segments (preambles), including development of several of Sufi epistemology's central themes.[55]

Toshihiku Izutsu observes that ʿAyn al-Quḍāt's epistemology rests on the principle of "a sharp distinction between knowing the reality of a thing through an immediate personal experience of it and knowing something *about* the thing....Thus to know something *about* God is completely different from knowing Him by coming into direct contact with the divine order of things."[56] More specifically, two of Hamadhānī's key epistemological themes are the direct relationship between intimate knowledge of oneself and *maʿrifa* of Muḥammad's very self, and the connection between *maʿrifa* of one's own self and the vision of God in the next life. He explains that as the individual mystic attains the station of inebriation with the "wine of *maʿrifa*," he or she comes into possession of the *ʿilm* and *maʿrifa* of the soul of Muḥammad himself. Hamadhānī is elaborating here on the meaning of the Ḥadīth "Whoever has seen me has seen God," suggesting that experiential knowledge of Muḥammad is integrally linked to the individual's potential to attain *maʿrifa* of God.

ʿAyn al-Quḍāt explains in detail the implications of this concept for travelers on the spiritual path. The wayfarer who is advanced on the journey confronts the paradox of bewilderment and incapacity in the midst of abundant grace, for he has been granted

> so much self-knowledge, so much *maʿrifa* of himself through knowledge of his Lord that he neither knows himself as one endowed with *maʿrifa* nor (Him as) the Object of *maʿrifa*. Did not Abū Bakr say concerning this that "the inability to apprehend the process of apprehension is itself apprehension?" This maxim means that *maʿrifa* and apprehension are what entirely consume the mystic, so that he

> cannot apprehend whether he is the one-who-apprehends or not. (And hence, the Ḥadīth): "Glory be to Him who has not appointed any other way to *maʿrifa* of Him but incapacity to know Him!"
>
> Not just anyone is given access to *maʿrifa* of His ineffable Essence. For whoever desires to acquire knowledge and *maʿrifa* of the Divine Essence must make the soul of his self-reality into a mirror, so that gazing thereupon, he will recognize the soul of Muḥammad. Then he will make the soul of Muḥammad into a mirror. (The Ḥadīth) "And I saw my Lord during the Ascension in the fairest of forms," signifies this mirror. Within this mirror you should find "faces on that day resplendent looking towards their Lord" (75:22–23). Then send up the cry that "they measure not the power of God with a true measure" (6:91) out into the world, for (as the Prophet said) "we have not known God as He truly deserved."...
>
> ...Edify yourself through *maʿrifa* of your self, for *maʿrifa* in this world is the seed (that ripens into) the *Visio Dei* hereafter. What have you heard? I say: whoever possesses *maʿrifa* today will perceive the divine Vision tomorrow.[57]

Sanāʾī of Ghazna

Three of the many great Sufi poets who wrote in Persian have also put their distinctive stamp on the evolving notions of *ʿilm* and *maʿrifa*. ʿAbū ʾl-Majd Sanāʾī (512/1118–548/1152), originally from Ghazna in present-day Afghanistan, was among the most influential Persian mystical poets. His didactic poetic masterwork, *The Enclosed Garden of Ultimate Reality (Ḥadīqat al-ḥaqīqa),* begins with a short section on *maʿrifa*, which functions as propaideutic to his treatment of acknowledging the divine transcendent unity *(tawḥīd)*. Sanāʾī says that reason can take one only as far as the door to knowledge of God, after which only grace can carry one forward. Since most human beings fail to attain *ʿilm* even of themselves at any depth, how much hope can there be of attaining *maʿrifa* of God? In any case, even at their best—for example, even at the lofty rank of the revealing archangel

Gabriel—neither intellect nor imagination can know God apart from intimacy with God. As Gabriel is reduced to a mere finch in God's presence, intellect must surrender its sense of control if there is to be any hope of *maʿrifa*.[58]

Farīd ad-Dīn ʿAṭṭār

Farīd ad-Dīn ʿAṭṭār (d.c. 627/1230) was a Persian-writing poet from Nishapur in northeastern Persia. He is most famous for the mystical-didactic epic *The Conference of the Birds (Manṭiq aṭ-ṭayr)*. Although his work is clearly not a theoretical treatise, much less a manual of Sufi spirituality, it tells its story of spiritual progress and discovery in large part as a journey through a series of seven valleys: quest, love, *maʿrifa*, detachment, acknowledgment of the divine transcendent unity, bewilderment, and poverty/annihilation. ʿAṭṭār describes the valley of *maʿrifa* as containing a unique road for each wayfarer precisely tailored to that individual's needs and degree of spiritual attainment. Paradoxically, however, it is not individuality that comes to the fore in this valley, for that depends on relatively superficial distinctions. The valley of *maʿrifa* is most of all like an ocean (of *ʿirfān*, a cognate of *maʿrifa*) into which all plunge and in which all lose the separateness that is part and parcel of rational processes. Unlike ordinary thought, which is self-motivated, *maʿrifa* requires a willingness to be guided. Here the poet seems to associate *maʿrifa* directly with *ʿilm*. By way of illustration of the Ḥadīth "Seek knowledge *(ʿilm)* even as far as China," ʿAṭṭār tells the story of a man in China who has turned to stone and who grieves continually because so few seek him out. He is Knowledge. But those who do not possess knowledge live in darkness, for knowledge is the only true light. He further associates *ʿilm* with love.[59]

Jalāl ad-Dīn Rūmī

One of the most celebrated Sufi authors of the thirteenth century was the poet Jalāl ad-Dīn Rūmī (d. 672/1273). Born in Balkh, in present-day Afghanistan, Rūmī spent most of his life in the central Anatolian (modern Turkish) city of Konya. Although Rūmī was not primarily a systematic thinker and never produced the kind of compendia for which the authors presented here in translation are most famous, he made a unique contribution to issues relating to knowledge. In Rūmī's view the prophets model both the innate knowledge of which Ibn ʿArabī (see below) spoke a great deal, and the *maʿrifa* that has thrown off the yoke of imagination and attains to primary causes. Rūmī identifies *maʿrifa* as generally superior to *ʿilm*, for the former is available only through direct experience whereas the latter is typically mediated. He nevertheless accords a very important role to *ʿilm*: If an individual combines fundamental *ʿilm* with self-discipline *(zuhd)*, God will grant that person a "second *ʿilm*," which Rūmī seems to consider synonymous with both *maʿrifa* and love.

The kinds of complex teachings that Ibn ʿArabī communicates through the medium of highly allusive but very systematic prose, Rūmī expresses largely through poetic narratives. In every case he emphasizes the need for "utilitarian" knowledge of the sort that alone proceeds from a relationship with God. Derivative knowledge at which one arrives by dependence on intellect is loss rather than gain, for reason is a highway robber. Referring to the kind of innate knowledge of which Ibn ʿArabī speaks, Rūmī observes that appealing to the intellect is like asking for a ladder after one has climbed to the roof.[60]

Muḥyī ad-Dīn Ibn al-ʿArabī

Muḥyī ad-Dīn ibn al-ʿArabī (560/1165–638/1240) was one of Iberia's most famous Muslims and, along with Abū Ḥāmid al-Ghazālī, one of the most influential Muslim theologians of all time. Though Ibn ʿArabī's work is of such a massive scope that one can scarcely begin to hint at the breadth of his achievement, at least some brief mention of him is essential here. His thought is also notoriously difficult, but it is much more accessible thanks to the work of scholars like William Chittick.[61] Throughout his extensive writings Ibn ʿArabī uses the terms *ʿilm* and *maʿrifa*, along with their various cognates. Though he is familiar with the efforts of earlier authors to clarify differences between these concepts, he is not generally concerned with upholding the distinction. He is, nevertheless, keenly aware of a major difference between knowledge of outward realities and the profound understanding of inward truths. Like most of his predecessors,

Ibn ʿArabī regards the heart as the locus of knowing. Like Makkī and other Sufi authors, Ibn ʿArabī emphasizes that the only knowledge worth pursuing is the "useful" knowledge that has God and the sign-revealing cosmos as its objects. Such knowledge is beneficial precisely because it offers a map for the spiritual wayfarer. That always presupposes an essential ethical-ritual dimension informed by a subtle appreciation of the metaphorical and spiritual implications of all action.

Readers of Chittick's two superb anthologies of Ibn ʿArabī's writings will find themselves overwhelmed at the pervasiveness of the shaykh's concern with knowledge. One of Ibn ʿArabī's favorite Qur'ānic texts is that in which God commands Muḥammad, "Say: My Lord, increase me in knowledge" (20:114). Muḥammad is not to ask simply for the gift of knowledge, because, in Ibn ʿArabī's interpretation, God has made knowledge of Himself innate in every creature. One can, however, acquire more knowledge, both through the more restrictive and limited intellect *(ʿaql)* and the freer, more process-oriented heart *(qalb)*. Whereas the intellect knows through reflection, the heart knows through divine disclosure. Ibn ʿArabī ranks knowledge on three levels that have much in common with those distinguished by some of his predecessors: rational science that is proven or self-evident; knowledge of the spiritual states that one can attain only experientially; and the infused knowledge of divine secrets, to which only Prophets and Friends of God are given access through revelation. What separates the generality of religious folk from those further advanced spiritually is that the latter possess authentic knowledge thanks to divine self-disclosure, whereas the former know only the level of beliefs handed on to them by others. Several thousand miles east of Ibn ʿArabī's native Iberia, one of his contemporaries was responsible for a somewhat less cosmic but nonetheless major synthesis of mystical spirituality.

Abū Ḥafṣ ʿUmar as-Suhrawardī: *The Benefits of Intimate Knowledge*

Abū Ḥafṣ ʿUmar as-Suhrawardī (539/1145–632/1234) was born in the Persian city of Suhraward. At about the age of fifteen or sixteen (555/1160), he traveled to Baghdad, where he spent the remainder of his life studying and teaching. His legal training followed the Shāfiʿī school of jurisprudence. His uncle, Abū 'n-Najīb Ḍiyā' ad-Dīn ʿAbd al-Qāhir ibn ʿAbd Allāh as-Suhrawardī (490/1097–536/1168) had a *ribāṭ* (an institution often identified as a residential facility for Sufis) on the bank of the Tigris, to which a number of important Sufis attached themselves, including, most notably, the younger brother of Abū Ḥāmid al-Ghazālī, Aḥmad al-Ghazālī (d. 520/1126). Traditions of varying credibility suggest that Abū Ḥafṣ had important connections with his uncle as well as with a number of other influential Sufis, ʿAbd al-Qādir al-Jīlānī (d. 561/1166), Muʿīn ad-Dīn Chishtī (536–37/1141–43–633/1236), Ibn ʿArabī, Najm ad-Dīn ad-Dāyā ar-Rāzī (d. 654/1256), and the consummate Egyptian Sufi poet Ibn al-Fāriḍ (576/1181–632/1235), among the most famous.[62]

Suhrawardīi's major work, *The Benefits of Intimate Knowledge (ʿAwārif al-maʿārif),* is often acknowledged as the last of the classical Sufi compendia. As such, it shows signs of the influence of many of the earlier works, excerpted in translation below. In the original Arabic the text became a much-cited source among Sufis as far west as Spain and Morocco. Translated into Persian around the last third of the thirteenth century, the book became a standard textbook for Sufis of various organizations as far east as India. The work shows evidence of Suhrawardī's familiarity with the manuals of Sarrāj, Kalābādhī, Makkī, and Qushayrī.

Suhrawardī opens *ʿAwārif al-maʿārif* with one of the loveliest and most poetic chapters of its kind, "On the Origins of the Disciplines of the Sufis." He plunges directly into a discussion of explicitly Sufi modes of knowing, no longer concerned with arguing that they deserve a place in the larger picture of religious knowledge, but virtually presuming that. He does deal with the proponents of other levels of knowledge—scriptural exegetes, Ḥadīth specialists, and jurists—but cuts right to the chase: None of those specialists possesses the highest forms of knowledge. Throughout the chapter he sustains most remarkably the metaphor of knowledge as water flowing through the *wādīs* (seasonal river beds) of various kinds of people, according to their respective capacities. But the watercourses of those who renounce this world are widened to such a degree that their hearts become cisterns. Here he may have borrowed some imagery from Ghazālī's "Book of the Marvels of the Heart." Suhrawardī then develops an elaborate secondary metaphor, that of the creation of Muḥammad during which knowledge and wisdom were kneaded into his clay, from which humankind then became heirs to that knowledge. He then returns to the water/cistern metaphor and slips in a reference to the heart as a mirror.

The crux of his argument, insofar as he feels the need to defend Sufi modes of knowing at all, is to identify higher knowing as at root the most fundamental form of *fiqh fī 'd-dīn,* deeper religious understanding, and *fahm,* profound comprehension. Suhrawardī follows his general introduction with a chapter that focuses on Sufis as knowers, but without yet introducing the concept of *maʿrifa.* In chapter 2, "On the Superiority of the Sufis in Keen Attentiveness," he develops the notion that, because of their heightened ability to listen, Sufis are more receptive to knowledge than others. Their elevated receptivity results from their extinguishing the fires of the ego. Here he discusses *maʿrifa* significantly for the first time, suggesting that experiential knowledge, comprehension, and attentiveness are integrally connected.

Suhrawardī begins to develop the concept of *maʿrifa* two-thirds of the way through his second chapter in *The Benefits of Intimate Knowledge.* He launches that development with a discussion of the differences between *tafsīr* and *ta'wīl,* noting that whereas accuracy in the former depends on scientific knowledge *(ʿilm),* accuracy in the latter is directly proportional to the level of the interpreter's *maʿrifa.* He provides a fairly detailed commentary on the Ḥadīth that says every word has a *ḥadd* (the prescriptive or ethical sense) and a *maṭlaʿ* (or *muṭṭalaʿ*, the spiritual sense), which he describes as the point at which understanding of the word that has been revealed becomes an experiential knowledge of the Revealer Himself. Suhrawardī places greater emphasis on hermeneutical principles than any of the other manualists, and the issue deserves further comment here.

Ibn ʿAbbās (d.c. 68/687), an early exegete, distinguished four levels of meaning in the Qur'ān roughly analogous to the ancient Christian "fourfold sense of scripture"—literal, allegorical, moral (or tropological), and spiritual/eschatological (or anagogical). Later Sufi authors, such as Muḥāsibī, Sahl at-Tustarī, and now Suhrawardī, adapted the distinction for the purposes of mystical exegesis. The Sufi exegete Sulamī attributes a saying about the four senses to ʿAlī, whereas Suhrawardī traces a saying referring to the two levels of meaning and two "higher" senses of scripture—*ḥadd* and *maṭlaʿ*—to Muḥammad himself. The aforementioned saying indicates that the whole of scripture was revealed according to seven "readings," that every verse of the scripture has an outward and inward dimension, and that each "reading" has a *ḥadd* and a *maṭlaʿ*.[63] In any case, Suhrawardī concerns himself with only the *ḥadd* and *maṭlaʿ*, associating them with aspects of the interpreter's spiritual experience. I have occasionally rendered the two terms, respectively, as "fundamental meaning" and "apex of insight."

Chapter 3, "On the Excellence of the Sciences of the Sufis," delves in greater detail into the concept of *maʿrifa* as such, explaining that it is integrally connected with the degree to which one acts upon, and is changed by, what one knows. Suhrawardī argues that the Ḥadīth "Knowledge is a duty for all Muslims" actually refers to experiential knowledge and spiritual discernment. Following Sarrāj, he points out that since in all matters that require specific knowledge, any reasonable person will seek the advice of those who specialize in the relevant science, so one who needs help with experiential knowledge and spiritual discernment must seek out experts. To that theme he returns in chapter 56, "On the Sufi Disclosures concerning Intimate Self-knowledge," where Suhrawardī develops essential elements of his psychology. Finally, in chapter 57, "On the Experiential Knowledge, Analysis, and Discernment of Movements of the Spirit *(khawāṭir)*," he develops in detail the ways in which *maʿrifa* allows one to sort out and neutralize diabolically stimulated proclivities. These latter two chapters are not presented in translation here, both for lack of space and because, although they do deal with the concept of *maʿrifa*, they develop it in a very specific way related to discernment of spirits and are thus moving off onto a new tack from that of epistemology in general.

Part Three: Beyond the Classics

Suhrawardī was not the last author of an important pedagogical work that discussed epistemological themes of *ʿilm* and *maʿrifa*. The language of knowing, using both of those technical terms, remains central to contemporary spiritual seekers who pursue the Sufi path across the world today.[64] Influential late medieval and early modern authors from Morocco to Malaysia have produced pedagogical works that reflect significant influence of the classical Sufi manuals. Here are brief examples of three very different authors from several centuries and across the globe.

The sixteenth-seventeenth-century Ḥamza Fanṣūrī (d. 1035/ 1625) of Acheh (now on the Indonesian island of Sumatra), for example, composed several works that set him apart as probably the first author to translate the full spectrum of Sufi concepts into the Malay language. *His Secrets of Those Endowed with Maʿrifa (Asrār al-ʿārifīn)* meditates on the attributes of God and emphasizes that it is only through *maʿrifa* that one comes to know them truly. Sayings of Muḥammad that he quotes quite often are, "One who knows himself intimately knows his Lord intimately," and "Without *maʿrifa*, the ritual prayer is not valid." Like earlier Sufi authors—he cites Kalābādhī's manual in particular a number of times—Ḥamza insists that there is no distinction between Revealed Law and the Sufi Path, between the Path and the ultimate spiritual reality, and between that truth and *maʿrifa*.[65] Ḥamza also penned a collection of thirty-two lyric poems, in which the theme of knowledge is prominent, for knowledge *is* the way forward. *Maʿrifa* is the ultimate goal, and Ḥamza tells his followers it is not difficult to attain if only they follow from one spiritual station *(maqām)* to the next. He appears to consider *ʿilm* of union with God virtually synonymous with *maʿrifa*, and says that such *ʿilm* is close at hand, for God is closer than the jugular vein (50:16). Everywhere in the universe one can find signs that yield *maʿrifa*, and one who fails to find it there should concentrate on repentance.[66]

At the western end of the Mediterranean, the eighteenth-century Moroccan Aḥmad ibn ʿAjība (1160/1746–1224/1809), of the Darqāwī Sufi order, wrote a "glossary" of 143 Sufi technical terms, arranged more or less in ascending order, called the *Book of the Ascension in Perceiving the Realities of Sufism (Kitāb al-miʿrāj at-tashawwuf ila ḥaqā'iq at-taṣawwuf)*. He acknowledges that he has followed Qushayrī's *Treatise* in providing a list of technical terms by way of convenient summary of the *ʿilm* of Sufism. He also acknowledges, through frequent citation, the influence of fellow "Westerner" Ibn al-ʿArīf on his work. Ibn ʿAjība locates his brief entry on *maʿrifa* at number 19, just after contemplation and essential vision, and before reverential piety. *Maʿrifa,* he observes concisely, is the "permanent and solid matrix of contemplation, a perpetual vision with a ravished heart that sees only its Lord and Master and turns to nothing but Him." Curiously, Ibn ʿAjība's entry on *maʿrifa* is easily one of the shortest, and he devotes much greater attention to other more technical terms. Only toward the end of the glossary does he again allude to *maʿrifa*, and that is in a reference that suggests that he all but took this concept for granted. There Ibn ʿAjība clusters together three terms used synonymously to refer to practitioners of the Sufi Path—devotees *(ʿubbād)*, ascetics *(zuhhād),* and those endowed with *maʿrifa (ʿārifūn).*[67]

Aḥmad also wrote a most interesting and extensive "autobiographical" document, whose eighteenth chapter is dedicated to the shaykh's survey of knowledge, or, as he calls them, "the exoteric and esoteric disciplines." Ibn ʿAjība discusses these matters here in the course of his autobiography because, he claims, this is what he has mastered in his quest for learning. He divides the disciplines into the sciences of intellectual operations (for example, logic and arithmetic), linguistics (including grammar, poetics, and belles-lettres), the physical sciences (especially medicine and anatomy), and the religious disciplines (including law, theology, and Sufism). Muslims, he observes, have built upon the sciences of the ancients in nonreligious fields and then developed fresh approaches to the religious disciplines. All in all, this is a strikingly broad-minded survey of knowledge, sharing with earlier manualists such as Sarrāj a concern for laying out the widest possible context within which to situate the disciplines of the Sufis. Only at the very end of his survey does Ibn ʿAjība describe what he takes to be the summit of true knowledge. Referring to Sufism as "my" discipline, he alludes with considerable subtlety to the goal of the spiritual quest: contemplative vision.[68]

Finally, twentieth-century Iranian scholar Jaʿfar Sajjādī (d. 1417/1996) published a Persian *Dictionary of Mystical Vocabulary, Technical Expressions, and Terminology,* in which he included a lengthy article on *maʿrifa*. Much of the work is taken up with direct citations from the works of the great medieval mystical authors. Before citing Sufi authorities for several full pages, Sajjādī begins with a broader set of definitions of the various ways one can understand *maʿrifa* in contemporary terms. It can mean a form of perception that includes conception and cognition. Occasionally people explain *maʿrifa* as image formation, in which case they refer to the cognition of the result of perception as *ʿilm*. It can even occur in a deductive or inferential form, a meaning quite different from that of the classical Sufi texts. *Maʿrifa* might also refer to the renewed perception of something known once but later forgotten. He then proceeds to offer a host of definitions of the term by leading Sufis, much the way the medieval sources did, but drawing heavily from Persian poets.[69]

A fuller survey of mystical-epistemological themes would have examined the works of dozens of other significant figures who retain places of honor in the ranks of the great Sufis. My purpose here has been primarily to offer an initial sense of the persistent issues and underlying concerns of those medieval Sufis best known for their manuals of spirituality, all in the larger context of ongoing developments in classical and medieval Muslim treatments of knowledge in relation to the spiritual life. With that general background I hope that the primary sources will be better able now to speak for themselves.

In the translated material offered here the reader will encounter an extraordinary breadth of themes and personalities from medieval Islamic tradition. These treatises on mystical spirituality are concerned with far more than arcane metaphysical argument and rarified theoretical discussion. Their subjects include the full range of traditional religious disciplines. Together they offer a thematic overview of the development of Sufi thought in relation to the broader history of the traditional sciences, and of the role of Islam's most fundamental sources in that larger story. In that sense one can find in these texts a solid primary source introduction to the greater Islamic religious tradition. As for the colorful personalities described anecdotally, whose sayings and thoughts are so often cited in these texts, they represent an equally expansive spectrum of views and biases. Whatever Sufism's critics over the centuries may have considered sufficient reason for condemning Sufism outright, a reading of these texts would surely have challenged their criticisms.

1

Abū Naṣr as-Sarrāj: *The Book of Flashes (Kitāb al-lumaʿ)*

Here are fifteen brief chapters—somewhat less than 10 percent of his whole work—in which Sarrāj sets out his understanding of legitimate Sufi claims to credibility among the other Islamic religious disciplines. The foundation of his argument rests on the "sociology" of Islamic religious knowledge that Sarrāj discusses in most of the first dozen sections of the book. After affirming Sufism as an authentic religious discipline, he delves into the finer points of Sufi modes of knowing in later chapters. Where gaps occur between chapters devoted to epistemological issues, I will summarize sections not translated here.[1]

Chapter 1: [4] Explanation of the discipline of Sufism, the method of the Sufis, and their relationship to scholars of unassailable credibility

Shaykh Abū Naṣr said: Someone asked me to explain the science of Sufism and the method of the Sufis. He argued that people are of various opinions about it. Some praise it excessively and elevate it above its rightful place; some consider it beyond the limits of rational and scientific investigation. Others regard [5] it as little more than a pastime, a trifling game for the feeble-minded. Still others associate it with piety, asceticism, woolen garments, affectation in the use of idiosyncratic jargon, habits of dress, and other such things. Some go so far as to impale the Sufis on the gibbet of their own terminology by accusing them of free thinking and doctrinal error.

So he asked me to expand on how I understand the soundness of the principles of the Sufis' method, as supported and sanctioned by adherence to the Book of God, the exalted and glorified, by imitation of the Messenger of God, God's blessings and peace upon him, by ethical conduct modeled on that of the Companions and Followers,[2] and by behavior consistent with that of devout servants of God Most High. He asked me to record that in writing with proof that would corroborate the true and discredit the false, separate the serious from the frivolous, the sound from the sickly, and set the record straight about all these variant opinions as to whether theirs is a credible religious discipline.

I say, therefore—and from God alone comes success—that God, blessed and exalted, has laid down the foundations of religion and has removed uncertainty from the hearts of the faithful concerning His command that they adhere to His Book and be committed to the implications of the words He addressed to them, may His majesty be magnified, "And hold fast to the rope of God all together, and do not break into factions" (3:103); and "Assist one another in devotion and piety" (5:3). Next, God Most High mentioned those whom He lists among the most excellent believers and the loftiest in religion, ranking them just after His angels. He testified to their witnessing to His transcendent oneness, placing His angels second only to Himself, saying—may He be exalted and glorified—"God has testified that there is no deity but He, as have His angels and those endowed with knowledge of unassailable credibility" (3:18).

Tradition has it that the Prophet, God's blessings and peace upon him, said, "Those who possess *ʿilm* are the heirs of the Prophets." I am of the opinion—and God knows best—that those endowed with knowledge of unassailable credibility are the heirs of the prophets; it is they who are devoted to the Book of God Most High, who strive to follow God's Messenger, God's blessings and peace upon him, and who emulate the Companions and Followers in traveling the road of God Most High's devout Friends and upright servants. They are of three categories: scholars of the Ḥadīth, jurists, and Sufis. These are the three groups endowed with knowledge of unassailable credibility who are the heirs of the prophets. Thus, of the many varieties of knowledge, these three are religious disciplines: knowledge of the Qur'ān, knowledge of the Sunna, and the exposition [6] and knowledge of the realities of the faith. These three groups together share the aforementioned religious disciplines, which represent the sum of the religious sciences, and none of them departs from the three above-cited verses of the Book of God, exalted and glorified, or from the sayings of God's Messenger, God's blessings and peace upon him, or from the profound wisdom that has moved the heart of any of the Friends of God Most High.

That [state of affairs] is rooted in the "Ḥadīth of faith," in which the Prophet, God's blessings and peace upon him, asked Gabriel, peace be upon him, about the three principles, surrender *(islām),* faith *(imān),* and spirituality *(iḥsān)*—the external, the internal, and the ultimate spiritual reality. *Islām* is the outward, *imān* both outward and inward, and *iḥsān* the outward, the inward, and the ultimate spiritual reality.[3] The Prophet, God's blessings and peace upon him, said that *iḥsān* is serving God Most High as though you saw Him, but even if you don't see Him, He sees you, and Gabriel confirmed that. *ʿIlm* is linked to action, and action to sincerity. Sincerity means that the servant seeks the face of God, glorious and mighty, in his knowledge and his action. These three groups mentioned above differ in both theory and practice and are organizationally disparate. God Most High alluded to their disparity and their respective levels when He, may He be exalted and glorified, said, "(God will raise) in rank those possessed of knowledge" (58:11); and, "all have ranks according to what they have done" (46:19); and, "Observe how We have made some excel over others" (17:21). The Prophet, God's blessings and peace upon him, said, "People are alike, lined up like the teeth of a comb, none more excellent than another except in knowledge and piety."

Anyone who has a question concerning one of the principles of the religion and its ramifications, legal implications, spiritual meanings, sanctions, or stipulations, whether external or internal, has no choice but to have recourse to these three groups—the traditionists, the jurists, and the Sufis. Each of these groups has its distinctive brand of theory and practice, spiritual reality and spiritual state, each its own interpretation of knowledge and action, spiritual station and expression, profound comprehension and place, deeper understanding and approach to interpretation of the sources. Those who are learned in it have knowledge of it, and those who are not schooled in it do not. No one group can achieve a comprehensive grasp of theories and practices and spiritual states; each one has its spiritual station where God Most High has placed it, and its spiritual state where God, exalted and glorified, has situated it. I will explain to you, God Most High willing, to the best of my ability, how each of these groups pursues one or another theory [7] and practice, in what aspect each excels, and which of them is of the highest level. I will do so in a way that you will find intellectually appealing and understandable, if God Most High wishes.

Chapter 2: [7] Characteristics and distinguishing features of the traditionists with regard to transmission and insight into the Ḥadīth and their unique ways of knowing the subject

Said the shaykh, God be compassionate to him: The traditionists are concerned with understanding the outward meaning of the sayings of God's Messenger, God's blessings and peace upon him. They have asserted that this is the foundation of the religion because God Most High says, "Take what the Messenger gives you and refrain from what he forbids for you" (59:7). Therefore, when material of this sort came to their attention, they would travel from one land to another in search of transmitters of Ḥadīth. They would stay with them until they had received from them the traditions of God's Messenger, God's blessings and peace upon him. Collating what had been transmitted from the Companions and Followers, they then analyzed carefully what they had gathered about the Companions' and Followers' life stories and sayings, their views and differences of opinion as evidenced in their decisions, utterances, deeds, character, and personal spiritual qualities.

The scholars would then assess the authenticity of what they had transmitted orally, committed to memory, and written down—material handed on from one trustworthy person to another, one individual of integrity to another. They then carefully preserved that material. They determined the whereabouts of the transmitters who were involved in compiling each report and entry, noting their names, their surnames, and recording precisely their birth and death dates. As a result, they gathered data on how many Ḥadīths each of those individuals had transmitted, from whom they had received each Ḥadīth, and to whom each transmitter had related the Ḥadīth. They were able to determine who had communicated a Ḥadīth inaccurately, which individuals had erred by either inserting a letter or deleting a word, which individuals had done so intentionally, and which had simply made an honest mistake.

These Ḥadīth scholars thus ascertained the names of suspect transmitters caught in a lie about God's Messenger, God's blessings and peace upon him. They identified whose transmissions were sound and whose not, and who had transmitted Ḥadīths otherwise unattested or whose precise wording was unique and not found in others. By this method they made note of how many individuals had transmitted each variant Ḥadīth and indicated the weak links in its chain of transmission. Thus they organized categories, classifying the *sunnas*[4] into chapters. They distinguished between those that were judged "sound," those of questionable reliability, and those whose chain of transmission included an untrustworthy individual. The scholars narrowed their attention to those Ḥadīths that were transmitted, respectively, by the fewest [8] and by the greatest number. They identified Ḥadīths transmitted by leading figures in the cities, and categorized lesser, derivative transmitters as distinct from the greater, leading figures. These scholars possessed comprehensive knowledge of the flaws evidenced in the disparity of views among transmitters, whether in the form of addition or deletion, and of their place in the chain of transmission of *sunnas* and traditions; for these things form the basis of religious practice.

In that matter these Ḥadīth scholars are superior to the (generalist) religious scholars, so that by dint of greater learning, one of them can lay claim to accuracy and capacity of memory in handling the evidence, when it comes to impartiality and critical assessment, of rejection and acceptance of traditions, on the grounds that a text's testimony is consistent with what God's Messenger, God's blessings and peace upon him, said and did, commanded and forbade, enjoined and prayed for. God Most High has said, "Thus did We fashion you as a morally balanced community so that you might bear witness to humankind and so that the Messenger might be a witness to you all" (2:143). The traditionists are said to be the custodians of what the Messenger of God, God's blessings and peace upon him, and the Companions and Followers, said and did. The scriptural text "and so that the Messenger might be a witness to you all" therefore refers to their testimony to the Prophet's deeds, words, spiritual states, and moral character. The Prophet, God's blessings and peace upon him, has said, "Whoever knowingly lies about me will sit on his own couch in hell." And the Prophet, God's blessings and peace upon him, said, "May God make radiant the face of one who has heard a Ḥadīth from me and spreads it abroad," and so on. It is said that every traditionist bears on his countenance a glow as a result of the Prophet's prayer.

The traditionists have produced written sources containing the findings of their research. As has been widely attested, famous masters among them have enjoyed the acknowledgment of their contemporaries for their outstanding learning, surpassing intellect, and exemplary religious practice and faith. What I have said is sufficient for those who know, and it is God who grants success.

Chapter 3: [8] On the classifications of the legal scholars and the unique features of their methodology among the various disciplines

Said Shaykh Abū Naṣr, God be compassionate to him: As a category of those who possess knowledge, the legal scholars are superior to the traditionists. The two groups are comparable with respect to the general import [9] of their disciplines and their methods. But the legal scholars possess a specialized understanding and deeper interpretation of the Ḥadīth, steeping themselves in detailed investigation for setting forth religious regulations and sanctions and the principles of Revealed Law. With those concerns in mind, they distinguish between abrogating and abrogated texts,[5] between principles and particulars, separating the specific from the general, with reference to the scripture, the Sunna, consensus *(ijmāʿ),* and analogical reasoning *(qiyās).*[6] They then explain to the people the requirements of their religion on the basis of Qur'ān and tradition. Some requirements are no longer in force but are still on the books, while others not attested to in writing nevertheless retain the force of law. Some are expressed in general terms but are understood specifically, while others are couched as specific rules but are understood more generally. Some regulations address a collectivity of people but are interpreted as referring to individuals, while others address the individual but are taken to refer to groups.

Legal scholars marshal intellectual arguments against their opponents. They draw conclusions on the basis of evidence in shaping their arguments against those in error, to bolster the religion. They adhere to the text of the scripture or the text of the Sunna, or to analogical reasoning on the basis of the text, or to the consensus of the community. In response to anyone who disagrees with them, they argue by the rules of rational argument. To any who dispute with them they respond with the etiquette of debate. Should anyone take issue with them contentiously, they counter with equally trenchant rejoinder, matching one imputed weakness with another in return. Thus they put everything in its place, prioritize every definition according to its category, distinguishing among rational analogy, formal similarity, affinity, and parallelism.[7] As for things either commanded or forbidden, they differentiate as to which are required, which are recommended, which are to be avoided and cause for alarm, and which are urged and called for.

These scholars thus explain obscurities, untie knots, illumine paths, dispel ambiguities, bring forth branches from roots, expand the cryptic, unravel the densely packed, and evaluate religious sanctions judiciously. They do this so that, in the external requirements and sanctions of the Sharīʿa, one scholar does not follow another scholar blindly, nor the ignorant person an ignorant person, nor the socially elite individual an elite person, nor the common person a common person. Legal scholars keep watch over their ordinances for the Muslims. God Most High, may He be exalted and glorified, referred to them in His Book when He said, "Let parties from every contingent set out to dedicate themselves to understanding the religion."[8] And the Prophet,

God's blessings and peace upon him, said, "When God desires an individual's good, He gives that person deeper religious understanding."

Concerning their branch of learning and methods, legal scholars, too, have their written sources, as well as their renowned masters, [10] whose leadership their contemporaries acclaimed unanimously for their greater learning, insight, religious commitment, and trustworthiness. But a full explanation of that would be too lengthy, and the perspicacious reader will draw fuller conclusions from these brief hints. And in Allāh is our success.

Chapter 4: [10] On the classifications of the Sufis, their various approaches to *ʿilm* and action, and their outstanding virtues and excellent qualities

Said Shaykh Abū Naṣr, God be compassionate to him: The Sufis are analogous to the legal scholars and the traditionists in that they, also, have their groups with their distinctive opinions. They agree with the other groups of religious specialists on their disciplines and are not at odds on their meanings and methods, to the extent that they avoid innovation and the pursuit of personal whim, while conforming to the established pattern and example of tradition. They are allied in their assent to and affirmation of all aspects of their discipline and do not disagree on them.

Any Sufis who do not measure up to the qualifications of the legal scholars and traditionists in knowledge and insight and fail to amass the broad learning they command will have recourse to those other religious experts in the event any divinely revealed commandment or religious sanction should become unclear to them. Thus, when they are in agreement about such a thing, they are unanimous in what they profess together; and when they disagree, the Sufis have recourse, according to their method, to the best, the first, and the most complete option out of care for the religion. They give priority to what God has commanded His servants and avoid what God has forbidden them. Their way does not include stooping to licentious behavior, going in search of esoteric interpretations, the tendency toward a life of ease and dissipation, and the espousal of questionable views, all of which amount to a disregard for the religion and throwing caution to the wind. On the contrary, their way is to hold fast to what is fundamental and most complete in the matter of religion.

This is what I have come to know about the ways of the Sufis and their methods in their use of the exoteric sciences as practiced by and current among the classes of religious scholars and traditionists. Beyond that, they ascend to high ranks and have a propensity for noble spiritual states [11] and elevated spiritual abodes, which consist of various forms of worshipfulness, profound obedience, and exquisite moral character. The upshot of that is a unique and distinctive quality not shared by other religious scholars, jurists, and traditionists. A full analysis of that would require a lengthier explanation. I can elucidate for you only a sample of the whole reality, so that, God willing, you might infer from what I have said to what I have not said.

Here we skip Chapter 5: "On the unique understandings with which the Sufis construe conduct, spiritual states, and knowledge and which set them apart from the generality of religious scholars." Sarrāj does not advance specifically his treatment of knowledge in this chapter but focuses instead on more praxis-oriented ways in which the Sufis differ from other "learned" people.

Chapter 6: [13] On the special qualities of the Sufis among the categories of those who possess *ʿilm* with respect to other epistemological issues

Said Shaykh [Abū Naṣr], God be compassionate to him: Another unique feature of the Sufis, among the categories of the religiously learned, is their use of verses recited from the Book of God Most High, and of traditions transmitted from God's Messenger, God's blessings and peace upon him, which no scriptural verse has abrogated and whose authority no prophetic tradition or report has preempted. These call for lofty moral conduct and impel toward elevated spiritual states and noble deeds. They speak of high spiritual stations in the religion and exalted stages that distinguish one segment of believers and characterize a group of the Companions and Followers. Those verses and traditions embrace the behavior and moral values of the Messenger, God's blessings and peace upon him, as he says, "Indeed God has instilled in me good conduct and has highly refined my behavior." And God, exalted and glorified be He, says, "Indeed you are of exquisite moral character" (68:4).

These matters are to be found in the documents of the religious scholars and jurists, but here they lack the penetrating understanding and insight that they display in the other aspects of their discipline. Apart from the Sufis, no scholars of unassailable credibility have a share in the present topic apart from general affirmation and belief that it is true. These matters include such things as the reality and characteristics of repentance, the ranks of the penitent, and their spiritual realities; the details of piety and the spiritual states of the god-fearing; the classifications of those who trust in God; the stations [14] of those who experience spiritual contentment; and the ranks of the patient. They speak similarly of modesty and humility and love, fear and hope, desire and introspection, contrition and tranquility, certainty and spiritual satisfaction. The numbers of these spiritual states are virtually beyond counting, each of them with its own practitioners and classifications. Each has essential details, including [contemplative method, spiritual states, self-scrutiny, mysteries, inner combat, spiritual stations, discrete levels], unique intentionality, distinctive strength of will, resistance to lassitude, and being overwhelmed by ecstasy. And each of these has its definition, spiritual station, type of knowledge, and analysis, to the extent that God, exalted and glorified, apportions them.

The Sufis are also distinguished by their *ma'rifa* of the specific features of concupiscence and earthly expectation; and their insight into the ego-soul with its importunities and ephemeral proclivities, and into the subtleties of conceit, disguised lust, and covert idolatry. Sufis are unique in their understanding of the means for liberation from these things and for turning toward God the Exalted and Glorified, for sincerely taking refuge in God, and for persisting in spiritual needfulness, surrender, handing all over to God, and admitting one's lack of power and strength.

In addition, the Sufis have discovered deeper interpretations of knowledge that have eluded the jurists and religious scholars. They couch these subtleties in allusion and conceal them in technical expressions because of their sensitivity and delicacy. That is the case with their talk of obstacles, hindrances, obligations, concealments, arcane secrets, the stations of sincerity and the states of insight into mystery, the realities of thought and the degrees of nearness to God, the laying bare of acknowledgment of divine transcendent unity, the stages of acknowledging the divine simplicity, the realities of servanthood, the obliteration of temporal existence in pre-eternity,[9] the ephemeral nature of created things by contrast with the eternally ancient, the passing away of the vision of what one might accept as a substitute for God, and the perdurance of the vision of the giver [even as the vision of the gift passes away], the fading of the states and stations, the uniting of [the separated], the passing away of the experience of striving while the vision of the goal survives, [avoidance of the vision of what substitutes for God,] letting go of resistance, of raiding travelers on obliterated paths, and of wandering through [15] perilous wastelands.

Among the religious scholars of unassailable authority or integrity, the Sufis distinguish themselves in untying these knots and penetrating the problematic aspects of these things. They pursue these questions tenaciously and doggedly, and attack them with complete unselfishness. They do not desist until they have communicated about their flavor and taste, decrease and increase. They inquire of any who lay claim to one of these spiritual states as to their evidence for it, and discourse about the state's soundness or weakness. There is more here than a single person can mention even a little about, since it is so vast there is no way to encompass it.

Knowledge of all of this is found in the Book of God, exalted and glorified, and in the traditions of God's Messenger, God's blessings and peace upon him, and is familiar to specialists; and the religious scholars do not dispute that when they discuss these matters. However, a group of those who specialize in exoteric learning do take issue with the Sufis because the exotericists understand only those aspects of the Book of God Most High and the traditions of God's Messenger, God's blessings and peace upon him, that pertain to outward requirements and that support their polemic against their opponents. People nowadays are more inclined to that sort of thing because it more closely approximates what they want in leadership, gaining standing among the masses, and achieving worldly ends. You will see precious few occupying themselves with the learning I have been describing, for this is a unique *ʿilm* alloyed with bitterness and choking torment. At the sound of it knees weaken, the heart grows sad, eyes fill with tears, the great becomes small and the small great. But what an enterprise, what an experience, what savor, what an encounter does that knowledge bring! Ego has no share in the inward encounter, for the ego-soul is hemmed in by mortality, the fallibility of the senses, and the ephemeral nature of objects of desire. As a result, the religious scholars have eschewed this knowledge, engrossing themselves in cultivating a knowledge that lightens their burden and impels them toward permissiveness, license, and facile interpretation, a knowledge that is congenial with human tendencies and rests more lightly on human souls, bent as they are toward yielding to baser proclivities and turning aside from duty. God Most High knows best.

In the next chapter, Sarrāj seriously undertakes to defend the Sufis' detailed analysis of elements of the spiritual life. They base their analysis on the occurrence of specific terms and descriptions found in the Qur'ān and Ḥadīth, and Sarrāj is concerned with demonstrating that every aspect of Sufi psychology and epistemology has a firm basis in tradition and revelation.

Chapter 7: [16] A rejoinder to the claim that the Sufis are an ignorant lot and that the science of Sufism has no support from the Book and tradition

Said Shaykh [Imām Abū Naṣr], God be compassionate to him: The imāms agree unanimously that God, Blessed and Exalted, refers in

His Book to upright men and women, to humble men and women, as well as to the submissive, the pious, the sincere, those who do good, the fearful, the hopeful, the awestruck, the worshipful, the sojourners, the long-suffering, the spiritually content, the god-trusting, the self-abasing, the Friends of God, the god-fearing, the elect, the chosen, the devout, and those who are close to God. God Most High mentioned those who bear witness when He said, "or one who gives ear, that person is a witness" (54:37). And God Most High refers to the serene when he says, "Surely hearts become serene when they remember God" (13:28). God Most High also speaks of those who arrive ahead of others, those who are temperate, and those who hasten to good deeds.

And the Prophet, God's blessings and peace upon him, said, "In my (religious) community there are those spoken about and those addressed, and ʿUmar is one of them." And the Prophet, God's blessings and peace upon him, said, "Many are the disheveled, dusty ones, clad in a pair of rags, whose oath God would honor, and Barā' (d. 72/691) is one of them." To Wābiṣa he said, "Seek advice from your heart," and he did not say that to anyone else. And the Prophet, God's blessings and peace upon him, said, "As a result of the intercession of a man of my community, people as numerous as the tribes of Rabīʿa and Muḍar will enter the Garden. That man's name is Uways al-Qaranī."[10] And in the Ḥadīth we find also, "In my community there are those whom I know to be god-fearing when they recite Qur'ān, and Ṭalq ibn Ḥabīb (d.c. 90/178) is among them." Another saying of the Prophet, God's blessings and peace upon him, goes, "Seventy thousand of my community will enter the Garden without being called to account." "O Messenger of God," someone asked, "who are they?" He replied, "They are the ones who do not allow themselves to be branded[11] and put their trust not in sorcery but rely on their Lord."[12]

There are numerous traditions and accounts of this sort, and everyone agrees that all of the people mentioned in these texts were of the community of Muḥammad, God's blessings and peace upon him. Had they not been part of the community, and if they could not have existed in every age, then God Most High would not have mentioned them in His Book, nor would the Messenger of God, God's blessings and peace upon him, have described them. On the one hand, we have seen that the term "faith" applies to the collectivity of believers; [17]

on the other, those people stand out from the crowd as individuals with specific names. That is proof of their uniqueness among the generality of believers united under the term "faith." Not one of the imāms disputes that the prophets, on whom be peace, are of higher rank than these individuals (mentioned above) and dwell nearer to God Most High than these, and that they were human beings subject to all the same needs as other human beings for food, sleep, and ordinary cares. Nevertheless, there is a vast difference between the prophets, God's blessings be on them all, and the rest of these people I have been talking about. That is due to the existence of a secret between them and the One they serve, and to the increase in their certitude and their belief in what God Most High has communicated and apportioned to them. Only the prophets, upon whom be peace, are set apart from these individuals by the unique features of prophetic revelation, prophetic mission, and proofs of prophethood. No one else can compete with them in that respect. And God is the one who knows most fully.

Chapter 8: [17] On the counter argument of the Sufis to those who make a profession of legal scholarship, and an explanation, supported by evidence, of deep religious understanding

Said Shaykh [Abū Naṣr], God be compassionate to him: It is reported that the Prophet, God's blessings and peace upon him, said: "When God wishes the best for an individual, he grants that person deep religious understanding." It has come to my attention that someone said to Ḥasan al-Baṣrī,[13] God be compassionate to him, "So-and-so is a *faqīh*." Ḥasan replied, "And have you ever seen a *faqīh*? The *faqīh* is the one who has forsaken this world, prefers the next, and possesses spiritual insight into his religion." God Most High says, "So that they might gain profound religious understanding" (9:122). "Religion" is a term that encompasses all requirements, both external and internal. Erudition in the requirements of these spiritual states and the meanings of these spiritual stations mentioned earlier is every bit as useful as erudition in the legal fine points of divorce, the release of slaves, the vow of abstinence,[14] retaliation, oath-taking, and legal punishments. That is because these legal issues are unlikely, during an entire lifetime, to require specific knowledge of them. Should such issues arise, one who has a question about them simply relies on authorities on the subject and abides by the opinion of one [18] of the jurists. That obligation then is no longer binding on that person until some other issue should arise.

However, believers are in need of these spiritual states, stations, and inner struggles that the Sufis seek to understand and whose realities they discuss. They must gain an experiential knowledge of these things, and these matters are not time related. These topics include, for example, uprightness, sincerity, recollection, and avoidance of heedlessness. There is no prescribed moment for these. On the contrary, the godservant must in each moment and at all times be aware of his or her intention, desire, and interior impulse. In the case of a duty, one must attend to it; in the case of pleasure, one must fend it off. God Most High said to His pure Prophet Muḥammad, God's blessings and peace upon him, "Do not obey any person whose heart We have allowed to stray from mindfulness of Us, who responds only to passing desire and whose manner of life is dissolute" (18:28). Anyone who disregards one of these spiritual states does so at the cost of having his heart overcome by heedlessness.

Know that the inner significance of what they learn, and the insight into the details and realities of that learning that the Sufis discover, is necessarily greater than the meanings that the legal scholars find in external requirements, for this *ʿilm* of the Sufis is limitless. It encompasses allusions, manifestations, movements of spirit, gifts, and blessings, which its practitioners harvest from the ocean of divine largesse. The other ways of knowing are clearly circumscribed. All ways of knowing culminate in the science of Sufism, while the knowledge of Sufism leads only to some further aspect of the discipline of Sufism. There is no end to that knowledge, for there is no end to that science's object, namely, mystical revelations. By way of the understanding of His word and perception of His communication, Allāh Most High reveals what, and as, He chooses to the hearts of His Friends. God the exalted and glorified has said, "Proclaim: If the ocean were ink with which to write the words of my Lord, the ocean would be exhausted more quickly than the words of my Lord, even if We supplied another its equal in size" (18:109). And He said, "If you (pl.) are grateful, I will give you an increase" (14:7). Increase from God Most High is limitless, and gratitude is itself a grace that calls for thankfulness that, in turn, ensures further infinite increase. And in God is our success.

Chapter 9: [19] Concerning the acceptability of unique qualifications in religious learning and the uniqueness of each discipline to its practitioners, along with a refutation of those who deny the existence of a branch of *ʿilm* and decline to refer a matter to the appropriate specialists

Said the shaykh, God be compassionate to him: Quite a few religious scholars are averse to the idea of specializations within the science of things divinely revealed. In this community there is no dispute that God Most High commanded His Messenger, God's blessings and peace upon him, to communicate what was revealed to him, for He said, "O Messenger, communicate what has been sent down to you from your Lord" (5:67). And it has been reported that the Prophet, God's blessings and peace upon him, said, "If you knew what I know, you would laugh little and weep much." Therefore, if he had known what they did not know of the forms of knowledge that God had commanded him to communicate, he would have communicated it. And if his Companions had been allowed to question him about that knowledge, they would have questioned him.

Scholars agree that among the Companions of the Messenger of God, God's blessings and peace upon him, there were specialists in certain areas of knowledge. Ḥudhayfa,[15] for example, was a specialist in knowledge of the names of the hypocrites, which God's Messenger, God's blessings and peace upon him, had imparted to him in secret, even to the point that ʿUmar, God be pleased with him, asked Ḥudhayfa, "Am I one of them?"[16] It is reported from ʿAlī ibn Abī Ṭālib,[17] God be pleased with him, that he said, "God's Messenger, God's blessings and peace upon him, instructed me in seventy chapters of knowledge that he taught to none but me."

This subject is discussed fully at the end of this book (chapter 122 below). I have raised the issue here as well, because the knowledge shared in common by the Ḥadīth specialists, the legal scholars, and the Sufis is knowledge of the religion. Every class of scholars has written accounts, treatises, books, and teachings characteristic of its discipline. Every group of them has its renowned leaders whose contemporaries agree unanimously on their authority because of their superior learning and depth of understanding. No one disputes that when the traditionists have a problem within the scope of the science of Ḥadīth on the weakness of a tradition or identification of transmitters, they do not [20] have recourse to the legal scholars on the matter. Nor do the legal scholars have recourse to the traditionists if they encounter an obscure question on the legal details of setting a woman free, or a declaration of innocence, or domiciles, or final testaments.

A similar situation obtains when a difficult question arises in the science of those who discuss the heart's ecstasy, the legacy of mysteries, the devout deeds of hearts, and who describe the sciences and conduct their investigations into them in terms of subtle allusions and sublime spiritual meanings. They need not have recourse to any but a scholar specializing in these matters, namely, someone experienced in these spiritual states, one who has journeyed through them and has sought to steep himself in the knowledge of their specific details. Anyone who does otherwise is making a mistake. No one has any business droning on about the experience of people whose spiritual state he does not understand, in whose discipline he is not well versed, and whose goals and methods he does not comprehend. Such a person comes to a bad end, all the while thinking he is among those who offer sound advice. May God Most High grant us all protection from such people.

Here we skip chapters 10 and 11, in which Sarrāj digresses slightly to discuss the origin of the name Sufi and to refute the argument of some that "Sufism" is not mentioned in the earliest sources and is therefore a newfangled innovation and thus unacceptable.

Chapter 12: [23] An affirmation of inward knowledge and an explanation proving its soundness

Said the shaykh, God be compassionate to him: One faction of the exotericists will have nothing to do with the Sufis, saying, "We recognize only the discipline of the Revealed Law in its manifest meaning that the Book and the Sunna have brought us. Your talk about knowledge of the inner implications and knowledge of Sufism is meaningless." I respond—and it is God who grants success: knowledge of the Revealed Law is a unique science, and this one term encompasses the two concepts of transmission *(riwāya)* and comprehension *(dirāya)*. Together the two comprise the knowledge of the Revealed Law, and that in turn gives rise to both outward and inward deeds. To refer to religious knowledge exclusively as either outward or inward is, therefore, inappropriate. For when knowledge resides in the heart, it is inward, until it becomes manifest on the tongue. Once given verbal expression, it becomes outward.

Religious knowledge is both manifest and hidden, for it is the knowledge of the Revealed Law that both leads to and calls forth outward and inward deeds. Outward deeds include, for example, the movements of the bodily limbs involved in acts of worship and juridical stipulations. Ritual purification, daily ritual prayer, almsgiving, fasting, pilgrimage, supporting justifiable struggle against injustice, and the like, are known as the acts of worship. As for the juridical stipulations, they include such matters as specific punishments, divorce, freeing slaves, commercial transactions, inheritance, and retaliation. All of these pertain to the external organs or bodily limbs.

As for the inward deeds, they are, as it were, the acts of the heart. They include such spiritual stations and states as faith's assent, the act of faith itself, certitude, authenticity, sincerity, insight into mystery, trust in God, love, spiritual contentment, recollectedness, gratitude, repentance, humility, awe of God, contemplation, reflectiveness, introspection, fear, hope, patience, moderation, surrender, handing all over to God, nearness to God, desire, ecstasy, dread, sadness, [24] contrition, shame, confusion, acknowledging God's sublimity, acknowledging God's magnificence, and reverence. Each of these deeds, both outward and inward, has its own type of learning, "standing,"[18] explanation, deep comprehension, ultimate spiritual reality, and profound spiritual experience *(wajd).* Verses from the Qur'ān and traditions from the Messenger, God's blessings and peace upon him, substantiate the soundness of each of these deeds, both the outward and the inward. One who is learned in this knows it; one who is ignorant of it is unaware of it.

When I refer to inward knowledge, therefore, I mean knowledge of inward deeds that pertain to the interior organ, the heart. And when I refer to knowledge of the outward, I am indicating the knowledge of external acts such as pertain to the exterior organs, the limbs of the body. God Most High has said, "And He has showered upon you His grace both outwardly and inwardly" (31:20). In other words, the evident graces that God Most High bestows upon the physical limbs result in acts of obedience, while the hidden graces that God Most High lavishes upon the heart yield these spiritual states. The outward cannot get by independent of the inward, nor the inward apart from the outward. God, exalted and glorified, has said, "Had they but referred the matter to the Messenger or the competent authorities among them rather than gossiping about it among themselves, those among them capable of deeper interpretation would have known about it" (4:83). For the knowledge that is understood in depth is the inward knowledge, and that is the knowledge of the practitioners of Sufism, for theirs is a deeper interpretation of Qur'ān and Ḥadīth and other sources. God willing, I am providing here a glimpse of that.

Knowledge, therefore, is outward and inward, Qur'ān both outward and inward, the Ḥadīth of God's Messenger, God's blessings and peace upon him, outward and inward, Islam outward and inward. To support that understanding, our companions gather evidence and arguments from the Book and the Sunna and intellectual understanding. But an explanation of that would be lengthy and would progress from saying too little to saying too much, and I have said enough on the matter. In God is our success.

In chapters 13 through 15 Sarrāj again digresses to discuss Sufism in more general terms (chapters 13 and 14) and then offers a fairly lengthy chapter on Sufi views of the divine unity and the process by which a human being becomes united with the divine. He then returns to the subject of Sufi epistemology, now focusing specifically on the experiential aspect of mystical knowledge, maʿrifa.

Chapter 16: [35] Elaborating on what the Sufis have said about the spiritual reality of *maʿrifa* and the characteristics of one endowed with such experiential knowledge

Someone asked Abū Saʿīd al-Kharrāz,[19] God be compassionate to him, about experiential knowledge of God. He replied, "Experiential knowledge comes from two directions: from absolute largesse and unstinting effort." Someone asked Abū Turāb an-Nakhshabī,[20] God be compassionate to him, to describe the mystic, and he said, "That is one whom nothing vexes and because of whom everything is purified." Aḥmad ibn ʿAṭā',[21] God be compassionate to him, said, "*Maʿrifa* is of two types, insight into the divine truth *(ḥaqq)* and insight into ultimate reality *(ḥaqīqa)*. Insight into the divine truth entails *maʿrifa* of God's simple unity to the extent that God has manifested to humankind the divine names and attributes. As for insight into the ultimate reality, there is no path to it because of the inaccessibility of the divinely eternal [36] and the incomprehensibility of divine lordliness, as suggested by the divine word, 'And they cannot encompass Him with their knowledge' (20:110)."

Aḥmad's saying, "There is no path to it," means that there is no method to the experiential knowledge of the ultimate reality, because God Most High has manifested to His creatures only those names and attributes that He knew they were capable of grasping. That is so because creatures cannot bear even an atom of experiential knowledge of the ultimate reality of God. Creatures would be annihilated at the first, slightest hint of a scintilla of the overwhelming force of the divine sublimity. Who could sustain experiential knowledge of a Being of such attributes? For that reason someone has observed that none but He can know Him experientially, and no one other than He can love Him, for the divine transcendence is utterly beyond human comprehension and consciousness. God Most High has said, "And they encompass none of His knowledge" (2:255).

On this subject, the story is told of how Abū Bakr aṣ-Ṣiddīq,[22] peace be upon him, said, "Praised be the One who fashioned for His creatures no path to experiential knowledge of Him other than their very inability to know Him intimately." Someone asked Shiblī,[23] "When does the mystic come into a place of experiencing God?" He replied, "When the (single experience of) witnessing comes into being and its (multiple) evidences pass away, when the senses depart and sense perception melts away." Someone also asked him, "What marks the onset of this condition and what is its end?" He replied, "Its onset is experiential knowledge of Him and it ends with acknowledgment of His transcendent oneness." He said further, "A sign of experiential knowledge is seeing oneself in the firm grasp of the divine magnificence, overwhelmed by the divine omnipotence." Another sign of experiential knowledge is love, for one who knows God intimately, loves Him.

Someone asked Abū Yazīd Ṭayfūr ibn ʿĪsā al-Bisṭāmī,[24] God be compassionate to him, I am told, about the qualities of the mystic. He answered, "The color of water is the color of its container. If you pour it into a white container, you imagine the water is white. If you pour it into a black container, you think it is black. The same is true for yellow and red and the other colors. The spiritual states come and go alternately, but the master of the spiritual states is his Master." The shaykh said, Allāh be compassionate to him: The meaning of this, and God knows best, is that to the extent of its clarity the water [37] takes on the color of its container. The container's color may change, but not because of its purity and spiritual state. The person who inspects it has the impression of something white or black, as if the water were one with the container. So it is with the mystic and his characteristics in relation to God exalted and glorified: though the spiritual states may change, the mystic's secret self in relation to God remains one and the same.

Someone asked Junayd,[25] God be compassionate to him, concerning what is understood about those who possess experiential knowledge. He replied, "They elude the description of those who describe them." Someone else responded to a query about *maʿrifa* by saying, "It is the insight of hearts into God's uniqueness arising from the subtleties of God's experiential pedagogy." Someone asked Junayd, God be compassionate to him, "Abū 'l-Qāsim, what do the mystics want from God Most High?" He answered, "They want God to watch over them and take care of them." "To the contrary," said Muḥammad ibn al-Faḍl as-Samarqandī (d. 319/931), Allāh be compassionate to him, "they have no wants and no preferences, since they obtain what they obtain apart from wants and preferences. That is because the mystics exist in the One who brings them into being, and survive in the One who brings them into being, and pass away in the One who brings them into being." Someone asked Muḥammad ibn al-Faḍl, God be compassionate to him, about the orientation of the desire of the mystics, and he replied, "Their desire is oriented to the quality in which all the comely attributes culminate and through whose loss all repulsive qualities are repugnant, and that quality is integrity."

Someone asked Yaḥyā ibn Muʿādh,[26] God be compassionate to him, to describe the mystic, and he replied, "Whoever joins them leaves them."[27] Another time someone asked him to describe one endowed with experiential knowledge, and he answered, "A godservant who was here and then departed."

Someone asked Abū 'l-Ḥusayn an-Nūrī,[28] God be compassionate to him, "How is it that intellects cannot reach Allāh, while Allāh can be known only through the intellect?" He replied, "How can a being with temporal limits comprehend one who has no such limits? How can a being beset with frailties comprehend one who has no weakness or infirmity? Or how can one whose being is conditional know the one who has fashioned conditionality itself? Or how can one whose being presumes a 'where' know the one who has given 'where' a place and named it 'where'? In the same way, God has made the first first and the last last and named them 'first' and 'last.' Had He not made the first first and the last last, there would be no way of knowing 'firstness' and 'lastness.'" Then he said, "And what really is begininglessness without endlessness? There is no boundary between the two, just as firstness is lastness and lastness firstness. Likewise, outwardness and hiddenness, except that God at times causes you to experience disconnectedness and at times intense concentration, in order to renew the joy [38] and the vision of servanthood. For the person who knows God intimately in creation does not know Him through direct encounter. That is because the creation is the full expression of God's saying 'Be!,' whereas a direct encounter would manifest a forbidden sacredness not to be trifled with."

I say that his expression "direct encounter" refers to the heart's unmediated experience of certitude and witnessing of the realities of faith in the realm of mystery. The shaykh, God be compassionate to him, said: The meaning of what he is referring to—and only God Most High really knows—is that Allāh Most High is neither time-bound nor changeable. What God was is what God is, what God said is what God says. From God's perspective the nearest is like the farthest and the farthest like the nearest. Human beings, however, can attain experiential knowledge only as human beings. The vicissitudes of nearness and distance, of displeasure and contentment, are human characteristics that are not among God Most High's attributes. And Allāh knows best.

Aḥmad ibn ʿAṭa', God be compassionate to him, said in one of his comments on the meaning of *maʿrifa*—some also attribute the comment to Abū Bakr Muḥammad al-Wāsiṭī,[29] God be compassionate to him, but it is more accurately attributed to Ibn ʿAṭā'—"Things that appear repugnant do so by reason of God's hiddenness, and those that seem beautiful do so because of His divine manifestation. These are two characteristics that will continue without end just as they existed without beginning, for the two characteristics will become known both to those who are accepted and those who are rejected. The evidence of His divine manifestation becomes apparent, through its radiance, to those who are accepted, just as the evidence of His hiddenness becomes apparent through its darkness to those who have been rejected. Beyond that, the yellow hue of an ascetic's complexion and the shortened sleeves and donning the armor of the Sufi habit and the patched frock are of no use."

I say: The meaning of what Ibn ʿAṭā' has said is close to the observation of Abū Sulaymān ʿAbd ar-Raḥmān ad-Dārānī[30] in which he says, "It is not within the capability of human beings either to annoy or to please God with their actions. On the contrary, God is pleased with some people so that He inspires them to perform the deeds that result in spiritual contentment, while He is displeased with other folk so that He causes them to perform the deeds that are associated with the divine anger." The meaning of Ibn ʿAṭā''s saying, "Things that appear repugnant do so by reason of God's hiddenness," is that God remains aloof from those things. The saying "those things that seem beautiful do so because of His divine manifestation" means that God becomes present to those things [39] and approves of them. An illustration of that has come to us in the Ḥadīth according to which "God's Messenger came out holding two books, one in his right hand and one in his left, and said, 'This is the book of the people destined for Paradise, with their names and the names of their ancestors, and this is the book of the people destined for hellfire, with their names and the names of their ancestors.'"

Abū Bakr al-Wāsiṭī, God be compassionate to him, said, "When God makes Himself intimately known to His elect ones, their sense of self is obliterated from their ego-souls. Consequently, they have no experience of alienation resulting from proofs of the First One's granting them the signs of prosperity. It is like that for everyone to whom meaning is given after the fact." What that means—and Allāh is most knowledgeable—is that one who experiences the firstness, according to which he knows intimately what the object of his worship has imparted experientially to him, experiences thereby neither loneliness in his knowledge of what is other than God nor an intimate bond with Him.

Chapter 17: [39] On the qualities of one endowed with experiential knowledge and what the Sufis have said on this subject

Yaḥyā ibn Muʿādh ar-Rāzī, God be compassionate to him, said, "As long as the godservant seeks experiential knowledge, God will say, 'Choose nothing and do not invest yourself in your freedom of choice until you have achieved experiential knowledge.' Once one knows experientially and has become a mystic, then God will say to him, 'Choose or do not choose, as you wish, for if you choose, you will do so through Our freedom of choice, and if you abandon choosing, you will have abandoned it through Our freedom of choice. Whether in choosing or in the abandonment of choice, you exist through Us.'" Yaḥyā ibn Muʿādh likewise said, "This world is a bride, and whoever seeks her is her handmaid. But the one who rejects her through renunciation blackens her face and pulls out her hair and tears her clothing. However, the one who knows God experientially is completely preoccupied with the Master and pays no attention to her." He said further, "When the mystic abandons the etiquette associated with his experiential knowledge, he perishes among those who are perishing." And Dhū 'n-Nūn, God be compassionate to him, said, "The signs of the mystic are three: The light of his *maʿrifa* does not extinguish the light of his piety; he does not cling to inward knowledge that an outward duty nullifies; and the abundance of God Most High's graces and God's largesse do not induce the individual to rend [40] the veils of what God Most High has forbidden."

One of the mystics has said, "A person who describes experiential knowledge according to the children of the next world is not truly endowed with experiential knowledge; how then could one who acts in accord with the children of this world be endowed with experiential knowledge?" He also said, "If the mystic turns from his accustomed way toward creatures without God's permission, that person will be abandoned among God's creatures." And he said, "How can you know God intimately when awe of Him does not rule your heart? And how can you be mindful of God and love Him without experiencing His graciousness in your heart, heedless of what He had in mind for you before He created you?" I have heard Muḥammad ibn Aḥmad ibn Ḥamdūn al-Farrā' (d. 370/980–81) say, "I heard ʿAbd ar-Raḥmān al-Fārisī say in response to a question, that experiential knowledge reached perfection 'when multiplicity becomes unity, and when the (various) spiritual states and resting places are equalized, and when the appearance of distinctiveness has vanished.'" And Abū Naṣr (as-Sarrāj) said: That means that the godservant's mystical moment is but a single homogeneous instant, and that in all his spiritual states the godservant is in God and of God and removed from what is not God. When that occurs, this is his spiritual state.

Chapter 18: [40] Concerning the question "How did you come to know God intimately?" and the difference between the believer and one endowed with experiential knowledge

Someone asked Abū 'l-Ḥusayn an-Nūrī, God be compassionate to him, "How did you come to know God Most High intimately?" He replied, "Through God." Someone asked, "So what has that to do with the intellect?" He replied, "The intellect is powerless in that it can show the way only to what is powerless like itself. When God created the intellect, He asked it 'Who am I?' but intellect was silent. So God daubed its eyes with the *kohl* of the light of divine oneness. Then the intellect said, 'You are God!' So it is that the intellect cannot know God intimately except through God." Someone asked (Abū 'l-Ḥusayn) what was the first religious duty Allāh Most High required of His servants, so he replied, "*Maʿrifa,* as when God said 'I have created the jinns and human beings only that they might worship Me'" (51:56). Ibn ʿAbbās,[31] God be compassionate to him, however, read the text as "that they might know Me intimately." Someone asked one of the mystics, "What is *maʿrifa*?" and he replied, "The heart's verification of the divine oneness through all the divine attributes and names, affirming that God is uniquely characterized by might, power, authority, and magnificence as the living, [41] the eternal, 'to whom none is equal, and He is the all-hearing and all-seeing' (42:11), 'without asking how,'[32] without likeness or equal, with none parallel in origin or status, banishing from hearts all thought of competitors and peers and secondary causes."[33] Someone also said, "The root of experiential knowledge is a gift. *Maʿrifa* is a fire, while faith is a light; experiential knowledge is a thing discovered as a result of quest, while faith is something granted apart from effort."

The distinction between the believer and the one endowed with experiential knowledge is that the believer sees with the light of God, while the one who knows experientially sees directly through Allāh, glorified and exalted. Whereas the believer possesses a heart, the mystic does not. The believer's heart arrives at peace through the recollection of God, while the mystic finds no peace in anything other than

God. There are three types of experiential knowledge: the experiential knowledge of affirmation, that of ultimate spiritual reality, and that of contemplation. And the experiential knowledge of contemplation encompasses profound comprehension, knowledge, articulation, and speech. Many are the indications and ways of describing *maʿrifa*, but in brevity there is sufficiency and even abundant wealth for the person who seeks demonstration and guidance. And in God is success. It is reported that Ḥasan ibn ʿAlī ibn Ḥannūya ad-Dāmaghānī said that someone asked Abū Bakr aẓ-Ẓāhirābādī about experiential knowledge. He replied, "*Maʿrifa* is a term that refers to the presence in the heart of an acknowledgment of divine sublimity that prevents you from either imagining God in human form or denying God's attributes."[34]

In the next thirty-three brief chapters Sarrāj lays out various aspects of advanced spiritual development. These include, most importantly, his analysis of the various stations and states. He moves thereafter to a description of how the Sufis base their approach on the fundamentals. First, Sarrāj analyzes Sufi hermeneutics of the Qur'ān; next he devotes four chapters to their way of interpreting the life and meaning of the Prophet Muḥammad and of embodying the prophetic values in their lives. In the two chapters below Sarrāj returns to a discussion of how the "deeper interpretations" (mustanbaṭāt) *of the Sufis represent a distinctive, credible, and religiously authentic development in mystical epistemology.*

Chapter 51: [105] On how the elect derive sound deep interpretations in understanding the Qur'ān and Ḥadīth and other sources, and their methods of exegesis

The shaykh, God be compassionate to him, said, in response to the question of the meaning of "deep interpretations," that "deep interpretations" refers to what the specialists among those who approach ultimate reality derive in accord with both apparent and hidden meanings of the Book of God, glorified and exalted, and with both the apparent and hidden aspects of emulating God's Messenger, and the corresponding deeds both outward and inward. When, therefore, they act according to what they know of these matters, God Most High "bequeaths to them knowledge of what they had not previously known." That is the knowledge of mystical allusion and the knowledge of the legacies of action that God Most High reveals to the hearts of people of integrity. That knowledge embraces deeply hidden meanings, subtleties, and mysteries stored away for safe keeping, rarities of knowledge and extraordinary wisdom in understanding the Qur'ān and traditions of God's Messenger from the perspective of their spiritual states, their moments of peak spiritual experience, and the purity of their recollectedness. Allāh Most High has said, "Do they not strive to interiorize the Qur'ān, or are there locks on their hearts?" (47:24). The Prophet, God's blessings and peace upon him, said, "To those who act according to what they know God Most High bequeaths knowledge of what they had not known before." That is the knowledge unavailable to the other religious scholars. The locks on their hearts are the rust that has settled on their hearts because of the multiplicity of sins, pursuing passionate desires, love of this world, protracted heedlessness, intense cupidity, love of comfort, addiction to adulation and praise, along with other forms of inattentiveness, backsliding, intransigence, and faithlessness.

When, as a result of sincere repentance and compunction for sin, God Most High draws back these veils from the hearts, the locks on the hearts open and superabundant benefits arrive from the realm beyond ordinary experience. Then God gives expression to His superabundance of benefits through His interpreter, [106] the tongue that speaks of the marvels of wisdom and a wondrous knowledge. Once it has strewn its gems, the aspirants, pursuers, and seekers gather these gems with ears attentive and hearts intently present. Thus they live on, profiting from that and experiencing new life.

Allāh, glorified and exalted, said, "Do they not seek to interiorize the Qur'ān? Had it come from any but God they would have found in it copious contradictions" (4:82). God is indicating that, in their interiorizing of the Qur'ān, they arrive at deep interpretations. But had the

Qur'ān come from other than God, they would discover numerous conflicting statements. Then God said in the next verse, "And when a matter of security or fear comes to their attention, they publicize it. If only they had referred it to the Messenger and to those in authority among them, those among them who seek deeper meanings would have comprehended it" (4:83). God is referring here to the people of knowledge, and the expression "those in authority" here means "those endowed with *ʿilm*." Here God is clarifying a precise distinction between the generality of those endowed with knowledge and those endowed with knowledge who arrive at deeper interpretation.

Prophetic tradition includes a report that a man came to the Messenger of God, God's blessings and peace upon him, and said, "Messenger of God, teach me of the wonders of knowledge." So he replied, "What have you learned of the fundamentals of knowledge? Master the beginnings of learning, then come back so that I can teach you the wonders of knowledge"—as he has said elsewhere as well.

The jurists and religious scholars of important cities in every time have rendered well-known deeper interpretations of the verses of the Qur'ān and familiar prophetic traditions. These interpretations are ready to be advanced in support of questions to be debated among those scholars. One of them referred to this Ḥadīth, in which the Messenger of God, God's blessings and peace upon him, said, "Actions presuppose intentions, and every person is responsible for what he intends. Whoever migrates[35] toward God and His Messenger," as the Ḥadīth records, "will enter through three of the gates of knowledge." And this comes to pass only on the path of deeper interpretation. Similarly, all the rational arguments of the proponents of speculative theology are deeper interpretations. Those involved in that field consider all of that good and acceptable, since its purpose is victory for the truth and defeat of the false. Better still than that, however, are the deeper interpretations that the people of knowledge base on knowledge, on experience of ultimate reality, sincerity in the conduct of spiritual combat, ascetical practice, and pious deeds. These are people who seek to be near to God Most High through all manner of surrender, the people of ultimate truths.

Chapter 52: [107] On the reason for differences of opinion among the people of ultimate reality concerning the deeper interpretations of the meanings of their disciplines and their spiritual states

Said the shaykh, God be compassionate to him: Know this—and may Allāh confirm your understanding and remove self-deception from you: Those who experience spiritual states and the masters of hearts are also endowed with deeper interpretations of the meanings of their spiritual states, their disciplines, and their spiritual realities. They have developed deeper interpretations of the subtle, hidden meanings of the text of the Qur'ān and the text of the prophetic traditions, thereby disclosing fresh wisdom and hidden secrets. I will discuss some few aspects of that, God Most High willing. In addition, they differ in their deeper interpretations much as the exotericists do. However, the variant views of the exotericists lead to erroneous and misleading conclusions, whereas difference of opinion in the science of inner realities does not, for it is concerned with virtues, excellent qualities, nobility, spiritual states, moral conduct, and spiritual stations and levels.

It has been said that the breadth of opinion of the religious scholars is a [mercy. This means that difference of views among the religious scholars] in the science of outward matters is a mercy from God Most High. For the one who is correct contradicts one who is in error and demonstrates to the people the error of the one who disagrees, pointing out that person's disagreement with the one whose religious views are correct, so that they might keep their distance from the one in error. If that were not the case, the people would perish as their religion disappeared. But the variety of views among the people of spiritual realities is likewise a mercy from God Most High. Each of them speaks from the perspective of an individual spiritual moment, responds on the basis of his spiritual state, and makes allusions in view of his mystical experience. What they say, therefore, is useful to every one of the people of pious deeds, possessors of hearts, seekers and mystics, and that applies as well according to their respective differences, individuality, and levels of spiritual attainment.

What is recounted about Dhū 'n-Nūn, God be compassionate to him, will explain what I have said. Someone asked him about the one who truly embraces spiritual poverty, so he replied, ["That is the one who does not feel comfortable in anything but to whom (108) everything feels comfortable." Someone asked Abū ʿAbd Allāh al-Maghribī (d.c. 299/911–12) about the authentic spiritually poor individual,] and he responded, "The true spiritually poor person is one who owns all things and is owned by none." Someone asked Abū 'l-Ḥārith al-Awlāsī (d. 297/909–10) the same question, so he answered, "That is an individual who is intimate with nothing but to whom all things are familiar." And Yūsuf ibn al-Ḥusayn[36] answered the question by saying, "one who attends seriously to his own spiritual moment, but if during that moment he should cast a glance at a second moment, does not consider himself worthy of the name poor person." Ḥusayn ibn Manṣūr (al-Ḥallāj), God be compassionate to him, responded to the question by referring to "One who does not choose the circumstances of his life with a view to securing his own contentment." In response to an inquiry about the true poor person, Nūrī, God be compassionate to him, said, "The true poor person is one who is not suspicious of God Most High as a result of personal circumstances and who gives himself over to God in every spiritual state." Samnūn,[37] God be compassionate to him, answered that the true poor person "is one who feels comfortable with what he lacks as an ignorant person is comfortable with what he has, and is distressed over what he has the way an ignorant person is distressed over what he lacks." Abū Ḥafṣ an-Naysābūrī's,[38] God be compassionate to him, [answer was, "one who remains within the judgment of each instant, and when distraction overcomes him and takes him away from the judgment of his spiritual moment, he finds it distasteful." Junayd, God be compassionate to him, said the true poor person] is "one who is satisfied with no thing but in whom all things are satisfied." Likewise someone asked Murtaʿish an-Naysābūrī (d. 328/939), and he answered, "One whom lice devour and who hasn't so much as a peg with which to scratch himself."

These individuals differed in their responses much as they did in their personal spiritual moments and states, and that is all good. For every answer of theirs, there are people who find their responses fitting. Those answers are a benefit, a grace, and an enrichment and a mercy for them.

At this juncture Sarrāj applies what he has just said about "deeper interpretations" to distinctively Sufi readings of the Qur'ān and Sunna. Next, he develops several dozen brief praxis-oriented chapters that describe how the Sufis put into action their interpretations of the revelatory sources, as well as their emulation of Muḥammad's Companions. Finally, before moving toward an exposition of a still deeper level of Sufi thought as expressed in arcane and problematical sayings, Sarrāj returns to a key aspect of Sufi epistemology.

Chapter 122: [377] On the interpretation of the various disciplines and the problematical aspect of the "special disciplines" as religious scholars understand them, and an affirmation of mystical knowledge supported by proof

Said the shaykh, God be compassionate to him: Know that *ʿilm* outstrips the comprehension of those who seek to understand and the intellectual capacity of those who apply their intellects. Sufficient for you is the story of Moses and Khiḍr, given Moses' great stature and God's singling him out for conversation,[39] prophethood, prophetic inspiration, and commission as divine messenger.[40] God Most High has referred, in the clear text enunciated by the tongue of His veracious prophet Muḥammad, to the inability of Moses to comprehend the knowledge of one of His servants (that is, Khiḍr), when the Most High said, "one of Our servants to whom We had given mercy from Ourselves" and so on (18:65), so that Moses inquired of the servant saying, "Shall I follow you?" and so on (18:66).[41] The story illustrates God's confirmation of Moses and his eminence and protection against rejection by Khiḍr, though Khiḍr never measured up to Moses' stature as prophet, messenger, and God's conversant.

The Prophet, God's blessings and peace upon him, said, "If you knew what I know, you would laugh little and weep much. You would not take pleasure in women or dally on your couches. You would go out into the byways and pray fervently to God Most High. By God, I wish I were a tree that had been felled!"[42] This was narrated by Isrā'īl from Ibrāhīm ibn Mujāhir from Mujāhid from Muwarriq[43] from Abū Dharr[44] from the Prophet, God's blessings and peace upon him. In this account is an indication of the meaning of God's saying, "O [378] Messenger, communicate what has been sent down to you from your Lord" (5:67). He did not say, communicate that of which We have given you intimate knowledge. And if the Prophet's saying, "If you knew what I know," had referred to some of the knowledge he had been commanded to communicate, he would have communicated it. Had it been in their best interest to know it, he would have taught them.[45]

God Most High has singled out the Prophet, God's blessings and peace upon him, for three types of *ʿilm*: First, a knowledge evident to the elect and the general public alike, that is, the knowledge of legal stipulations, the command and the prohibition. Second, a knowledge reserved for a group of the Companions exclusively, and that is the knowledge Ḥudhayfa ibn al-Yamān, God be pleased with him, possessed, so that ʿUmar ibn al-Khaṭṭāb,[46] God be pleased with him, asked him, "Am I among the hypocrites?" In that vein also it is reported that ʿAlī ibn Abī Ṭālib, God be pleased with him, said, "The Messenger of God, God's blessings and peace upon him, instructed me in seven chapters of knowledge that none but me has come to know." And whenever one of the Companions of God's Messenger had a problem with something, he would have recourse to ʿAlī ibn Abī Ṭālib, God be pleased with him, about that. Third, a knowledge reserved for God's Messenger, God's blessings and peace upon him, in which none of his Companions shared, and that is the knowledge of which he remarked, "If you knew what I know." For that reason I have said no one should think that he possesses all types of knowledge, so that he is mistaken in his opinion of what the elect say, proclaiming them unbelievers and heretics. He himself, meanwhile, is entirely lacking in experience of their spiritual states and direct contact with their spiritual realities and deeds.

There are four parts to the disciplines of divinely Revealed Law. The first part is the knowledge of transmitting and traditions and prophetic narratives. That is the knowledge handed down from trustworthy person to trustworthy person. The second part is the systematic knowledge that constitutes the discipline of jurisprudence and legal regulations, the knowledge shared by religious scholars and jurists. The third part is the science of analogical reasoning, speculative thinking, and argumentation with opponents. This is the knowledge of dialectic and establishing proof against innovators and those in error, in support of the religion. The fourth part is the highest and most noble of them, and it is the science of spiritual realities and experiences and the knowledge of pious deeds. This includes spiritual combat, sincerity in obedience, and turning one's face toward God from every quarter, [379] complete attachment to Him in each instant, genuineness of intentions and desires, purity of innermost thoughts from corruption, reliance on the all-sufficiency of the Maker of the heavens, the death of the soul as a result of violations, sincerity in experiencing the spiritual states and stations, proper demeanor in solitude before God both interiorly and in external matters, contentment with mere sufficiency when need is overwhelming, leaving this world aside and abandoning what it offers in quest of higher levels and of attaining wondrous benefits.

One who is in error concerning the discipline of transmission of tradition would not inquire of a specialist in the systematic discipline of jurisprudence about his failing. Someone who is mistaken about a matter of the technical discipline of jurisprudence would not inquire of a specialist in the discipline of transmission of tradition about his lack of knowledge. Nor would a person who lacks knowledge about an issue in the science of analogical reasoning and speculative thinking inquire of a specialist in the disciplines of tradition or systematic jurisprudence about his deficiency. In a similar vein, one who lacks knowledge of some aspect of the discipline of mystical realities and spiritual states would inquire only of a person knowledgeable in those things, one whose understanding of them was complete. It is possible also that one might encounter all these disciplines among specialists in mystical realities. It is not possible, however, to find knowledge of mystical realities among the other specialists except as God wills, because knowledge of mystical realities is the fruit of all the disciplines and the ultimate end of the sum total of the disciplines.

The final objective of all the disciplines is knowledge of mystical realities. When someone ends up there, that person falls into a limitless ocean that is the science of hearts, the science of experiential knowledge, the science of mysteries, the science of the inward, the science of Sufism, the science of spiritual states, and the science of pious deeds. Whatever aspect you choose, its meaning is but one. God Most High said, "Proclaim: If the ocean were ink to write the words of my Lord, the ocean would run out before the words of my Lord, even if We provided another like it" (18:109).

Do you not see that these people do not disavow any aspect of the other branches of knowledge, whereas the practitioners of the other disciplines devalue the disciplines of the Sufis, except as God wills? Whenever any of these other specialists penetrates deeply into his branch of knowledge, so that he becomes a master in understanding it, he is the leader of his companions. They will inevitably have recourse to him with whatever puzzles them. But when these four parts of knowledge come together in one [380] person, then he is the complete imām, the axis, the proof, and the one who summons to the path and the pilgrim's goal. Thus it has been reported that ʿAlī ibn Abī Ṭālib, God be compassionate to him, said in a conversation he had with Kumayl ibn Ziyād (d.c. 82/701), "O God, the earth will never lack individuals who stand firm for the proofs of God, lest His signs be rendered false and His authority refuted. These are the fewest in number but of the greatest stature in God's eyes."[47]

I have come full circle to the meaning of the paradoxical saying[48] and the interpretation of the paradoxical sayings. Ecstatic utterance is the least of what one discovers among the perfected ones. That is because these people are firmly grounded in their spiritual perceptions, for only that person penetrates the theopathic utterance who is at a beginning and whose desire is to arrive at perfection and the final destination. His beginning is, therefore, the ending of desires, and that, in turn, is in essence the beginning of the goal and the perfection and the completion. And Allāh knows best what is correct.[49]

2

Abū Bakr al-Kalābādhī: *The Exploration of Sufi Teachings (Kitāb at-taʿarruf)*

First, Kalābādhī summarizes the critical aspects of what he takes to be the most widely held opinions about the subject in general. Then he follows up immediately with a precis of ways in which major Sufis disagreed on the general meaning of maʿrifa. *Forty chapters later Kalābādhī returns to the topic, now focusing in greater detail on certain more refined characteristics of experiential knowledge and the marks of individuals endowed with* maʿrifa.[1]

Chapter 21: Their (the Sufis') teaching on experiential knowledge of God

[78] They are united in the view that God alone is the guide to God, and that the role of the intellect is to provide a path for the intelligent person in need of a guide. Since the intellect is created in time, it can provide guidance only to other temporal realities. A man asked (Abū 'l-Ḥusayn) Nūrī, "What is the guide to God?" He replied, "God." The man then asked, "Then what about the intellect?" [79] Nūrī replied, "The intellect is limited, and that which is subject to limitation can lead only to other limited things." Ibn ʿAṭā' said, "The intellect is a means to serving God, not for arrogating lordliness to oneself." Someone else said, "The intellect enjoys free run of creation, but when it gets a glimpse of the Creator, it melts." Abū Bakr al-Qaḥtabī said,

"What intellects manage to master is under their sway, except with respect to the fundamental evidence;[2] for if God had not graciously disclosed Himself to them, intellects would never have noticed the fundamental evidence in the first place." Sources pass on to us the words of an eminent Sufi (Ḥallāj):

> Anyone who searches for God under the intellect's tutelage
> God consigns to mindless self-absorption.
> Corrupted by the deceptions of the innermost self,
> the seeker asks in utter bewilderment, "Does He exist?"

An eminent Sufi has said, "Only the individual to whom He has disclosed Himself has experiential knowledge of God. Only the person to whom He has proclaimed His transcendent unity can affirm that transcendence. Only the one to whom God has been gracious can believe in Him. Only the person who has experienced an interior manifestation of God can describe God. Only the individual whom God draws to Himself arrives in God's presence. And that person alone whom God has bound to Himself can be utterly devoted to God." The phrase "to whom He has disclosed Himself" means "to whom God has disclosed Himself," and the phrase "to whom He has proclaimed His unity" means "to whom God has shown that He is one."

Junayd said, "*Maʿrifa* is of two kinds: the *maʿrifa* born of self-disclosure and the *maʿrifa* based on instruction."[3] Experiential knowledge born of (God's) self-disclosure means that God makes Himself known to individuals and through this gives them insight into things, as Abraham said, "I love not things (e.g., heavenly luminaries) that set" (6:76). "Instruction" means that God shows individuals the traces of His power "on the horizons and within themselves" (41:53; see also 51:20–21), and then instills a grace in them whereby created things demonstrate to them that there is a Creator.[4] This latter experiential knowledge is the common heritage of believers, whereas the former is that of the few, for no person truly knows God experientially except through God's direct agency.

In this connection Muḥammad ibn Wāsiʿ[5] said, "I have never seen anything without seeing God in it." [80] Someone else said, "Never have I seen anything without seeing God before it." Ibn ʿAṭā' said, "God has disclosed Himself to the generality of people through His creation, as His word suggests, 'Do they not observe how the camel is fashioned?'" (88:17).[6] To the chosen few, on the other hand, God has disclosed Himself through His speech and attributes, as when He said, "Do they not reflect on the Qur'ān?" (4:82), and "And We will send down healing and mercy for the believers from the Qur'ān" (17:82), and "it is to God that the Most Beautiful Names refer" (7:180). And to the prophets God has disclosed Himself through His very Self, as He has said, "Thus have We revealed to you a spirit at Our command" (42:52), and "Have you not noticed how your Lord lengthens the shadow?" (25:45)." One of the greatest of the mystics (Ḥallāj) has said:

> Between me and the Truth there remains neither
> discursive explanation nor evidence nor proven signs.
> Here the rising sun of Truth, disclosed in brilliance,
> has outshone all that, bringing it to nought with its authority.[7]
> None knows God experientially but the one to whom God has revealed Himself,
> for the ephemeral upstart cannot know intimately the eternally ancient.
> The Creator's handiwork cannot give proof of Him—
> your view of the ephemeral is deflected like an arrow from its mark across the vastness of time.
> Firm indication of God comes from Him and through Him
> to one who witnesses the Truth as He reveals it in sending down the power of discrimination (i.e., the Qur'ān).
> Firm indication of God from Him and through Him and toward Him
> we have found in truth, indeed a knowledge clear.
> This is my existence, my affirmation, and my conviction;
> thus God brings into one my affirmation of God's transcendent unity and my faith.
> This is the way dwellers in the divine singularity express themselves

when they have known God intimately in secret and in public.
This is the essence of the essence of those who find ecstasy in God,
those of like spirit, my companions and intimate friends.

[81] One of the great ones has said, "God discloses Himself to us through Himself, and has pointed us toward experiential knowledge of Him through Himself. As a result, testifying to experiential knowledge arises from experiential knowledge after the One who discloses Himself bestows experiential knowledge on an individual." That means that there is no cause of experiential knowledge other than God's self-disclosure to the mystic so that he experiences God intimately by means of that disclosure. One of the leading shaykhs has said, "The intellect is capable of grasping the manifestation of created things as such by approaching that evidence directly. God, on the other hand, transcends the intellect's direct approach and has Himself infused in us the awareness that He is our Lord, in that He asked, 'Am I not your Lord?' (7:172). He did not ask, when first He presented Himself as the Infuser of Knowledge, 'Who am I?'—a question that would have given human intellects occasion to approach Him directly. God is, therefore, separate from intellects, transcends apprehension, and is beyond intellectual verification."

They agree that only one endowed with intellect can know God, since the intellect is the means by which the godservant possesses whatever knowledge of God he has, even though one cannot arrive at knowledge of God on one's own. Abū Bakr as-Sabbāk said, "When God created the intellect, He asked it, 'Who am I?' But the intellect remained silent, so God daubed its eyes with the *kohl* of the light of divine oneness, so that it opened its eyes and said, 'You are God and there is no deity but You.'" In other words, the intellect was incapable of knowing God experientially except with the help of God.

Chapter 22: Their (the Sufis') disagreement about *maʿrifa*

They hold diverse views concerning the nature of *maʿrifa* and its relationship to *ʿilm*. Junayd said, "*Maʿrifa* means awareness of your ignorance when God's *ʿilm* arrives." Someone requested, "Expand this for us further," so he replied, "God is both the source and goal of experiential knowledge."[8] In other words, one is ignorant of God so long as one regards oneself as a distinct entity and knows Him experientially only when one acknowledges Him as all that exists." Or as Sahl (at-Tustarī)[9] put it, "*Maʿrifa* is the intimate awareness of one's ignorance." [82] Sahl said further, "*ʿIlm* is confirmed by *maʿrifa*, and the intellect rests on *ʿilm*, whereas *maʿrifa* ratifies itself." What this means is that when God infuses in a godservant the *maʿrifa* of God, so that the individual becomes aware of God through God's self-disclosure, God subsequently makes *ʿilm* possible in the individual. In other words, the individual arrives at *ʿilm* by means of *maʿrifa*, and the intellect processes the *ʿilm* that God has brought into being in it.

Another Sufi has said, "Investigation of the outward meanings of things yields *ʿilm*, while investigation of their inward meanings by means of revelatory disclosure yields *maʿrifa*." Yet another has said, "God has made *ʿilm* available to the generality of people but has reserved *maʿrifa* for His Friends." On the contrary, according to Abū Bakr al-Warrāq,[10] "*Maʿrifa* means cognition of the outward forms and names of things, whereas *ʿilm* refers to knowledge of the inner realities of things." Abū Saʿīd al-Kharrāz said, "Generic *maʿrifa* of God is the *ʿilm* of the search for God prior to actually finding Him, while the specific *ʿilm* of God comes after one has found Him. Therefore, the specific *ʿilm* of God is more hidden and refined than the generic *maʿrifa* of God." (Abū 'l-Qāsim) Fāris (d. after 340/951), on the other hand, said, "*Maʿrifa* is total absorption in the being of the one known." Someone else has said, "*Maʿrifa* means holding in contempt all assessments but God's and acknowledging no value system but God's."

Someone asked Dhū 'n-Nūn, "How did you attain experiential knowledge of your Lord?" He replied, "Whenever the thought of disobedience crossed my mind, followed by the thought of God's majesty,

I experienced shame for it." In other words, he interpreted his experience of the nearness of God as a proof of his experiential knowledge of Him. Someone asked ʿUlayyān, "How is your relationship with the Master?" He said in reply, "I have not turned away from Him since I attained experiential knowledge of Him." [83] The questioner asked again, "How long have you been endowed with experiential knowledge?" "Since they dubbed me 'Crazy,'" he responded. In other words, he interpreted his awe before God's might as an indication of his experiential knowledge of Him. Sahl said, "Glory be to the One about whom godservants can possess experiential knowledge only through awareness of their inability to attain experiential knowledge of Him."

Chapter 60: Their (the Sufis') views on the spiritual realities of *maʿrifa*

[158] One of the shaykhs said, "There are two kinds of intimate awareness: intimate awareness of divine truth and intimate awareness of ultimate spiritual reality. The intimate awareness of divine truth, on the one hand, means affirming the priority of God's oneness above the attributes He has made manifest. As for the intimate awareness of ultimate spiritual reality, it involves realization that there is no method for attaining such an awareness because no mind can comprehend the divine transcendence or embrace fully the divine sublimity. God has said, 'And they do not encompass Him with their knowledge' (20:110). He is the transcendent One, the spiritual realities of whose characteristics and attributes no one can grasp."

One of the leading Sufis said, "Intimate knowledge involves calling forth the innermost self through all manner of reflection. It is part of the process of assessing the ecstatic experiences resulting from invoking God in connection with unfolding signs of divine revelation." By that he means that the innermost self experiences the grandeur of God, the magnification of His reality, and the glorification of His power in a way that eludes articulation. Someone asked Junayd about intimate knowledge, and he answered, "It is the innermost self's ambivalence as to whether to proclaim God grand beyond comprehension or majestic beyond grasping." Someone else asked that question, and he replied, "*Maʿrifa* means knowing that God is the opposite of whatever your heart can picture. And how perplexing it is that God shares no human qualities and that no human being has any share in divine qualities! For the mystic is a being who goes in and out of the state of nonbeing. No mode of expression is adequate to deal with God, since created things came after God, and what comes into existence later is incapable of comprehending what came before it." [159] Junayd's words, "the mystic is a being that goes in and out of the state of nonbeing," are referring to the individual in that spiritual state, for Junayd says that the individual exists to outward appearances, but as for attributes and characteristics he is as good as nonexistent. Junayd also said, "Experiential knowledge is the awareness, through a passing spiritual impulse, of the implications of one's impending return to God: The mystic had best avoid sins of both commission and omission." In other words, the mystic is not witnessing his actual present spiritual state, but rather has a glimpse of God's prior knowledge of him and a realization that he will return to that prior condition, aware that both in service and failure he is at God's bidding.

One Sufi said of experiential knowledge, "When it descends into the inmost self, the inmost self is incapable of dealing with it, much as the sun's rays prevent one from perceiving it from periphery to center." Ibn al-Farghānī[11] said, "One who understands the mere outlines of a reality becomes puffed up; one who perceives the reality's stamp[12] becomes perplexed; one who knows what has already been arranged, stops in his tracks; one who attains experiential knowledge of God remains at rest; and one who knows the Master through experiential knowledge humbles himself." This means that a person who testifies to his own religious observance before God is full of himself; someone who witnesses what God has prepared for him in advance is stymied because he does not comprehend what God knows of him or what the Pen has written about him; one who is aware that he cannot hasten or postpone what his allotted portion holds in store for him is no longer able to search for alternative possibilities; one who possesses experiential knowledge of God's power over him and sufficiency for him is self-possessed and unruffled by fearsome realities or deficits;

and one who knows through *maʿrifa* that God is in charge of his affairs experiences humility before God's judgments and decrees.

An outstanding individual has said, "When God grants a person experiential knowledge of Godself, God puts a hold on that person's intuitive awareness so that he experiences neither love nor fear nor hope nor poverty nor sufficiency, since these things are not ultimate concerns and God transcends human goals." In other words, the individual is not aware of these spiritual states for they are the individual's own qualities, and his characteristics are so limited as to fall far short of what befits God. [160] One of the great ones is said to have composed these lines:

> You have watched over me and kept me safe,
> holding me clear of the cesspool of evil.
> In the heat of dispute you are my rebuttal,
> and in my thirst it is you alone who quench.
> When the mystic mounts the steed of experiential knowledge, he is borne aloft
> in secret toward a perspective from on high,
> Thence to be submerged in an abundant reward
> and there engulfed in revelatory insight.
> He breaks the seals of arcane truths by which
> anxious intimate hearts come back to life.
> But one so dwarfed in the bewilderment of that encounter
> you would perceive as dead even as he remained living.

In other words, the individual is so completely overwhelmed by the experience of God's grandeur and majesty that you would perceive him, though alive, to be as if dead and passing away as he becomes aware of what he now has, for he discovers he can neither hasten nor postpone his destiny.

Chapter 62: Their (the Sufis') ways of describing the individual endowed with experiential knowledge

[162] Someone asked Ḥasan ibn ʿAlī ibn Yazdānyār,[13] "When does the person endowed with *maʿrifa* experience God?" He answered, "When the real evidence is manifest, and the counterfeits pass away, and the senses lose their purchase, and sincerity becomes irrelevant." His words "real evidence is manifest" refer to the evidence of what God has done with you previously, His attentiveness and largesse in infused knowledge of Him, conviction of His oneness, and belief in Him. Awareness of all of that sends [163] attention to your own deeds, devotion, and obedience into oblivion. As a result, you realize how the "much" that apparently originates with the self is engulfed in the "little" that apparently originates with God; and, in fact, what originates with the self is not the "much." His words "the counterfeits pass away" refer to the individual's no longer adverting to whether other people represent threat or advantage, criticism or adulation. His reference to the senses' loss of force alludes to God's saying, "He speaks through Me and he sees through Me." When he says that sincerity becomes irrelevant, he means that when the individual takes stock of his own qualities, he no longer considers himself sincere nor does he judge his actions, past or to come, as sincere, since his personal qualities are contingent just as he himself is.

Someone asked Dhū 'n-Nūn about the ultimate fate of the one endowed with experiential knowledge, and he replied, "To become as he was, where he was, before he came into being." In other words, one endowed with *maʿrifa* experiences God and the divine activity rather than himself and his own deeds. Someone else said, "The person who has the keenest experiential knowledge of God is the one whose perplexity is the most intense." Someone asked Dhū 'n-Nūn, "What is the first hurdle one endowed with experiential knowledge has to clear?" He answered, "Perplexity, followed by radical spiritual poverty, then arrival in God's presence, followed by more perplexity." Initial perplexity follows from God's actions and beneficence toward the individual, when he realizes that his gratitude is no match for the divine largesse. He knows that gratitude is a compulsory response for that, but that if he is thankful, even his gratitude is a grace for which he must give thanks. He does not regard his deeds as worthy possessions with which to meet God but despises them as no more than what was required of him and in no way optional for him.

They say Shiblī stood up one day to perform the ritual prayer. After a long pause he performed the ritual prayer. When he had completed the prayer, he said, "How difficult a dilemma! If I pray, it implies that I am rejecting what God has in store for me; if I do not pray, it implies that I am ungrateful for what God has already given me." In other words, "I am contradicting the scope of the divine largesse and the completeness of the divine abundance by juxtaposing that to my own puny gesture of thanks." [164] Then Shiblī recited these verses:

Praise be to God that I am
like a frog that dwells in the sea:
For it either gives voice, and its mouth is filled
or it remains silent and dies in obscurity.

As for the second perplexity, it occurs in the trackless deserts of divine transcendent unity where the mystic's understanding is led astray and his intellect disappears before the immensity of divine power and awe-inspiring magnificence. As the saying goes, "On this side of the divine transcendent unity are trackless wastes where discursive thinking goes off course." Abū 's-Sawdā asked one of the great ones, "Does the one endowed with experiential knowledge have a specific mystical moment?" "No," he answered. "Why not?" came the inquirer's reply. "Because the mystical moment is a respite in which one takes a breather from anxious care, whereas experiential knowledge happens in successive waves that overwhelm one while alternately lifting and dashing the mystic, so that his moment is dark and forbidding." He then said,

Maʿrifa requires of you total self-effacement, as when
the seeker of God from the outset restricts his gaze from wandering.

Fāris said, "One endowed with experiential knowledge is one whose knowledge is an inward state and whose outward movements result from his being taken over by God." Someone asked Junayd what a possessor of experiential knowledge is like, and he replied, "Water assumes the color of its container." In other words, one endowed with experiential knowledge exists in every spiritual state as is most appropriate, and since his spiritual states vary, they say "he is the son of the moment." Someone asked Dhū 'n-Nūn what a mystic is, and he answered, "He was here but has gone." He meant that one does not see a person endowed with experiential knowledge in the same spiritual state on two occasions because someone other than the mystic is directing him. Ibn ʿAṭā' is credited with the verse,

If fated time spoke with a tongue it would tell how
 I swagger, sweeping wide the hem of passionate love's cloak.
But impersonal time has no knowledge of my substance and status,
 never suspecting what a moving target I am.

[165] Sahl ibn ʿAbd Allāh (at-Tustarī) said, "The first station in experiential knowledge is the servant's being given a certitude in his inmost being that bestows rest on his limbs, and a trust in his limbs that makes him at peace in his surroundings, and a vitality in his heart that gives him victory over what has yet to be." One endowed with experiential knowledge, therefore, is one who has taken pains to fulfill his responsibilities toward God and has realized experientially what he has received from God, so that his return from things to God is sure. God has said, "You will see their eyes overflow with tears from what they recognize as the Truth" (5:83). It is possible that the phrase "what they recognize" refers to their experiential knowledge of God's kindness and goodness, His attending to them and turning toward them, and His singling them out from among others like them. When the Prophet said to Ubayy ibn Kaʿb,[14] "God has ordered me to make a Qur'ānic recitation to you," [166] Ubayy asked, "O Messenger of God, was I mentioned among them?" He responded, "Yes," and Ubayy wept, for he could envision no spiritual state in which to come before

God, no thankfulness commensurate with the divine largesse, no mindfulness worthy of God. So he went off alone and wept.

The Prophet said to Ḥāritha,[15] "Your knowledge comes from experience, so persevere in that," thus associating him with experiential knowledge and enjoining him to be steadfast, but without specifying a particular course of action. Someone asked Dhū 'n-Nūn about the one endowed with experiential knowledge, and he replied, "He is a man who is solitary even in the company of others." Sahl said, "Those who are intimately aware of God are like the people of Aʿrāf who 'would recognize everyone by their characteristic features' (7:46).[16] God has assigned them a station and suspended them over the two dwelling places, thus giving them experiential knowledge of the two kingdoms." The following verses are attributed to one of the Sufis:

How thoughts of people who have lived their destinies and passed on saddens me;
though striving long to emulate them, I have not equaled them.
They were hidden even amid the pomp of kings, and whoever
caught a glimpse of them said, "They are emaciated and formless."[17]

3

Abū Ṭālib al-Makkī: *The Book of Knowledge (Kitāb al-ʿilm)*: Part Thirty-One of *The Sustenance of Hearts (Qūt al-qulūb)*

Abū Ṭālib al-Makkī's treatment of knowledge is the most expansive of the texts translated here. It is also the most broadly tradition-based in the sense that Makkī regards the early history of Islam as the source of knowledge paradigms more explicitly than do the other authors represented. The other texts do, of course, make reference to countless historical characters and events, in addition to their copious citation of Qur'ān, Ḥadīth, and the sayings of famous Sufis. Defying easy characterization, Makkī's approach is distinctive in part because he so prominently canonizes the way of the salaf, *the ancestors in faith, as the standard of belief and action, while the other authors generally do not showcase the traditionalist paradigm to that degree. At the same time Makkī consistently argues for a flexibility and vitality in that traditionalist paradigm that will surprise many twenty-first-century readers.*

He begins with a list of the main themes he intends to discuss. His initial section takes the form of a commentary on the various meanings of the two most important Ḥadīths on the subject of knowledge. Makkī sets out to survey the various interpretations of the traditions and eases into his own position on the first Ḥadīth but never directly addresses the second. He then moves on to discuss, more or less in order, the topics at the top of his "table of contents":[1]

- *concerning the excellence of* ʿilm;
- *the characteristics of those who possess* ʿilm;
- *the superiority of the science of* maʿrifa *over other disciplines;*
- *an exposition of the ways of the upright religious scholars among the pious ancestors in faith;*
- *an explanation of the excellence of the sciences of silence;*
- *on the way of the devout in knowledge;*
- *the difference between knowledge of inward reality and of outward reality, and between those who possess knowledge of this world and those who possess knowledge of the next;*
- *on the superiority of the proponents of* maʿrifa *over externalists;*
- *discussion of the wicked religious scholars who use their disciplines for worldly ends;*
- *description of knowledge and of the method of instruction;*
- *the blameworthy elements that people have recently introduced via popular narrative traditions and public discourse;*
- *a segment on how people have innovated idiosyncratic speech and action not in accord with the ancestors in faith;*
- *an exposition of the superiority of faith and certitude over the other sciences; and*
- *a caution against personal opinion.*

[234] Discussion of the meaning of the Prophet's saying, "The quest for knowledge is a religious duty for every Muslim," and the other Ḥadīth, "Seek knowledge, even as far as China"

"The quest for knowledge is a religious duty for every Muslim." Our teacher Abū Muḥammad Sahl (at-Tustarī) said: "By that the Prophet meant the science of a spiritual state." He means the knowledge of the godservant's spiritual state in the spiritual station in which he has been placed, because he knows the demands of the spiritual state that constitutes his relationship to God, especially in his life both here and hereafter, so that he fulfills God's obligations for him accordingly.

One of the mystics said, "What that means is the quest for knowledge of the mystical moment and the godservant's performance of the requirements of the present moment and of what is demanded of him each moment of his day." A religious scholar of Syria said: "By that he means the quest for the knowledge of sincerity and the *maʿrifa* of the ego-soul's sinful propensities and its insinuations, and the *maʿrifa* of the stratagems of the enemy and of his ruses, deceptions, and arrogance, and of that which either renders one's deeds appropriate or vitiates them." All of that is a religious duty insofar as sincerity in one's acts is a duty, and to the degree that the Prophet teaches about the malice of Iblīs and enjoins one to counteract his evil designs—this according to ʿAbd ar-Raḥīm ibn Yaḥyā al-Urmawī[2] and some of his disciples.

Concerning the interpretation of this Ḥadīth, one of the Basrans has said: "The quest for the science of hearts and the experiential awareness and analysis of passing thoughts and of their various types is a duty, since they include the messengers of Allāh to the servant as well as the whisperings of the enemy and the ego-soul. The individual can thus act in accord with what comes from God, and that includes the implementation of what comes from Him to the servant and probing the efficacy of the individual's struggle with his ego-soul in its rejection of the whisperings. For these inward movements mark the beginning of the intention that is the precursor of every action; from it all deeds arise and according to its strength actions multiply. One must therefore distinguish the call of the angel from that of the Enemy, the inward movement of the spirit from the whispering of the ego-self, and certain knowledge from the reproaches of the intellect, in order, thereby, to distinguish among the originating circumstances. This is a duty according to these people, and it is the position of Mālik ibn Dīnār,[3] Farqad as-Sabakhī,[4] ʿAbd al-Wāḥid ibn Zayd,[5] and their pious followers. Ḥasan al-Baṣrī, their teacher, had previously asserted that and they adopted the sciences of the heart from him.

According to religious devotees among the people of Syria, [235] the quest for knowledge of what is religiously permitted is a duty, since God commanded it. Muslims are of one mind concerning the corruption of one who consumes forbidden food. An account clarifying this has come to us, saying, "Quest for knowledge of the religiously permitted is a duty beyond the duty." Ibrāhīm ibn Adham,[6] Yūsuf ibn Asbāṭ,[7] Wuhayb ibn al-Ward,[8] and Shuʿayb ibn Ḥarb[9] incline toward this opinion. One of this group who possessed experiential knowledge, said, "It means that the quest for *ʿilm* of inward realities is a duty for those endowed with it." Someone said, "This is a unique duty for the possessors of heart, people who seek to act upon it and of whom it is required in a way that does not apply to the generality of Muslims."

This is clearly articulated in the Ḥadīth "Learn certitude," which means, "Seek the knowledge of certitude." But the knowledge of certitude cannot be found except among those who have certitude. It is among the deeds of those who possess certitude and is found uniquely in the hearts of those endowed with experiential knowledge. This is the useful knowledge that constitutes the godservant's spiritual state and station before God, just as the saying of the Prophet testifies: "An inward knowledge is in the heart." This refers to that beneficial knowledge, and this is an interpretation upon which others have agreed. Jundab (ibn ʿAbd Allāh) said, "When we were with the Messenger of Allāh, he taught us the faith, and then he taught us the Qur'ān, so that our faith increased. But a time will come when people learn the Qur'ān before the faith, and our instructing them in the faith will assist them." This is the view of the austere devotees among the people of Basra.

According to one of the religious forebears, this means the quest of a knowledge of that which cannot be ignored, namely, the knowledge of the divine transcendent unity, of the ethical principles of commanding the good and forbidding the evil, and of the difference between the permitted and the forbidden. For there is no goal for the other sciences beyond this, and the term "*ʿilm*" is applied to them all to the extent that they are dealing with things known. They concur that instruction in matters beyond what I have mentioned is not a duty, even if it is in some way excellent or commendable. A legal scholar of Kufa said, "It refers to the quest for a knowledge of buying and selling, and of marriage and divorce. If someone wants to enter into one of these transactions, it then becomes a duty for that person, upon entering into it, to seek knowledge of it." As ʿUmar ibn al-Khaṭṭāb said, "Let none do business in our market except one who is familiar with the law, lest he be vulnerable to the charge of usury whether intended or not." As the saying goes, "Gain an understanding of the law, then do business." Sufyān ath-Thawrī,[10] Abū Ḥanīfa,[11] and their companions are inclined to this view.

One Khurāsānī religious scholar of earlier days said, "Suppose that a man is at home and wants to do something that has to do with religion, or that there crosses his mind an issue that has to do with God that imposes on him an obligation of worship or belief or action. But he is unable to ignore that, and he is allowed neither to take action on it according to his personal opinion nor to evaluate it according to preference. He must, therefore, put on his sandals and head out to inquire of the most learned of his fellow citizens, asking him about that matter when it arises. This, then, is a religious duty. This opinion has been attributed to Ibn al-Mubārak[12] and some of the Ḥadīth specialists.

Others, however, have said that this Ḥadīth means that the quest for the knowledge of God's transcendent unity is a duty, but they are at odds concerning how the quest is to be conducted and the nature of the goal. Some of them argue for the method of deductive proof and deliberation; others argue for the method of scientific investigation and speculative thinking; still others for that of divine assistance and tradition. A faction among these people say that it is solely a matter of a search for knowledge about ambiguous and confusing issues, to the degree that when the godservant hears of them he finds them problematic, and the search is not incumbent on him if he is unaware of them. On the principle of acceptance and in accord with the belief of the generality of Muslims, he will not entertain in his mind any doubts nor ruminate on them [236] in the center of his being. At this juncture he is permitted to abandon investigation. Should he hear, however, of anything of that sort that burdens his heart and about which he lacks clarity, certainty, and whose truth or falsehood he is at a loss to evaluate, it is not permissible for him to remain silent about the issue, lest he assent to an untruth or deny a truth.

At this point, the individual is duty-bound to inquire of those who are informed about the matter, seeking to be informed to the point that he is sure he believes the truth and rejects the falsehood of the matter. One does not abandon the quest so as to remain vague and thus follow one's whim, or become doubtful concerning matters of religion so that he swerves from the path of the believers or assents to an innovation, thereby departing unawares from the Sunna and the belief system of the community. Abū Bakr aṣ-Ṣiddīq was referring to this in his prayer, "O God, show us the truth as true, so that we may pursue it; and show us the false as false, so that we might avoid it; and do not leave the matter confusing for us, lest we proceed on a whim." This is the position of Abū Thawr Ibrāhīm ibn Khālid al-Kalbī,[13] Dāwūd ibn ʿAlī, Ḥusayn al-Karābīsī (d.c. 245/859), and Ḥārith ibn Asad al-Muḥāsībī,[14] and their disciples among the speculative theologians.

These are the opinions of the religious scholars concerning the meaning of this tradition. Our information is based on our knowledge of their views, taking into consideration every faction's interpretation as supported by every relevant citation. The specific articulation is ours, the underlying meaning theirs; and this is altogether good and appropriate. Even though all of these people have differing views as to the interpretation of the Ḥadīth's precise wording, they nevertheless concur as to its meaning. Exceptions to that include the exotericists among them, who interpret it according to what they know, whereas the esotericists search for the inner meaning according to their knowledge. And, make no mistake about it, the exotericists and esotericists represent two different ways of knowing, neither of which can get along without the other, as in the relationship between Islam and faith. One depends on the other as do the body and the heart, neither of them able to disentangle itself from its partner. Though these groups differ in their explanations, they agree that the Prophet did not mean either a quest for knowledge of judgments of law and legal advisories, or knowledge of theological controversies or legal methodologies, or the books of Ḥadīth. No legal duty is attached to any of these, even though God does not exempt from those things individuals whom He has charged with looking after them.

My own view on the true meaning of the Ḥadīth—but God is most knowledgeable—is that the Prophet's saying "The quest for knowledge is a duty" refers to the five obligations on which Islam is founded, to the extent that no other obligations are binding upon Muslims. No action is sound apart from knowledge of it, for the beginning of action is knowledge of it. Knowledge of the deed, therefore, is a duty to the extent that the action itself is a duty. Since Muslims are required only these five deeds, the quest for knowledge of these five becomes obligatory, as the duty itself is obligatory. Knowledge of the divine transcendent unity is at issue here, since the first of the five obligations is the confession of faith, "There is no deity but God," along with the affirmation of His attributes united with His essence and the denial of attributes distinct from God. All of that pertains to the knowledge of the attestation, "There is no deity but God." The knowledge of sincerity is related to the soundness of Islam, since no one can be a Muslim without sincerity of action. As the Prophet has said, "There are three things by which the heart of a Muslim is not fettered: sincerity of action done for God...(good counsel for Muslim leaders, and holding fast to the community)." He therefore began with sincerity of action and made it a condition for Islam.

The fundamental point here is that he is not referring to knowledge of everything that can be known on the basis of consensus of the whole community. He does not mean, for example, the sciences of medicine, astronomy, grammar, poetry, or warfare. These [237] are known as sciences because their subject matter is known and their specialists possess knowledge of them. The Revealed Law, on the other hand, does not deal with specific stipulations, and the community is in agreement that this is not a question of knowledge of legal opinions and judgments, nor a knowledge of the differences among the schools of legal methodology and the divergence of opinions among scholars. All of these are known as sciences among their practitioners. Some of them are a duty given a sufficient collectivity of Muslims, but none has any force with respect to individuals.[15]

The prophetic tradition employs the general term for knowledge: "The quest for *ʿilm* (in general) is a duty." But then his saying "for every Muslim" after saying "seek knowledge (even as far as China)" implies that the mention of *ʿilm* is in fact specific knowledge. It seems, therefore, given the definite article—by which I mean the letters "a" and "l"—prefixed to the noun "knowledge" *(al-ʿilm)*, that it lends the meaning of specific and generally known knowledge. In the absence of these considerations one could equally argue that the Prophet's saying, "The quest for knowledge is a duty for every Muslim," refers to seeking knowledge of that on which Islam is founded, knowledge of which is required of Muslims. A clear indication of this is what Muḥammad said to the Bedouin when asked, "Tell me what Allāh requires of me," or in another version, "Tell us with what message God has sent you to us." The Prophet then told him about the double confession of faith, the five ritual prayers, alms, fasting during the month of Ramaḍān, and pilgrimage to the sacred house in Mecca. So the Bedouin asked, "Anything else?" Muḥammad answered, "No, only that you do so obediently." Said the Bedouin, "By God, I will neither add nor subtract a thing!" So Muḥammad said, "If that man is sincere, he will flourish and enter Paradise." Therefore, knowledge of these five pillars is a duty to the extent that the content of that knowledge is required, since there can be no action without knowledge.

God has said, "Apart from those who testify to the truth and are knowledgeable" (43:86); similarly, "Until you understand what you are saying" (4:43); and "Do you have knowledge? Then bring it forth for us. Indeed, you follow only conjecture" (6:148); and "But those who do evil follow their own whims without knowledge, but who will guide those whom God leads astray?" (30:29); and "Do not pursue the whims of those who do not know. They will avail you nothing from God's perspective" (45:18–19). And God has said: "Understand that the Qur'ān is revealed containing the knowledge of God, and that there is no deity but He" (11:14); and "If you do not know, then ask the people who have been reminded" (16:43). With these verses, therefore, God enjoins the quest for knowledge, and in the traditions concerning the five foundations of Islam, the Messenger of God made these deeds a duty. Then he made the general statement, "The quest for knowledge is a duty," and further specified it by adding "for every Muslim."

Interpretation and detailed study yield the conclusion that it is the knowledge of these five pillars that are the foundation of Islam that is a duty since the five are a duty.

Tradition concerning the Messenger of God has come down to us by way of a Ḥadīth from a Follower that lacks the name of the Companion from whom he received it, that he once came across a man around whom a crowd was gathering, and asked, "What is this?" They replied, "A most learned man!" So he asked, "Learned about what?" They replied, "About poetry and genealogies and the campaigns of the pre-Islamic Arabs." So he observed, "This is a knowledge the ignorance of which won't hurt you." Another version has, "A knowledge that won't help and an ignorance that won't hurt." A tradition has come down to us, "There is knowledge that is (in fact) ignorance, and words that are inappropriate." In another tradition, "A little help from God is better than a lot of knowledge." And in a less soundly attested tradition, "Everything requires knowledge, but knowledge requires the help of God." And in a well-known Ḥadīth [238] his words are, "I seek refuge in You from unprofitable knowledge." He calls it "knowledge" because it has the quality of something known and because those who cultivate it are, in the eyes of their associates, learned. However, he then denies that it is useful and seeks refuge in God from it.

We have received a tradition that says, "Satan often gets the better of you when it comes to knowledge." We asked, "O Messenger of God, how is it that he gets the better of us in knowledge?" He replied, "He says, 'Seek knowledge, but take no action until you know completely.' So the individual prattles on about knowledge, postponing action so that he dies without ever acting on it." This tradition makes two points. The first is that it refers to the quest for superfluous knowledge that will have no utility in the next life: the quest for it does not bring one closer to God. The second is that the knowledge that it extolls and recommends is that which requires action, for the Prophet commands no action apart from knowledge and he has no problem with a quest for knowledge in service of action. Haven't you heard what he has said in another tradition, "I prefer excellence in knowledge over excellence in action, and the best part of your religious practice is spiritual reticence."

In the following section, Makkī begins by framing the problem in relation to legal disciplines, gives evidence from Ḥadīths, and then bolsters his case with dream accounts and sayings of early Sufis.

Discussion of the superiority of the science of *maʿrifa* and certitude over the other sciences, and a disclosure of the way(s) of the learned and righteous ancestors in faith [among the learned ones of this world and the next]

The Messenger of God was taken from among thousands of his companions, all of whom possessed knowledge of God, were given deep comprehension through God, and were beneficiaries of God's good pleasure. Even so, barely ten men among them were professionally concerned with legal opinions, or issued legal judgments or decisions. When someone asked Ibn ʿUmar[16] about legal opinions, he replied, "Go to the official who is responsible for public matters and lay that burden on his neck!" That tradition was transmitted from Anas (ibn Mālik)[17] and then from the collectivity of the Companions and those who followed them in spirituality. Ibn Masʿūd[18] used to say, "Anyone who delivers legal opinions to every legal inquiry the people make is certainly crazy." When someone asked Ibn ʿUmar about ten issues, he would respond on one matter and keep silent about the other nine. By contrast, Ibn ʿAbbās, when asked about ten matters, would respond about nine and keep quiet about the one remaining. Some legal scholars have said "I do not know" more often than "I know"—Sufyān ath-Thawrī, Mālik ibn Anas,[19] Aḥmad ibn Ḥanbal,[20] Fuḍayl ibn ʿIyāḍ,[21] and Bishr al-Ḥāfī,[22] to name a few. When they held public sessions, they would respond to some questions and keep silent on others, and did not answer every question put to them.

We have a tradition from ʿAbd ar-Raḥmān ibn Abī Laylā[23] in which he said, "I came upon 120 Companions of the Messenger of God in this mosque, and every one of them, on being asked about a Ḥadīth or legal opinion, preferred that his brother handle it for him." According to another version, "If one of them was presented with a question, he would pass it along to the next person and he to the next until it came back round to the one who had posed it in the first place." A tradition has come down to us from Ibn Masʿūd and Ibn ʿUmar and others among the Followers with an unbroken chain of transmitters back to the Prophet, "Only three persons offer legal opinions to the people: a ruler, a deputy, or someone who is putting on airs."[24] To be more specific, [239] the ruler is one who discourses on the knowledge of legal advisories and statutes, as, for example, when people ask rulers and they make a legal pronouncement. The deputy is one who receives an order from the ruler, who puts the deputy in his stead, seeking assistance through the deputy's involvement with the ruler's subjects. The showoff is the storyteller who narrates the tales of people of old and relates traditions from bygone days. That is unnecessary nowadays and is not an authorized form of knowledge, and is subject to embellishment and abridgement and divergent interpretations. As a result, narrative tales are unacceptable and the storyteller has joined the ranks of the showoffs.[25]

The specific terminology of another Ḥadīth bears on the interpretation of the above Ḥadīth's inner meaning: "Only three people discourse to the public: a ruler, a deputy, or an impostor." Here are the kinds of things they say: A ruler is one who makes legal advisories concerning judgments and statutes, as I have already mentioned. The term "deputy" here means one who has knowledge of God and who denies himself in worldly matters, and who discusses the knowledge of the faith and certitude in knowledge of the Qur'ān, and encourages people to deeds of religious piety at the command of God. God grants him permission for that in His words, "And when God took the covenant of those to whom He had given the Book, saying to them, 'You are to make it clear to the people and not to conceal it'" (3:187). Abū Hurayra[26] and others used to say, "If these two verses were not in the Book of God, I would never have communicated a Ḥadīth to you." Then he would recite these verses and the verses prior to them, and say, "The Messenger of God said, 'God has given no learned person knowledge without binding him by the covenant to which He bound the prophets, namely, that he should make it clear and not conceal it.'"

The hypocrite, on the other hand, is one who talks about the worldly sciences and expresses himself out of caprice, seeking thereby to win people's hearts and secure through his rhetoric an increase of worldly profit and status.

One of the religious scholars said, "The Companions and Followers urged each other to excel with respect to four things: executorship, taking charge of some valuable entrusted to someone, last testaments, and legal advisories." One of them said, "The individual who is quickest to issue a legal advisory is the one who knows the least, while the one who most steadfastly resists rushing to offer a *fatwā* and refrains from that is the most admirable." Thus said one of the ancestors in faith, "The Companions and Followers occupied themselves with excellence in five things: reciting Qur'ān, building mosques, recollecting God, commanding the good, and forbidding the evil." According to a tradition from God's Messenger "Every word of a human being is a burden rather than a benefit, except for these three: commanding the good, forbidding the evil, and reminding people of God." And God, the truest of speakers, has said, "There is no good in most of their conversations, except that of a person who exhorts (others) to a deed of optional charity[27] or morally upright action or reconciliation among the people" (4:114). One of the Ḥadīth specialists saw in a dream a deceased legal scholar of Kufa, who was among the proponents of personal judgment. The dreamer said, "I asked him, 'What have you discovered about your view on formal legal opinion and personal judgment?' In embarrassment he turned away from the dreamer and replied, 'We found it was nothing and have nothing good to say about its consequences.'"

We have received a tradition from ʿAlī ibn Naṣr ibn ʿAlī al-Jahḍamī (d. 187/803) that his father said, "As I slept, I saw Khalīl ibn Aḥmad (d. between 160/776 and 175/791) after his death, so I said to myself, 'I'll never find a more intelligent person than Khalīl—I must put a question to him!' Then he asked me, 'Do you want to know what I know? I regard it as nothing. Nothing I have known is more useful than the phrases, "Glory be to God," "God be praised," "There is no deity but God," and "God is supreme."'" We have received the tradition that one of the shaykhs said, "I saw one of the religious scholars in a dream, so I asked him, 'What is the point [240] of these sciences about which we debate and speculate?' He opened his hand, blew on it and said, 'All of them are carried away like so much "scattered dust" (25:23). Nothing has been of use to me apart from two cycles of ritual prostration that I was moved to perform in the middle of the night.'"

I have received a tradition from Abū Dāwūd as-Sijistānī (d. 275/889), saying, "One of our companions had searched out many Ḥadīths and was thoroughly familiar with them. After he died, I saw him in a dream, so I asked, 'How has God dealt with you?' He said nothing, so I repeated my question. Again he was silent, so I asked, 'Has God forgiven you?' He replied, 'No.' I asked, 'Why not?' Said he, 'My sins abound and my excuses are meager. Still, I have been promised good things, so I go on hoping for good.' I asked, 'Which deeds did you find the most excellent here in this world?' He responded, 'Qur'ān recitation and ritual prayer in the middle of the night.' I inquired further, 'And is it better to recite Qur'ān or have it recited to you?' Said he, 'To recite it myself.' I asked, 'And what do you think of our saying, "This person is reliable and that one inaccurate in transmitting?"' He answered, 'If your intention in saying that is sincere, classifying transmitters that way goes neither for you nor against you.'"

One of the shaykhs passed along a tradition to me, saying, "Aḥmad ibn ʿUmar al-Khulqānī told me, 'I saw in my dream that I was going along on a path when a man happened upon me. He approached me and said, "Even when you are obedient, most people on earth will lead you astray from the way of God." I asked, "Do you mean me?" He answered, "You and anyone who comes after you." I turned away and, lo and behold, there was Sarī (as-Saqaṭī). So I left the man and approached Sarī and said, "This is our teacher and mentor who educated us in the world below." Then I said to him, "Abū 'l-Ḥasan (Sarī), you have gone to God, so fill us in as to what deed God has accepted." At that he took my hand and said, "Come!" So I went with him to a structure like the Kaʿba and we stopped beside it. Suddenly an individual looked down at us from the building, and that place was resplendent because of him. Sarī gestured toward him and boosted me up toward him. Sarī was small of stature and so was I, so the individual who was up on the building extended his hand. I grabbed it and he lifted me up to himself. I could not open my eyes against the lights in that place. Then he said to me, "I heard your conversation with the shaykh. If you make use of every created thing that the Qur'ān praises and avoid every created thing the Qur'ān condemns, it will serve you well.'""

Tradition has it that Sarī as-Saqaṭī said, "A young man was doggedly pursuing exoteric knowledge. Then he gave up on that and single-mindedly dedicated himself to devotion. So I inquired about him and found that he had withdrawn from society and was staying in his house, intent on worship. I said to him, 'You were avidly in search of exoteric knowledge. Why did you break off that concern?' He answered, 'I saw in a dream someone who was saying to me, "How much knowledge you have squandered! May God squander you!" Then I said, "But I have kept it!" Came the response, "Keeping knowledge involves acting upon it." So I abandoned the quest and devoted myself to regarding knowledge in terms of action.'" Ibn Masʿūd used to say, "Knowledge is not a question of transmitting a great deal; knowledge is God-awareness." Another person who possessed deep comprehension said, "*ʿIlm* is a light that God casts into the heart." Ḥasan al-Baṣrī used to say, "Know what you wish, but by God, God most High will not reward you for it unless you act upon it. Persons of little substance are concerned with transmission of tradition; the truly learned are concerned with observance."[28] [241] We have also received a tradition about him (Ḥasan), in which he said, "God does not care about the person who talks and transmits texts; he cares about people of profound comprehension and awareness." Abū Ḥaṣīn (d.c. 128/745) said, "If one of them had offered a legal opinion on a question and it came to the attention of ʿUmar ibn al-Khaṭṭāb, he would have gathered those who had participated in the Battle of Badr."[29] Someone else said, "If someone asked one of them a question about something, he would hasten to offer a legal opinion, even though if someone had asked the people who had participated in the Battle of Badr about it, it would have stumped them."

ʿAbd ar-Raḥmān ibn Yaḥyā al-Aswad and other religious scholars said, "Knowledge of religious statutes and legal opinions used to be the province of governors and rulers, and the public consulted them on these things. Then the situation deteriorated and the governors were no longer able to function that way because of their inclination to this world and their involvement in wars. So they came to rely for help in these matters on the exoteric scholars and those who issued legal advisories in the mosques. Then, when the ruler sat to hear legal claims, specialists in legal advice sat to his right and his left, and he would consult them both concerning rulings and statutes. He ordered his assistants to act likewise. Some among the people, then, learned the science of legal advisories and rulings, so that the governor could seek their assistance concerning legal statutes and rulings. Eventually, legal advisors multiplied as a result of worldly desires and the quest for leadership status. Then matters deteriorated further until the governors ceased to ask the assistance of the scholars."

A tradition from ʿUmar, when he wrote to Abū Masʿūd ʿUqba ibn ʿAmr (d. 40/660), clarifies: "Have I not been informed that you gave the people a legal opinion though you are neither a ruler nor a deputy?" Similarly, in a Ḥadīth Ibn ʿĀmir al-Hawzānī said, "I was making the Ḥajj with Muʿāwiya,[30] and, when we came to Mecca, we heard tell of a certain client of the tribe of Makhzūm[31] who was issuing legal rulings and legal advisories to the people. Muʿāwiya sent a message to him inquiring, 'Have you received an order to do this?' 'No,' he replied. So Muʿāwiya asked, 'Then what prompts you to do it?' He answered, 'We issue legal advisories and spread our knowledge.' So Muʿāwiya said, 'Had I come to you before now, I would have had your hand cut off (as if you were a thief).' Then he forbade him to do it any more."

They did not generally say that about the science of hearts, or the science of the faith or of certitude. On the contrary, ʿUmar would write to his military commanders, "Guard what you have heard from the obedient ones, for to them true matters have been manifested." ʿUmar used to sit among the spiritual seekers and listen to them. According to a tradition, "When you see a man who has received the gifts of silence and asceticism, get close to him, for he has received wisdom." One of the Ḥadīth specialists said, "I saw Sufyān ath-Thawrī sad, so I asked him about that. He replied wearily, 'We have become nothing but merchandise for the denizens of this world!' 'How so?' I asked. He replied, 'One of them has a use for us until, once he has become familiar with us and profited from us, someone makes him a boss or a chamberlain or a household manager.'" Ḥasan (al-Baṣrī) used to say, "People have come to learn this knowledge who have no connection through it to the next world. God preserves the knowledge through them for the sake of the community, lest it be lost entirely." Ma'mūn[32] said, "But for three things, this world would go to ruin: were it not for concupiscence, progeny would die off; and were it not for the love of amassing wealth, means of subsistence would cease; and were it not for the love of leadership, knowledge would vanish." All of this describes those who seek this world and the proponents of the science of tongues.

As for those seeking the next life who are the proponents of *maʿrifa* and certitude, they flee from rulers and their followers and minions among the people of this world. They belittle the learned of this world, discredit them, and avoid their company. (ʿAbd ar-Raḥmān) Ibn Abī Laylā said, "I came upon 120 of the Companions in this mosque. Not one of them, who when questioned about a Ḥadīth or [242] asked to enunciate a legal opinion, but preferred that his companion take over for him." He once said, "I encountered three hundred people, and if one of them was questioned about a legal opinion or the Ḥadīth, he referred it to the next person, who passed it to his companion, and they went on passing around the legal issue in question. But when one of them was questioned about a problem in the science of the Qur'ān or of certitude or the faith, he would not as a rule pass it off to his companion and was not reticent about answering."

God has said, "When you do not know, then inquire of the people of recollection" (16:43, 21:7). They are the people ever-mindful of God and the people of the divine transcendent unity and of understanding from God. They have not acquired this knowledge through the study of books, nor received it from one another by word of mouth. They were people of action and elegant deeds of devotion, so that when one of them was entirely dedicated to, and occupied with, God, he sought to labor in the service of the Master through deeds of the heart. They were with Him in seclusion before Him, remembering nothing but Him and occupying themselves with Him alone. And, when they appeared in public and someone questioned them, God inspired them with right guidance and accommodated them with the perfectly apposite response. He gave them wisdom as the heritage of the inward deeds arising from their pure hearts, pellucid minds, and lofty aspirations.

He chose, in His exquisite providence, to inspire in them the spiritual reality of knowledge, and to disclose to them the hidden mystery, since they chose to serve Him and dedicated themselves to Him through worthy deeds of devotion. Thus, they would respond to any question put to them, through the beauty of God's predilection and His comely imprint upon them. They would discourse of the knowledge of the divine power, bring to light the quality of wisdom, articulate the sciences of the faith, and reveal the inner meanings of the Qur'ān. This, then, is the knowledge that is beneficial in the relationship between the servant and God, through which one meets God, about which one inquires of God, and for which God rewards the individual. That knowledge is the balance-scale that weighs all actions at judgment day. In proportion to the servant's knowledge of his Lord, his actions in general weigh more and his good deeds are counted twice. This is how the individual becomes, in the eyes of God, among those who draw near, since from God's perspective he is one of those who possess certitude.

These are the people of spiritual realities whom ʿAlī described, elevating them over all creatures. He characterized them by saying, "Hearts are receptacles, and the best of them are the most capacious. People are of three kinds: those learned about their Lord, those who seek knowledge along the path of salvation, and the common rabble that chase after every con artist, bend with every breeze, do not seek to be illumined by the light of knowledge, and do not take refuge in a firm foundation. Knowledge is better than possessions, for knowledge keeps watch over you, whereas you must keep watch over wealth. Knowledge is purified by action, whereas consumption diminishes wealth. The love of knowledge is a religion through which one serves God. It anchors the individual in obedience throughout his life and speaks well of him after his death. Knowledge passes judgment, whereas wealth is subject to judgment. Wealth's utility dwindles as it diminishes. The treasury of riches perishes while its owners live, whereas the learned survive as long as time itself goes on."

Then ʿAlī sighed deeply and said, "Now that is an abundant knowledge! If only I could find one able to bear it. Of course, I can easily find a clever person who is not trustworthy, who affects the performance of religious deeds in search of worldly goals, who brags about the favors God bestows on His Friends, who makes a show of himself by demonstrations of God's proofs before people, or who tags along with the people of the Truth while nurturing doubt in his heart at the first inkling of ambiguity, and who has no spiritual insight. [243] Neither of the following two types are guardians of the religion—neither the person who is accustomed to pleasure and easily swayed toward satisfying his cravings, nor one who is seduced into accumulating and hoarding wealth and is in thrall to his whims. They are very much like grazing cattle. O God, thus let this vain knowledge die when those who possess it die. But the earth will never lack one who puts forth proof on behalf of God—whether out in the open and known, or in fear and under duress—so that the proofs and elucidations of God might not come to nought. But how many are they, and where are these people? Though they be few in number, their influence is enormous. Though one cannot detect their intrinsic characters, their likenesses exist in the hearts of humankind. Through them God guards the proofs He safely deposits in the hearts of those similar to them and implants in the hearts of those resembling them. Through their agency, the knowledge of the essential realities takes hold, so that they touch the spirit of certitude. What the pampered consider rough, they consider gentle, and they become intimate with what the heedless find repellent. They keep this world company in bodies whose spirits are connected to the loftiest abode. These are the Friends of God among His creatures, His agents on His earth and those who invite to His religion." Then ʿAlī wept and said, "What I would give for a glimpse of them!"

All of these are features of those who possess knowledge of the next world. They are characteristics of the knowledge of inward reality and the science of hearts, not of the science of tongues. That is how Muʿādh ibn Jabal[33] has characterized them in his description of the knowledge of God, in a Ḥadīth transmitted to us from Rajā' ibn Ḥaywa ibn ʿAbd ar-Raḥmān ibn Ghanam (d. 112/730) from Muʿādh himself: "Learn this knowledge, for learning it for God's sake is God-wariness; searching for it is worship; studying it is praise; seeking it is *jihād*; teaching it to one who does not know it is a gift of charity. Granting knowledge to those worthy of it is nearness to God, intimacy with the divine oneness, a companion in the midst of loneliness, a guide amid both joy and sorrow, adornment when divested of one's honor, nearness in the midst of strangers, and the lighthouse illumining the way to Paradise. Through knowledge God raises up peoples, making them on the path good models and guides so that people can emulate them, and signs toward what is good whose traces people can follow. The people observe the deeds of these exemplars and take guidance from their actions, ending up at the goal that is their exemplars' way of thinking. The angels long for their companionship and stroke their wings over them until everything wet and dry asks forgiveness for them—the creatures and fish of the sea, the dry land's beasts of prey and livestock, the firmament and its stars. For knowledge is the life of human hearts out of blindness, the light of the eyes out of darkness, and the strength of bodies out of weakness. Through knowledge the servant arrives at the dwelling places of the pious and the loftiest spiritual stations. Reflection upon knowledge is food during fasting; through studying it and acting upon it one obeys God; through it one worships; through it one acknowledges the divine transcendent unity; through it one does deeds of piety; through it blood relatives come together. Knowledge is a guide and action is its follower. It inspires the blessed while it is denied the wicked." These, then, are the characteristics of the otherworldly scholars, and the attributes of inward knowledge.

ʿUmar ibn ʿAbd al-ʿAzīz[34] was one of the most excellent rulers after the four Rightly Guided Caliphs. We have received a tradition from Zakarīyā ibn Yaḥyā aṭ-Ṭā'ī (d. 251/865) in which he said, "My uncle Zajr ibn Ḥiṣn passed on to me the tradition that ʿUmar ibn ʿAbd al-ʿAzīz wrote to Ḥasan (al-Baṣrī), 'Now then, show me a group of people I can ask for assistance concerning the command of God.' Ḥasan wrote back, 'As for the people of the religion, they will never want to deal with you, but as for the people of this world, you will never want to deal with them. You must associate with the high-born, for they [244] will uphold their nobility lest they besmirch it with treachery.'" Ḥasan used to talk disparagingly about some of the religious scholars of Basra, and Abū Ḥāzim al-Madanī and Rabīʿa al-Madanī[35] used to find fault with the religious scholars of the Banū Marwān.[36] And (Sufyān) ath-Thawrī, Ibn al-Mubārak, Ayyūb, and (ʿAbd Allāh) Ibn ʿAwn (ibn Artabān, d. 151/768) let their views be known about certain worldly scholars of Kufa, as did Fuḍayl, Ibrāhīm ibn Adham, and Yūsuf ibn Asbāṭ about some worldly learned individuals among the people of Mecca and Syria, whose names I am loathe to mention since reticence here is the better part of tact.

Bishr (al-Ḥāfī) used to say, "(The technical phrase) 'It has been handed down to us' is one of the gates of this world. So, when you hear a man say, 'It has been handed down to us,' he is really saying, 'Make room for me.'" Sufyān ath-Thawrī, (Bishr's) imām before him, used to say to the proponents of exoteric knowledge, "The quest for exoteric knowledge isn't a source of provisions for the next life." ('Abd Allāh) Ibn Wahb (d. 197/812) said, "Someone mentioned the quest for knowledge in the presence of Mālik (ibn Anas), and Mālik observed, 'The quest for knowledge is beautiful, and expatiating on it is beautiful, so long as one's intention in doing so is sound. But pay attention to what is required of you from the time you awake to the time you retire, and from evening until morning, and then prefer nothing over it." Abū Sulaymān ad-Dārānī said, "When a man goes in search of Ḥadīth or gets married or travels to seek the means of livelihood, he has relied on this world."

But as for the knowledge of the faith and the divine transcendent unity, and the science of *ma'rifa* and certitude, that belongs to every sure believer whose *islām* is beautiful. That is one's spiritual station, as God sees it, one's spiritual state before God, and one's portion from God with respect to the levels of Paradise. Through that means the individual becomes, from God's perspective, one of those who draw near to God, and the knowledge of God and faith in Him are two things joined inseparably. As for the knowledge of God, it is the balance-scale through which one distinguishes the growth of faith from its diminishment. For knowledge is the outward aspect of faith in that it reveals and makes faith visible, whereas faith is the inward aspect of knowledge in that it bestirs and enkindles knowledge. Faith is the support and vision of knowledge, while knowledge is the power and tongue of faith. Faith's weakness and strength, its increase and diminution, are directly proportionate to the waxing or waning, the vigor or infirmity, of knowledge.

In his advice to his son, the Sage Luqmān[37] said, "O my son, just as the seed cannot flourish without water and soil, so the faith cannot flourish without knowledge and action." The relationship among contemplative vision, *ma'rifa*, certitude, and faith is similar to that among the final food product (derived respectively) from flower meal, from grist, from wheat. The wheat contains all of that in itself. As faith is the root of which contemplative vision is the highest branch, so the wheat is the root of these developments whose highest branch is the final edible product. These spiritual stations exist within the lights of faith, and the knowledge of certitude undergirds them. Experiential knowledge, furthermore, is of two degrees, one related to hearing and the other related to seeing. *Maʿrifa* through hearing is connected to Islam in that people hear about God and thus come to know Him experientially. But *maʿrifa* through seeing is associated with contemplative vision, in that it is the essence of certitude.

Contemplative vision likewise is of two degrees, namely, contemplative vision related through demonstrative proof and contemplative vision through signs. Vision through demonstrative proof precedes *maʿrifa* and consists in the knowledge of information that derives from hearing, and whose tongue is the word. One who finds it does so through knowledge from which certitude arises, as in the word of God, "Sure news...I have found" (27:22–23).[38] This knowledge precedes the "finding" and is the knowledge of hearing. Instruction is its means and the saying of the Prophet is related to it, "Learn the knowledge of certitude!" In other words, keep the company of those endowed with certitude [245] and hear of the knowledge of certitude from them, for they are the ones who know it.

Contemplative vision through signs, on the other hand, comes after the experiential knowledge that derives from seeing. This is certitude, and its tongue is the experience of ecstatic finding and being found. The individual who "finds" this experience finds proximity, and after this "being found" there is a knowledge of the essence of certitude. God takes care of this individual with the aid of His light and power. Pertinent here is the saying of the Prophet, "I have experienced its chill, and thus I know it."[39] This knowledge subsequent to the experience of finding and being found arises from the essence of certitude by means of certitude, and it is one of the deeds of hearts. These are endowed with knowledge of the next life, the people of the realm of Lordly Dominion,[40] who possess hearts. They are among the Companions of the Right Hand,[41] who draw near to God. Exoteric knowledge, on the other hand, belongs to the knowledge of earthly sovereignty, and it is one of the deeds of the tongue. Those who possess knowledge of it are kin to this world, though the upright persons among them are Companions of the Right Hand.

A man came to Muʿādh ibn Jabal and said, "Tell me about two kinds of people: one of them is given totally to the struggle[42] in worship of God, prolific in good works, and guilty of few sins. But he is weak in certitude and subject to doubts in his daily affairs." Muʿādh then said, "Surely his doubts cancel out his good works." The man went on, "Now tell me now about an individual who has few good works to his credit, and who, though strong in certitude, is nevertheless a prolific sinner." Muʿādh was silent, so the man said, "By God, if the first man's doubts cancel out his deeds of piety, surely all of this man's sins would cancel out his certitude?" Then Muʿādh grabbed his hand, stood bolt upright, and said, "I have never seen one with greater understanding than this man." A Ḥadīth with a complete chain of transmitters, comments on the meaning of this. In the Ḥadīth someone inquired, "Messenger of God, what about an individual of fine certitude but many sins, and one thoroughly dedicated to worship but with meager certitude?" He replied, "No human being is sinless, but when someone is naturally disposed to intelligence and has certitude by temperament, his sins do him no harm; for whenever he sins, he repents, asks forgiveness, and feels contrition. Thus his sins are covered, leaving him a surplus of grace that will gain him entry to Paradise."

We have received the following Ḥadīth of Abū Umāma (d.c. 86/705) from God's Messenger: "At the very least, what you have been given includes certitude and firm patience. For one who receives his share of these two, it does not matter that he neglects night vigil and daytime fasting." In his advice to his son, Luqmān said, "My little son, knowledge without certitude is not possible, and a person cannot act except to the extent of his certitude. One who acts does not fail unless his certitude is insufficient." Weak action done with certitude is preferable to strong action accompanied by weak certitude. When a person's certitude is weak, minor sinfulness can vanquish him. Yaḥyā ibn Muʿādh used to say, "For affirming the divine transcendent unity there is light, and for idolatry there is fire; but the light of divine unity incinerates the evils of those who affirm it more completely than does the fire of idolatry the idolaters' good deeds."

There are three stations in certitude: first, certitude resulting from direct observation, about whose information there is no dispute, for one who knows in this manner is informed definitively. This is a characteristic of the completely veracious ones and the witnesses. Then there is the certitude of affirmation and assent, and this has to do with reports from others. One who knows this is one who accepts the report. This is the certitude of believers, and they are the pious ones "among whom are the upright and those who are not" (7:168), according to the words of the Most High, "and it only increased their faith and surrender" (33:22). The certainty of these people may weaken with the lack of basic necessities and the disruption of familiar circumstances, whereas their certitude grows stronger with better conditions and a more accustomed flow of circumstances. They are able to see only secondary causes and are aware of the truth only in specific contexts. They are social creatures, and they experience diminishment and alienation in their loss of social relations. Among these people there is variation in certitude; they waver, fluctuate, and diminish as do their exterior circumstances.

[246] The Third Station of Certitude

The third dimension of certitude is the certitude of opinion. This grows stronger through the arguments of religious knowledge and reports of traditions and the pronouncements of the religious scholars. These people experience increase from God in the portion they receive from Him. It weakens as a result of loss of proofs and the silence of teachers. This is the certitude of demonstrative argumentation, whose sciences are based on rational understanding. This is the certitude of the speculative theologians within the larger Muslim population, and more specifically among the proponents of individual assessment, the rational sciences, analogical reasoning, and speculative inquiry.

Everyone who possesses certitude concerning the existence of God thereby possesses knowledge of the divine transcendent unity and *maʿrifa*. But such a person's discursive and experiential knowledge is proportional to his certitude. His certitude is in accord with the purity and strength of his faith, which in turn depends on his deeds of worship and religious observance. The loftiest of the sciences is the knowledge of contemplative vision deriving from the essence of certitude. This is reserved for those who draw near to God in the stations of proximity to Him, in the conversations of their spiritual sessions and the shelter of their intimacy, and in the gentle nature of their affection. The most accessible of the sciences is the knowledge of surrender and acceptance without disavowal and without doubts. This belongs to the generality of believers and is an aspect of the knowledge of faith and of the highest affirmation of religious truth. It is the province of the Companions of the Right Hand. Between these two are the refined spiritual stations, from the highest categories of those who draw near to God to the intermediate spiritual stations, and from the most accessible ranks of the Companions of the Right Hand to the highest of the intermediate higher stations.

Discussion of the various sciences of silence and the path of the spiritually reticent in the religious disciplines

According to a tradition that has come down to us, "There are three aspects of knowledge: a book that speaks, an unwavering Sunna, and I don't know." According to Shaʿbī,[43] Muḥammad said, "'I don't know' is the half of knowledge." In other words, this is spiritual reticence. (Sufyān) ath-Thawrī used to say, "Knowledge does indeed involve authorization from a reliable person; but as for strengthening it, every individual can improve on it." By that he meant that spiritual reticence and success in ordinary affairs is the way the believers live, even if they are not formally learned. Spiritual reticence means hesitating to forge ahead with a frontal assault on ambiguities and coming to a tranquil or silent halt in the face of problematical issues. Certitude, on the other hand, means going forward with spiritual insight and firmness and making decisions on the basis of knowledge and information. This, then, is how religious scholars firmly established in their knowledge proceed, as they alone can do well.

ʿAlī said to his son Muḥammad ibn al-Ḥanafīya,[44] whom he had let go ahead of him during the Battle of the Camel,[45] "Go on! Go on!" Muḥammad hesitated and (ʿAlī) struck him with the shaft of the spear. Then Muḥammad, his son, turned to him and said, "By God, this is the dark, blind insurrection!" So ʿAlī struck him with his spear and said, "Get going! You have no mother. Is there an insurrection whose leader and promoter is your father?" When the man said, "I don't know," he was acting upon his knowledge and proceeding on the basis of his spiritual state. As a result, his reward was equal to that of a person who knows and proceeds according to his spiritual state and acts on his knowledge, thereby clarifying it. Thus, the expression, "I don't know" is half of knowledge, so that the recompense of a person who remains silent out of spiritual reticence for God is equal to that of one who talks openly with knowledge for God. ʿAlī ibn al-Ḥusayn[46] and Muḥammad ibn ʿAjlān (d. 148/765) said, "When a learned person mistakenly says, 'I don't know,' those who oppose him act appropriately." Mālik (ibn Anas) and Shāfiʿī[47] said so after these two.

You must understand that knowledge and ignorance are like the disparity among human beings with respect to madness and intelligence. There are categories of both mad and intelligent persons, just as there are categories of ignorant and learned persons. The best endowed [247] among the ignorant are like the run-of-the-mill scholars, and they confuse the generality of people so that they begin to consider them learned, while as far as those who are knowledgeable of God are concerned, their ignorance is evident. Similarly, those endowed with experiential knowledge are held in suspicion by the generality of religious scholars but are visible to those who possess certitude. One of the learned has said, "*ʿIlm* is of two kinds: the knowledge of rulers and the knowledge of the god-fearing. The knowledge of rulers is the knowledge of legal edicts, whereas the knowledge of the god-fearing is that of certitude and *maʿrifa*."

God has said by way of a description of the knowledge of believers and a discussion of the knowledge of faith, "God will elevate in ranks those among you who believe and to whom knowledge has been given" (58:11). He has thereby construed the believers as learned and indicated that there is no distinction between knowledge and faith. According to linguists, the "and" here communicates praise rather than conjunction. When the Arabs praise someone's characteristics, they introduce the word *and* by way of intensification. So, for example, they say, "So-and-so is intelligent and knowledgeable and refined." In the same vein, God said, "But those among you who are well-grounded in knowledge and who are believers [who believe in what was sent down to you and what was sent down previously] and who perform the ritual prayer and who give alms" (4:162), all by way of description. So the believers are the ones who are "well-grounded in knowledge" and who perform ritual prayer and give alms as well. All of this is a description of those who are "well-grounded in knowledge," and for that reason God's words "and who perform ritual prayer" are in the accusative (as the direct object of the first verb) because they are words of praise, and the Arabs use the accusative and the nominative to express praise.

In the same vein God said, "And those well-grounded in knowledge say 'We believe in the scripture'" (3:7). He has described the learned as endowed with faith just as He has described the believers as endowed with knowledge. So also God's words, "And those to whom knowledge and faith were given say..." (30:56). Also to the point is this Ḥadīth from Anas (ibn Mālik) from the Prophet, "Mine is a community of five generations of forty years each. My generation and that of my Companions are people of knowledge and faith; those who succeed them up to eighty years, people of piety and fear of God; and those who succeed them up to 120 years, people of union and compassion." He thereby connected knowledge and faith and gave them precedence over the other generations.

(On the Way of the Devout in Knowledge)

God connected faith with the Qur'ān, which is knowledge, as He linked the Qur'ān with faith, when He said, "He has inscribed faith in their hearts and strengthened them with a spirit from Him" (58:22). It is said that it is the Qur'ān that God has so inscribed. Now the "Him" refers to God, according to most interpretations. As He has said, "You did not know what the scripture was, nor the faith, but We made it a light" (42:52). Therefore the people of faith are the people of the Qur'ān and the people of the Qur'ān are the people of God and His chosen ones. Mahdī[48] asked Sufyān ibn al-Ḥusayn when he visited him, "Are you one of the learned ones?" He was one of the learned ones, but he did not answer, so Mahdī repeated the question. Still Sufyān was silent. Someone asked Sufyān, "Do you not respond to the Commander of the Faithful?" He replied, "He asked me an unanswerable question. Had I said 'I am not a learned one,' after reciting the Book of God, I would have been a liar. But if I had said, 'I am a learned one,' I would be an ignorant person." Abū Jaʿfar ar-Rāzī passed on a tradition from Rabīʿ ibn Anas (d.c. 139/756) about God's word, "Indeed, those among His servants who possess knowledge fear God" (35:28), commenting, "Whoever does not fear God is not a learned person." Are you not aware that David said, "You have made knowledge fear of You, and wisdom faith in You. One who does not [248] fear You does not know, and one who does not believe has no judgment." ʿAbd Allāh ibn Rawāḥa[49] called knowledge faith and used to say to his companions, "Sit down with us and let us believe for a while." They would then discuss together the knowledge of faith.

God has given believers hearing and sight and heart, for these are the avenues to knowledge along which they find and gain knowledge. These are the roots of knowledge and grace that God bestows on humankind and for which He expects gratitude. So He has said, "And when God brought you out of your mothers' wombs you knew nothing, and He gave you hearing and sight and hearts that perhaps you might give thanks" (16:78). On those three bases, therefore, He has established knowledge, after precluding it from the unborn. And God said, by way of description of the person who does not believe and denial that such a person enjoys the benefits of knowledge through (the three faculties), "And we have made for them hearing, sight, and heart, but their hearing, sight and heart did not avail them in the least, since they continued to disavow the signs of God" (46:26). But the person who believes in the signs of God benefits from his hearing, sight, and heart, and the paths of knowledge are open to him. God has also said concerning the meaning of that, "And do not involve yourself in things of which you have no knowledge, for hearing, sight, and heart will all be called to account for that" (17:36). If knowledge did not depend on the hearing, sight, and heart, God would not have proscribed what these faculties do not know. So, in God's forbidding the pursuit of and adherence to what these faculties do not know, there is an affirmation of what one does know through them. Every believer possesses hearing, sight, and heart, and is thus knowledgeable through God's largesse and mercy.

In this context, God has given this community preference over other communities and singled it out in three respects. First is the perdurance of chains of transmitters in which each successive link is joined without hiatus through the forebears in faith to our Prophet Muḥammad and to any of our religious scholars of the past. They then transcribed the pages (of the text of the Qur'ān), and whenever a page was worn out, a new one replaced it, thus continuing the tradition of knowledge. Second is the memorizing of the Book of God sent down from the upper realm of mystery, whereas previously other communities had recited their scriptures while reading. Apart from this scripture of ours, no book revealed by God has been entirely committed to memory, except for the Torah with which God inspired Ezra after Nebuchadnezzar burned all of it during the destruction of the Temple. For that reason, they say a descendant of the Jews is the son of God—God is far exalted above such a thing—since God chose him and bestowed on him alone knowledge of the whole Torah from memory.[50] Third, every believer of this community is asked about the knowledge of the faith, and people hear what he says and benefit from his view and his knowledge even when he is young. Previously, however, people listened only to their rabbis and priests and monks and not to any others among the people. And He increased (the Muslim community) in a fourth respect, namely, firmness of faith, over the community of Moses, so that no doubt beset them and no idolatry possessed them, even when their hearts were turning about in sinful rebellion; while the hearts of the community of Moses where immersed in doubt and idolatry just as their hearts were overturned in sinful rebellion. And the hearts of the community of Moses were overturned in doubt and idolatry just as their bodily members were overturned in sinful rebellion. So they said, "O Moses, make us a god like their gods" (7:138), and after that they saw the great sign of the parting of the sea, their passage through it on dry paths, their salvation from drowning, and the destruction of Pharaoh.

[249] We have received a tradition that one of the revealed scriptures says, "O children of Israel, do not say: knowledge is in heaven, who will bring it down? Or at the ends of the earth, who will get it? Or

beyond the seas, who will cross over and bring it? Knowledge is fixed in your hearts.[51] In my presence be schooled in the demeanor of the spiritual ones and be molded in the moral character of the righteous ones. I will make that knowledge manifest as a light in your hearts so that it fills you to overflowing." It is written in the (non-canonical) gospel, "Do not look for knowledge of what you have not acted upon until you have acted upon what you already know." And in our traditions we find, "To the person who acts upon what he knows, God bequeaths knowledge of what he does not know." In fact, someone has said, "To one who acts upon a tenth of what he knows, God gives as an inheritance a knowledge of that about which he knows nothing." We have a tradition from Ḥudhayfa ibn al-Yamān, "The time has come when a person who neglects a tenth of what he knows perishes, but after you will come a time when a person who acts on a tenth of what he knows will be saved." This is due to a scarcity of those who act and a plethora of foolish people. Our scripture provides concise, pithy sayings: "Fear God and God will instruct you" (2:282); "Fear God and know" (2:194); "Fear God and hear" (5:108).

Understand that a person who acts on what he knows or communicates about it, so that he attains the ultimate spiritual reality as God sees it, wins a double reward: the reward of divine assistance and the reward of action, and this is the spiritual station of those endowed with experiential knowledge. A person who talks and acts ignorantly, thereby missing out on the ultimate spiritual reality, bears two burdens, and this is the spiritual station of the ignorant. And a person who acts on or talks about traditional knowledge, but falls short of the ultimate spiritual reality, wins a reward for the sake of knowledge, and this is the spiritual station of those endowed with outward knowledge. A person who speaks or performs an action in ignorance, but nevertheless attains ultimate spiritual reality, bears a burden because of his abandoning the quest for knowledge, and this is the spiritual station of the ignorant godservants.

The learned person is like a judge. The Prophet divided judges into three groups, when he said, "Judges are of three sorts: a judge who judges truly and knowledgeably, and is bound for Heaven; a judge who knowingly passes unjust judgment, or one who does so unknowingly, both of whom are bound for Hell." One of the finest interpretations I have heard concerning the words of God, "O Children of Adam, We have sent down upon you raiment with which to cover your shame" (7:26), is that the raiment is knowledge, while plumage is certitude, and the garment of the fear of God is humility. A tradition has come to us from Wahb ibn Munabbih al-Yamānī[52] concerning the meaning of this text: "Faith is naked; its raiment is the fear of God, its adornment is humility, and its fruit is knowledge." Ḥamza al-Khurāsānī traced its chain to (Sufyān) ath-Thawrī and brought it forward to ʿAbd Allāh (ibn ʿAbbās) from the Prophet.

We have it attested also in an unbroken line of transmission that Miʿsar (ibn Kidām) (d.c. 153/770) passed on a tradition from Saʿd ibn Ibrāhīm (d.c. 125/742), in which someone inquired of him, "Which of the citizens of Medina is endowed with the deepest understanding?" and he replied, "The one whose fear of God is the greatest." One of the religious scholars said, "If someone were to ask me who was the most learned of the people, I would reply, the most spiritually reticent of them. And if someone were to ask me which of the citizens of this city was the best, I would ask, 'Do you know which of them it is who gives them the most sincere counsel?' And if they replied, 'Yes,' I would say, 'He is the best of them.'" Someone else has said, "Should someone ask me who was the most fatuous person, I would grab a judge by the hand and say, 'This one.'" God has said, "Fear God and hear" (5:108), and "Fear God and say a word that hits the mark" (33:70). So the Most High has turned fear of God into the key of the apposite word, and of well-guided knowledge and of well-founded hearing. It is the testament of God to those before our time, and to us, in which God says, "We have instructed those who have received the Book before your time, as well as you, to fear God" (4:131). This verse [250] is the pivot of the Qur'ān, around which it revolves like a millstone around its wooden axes. A tradition has been reported to us from Jesus, "How can someone who is devoted to this world belong to the people of knowledge whose destination is the next life? And how can someone who seeks discourse by which to inform others, but does not seek it in order to put it into action, belong to the people of knowledge?" Ḍaḥḥāk ibn Muzāhim[53] said, "I have come across people who learned nothing from one another but spiritual reticence, but these days they study theoretical discourse."

According to a Ḥadīth, "No people has fallen into error after being well-guided without degenerating into vain disputes. Then the Prophet recited the Qur'ānic text, 'They engage you (Jesus) only through vain debate. They are truly a contentious people.'" (43:58) Another Ḥadīth cites the Qur'ān and then comments on His words, "'But those whose hearts deviate (from the true interpretation)...' (3:7) are the proponents of disputation to whom God referred in the earlier cited verse, so beware of them." From one of the ancestors in faith comes the tradition, "At the end of time there will be religious scholars to whom the door of action will be shut, but to whom the door of disputation will be opened." And according to another tradition, "Yours is a time in which you will be inspired to action, but there will come a people inspired to disputation." From Ibn Mas'ūd comes the tradition, "You live in a time when the best of you is the one who acts with alacrity, but after you will come a time when the best of you is the one who behaves cautiously." In other words, during the first Islamic century there was revelation of the truth and certitude; but after that, in this our time, ambiguity and obscurity abound and innovations are introduced the way night steals over people on a journey. Matters are difficult, except for the individual who is intimately familiar with the ways of the ancestors in faith and thus steers clear of innovation altogether.

From one of the learned we have received the tradition, "When God desires good for a godservant He opens to him the door of action and closes to him the door of disputation. And when God desires evil for a servant, He shuts the door of action to him and opens for him the door of disputation." And a famous Ḥadīth from God's Messenger says, "God considers those who argue the most contentiously the most despicable of all people." We find in another tradition, "Shame and hesitation in speech are two branches of the faith, while obscene language and facile discourse are two branches of hypocrisy." By way of commentary one text explains, "Hesitation in speech is that of the tongue rather than of the heart." In another report passed on by Ḥakam ibn 'Utayba from 'Abd ar-Raḥmān ibn Abī Laylā, the Prophet said, "Any people with the gift of eloquence will abstain from action." According to a Ḥadīth, "God loathes the glib person who rolls discourse around on his tongue the way a cow chews its cud." Aḥmad ibn

Ḥanbal used to say, "Knowledge is that which comes from above," that is, an inspiration without ordinary pedagogy. He also said, "The learned among the speculative theologians are heretics." Before him, Abū Yūsuf[54] said, "Anyone who seeks knowledge in speculative theology engages in heresy."

A further exposition of the superiority of inward knowledge over outward

Here I will discuss the knowledge that the religious scholars have extolled and whose significance they have underscored. They regard this knowledge as a characteristic of the learned person and commend such a person for it. The Prophetic traditions testify to its excellence and authorize it, and the traditional reports laud its proponents. These sources indicate that it is knowledge of God, that it leads to God, and that it returns one to Him. The person who confesses the divine transcendent unity does so through the knowledge of faith and certitude, and through the science of [251] *maʿrifa* and deeds of worship. This knowledge does not lead one to the other disciplines of legal opinion and legal statutes. The scholars talk of "one who acts on his knowledge" and discuss action in relation to knowledge. They characterize it overall as fear of God and humility.

This, then, is the knowledge of hearts, not the knowledge of the tongue. It involves action and produces deeds of worship related to the works of faith. The deeds of hearts are spiritual stations of certitude and characteristics of those possessed of certitude. They are analogous to the righteous actions of the bodily members that result from increased faith. It is to this that the masters among the proponents of spiritual poverty and self-denial, and those who live by trust in God and fear, as well as those who experience longing and love, are referring. They do not mean that when a person has knowledge of statutes and legal rulings he is constrained to act on that knowledge, so that he is obliged to engage their stipulations in order to act according to them. He is not required, for example, to seek the office of magistrate so that he can adjudicate claims between people, if he has knowledge of these things; nor to purchase goods and engage in selling and buying, if he has knowledge of almsgiving and commercial transactions; or to marry a wife and divorce her just because he has knowledge about marriage and divorce, in order to be in these matters a person who puts his knowledge of them into action. No one has made such a claim; in fact, tradition has forbidden and censured that far more often than one can mention. The proponents of these sciences are characterized by a preference for this world and acquisitiveness, and they like to hobnob with rulers so that they can exchange favors with them. It therefore goes without saying that it is not these people one means when referring to knowledge, and that fear of God and asceticism are not their hallmarks.

In the same vein, most of the ancestors in the faith held knowledge superior to action, as in their sayings, "An atom of knowledge is more excellent than thus-and-so much action"; and "Two ritual prayer cycles of a learned person are more excellent than a thousand of a devotee." And according to a Ḥadīth of Abū Saʿīd al-Khudrī[55] from God's Messenger, "The learned person is superior to the devotee as I am superior to my community." And a well-attested version reads, "as the moon is superior to the other stars." A tradition of Ibn ʿAbbās and Saʿd,[56] which we have received with unbroken transmission back to the Prophet, says, "A single learned person is harder on Satan than a thousand devout ones." Something similar is said about the scholar's death, namely, that it is dearer to God than the deaths of a thousand pious persons.

The point is that knowledge of God is superior to action, for knowledge of God is an attribute of faith and an aspect of the certitude that is more precious than anything that comes down from the heavens. Nothing measures up to it, and no action is sound or acceptable apart from it. It is the measure of all acts in whose scale deeds are weighed, some more worthy than others, some weightier on the scales than others. And those who act are elevated to lofty ranks, some higher than the others. God has said, "And We have brought them a scripture, which We have laid out in detail on the basis of knowledge" (7:52). And the Most High has said, "We will narrate their story on the basis of knowledge" (7:7); and the Most High continued, "And on that day the scale will register true, and those whose scales weigh heavily with good deeds…"(7:8).[57] And the benefit that accrues from knowledge that is nearest to lordliness is more excellent. Action is an attribute of the agent, and it is germane to deeds of worship. They do not mean, however, that legal opinions, statutes, and rulings—in which people have a vested interest and from which they benefit—are superior to spiritual deeds in relation to God on the level of the heart. These latter include the spiritual stations of trust, satisfaction, and love, which, in turn, result from the examination of certitude, which, in turn, are the stations of those who have drawn near to God. A scholar does not make such claims.

A Ḥadīth has been passed along to us from ʿAbd ar-Raḥmān ibn Ghanm (d. 78/697) from Muʿādh ibn Jabal, that God's Messenger said, [252] "The people closest to the level of prophethood are the people of knowledge and the people of *jihād*. The people of knowledge lead humankind to that which the Messengers have brought, whereas the people of combat engage in battle with their swords on behalf of that which the Messengers have brought." Do you not see how God has fashioned knowledge into a guide to God, and outward combat as well? Likewise a tradition has come to us that "the first to make intercession are the prophets, [then those who possess knowledge,] then the martyrs." And according to a tradition, "The prophets are one step above the truly learned, and the learned are two steps above the martyrs." Concerning the meaning of the words of God, "God has elevated in ranks those among you who believe and those who have been given knowledge" (58:11), Ibn ʿAbbās said, "The learned ones are of many degrees and seven hundred ranks above those who believe; and between every two degrees is a span of five hundred years." When ʿUmar died, Ibn Masʿūd said, "In my estimation, he took nine-tenths of knowledge with him." Someone interjected, "You say this even while the majority of the Companions of the Prophet are still among us?" He replied, "I am not talking about the knowledge you want; I mean, rather, the knowledge of God." He thus established that knowledge of the innumerable knowable objects is not authentic knowledge, and that knowledge of God is superior to nine-tenths of the various other forms of knowledge.

The value of outward knowledge does not greatly exceed that of actions, in that it is itself one of the outward acts because it is a characteristic of the tongue and because it belongs to the generality of Muslims. The highest of its spiritual stations is sincerity, and if it eludes them, then it is worldliness like the other passions. Sincerity is the first spiritual state of knowledge of God in terms of inward knowledge. There is, however, no end to their spiritual stations, all the way to the loftiest stations of those who know God experientially and the ranks of the veracious ones.

[253] A chapter discussing the difference between those who possess knowledge of this world and those who possess knowledge of the next, and a censure of the wicked scholars who use their sciences to consume this world's goods

Religious scholars have made a distinction between knowing God and knowing God's command. They have also distinguished between those who are learned about this world and those endowed with knowledge of the next life. Sufyān (ath-Thawrī) said, "There are three types of learned people: one who has knowledge of God and of God's command, and that is the person of complete knowledge; one who has knowledge of God but not of God's command, and that is the pious and god-fearing person; and one who has knowledge of God's command but not of God Himself, and that is the profligate scholar." Another saying also mentions, "one who has knowledge for God's sake, and who acts upon his knowledge; and one who has knowledge about the 'Days of God' (14:5, 45:14),[58] and who experiences fear and hope."

Someone asked Sufyān what knowledge is, and he replied, "It is spiritual reticence." Someone asked, "And what is spiritual reticence?" He answered, "The quest for the knowledge by which one recognizes spiritual reticence." According to the people generally, that means protracted silence and few words. In my view that is not the case; rather, the learned person who speaks is preferable to one who keeps silent. Tradition has come down to us that Luqmān said in his advice, "There are three indications of knowledge: knowledge of God, of what God loves, and of what He hates." He thus construed these three as the essence of knowledge and evidence of its existence.

Here are some things that provide you evidence as to the distinction between those who are learned in matters of this world and those who have knowledge of the next life: Whenever someone sees a truly learned person, but does not know him as such, the signs of his knowledge will not be evident to him, for none will recognize that he is a learned person except those who have knowledge of God. They are identifiable through their characteristic humility, tranquility, lowliness, and self-effacement. These constitute the "distinctive hue" that God bestows on His Friends and the vesture with which He clothes those who have knowledge of Him. "And who is better at conferring a distinctive hue than God?" (2:138). In that respect they are like craftsmen, for whenever anyone sees a craftsman but does not recognize him as such, he does not recognize the craftsman's work as distinct from other works. Only a fellow craftsman can see the difference between him and other craftsmen. One recognizes the craftsman by his product, for it is his outward characteristic and makes him known in that it becomes, through the results of his activity, like a uniform and a distinguishing mark of what would otherwise be anonymity.[59] As someone has said, "The finest garment God confers on a godservant is humility in tranquility, which is the raiment of the Prophets and the outward mark of the most righteous and the truly learned."

The most learned people are those who have knowledge of the subtle things that God loves and the secret things that He hates. They are the people whose hearts have a penetrating understanding of God and who have experiential knowledge of Him. Sahl (at-Tustarī) used to say, "Learned people are of three kinds: one who has knowledge of God; one who has knowledge oriented to (acting in accord with the will of) God; and one who has knowledge of God's statutes." In other words, one who has knowledge about God is one who knows God experientially and with certitude; one who has knowledge for God is one who is knowledgeable through the knowledge of sincerity, spiritual states, and deeds of worship; and one who knows the statutes of

God is one who has knowledge of the particularities of what is allowed and what is forbidden.

I will elaborate on that with reference to the senses of Sahl's utterances and with an intimate understanding of his overall approach. He once said in a more expansive explanation [254] than this, "Those who have knowledge of God but not of God's command or of the 'Days of God,' are the believers; those who have knowledge of the command of God, but not of the 'Days of God,' are they who issue legal opinions concerning the permitted and the forbidden; and those who have knowledge of God and of the 'Days of God' are the veracious ones." His saying "about the 'Days of God'" means "about His hidden graces and His inscrutable reproaches." He then said, "All people other than the learned are dead; and the learned are asleep, except for those who fear God; and those who fear God are cut off (from society in general), except for the lovers; and the lovers are living witnesses who give God precedence over every spiritual state." And Sahl used to say, "Seekers of knowledge are of three kinds: one seeks it in order to act upon it; another seeks it in order to recognize differences of opinion, in order thereby to exercise spiritual reticence and circumspection; and the third seeks it for an understanding of obscure interpretations that will allow him to interpret what is forbidden so as to render it permissible. This last individual thereby destroys the truth with his own hands."

A tradition has been passed along to me, that at the beginning of the year Abū Yūsuf endowed his wife with his possessions and then asked her to give him her possessions, so that the two of them would be absolved of required almsgiving.[60] Someone mentioned that to Abū Ḥanīfa, and he answered, "That is a result of his knowledge of technical loopholes." Even so, people seek knowledge to understand spiritual reticence and circumspection in religion, and this is useful knowledge. But if a person seeks something like this and pursues a tendentious interpretation, ignorance would be preferable. Such knowledge becomes detrimental and something from which the Messenger sought refuge.

We have a tradition from ʿUmar and others, "How numerous are the profligate scholars and the ignorant godservants! Beware the profligate among the scholars and the ignorant among those who devote themselves to worship!" Likewise from ʿUmar, and transmitted to us with unbroken chain, "Beware every hypocrite of learned tongue, who talks about what is familiar to you and does what you abhor!" We have also received this tradition from him, "Learn knowledge, and learn for the sake of knowledge tranquility and mildness. Humble yourselves before those from whom you learn, so that those who learn from you might humble themselves before you. Do not be overweening scholars, lest your knowledge rest upon your ignorance." We have a tradition from ʿAlī and Ibn ʿAbbās, and from Kaʿb al-Aḥbār,[61] "At the end of time there will be scholars who encourage the people to withdraw from this world while they themselves do not do so; who encourage the people to fear God while they themselves do not fear Him; and who forbid them to keep the company of rulers while they do not so restrict themselves. They prefer this world to the next and devour this world's goods with their tongues, hoarding wealth for themselves while keeping it away from the poor. They guard their knowledge jealously from one another the way women guard their men, so that they are roused to anger should one's companion spend time with another. That is their portion of knowledge."

According to a Ḥadīth of ʿAlī, "Their learned ones are the most wicked of creatures, for strife begins with them and returns among them." A Ḥadīth of Ibn ʿAbbās says, "They are the bold enemies of the Merciful." We have received a tradition from ʿAlī, "Only two men give me trouble in Islam: a profligate scholar and a novelty-contriving ascetic. The profligate scholar begrudges the people his knowledge because they recognize his depravity, while the contriving ascetic titillates the people with his novel practices when they observe his asceticism." Ṣāliḥ ibn al-Ḥassān al-Baṣrī said, "I came upon the elders while they were taking refuge in God from the profligate scholar of the Sunna." Fuḍayl ibn ʿIyāḍ said, "The learned are of two sorts: one who has knowledge of this world and the other knowledge of the next. The knowledge of one learned in matters of this world is out in the open, while that of one learned in matters of the next is veiled. Seek out the one knowledgeable of the next world and be on guard against the one knowledgeable of this world. Do not let his intoxicating wine hinder your progress." Then Fuḍayl recited the Qur'ānic verse, "Many are the priests and monks who deceitfully devour the possessions of humankind [255] and hinder them from the way of God" (9:34).

Fuḍayl commented further, "The priests are the scholars, and the monks are the ascetics."

Sahl ibn ʿAbd Allāh (at-Tustarī) said, "Seekers of knowledge are of three kinds: One seeks the knowledge of spiritual reticence for fear of being vulnerable to ambiguities, so he forgoes the permitted in fear of the forbidden. Such is the god-fearing ascetic. Another seeks the knowledge of the disparity and multiplicity of views: He avoids what is clearly obligatory upon him and opts for that which God has made permissible in His largesse, and avails himself of dispensations.[62] Still another inquires about something, is told that it is not permissible, and asks further, 'How can I can contrive to make it permissible for me?' So he asks the religious scholars to inform him of the divergent views and ambiguous interpretations. Such a person thereby causes the destruction of humankind with his own hands, after compassing his own ruin. These are the corrupt scholars."

Understand that everyone in love with this world who communicates knowledge devours wealth through deceit and falsehood. And everyone who consumes the possessions of the people through deceit inevitably diverts them from the way of God (as in Q 9:34). And even if that is not apparent in what a person says, you will, nevertheless, recognize it in nuanced allusions to minute details of tactics designed to steer people away from the company of others, and in subtle ways of deterring them from the paths to the next life. For the love of this world and the victory of caprice predispose one to that, willy-nilly. A truly learned individual has said, "God loves the learned person who humbles himself and loathes those among the learned who are overbearing. God bequeaths wisdom as an inheritance to those who humble themselves before God." According to a tradition from Ibn Masʿūd, "God abhors the fat rabbi." And God's Messenger said to Mālik ibn aṣ-Ṣayf, a Jewish religious authority, "On your solemn honor before God, do you not find in what God revealed to Moses that God abhors the fat rabbi?" Now Ibn aṣ-Ṣayf was corpulent, so he became angry at that and replied, citing the Qur'ān, "God has not sent anything down to a human being" (6:91). So this verse was sent down as a clarification of his false assertion, "Proclaim: Who has sent down the scripture that Moses has brought as a light (and guidance for humankind)?" (6:91) So Ibn aṣ-Ṣayf's companion said to him, "Woe to you! What you have said repudiates the scripture of Moses!" So he replied, "He picked a fight with me, so I said that."

Someone said, "God has not given a godservant knowledge without simultaneously giving him gentleness, humility, good disposition, and affability." That is the mark of useful knowledge. We have received a tradition on the meaning of that, saying, "The person to whom God grants asceticism, humility, and good disposition is the leader of the god-fearing." Ḥasan (al-Baṣrī) used to say, "Gentleness is the minister of knowledge, affability is its father, and humility its raiment." According to a tradition about David, "God revealed to him, 'David, do not ask Me about a knowledgeable person who is intoxicated with this world and has diverted you from the path of loving Me. Such are the highway robbers of My servants who seek Me. David, the least severe thing that I do to the learned person, if he gives his own desires precedence over love for Me, is to forbid him the delights of intimate conversation with Me. David, should you see someone in search of Me, become his servant. David, when someone brings back to Me a person seeking refuge, I take note that he is a brilliant scholar; and I will never punish one whom I note down as a brilliant scholar.'"

We have a tradition from Jesus, "Wicked scholars are like a boulder that has tumbled into the mouth of a river: it neither drinks the water nor allows the water to be directed to irrigate a cultivated field." That is how those worldly scholars block the path to the next life: They neither move along nor allow godservants to journey on to God. He also said, "Wicked scholars are like [256] a sewer pipe: externally beautiful and internally foul-smelling; or like pretentious funeral monuments: imposing mansions on the outside, charnel houses within."[63]

Bishr al-Ḥārith (al-Ḥāfī) said, "When someone aspires to leadership among the religious scholars and approaches God, to God's great displeasure, he is despised in heaven and on earth." Awzāʿī handed down a tradition that Bilāl ibn Saʿd (d. between 105/724 and 124/743) used to say, "People of your ilk look at the royal guard and the courtiers, take refuge in God from being like that, and loathe that state. On the other hand, they look at a worldly scholar who puts on airs before the people and eagerly anticipates the objects of his desire and a position of leadership, but do not spurn him. Yet this scholar was more deserving of disgust than that royal guard." Abū Muḥammad

(Sahl at-Tustarī) said, "Do not undertake the accomplishment of any deed, religious or secular, without consulting the truly learned, for only then will you ultimately gain the praise of God." Someone asked, "Abū Muḥammad, who are the truly learned?" He replied, "Those who prefer the next world to this, and God to themselves." And ʿUmar said in his last testament, "Be reflective in all your affairs like those who fear God."

Tradition has come to us in the historical documents about the Israelites that one of the wise ones compiled 360 volumes on wisdom, and thus became known as the Sage. God therefore revealed to their prophet, "Say to so-and-so, 'You have filled the earth with idle chatter and you have not acquitted yourself before me in any of that. Therefore, I do not accept any of your babbling.'" The man then became downcast and sad as a result and abandoned that way of acting. He mingled among the public, strolled in the markets, and looked after the children of Israel. Thus did he attain spiritual humility. So God revealed to the prophet, "Tell that person, 'Now you have measured up to what pleases me.'"

One of the learned said, "The learned are of two types: the public scholar and the private scholar. The public scholar is one who issues legal opinions concerning the permitted and the forbidden, and keeps the company of the high and mighty. The private scholar, on the other hand, is one who knows the science of the divine transcendent unity and experiential knowledge. The latter type keep to their secluded corners.[64] Someone said, "Imām Aḥmad ibn Ḥanbal is like the Tigris River—everybody is familiar with it. But Bishr ibn al-Ḥārith (al-Ḥāfī) is like a pleasant hidden spring—people head for it one at a time." Ḥammād ibn Zayd (d. 179/795) said, "Someone asked Ayyūb,[65] 'Is knowledge more plentiful these days than in the past?' He replied, 'Knowledge was more abundant in the past; nowadays words are in greater supply.'" He thus distinguished between knowledge and discourse. People used to say, "So-and-so is a learned person, and so-and-so is a talker; so-and-so talks more, but so-and-so is more knowledgeable." Abū Sulaymān (ad-Dārānī) used to say, "*Maʿrifa* is closer to silence than to speech." One of those who possessed experiential knowledge said, "This type of knowledge has two parts: half of it keeps quiet, and as for the other half, you know where you can deposit it." Someone else has added, "Half of it is ecstasy, and half reflection," meaning reflection and contemplation.

Someone asked Sufyān (ath-Thawrī) what a learned person is, and he answered, "Someone who puts knowledge in its place, so that all things exist in due proportion." One of the sages said, "When knowledge abounds, talk is scarce." Ibrāhīm al-Khawwāṣ[66] said, "As the Sufi's knowledge waxes, so wanes his inner spiritual openness." One of our spiritual masters said, "I asked Junayd, 'Abū 'l-Qāsim, are there tongues without hearts?' 'Plenty,' he replied. I asked, 'Are there hearts without tongues?' 'There are,' he answered, 'but a tongue without a heart is a an affliction, while a heart without a tongue is a blessing.' I asked, 'And when tongue and heart are together?' 'That,' said he, 'is butter [257] with the finest dates,'" meaning (butter with) date syrup.

We have a tradition, lacking full *isnād,* from Sufyān (ath-Thawrī) from Mālik ibn Mighwal (d.c. 157/773), who said, "Someone asked, 'Messenger of God, what is the most excellent deed?' He replied, 'Avoiding forbidden things, while your mouth is moistened with the remembrance of God.' Someone asked, 'Messenger of God, who is the best companion?' He answered, 'A companion who supports you when you engage in recollection, and who spurs you to recollection you when you forget.' Someone asked, 'Who is the most evil companion?' Said he, 'One who does not urge you to recollection when you are silent, and who does not support you when you recollect.' Someone else asked, 'And who is the most learned person?' (Muḥammad) answered, 'The one whose fear of God is the most intense.' They said, 'Tell us about the best among us so that we can keep company with them.' He answered, 'People at the sight of whom one remembers God.' They said, 'And who is the worst person, Messenger of God?' He replied, 'O God forgive!' They continued, 'Messenger of God, tell us more about that.' He answered, 'Religious scholars who have become corrupted.'"

ʿAlī described worldly scholars who speak out of personal opinion and caprice in an extraordinary manner—we have the tradition from Khālid ibn Ṭalīq, from his father, and his father, ʿImrān ibn Ḥusayn (d. 52/672): "ʿAlī ibn Abī Ṭālib addressed us and said, 'My responsibility is a pledge, and I stand behind it. No people's seed of the fear of God withers, and no rootstock thirsts for guidance. The most ignorant person is the one who is not aware of his standing—and that is some ignorance, to be unaware of one's spiritual standing! From God's perspective, the most hateful of creatures is a person who collects knowledge, raiding under cover of darkness, causing trial and tribulation, blind to what is hidden in tranquility. The most contemptible people, and those who have the most in common with such a person, consider him learned, even though he has not gained any knowledge for a single entire day. He sets out early in the morning, amassing that which, though available in abundance, is of little use. When he has slaked his thirst with tainted water and has multiplied fruitless acts, he sits with the people issuing legal opinions with the intent of clarifying what others find obscure. Should he be confronted with a puzzling issue, he addresses it from his idiosyncratic perspective. In his dispelling of ambiguities he is as tenuous as the spider's webbing, for he does not know whether he has missed the mark or hit it. The foolishness drags on, a dark madness in which he offers no excuse for what he does not know, and he thus gets away unscathed. He never takes a firm convincing bite out of knowledge, yet he manages to come away with the prize. People shed tears of blood for him, inheritances cry out for him; because of his rulings, people consider forbidden women permissible. By God, such a person is incapable of giving out what he has received, nor is he equal to that which overpowers him. These are the ones destined to wail and weep all the days of their lives in this world.'"

ʿAlī also described those learned about the next life in the Ḥadīth of Kumayl ibn Ziyād, in which he said, "People are of three kinds: one who possesses spiritual knowledge"—that is, one who possesses knowledge of Lordliness so that ʿAlī made attribution to a Lord, the way God has referred to them in His word, "Be you all Lordly ones in that you are those who know the scripture (and in that you have studied it intensively)" (3:79). He thus calls "Lordly" both the one who possesses knowledge of His scripture, and the one who studies it intensely. This person therefore integrates knowledge and action, so it is said that the one who possesses Lordly knowledge is the one who knows and acts and teaches the people what is good. He said "that is the one who is called mighty in the realm of heaven." And about His giving them precedence God has said, "Why then do their divines and scriptural specialists not deter them (from delivering their sinful teachings and eating what is forbidden)?" (5:63).

So the Lordly ones have precedence over the religious authorities who possess knowledge of the scripture. In this context we have received a tradition from Mujāhid,[67] "The Lordly ones are one step above the authorities on scripture." Someone else said, "The scriptural authorities are one step above the monks," that is, those who possess the knowledge of hearts [258] outrank those who possess the knowledge that can be articulated, while those who possess knowledge of the scripture are superior in rank to devotees. God has linked them to His prophets as their helpers and regards them as long-suffering, when He says, "How many a prophet has done battle, and alongside them countless Lordly ones" (3:146). He proceeds, in the remainder of the verse, to describe them as firmly committed to His command, staunch in His religion, and long-suffering in the face of His judgment. The word "Lordly ones" *(ribbiyūna)* is the plural of "Lordly one" *(ribbiy^{un})*. One says *ribbiy^{un}* and *rabbāniy^{un}*, so the plural of *ribbiy^{un}* is *ribbiyūna* and that of *rabbāniy^{un}* is *rabbāniyūna.*

In that vein, the tradition has come down from God's Messenger, "On the day of Resurrection the prophets will intercede, then the learned ones, then the martyrs." He has thus given the learned precedence over the martyrs, for the learned one is the leader of a community, and his reward commensurate with that of his community, whereas the martyr acts on his own behalf. According to another traditional report, "The ink of scholars will be weighed in the scale with the blood of martyrs." The martyr's loftiest spiritual aspect is his blood, whereas the lowest attribute of the scholar is his ink. But God compared them with each other and the scholar came out ahead of the martyr in his loftiest spiritual station. ʿAlī used to say, "The scholar is more excellent than one who fasts or keeps night vigil or engages in *jihād* in the cause of God, and when a learned one dies he leaves a vacuum in Islam that only one of his successors can fill." A tradition supported completely back to Muḥammad elaborates, saying, "When a learned one dies, he leaves a vacuum in Islam that nothing can fill as long as the night banishes the day. A scholar's death means that a star has gone dark, outstripping in importance even the extinction of a whole tribe."

Then ʿAlī said, in the Ḥadīth of Kumayl, referring to the second type of person, "The one who seeks knowledge toward salvation." He refers to the seeker in quest of knowledge who wants to learn from those who possess knowledge of God about the path of pious deeds and sincerity in relation to the quest for wholeness and salvation from ignorance in this world and from punishment in the next. He then added, "And the swarming winged insects." The "winged insects" are moths that, out of ignorance, dive into the flame. The singular of the term *(hamaj*^{un}*)* is *hamajat*^{un}. "Swarming" means trivial, fickle, and lacking understanding: craving agitates him, irascibility carries him away, self-satisfaction gives him the illusion of cleverness, and he displays his hubris arrogantly. On that account ʿAlī wept and said, "Thus does knowledge perish when one to whom it is entrusted dies." Then he sighed as he referred to the Lordly ones, saying, "Oh, how I long to have a glimpse of them!"—meaning the Lordly ones among the learned. I have discussed this Ḥadīth in its entirety in a previous section. Those whom he laments longingly are those for whom the Messenger of God had longed before him, when he said, "Oh, how I long to meet my brothers! How I wish I could see my brothers!" Then he said, "They are the people who will come after you," and described them (see pp. 128–29).

They are, then, his brothers, for their hearts are in accord with the hearts of the prophets and by natural temperament they possess the attributes of the faith. They are the *Abdāl*[68] of this community. Their qualities defy description, and they are of three categories: the perfectly truthful, the witnesses, and the righteous. Some of their hearts are in tune with the heart of Abraham the Khalīl (God's intimate friend); some of their hearts are in tune with that of Moses the Kalīm (God's conversant), Jesus the Spirit (of God), and Muḥammad the Beloved (of God); while still others' hearts are in tune with those of Gabriel, Michael, and Isrāfil.

Brotherhood between two parties is a matter of affinity and close resemblance in deeds and natural temperament, as God has said, "Have you not noticed how the hypocrites say to their infidel brothers among the people of the Book…?" (59:11).[69] Since they share at heart the inner characteristics of unbelief and adherence to what is dubious, God refers to them [259] as brothers. In a similar vein, God has said, "The squanderers are brothers of the Satans" (17:27). These have nothing in common with respect to creaturely characteristics, nor do they share either common fatherhood or motherhood, for the Satans are the spawn of Iblīs while the squanderers are descendants of Adam. Nevertheless, since their hearts are similar with respect to affective propensities, natural temperament, and deeds, theirs is a brotherly affinity.

The understanding of one who possesses knowledge of the next life, on the other hand, is resplendent from the lights of his heart, and his spiritual comprehension is informed by what he has discovered through his learning and contemplation. His natural temperament takes on the qualities of his certitude and power, and his path and journeying are on the highroad of the Prophet's example and way. He is thus among his brothers and the brothers of the prophets whom God's Messenger longed to see. They are the strangers among the multitude, of whom Muḥammad said, "Islam began as a stranger and will end as a stranger. Happy are the strangers!" Someone asked, "And who are the strangers?" He replied, "Those who remain upright while humankind becomes corrupt." Another version says, "Those who continue to honor aspects of my Sunna that most people have distorted, and who keep alive aspects of my Sunna that most people have killed." In other words, they show forth the Prophet's Path, which most people have abandoned, and of which they are ignorant. According to another tradition, "They are those who adhere to my Sunna and to the way you live now." And in another Ḥadīth, "The strangers are persons few in number and upright, among numerous wicked people, more of whom hate them than love them." So the strangers are those whom God has blessed with the friendship of the prophets in the highest heights, and of whom He said, "With those upon whom God has bestowed His grace, the prophets…" on down to His word "friends" (4:69).[70] (Sufyān) ath-Thawrī used to say, "When you see a learned person who has many intimate friends, know that he is spreading confusion." He also said, "If you see a man beloved of his brothers and praised by his neighbors, you can be sure that he is a publicity seeker."

God has described wicked scholars as consuming this world with knowledge. By contrast He has described those who possess knowledge of the next life as god-fearing and self-disciplined. And concerning the worldly scholars He has said, "God accepted a covenant with those who had received the Book (enjoining them) to make (the scripture) clear to the people and not to conceal it; but they cast it behind their backs and traded it for a paltry price" (3:187). Characterizing those who possess knowledge of the next life, God has said, "Indeed among the people of the Book are those who believe in God and what He has revealed to you..." continuing on to His words, "they have their reward in God's eyes" (3:199).[71]

We have received a tradition through Ḍaḥḥāk (ibn Muzāhim) and Ibn ʿAbbās from the Prophet, "Among the learned ones of this community are two kinds of people. First is the one to whom God has given knowledge and who then dispenses it liberally to humankind without expecting anything in return and without selling it for a price. For that reason the birds of the sky, the fishes of the sea, the beasts of the earth, and the highest-ranking recording angels call down blessings upon him. Such a person will come before God on Resurrection Day as a *Sayyid* and a *Sharīf*[72] and thus become an intimate friend of the Messengers. Then there is the person to whom God has given knowledge in this world, but who then withholds it from the servants of God, expects something in return for it, and sells it for a price. On Resurrection Day such a person will come as one restrained in harness from the fire, while a crier calls out above all creatures, 'This is what's-his-name to whom God gave knowledge in this world, but who then withheld it from the servants of God, expected something in return for it, and sold it for a price. He will be punished until God has finished calling humankind to account.'"

One of the most egregious examples I have heard of someone using knowledge to devour this world's goods is a story passed along by ʿUbayd ibn Wāqid from ʿUthmān ibn Abī Sulaymān, who said, "There was a man who worked for Moses who used to claim, 'Moses, God's dear friend, told me...,' and 'Moses, God's confidant, told me...,' [260] and 'Moses, who conversed with God, told me...,' until he became wealthy and his possessions multiplied. Moses lost touch with him and started inquiring about him, but found not a trace. Then, one day, a man came along carrying a pig with a black cord around its neck. Moses asked him, 'Do you know so-and-so,' and he replied, 'Yes, he's the pig here.' Moses said, 'Sir, I request that you return him to his former state so that I can question him about how this happened to him.' Then God revealed to him, 'O Moses, had you entreated me as Adam and the other Prophets entreated me, I would not have responded to your call. But I will explain it to you: I did this to him because he used religion for worldly gain.'"

We have a tradition from Ḥasan (al-Baṣrī), that one day, as he left his study circle, a man from Khurasan requested a permission from him. He placed before him a purse containing five thousand dirhams and produced from under his arm a parcel containing ten garments of fine Khurāsānī linen. So Ḥasan asked, "What's this?" He replied, "Abū Saʿīd, this is for spending and this is for wearing." Replied Ḥasan, "May God forgive you! Keep your money and your clothes. We don't need that. Anyone who holds a study circle such as this one of mine and accepts from people something like this, on the day he meets God, he will meet Him in disgrace." And according to a tradition, "Indeed, though people may praise an individual from east to west, God regards that person as of no greater value than the weight of a gnat's wing." As for the worldly scholars who seek this world through their knowledge, who consume it by exploiting religion, who choose their friends and companions from among the children of nobility, who aggrandize them and love this world, and who devote themselves to it gladly and cheerfully—in every age they will be known by their characteristics, by the style of their pronouncements, and by their demeanor.

We have received a harsh tradition about the spiritual stations of the wicked scholars. We take refuge in God from their ilk and ask Him not to afflict us with any of their spiritual circumstances. We have received this tradition in one version with an unbroken chain of transmission back to the Prophet, and in another with a line of transmission back as far as Muʿādh ibn Jabal; I prefer the latter. We have a tradition from Mindal ibn ʿAlī and Abū Nuʿaym ash-Shāmī and Muḥammad ibn Ziyād, in which Muʿādh ibn Jabal says, "God's Messenger said," though I stop the chain of transmission with Muʿādh, who said, "A temptation for the learned person is to prefer talking over listening. Talking allows scope for elegant expression and embellishment, so that one cannot readily pinpoint a speaker's error. Silence, on the other hand, yields integrity and knowledge. Some scholars hoard their knowledge and do not like people to discover it from someone else. Such a person is destined for the first level of Hellfire. Other scholars take their knowledge as authority to rule over others, so that, should anyone reject some aspect of their knowledge or doubt the truth of what they know, they become angry. Such people are destined for the second level of Hellfire. Still other scholars deem their pronouncements and the arcane aspects of their knowledge appropriate only for the well-connected and affluent, regarding those who need their knowledge as unworthy of it. These are destined for the third level of Hellfire. Some scholars, again, appoint themselves as legal advisors and proceed to issue faulty legal opinions. And God loathes people who perpetrate fraud. They are destined for the fourth level of Hellfire. Yet other scholars discourse using the terminology of the Jews and Christians, so that their learning is replete with that. These are destined for the fifth level of Hellfire. Then there are the scholars who take their learning to be no more than a mark of manly virtue, magnanimity, and reputation among the people. Such people are destined for the sixth level of Hellfire. Vanity and narcissism motivate some learned persons, so that, when they admonish others, they make stringent demands, but when others admonish them, they respond with disdain. [261] These are destined for the seventh level of Hellfire. Consider silence mandatory, for with it you will overcome Satan. Take care not to be amused when there is nothing worth laughing at, and not to set off without a destination in mind."

We have received a Ḥadīth that makes reference to the characteristics of those who possess knowledge of the next life. It encompasses the principles of the spiritual stations of the faith and the means of religion and certitude for which humanity cries out. We have a tradition from Shaqīq ibn Ibrāhīm al-Balkhī[73] from ʿAbbād ibn Kathīr (d.c. 140/757), from Abū 'z-Zubayr (d. 126/743), from Jābir,[74] who attributed it to God's Messenger. I, however, judge the chain to end with Jābir ibn ʿAbd Allāh, who said, "Do not associate with every learned person, but only with those who call you to progress in five areas: from doubt to certitude, from vainglory to sincerity, from craving to asceticism, from haughtiness to self-effacement, and from hostility to amicable admonition."

It is evident that certain knowledge, as well as the science of *maʿrifa* and guidance, is the very knowledge that the ancestors in faith had in mind, in that the Companions and the Followers were on their guard against losing that knowledge. They feared being deprived of it and spoke about its elimination and scarcity at the end of time. What they were talking about was the knowledge of hearts and contemplation that is the result of fear of God, as well as about the science of experiential knowledge and certitude that arises from increased faith and is the fruit of guidance. Once the god-fearing are no more, and those who exercise self-scrutiny are scarce, and the ascetical people have disappeared, these disciplines will have vanished, for they depend on these people for their existence. Such people are the masters and communicators of these sciences, which in turn are the spiritual states that undergird them and their path along which they travel. It was because of their *maʿrifa* of the preciousness of that knowledge that the Companions and the Followers grieved over its loss.

God has described the truly learned as people who renounce and think little of this world, and who perform and believe in righteous deeds. Conversely, the people of this world are characterized as lusting after it and making much of it, as when the Most High said in this connection, "So Qārūn went out among his people in his adornment. Those who desire the life of this world said, 'O that we had the likes of what Qārūn has been given, for his indeed is a prodigious fortune!' But those who had been given knowledge said, 'Woe to you, for better is God's reward for those who believe and do righteous deeds.'" Then He said, "None but the long-suffering will attain that" (28:79–80). In other words, none will attain this wisdom except those who renounce the worldly adornment with which Qārūn went out.

We have received a tradition from Jundab ibn ʿAbd Allāh al-Bajalī, "As impressionable young people, we were in the presence of God's Messenger and we learned about the faith before the Qur'ān, and then we learned the Qur'ān, so that we grew in faith." And from Ibn Masʿūd, "The Qur'ān was revealed in order that people would act upon it, and you have engaged in the act of studying it. There will come a people who will make it as straight as spears, and they will not be among the best of you." According to another version, "They make it straight as an arrow so as to anticipate it rather than wait for it."

We have a tradition from Ibn ʿUmar and others, "There was a period during our lifetime when one of us received the faith before the Qur'ān. A particular sūra was revealed so that he learned what it held permitted and what forbidden, and which of its contents constituted an injunction and which a rejection. He learned what aspects of it had to be left undecided, the way you learn the Qur'ān nowadays. And I have seen individuals who received the Qur'ān before the faith, and who could recite its contents from the first sūra to its conclusion, without knowing what it enjoined and what it rejected, or concerning what aspects of it one needed to remain undecided, and who tossed it off as one discards spoiled dates." Another report comments on the meaning of this: "We were [262] Companions of God's Messenger who received the faith before the Qur'ān. After you there will come a people to whom the Qur'ān will be given before the faith. They will articulate its letters properly but they will fail to grasp its meanings. They will say, 'We have recited Qur'ān, and who recites more excellently than we? We are knowledgeable, and who is more learned than we?' That is the extent of their reception of the Qur'ān." And according to another version, "They are the vilest of this community."

As for the knowledge that has been handed down, which the successors of the ancestors in faith have transmitted, and the reports recorded in the books and put down on the folios, which the most ancient among our forbears heard—this is the knowledge of legal statutes and opinions, and the knowledge of Islam and legal rulings. Its method is hearing, its key is deductive inference, and its storehouse is the intellect. It is recorded in the books and written elegantly on paper. The small learn it from the great through oral tradition, and it will remain as long as Islam remains and exist so long as Muslims exist. For it is the proof of God for His servants and the pilgrim's goal for the whole of His creation. Its manifestation is guaranteed, but it can be manifested only through those who bear the burden of manifesting it and handing it down. So the Most High has said, "To make manifest the religion in its entirety, even though the idolaters abhor it" (9:33). In this connection the Messenger has said, "And a knowledge manifest by the tongue...," such is the proof of God before His creation. Muḥammad said to his Companions, "You hear and others hear from you, and others hear from those who have heard from you." Muḥammad has thereby informed us about the knowledge yet to come that has been manifestly set down in the books, knowledge that is the outward aspect of the religion, ignorance or lack of which gives rise to idolatry. Just so has God assured the survival of Islam in the face of the idolaters' denial.

Muḥammad said, "God be merciful to one who has heard a Ḥadīth from me and imparts it just as he has heard it. Many are the purveyors of *fiqh* who have no deep understanding of it. Many are they who convey religious understanding to those whose understanding is deeper than their own." Muḥammad has thereby informed us that the purveyor of religious knowledge can lack an understanding heart if he does not act upon his knowledge, and that such a person conveys knowledge to those who have deeper understanding than he has, if the one to whom he conveys it acts upon it [once he has appropriated it]. As Muḥammad said in another tradition, "Many are those who impart knowledge whose appropriation of it is more profound than that of those who heard it from me directly." He thus praises such a person for acting according to his knowledge once he has appropriated it, for this individual keeps it in mind and reflects upon it even if he has not heard it directly from the Prophet.

God has said, "...and that the ears that hear it might appropriate it profoundly" (69:12), referring to the ear of the heart that holds in memory what it has heard and that ponders what it has taken in. As the Most High has said, "In that, there is a reminder for one who has a heart or listens and is a witness" (50:37). He means one who is listening attentively to one who has heard, and witnesses with his heart that which the one from whom he hears this knowledge has actually witnessed. According to an exegetical commentary on the Most High's words, "...and that the ears that hear it might appropriate it profoundly" (69:12), this means an ear that has understood from God His injunction and His forbidding, and has interiorized it and acted upon it. So the Most High has characterized the believers, whose very selves He has purchased (9:111), saying at the conclusion of a description of them, "those who observe God's sanctions" (9:112).

We have received a tradition from ʿAlī, "Seek knowledge, so that you can gain *maʿrifa* by means of it. Act upon it and become its proponents." He also said, "When you hear of knowledge, keep it to yourself and do not get it mixed up with light banter lest hearts reject it." One of the ancestors in faith said, "Anyone who emits a laugh, spits out a bit of knowledge." Khalīl ibn Aḥmad said, "Knowledge is not merely what fits in a book satchel; knowledge is that which the center of one's being appropriates to itself." When a knowledgeable person combines in himself [263] three things, namely, long-suffering, humility, and pleasant disposition, the blessing upon the one who learns from him is complete. And when the one who learns combines in himself three things, namely, understanding, proper demeanor, and excellent comprehension, then the blessing upon the learned person is complete. [And God knows best.]

Discussion of the characteristics of traditional knowledge and the path of the ancestors in faith, and a censure of the new, more recently introduced popular narratives and public discourse

One who possesses knowledge of God must have five things that are the hallmarks of those endowed with knowledge of the next life: fear of God, awe in God's presence, meekness, noble character, and self-denial. God has said, "Those among God's servants who possess knowledge, experience dread in God's presence" (35:28); and "Those who humble themselves before God..." (3:199). Likewise meekness and positive disposition are essential, as God said (addressing Muḥammad), "And lower your wing gently toward the believers, and say: 'I am the clear warner'" (15:88–89). The Most High has said, "So it is inherent in the mercy of God that you be gentle to them" (3:159). And as for self-denial in this world, God has said, "Those who have been given knowledge said, 'Woe unto you! The reward of God is best (for those who believe and do good works)'" (28:80). The individual in whom these characteristics are evident is among those who possess knowledge of God.

Know that one can discern the possessor of knowledge in the context of addressing religious dilemmas. People need the individual who possesses experiential knowledge when doubts take hold of the center of their being, as ʿAbd Allāh ibn Masʿūd said, "When one of you experiences internal consternation, good will always come of it so long as that person finds someone who can offer solid information on the matter and heal the one suffering from it. But, by God, we are on the verge of a time when you will not find such a person." In this connection God's Messenger asked ʿAbd Allāh ibn Masʿūd, "Who is the most learned person?" He replied, "God and his Messenger know that best." So Muḥammad continued, "The one who, even when he is too young to walk, is the most knowledgeable concerning the truth when matters are ambiguous and dilemmas arise, or when people are at odds with each other, even if the knowledgeable person is limited in his ability to act."[75] We have received a tradition from ʿImrān ibn Ḥusayn, "Indeed God loves the penetrating gaze when doubts descend, and complete rational understanding amid the onslaught of passions. He loves generosity even with something so small as dates, and He loves valor even if one is merely killing a snake."

In this age of ours we have come to a situation such as Ibn Masʿūd feared: Imagine that a dilemma were to arise with respect to affirming God's transcendent unity, or a doubt preoccupied a believer to the center of his being concerning God's attributes, and you sought a disclosure of the truth of the matter in terms of what the rightly guided heart witnesses—a heart that God has made to prosper and the center of whose being God has expanded with guidance and cleansed with snow.[76] Suppose further that such a thing were rare in this time of yours, so that in seeking a disclosure about it you found yourself having to choose among five types of people.[77]

First is the wayward innovator who informs you of his view on the basis of whim, thereby adding to your confusion. Second is the speculative theologian who purveys legal opinions to you on the basis both of his meager knowledge of the proofs of those who possess certitude and of his rational understanding of the outward dimension of religion. This, however, is itself an ambiguous matter: How can one elucidate one ambiguous matter with another?

Third, there is the itinerant, errant Sufi who makes ecstatic utterances, who takes you beyond the Book and the Sunna, since he does not care about them, and who opposes the teachings of the imāms, though he pays them no heed. He answers you with supposition, diabolical insinuation, conjecture, pretense, and obfuscation. He obliterates being and place, turns knowledge and ethical standards topsy-turvy, and dispenses with names and forms. These people wander aimlessly in trackless desert wilderness, never settling down along the beaten path. They are submerged in the ocean of divine transcendent unity, but they stand neither as guides for those who possess certitude nor as proof [for the god-fearing.] This person's teaching is vapid, for he has no proof and does not travel by the established [264] road.

Fourth, there is the one who issues legal advisories, who considers himself learned, and whose cronies feature him a person of deeper understanding. He says, "This is among the requirements of the next life and an aspect of the knowledge of the unseen world, but we don't talk about it because it isn't our charge." He nevertheless multiplies his arguments and discourses about what is not his charge and holds disputations concerning things the ancestors in faith never discussed. He studies and acquires a knowledge that is little more than an affectation. As a result, the hapless one does not know that he is charged with dedicating himself to the knowledge of the faith, the ultimate reality of the divine transcendent unity, the *maʿrifa* of sincerity in pious deeds, and the knowledge of things that undermine sincerity. He sidesteps all of that even before engaging in it, unaware that what he is striving for truly is incumbent upon him. Knowledge of the faith, integrity of the affirmation of God's transcendent unity, sincerity of worship in relation to Lordliness, the disengagement of actions from worldly craving, and the associated works of hearts—all of that composes deep religious understanding and epitomizes the qualities of believers, since one is enjoined in these matters to take great care, as in the words of the Most High, "To acquire deep religious understanding and to admonish their people...[when they return to them so that perhaps they might take precautions]" (9:122). The Messenger said, "Learn certitude and I will learn along with you." And the Companions said, "We learned the faith, then we learned the Qur'ān, so that we grew in faith." This, then, is an abundance of guidance through certitude and an augmentation of the believers in the faith, as the Most High has said, "So He increased their faith" (3:173). God has also said, "And God increases the guidance of those who are guided" (19:76).

But that type of person does not realize that the proper demeanor in pious deeds, which results from experiential knowledge and certitude, is among the qualities of those who possess certitude. That is the interior state of the godservant in the spiritual station that characterizes his relationship to his Lord, his share from his Lord, and his portion of abundance in his life hereafter. It is intimately bound to the pure confession of God's transcendent unity, which is in turn inextricably linked to the faith over against insidious types of polytheism and varieties of hypocrisy. It is connected to mandatory duties, and the most fundamental requirement of all is sincerity in pious deeds. Any knowledge other than this, which he loves and is dear to his heart, from among the varieties of superfluous knowledge and strange sciences, deals only with human concerns and necessities and is a distraction from religious duty and a vain preoccupation.

But due to a lack of experiential awareness of the reality of beneficial knowledge, this heedless person prefers that which he has come to consider worthy of his quest for worthless knowledge whose goal he holds so dear. He accords priority to the needs and states of others over his own needs and spiritual state. He occupies himself with their claim on him in the immediacy of their mundane affairs and in legal opinions and does not work toward his own more plentiful portion promised him by his Lord in the life to come, which "is better and more lasting" (87:17), since it is there he is destined to return and there will have his everlasting dwelling. For he prefers proximity to others over nearness to his Lord and abandons all but a part of his own share with God in favor of involvement with them. He would rather free himself for them than free his own heart for tomorrow by occupying himself with the service of his Master and seeking His good pleasure. Instead, he is distracted from attaining virtue in his heart by the virtuous things they say about him, and from his own inward spiritual state by their outward circumstances.

The causes for what ails him are the love of the role of leader; the quest for status in the eyes of the people, together with the rank that goes with governance; and the thirst for worldly acquisitions and the adulation they bring. Add to that his meager spiritual desire and weak intention with respect to the lasting benefits and treasures of the next life. He fritters away his days in favor of their days, he squanders his life in response to their cravings, so that those who are utterly ignorant of learning will call him a learned man, and so that he will be, in the hearts and opinions of fools, an important person! So he arrives at the Resurrection bankrupt, for he appears bereft, by contrast with the portion of those who have drawn near to God. For those who act, win nearness to God; and those who know, experience the refreshment of contentment. [265] But how and whence could one win the portion allotted to another? For God has made a doer for every deed and a knower for every kind of knowledge: "Their allotted portion comes to them from the Book of Deeds" (7:37). Every thing does readily that for which it was created, and this is the final word on the subject.

In addition, there is no disagreement among members of the community of believers: Knowledge of the divine transcendent unity is a requirement, particularly when doubts arise and dilemmas become evident. People do, however, differ with respect to answers to two questions: What is the divine transcendent unity? and How does one seek it and arrive at it? Some say through investigation and search; others, through deductive inference and speculative analysis; still others, through hearing and passing along tradition. And some of them say, through divine accommodation and surrender. Some say that it is to be encountered through vulnerability and inability to arrive at their goals.

The fifth type of person among those who possess knowledge is one who has mastered Ḥadīth and traditions and who communicates by passing along sacred reports. When you inquire, such a person says to you, "Commit yourself to surrender, and teach the Ḥadīth as it has come to you without examining it." This is how the legal advisor with integrity transmits material, and he is the best of those who point to the path and is in temperament most like the forebears of the general public. He does not believe in claiming certitude or in the *maʿrifa* of profoundest truths in relation to what he communicates, nor does he pay close attention as he describes the meaning of what he passes along to others. In relation to knowledge, his role is that of a reporter, and in relation to Ḥadīth and traditional accounts, that of a conduit that conveys only the information he has received without seeking deeper understanding of what he has communicated. He is, therefore, "in the presence of a clear indication from his Lord" but that indication is not "followed by a witness from Him" (11:17).

Zuhrī[78] used to say, "So-and-so transmitted a Ḥadīth to us, and he was among the vessels of knowledge." He did not say, "He was a learned person." And Mālik ibn Anas used to say, "I encountered seven shaykhs among the Followers, among whom some were godservants, some individuals whose prayers of petition were heard by God, and others who prayed for rain on behalf of others; but I took away no knowledge at all from them." Someone asked, "Why so?" He replied, "Because they were not among those who knew about these matters." According to another version, "They did not understand what they were passing along and possessed no *fiqh* of the inquirer's question." Mālik said, "Ibn Shihāb az-Zuhrī came among us, while he was still young, and such a throng had gathered that we could not get near him, for he was knowledgeable about what he was transmitting." This is the meaning of what has been transmitted from God's Messenger, "Many are those who are responsible for deeper understanding but who do not have it, and many are those who convey *fiqh* to those who possess more of it than they do."

One of the ancestors in faith said, "Those who are not aware of the disparity of views among the scholars concerning knowledge are not committed to knowledge." Others said, "One who is not familiar with the disparity of views among the scholars is not permitted to issue legal advisories and is not called a possessor of knowledge." Qatāda[79] and Saʿīd ibn Jubayr[80] said, "The most learned person is one who is the most cognizant of diversity of views among people." Someone asked Imām Aḥmad (ibn Ḥanbal), "When a man has written down a hundred thousand Ḥadīths, is he authorized to issue legal advisories?" "No," he replied. Someone asked, "What about two hundred thousand?" "No," he answered. Someone asked, "How about three hundred thousand?" Said he, "I hope so."

It is written in the Torah, "The skilled physician succeeds at healing the inner ailment."[81] Salmān al-Fārisī[82] wrote from Madā'in to Abū 'd-Dardā',[83] after God's Messenger had linked them in brotherhood, "My brother, it has come to my attention that someone has appointed you as a physician to treat the infirm. Watch out! If you are a physician, speak, for your word brings healing. But if you are only a quack, for God's sake, don't murder a Muslim!" Abū 'd-Dardā' was inclined to [266] hesitate after that, whenever someone asked him about something. An individual asked him about something, so he gave a response and then said, "Disregard it." So the individual said to him, "Repeat it to me," so he repeated it, and the man said, "By God, a charlatan!" So Abū 'd-Dardā' took his response back.

Rest assured that the saying has come down from God's Messenger, "One who practices medicine without possessing a knowledge of medicine and kills someone is responsible for that." Ibn ʿAbbās used to say, "Ask Jābir ibn Zayd.[84] Were the people of Basra to acccept his legal pronouncements, he would exercise latitude even for them, and he was among the pious Followers." When someone asked Ibn ʿUmar about something, he would say, "Ask Saʿīd ibn al-Musayyib!"[85] And Anas ibn Mālik used to say, "Ask our Master Ḥasan (al-Baṣrī), for he remembers, whereas we have forgotten." One of the Basrans said, "One of the Companions of God's Messenger came among us, so we went to Ḥasan and said, 'Should we not go to this Companion and ask him about a Ḥadīth of God's Messenger and you accompany us?' 'Yes,' he replied, 'let's go.' So we began to inquire of the Companion about the Ḥadīth of God's Messenger, and he started to teach us Ḥadīth until he had communicated twenty Ḥadīths to us. Ḥasan listened and was attentive to him. Then Ḥasan got down on his knees and said, 'Companion of God's Messenger, provide us with a commentary on what you have handed on to us from God's Messenger so that we gain deeper understanding of it.' But the Companion was silent, and then said, 'I know only what I have heard.' So Ḥasan began to comment on what the Companion had recited. 'As for the first Ḥadīth he communicated to us,' he began, 'its explanation is such-and-such; and the commentary on the second is thus and so…' until he had dealt with each of the Ḥadīths as the Companion had communicated to us, and informed us of its interpretation. And we knew not whether to be more amazed at the accuracy of his memory and command of the Ḥadīth or at his erudite explication. At that the Companion grabbed a handful of pebbles and pelted us with them, then said, 'You seek knowledge from me with this learned person in your midst!?'"

Those Companions of the Prophet referred matters relating to legal opinions and outward knowledge to those of lesser estate and rank than themselves, but who, nevertheless, were superior to them in the knowledge of the divine transcendent unity and *maʿrifa* and faith. The latter did not have recourse to the Companions in ambiguous matters, nor did they defer to them in respect to the science of experiential knowledge and certitude. Hence the saying, "Knowledge is a light that God casts into the hearts of His friends." Thus are some persons accorded preferential treatment over others like them, as, for example, when youth are singled out over elders, and those among the Followers who came after the ancestors in faith. It is often the case that obscure and unassuming persons are ennobled in order to bring them to notice by aggrandizing and elevating them, as God has said, "We chose to grant favor to those downtrodden on the earth and make them leaders" (28:5).

When the light occurs in the center of one's being, the heart is expanded with knowledge and sees with certitude, so that the tongue speaks with authentic elucidation. This is the wisdom that God places in the hearts of His friends, just as the interpretation of the word of the Exalted and Majestic One has it, "We gave him (King David) wisdom and discerning, articulate speech" (38:20). Interpreters say that discernment means knowing exactly what to say, so that it is as though God gives the individual success in spiritual reality as God sees it, and the Most High has said, "He bestows wisdom on whom He will, and one to whom wisdom is given receives immense good" (2:269). Interpreters say that person receives profound comprehension and sagacity.

[267] God's Messenger was talking about divine guidance when he recited the word of God, "When God wishes to guide someone, He expands the center of that person's being toward surrender" (6:125). Someone asked, "O Messenger of God, what is this 'expansion'?" He replied, "When the light descends into the heart, it expands its center so that it becomes spacious." Someone asked, "And is there some indication of that?" Replied the Prophet, "Yes: withdrawal from the abode of delusion, repairing to the abode of timelessness, and being prepared for death before its arrival." Then he mentioned as conditions self-denial in this world and willingness to serve the Master.

Outstanding success and accuracy in knowledge are gifts from God and a mark of preferential treatment with which God singles out whom He will. Someone asked Abū Mūsā al-Ashʿarī,[86] when he was the Amīr of Kufa, concerning the whereabouts of a man who was killed in the cause of God while advancing rather than retreating. Abū Mūsā replied, "In Heaven." Ibn Masʿūd said to the inquirer, "Repeat your question to the Amīr; perhaps he did not fully understand your question." The inquirer said, "I said, 'O Amīr, what do you say about the whereabouts of a man fighting in the way of God who is killed while attacking rather than retreating?'" Abū Mūsā said, "In Heaven." Ibn Masʿūd said, "Repeat your question to the Amīr, for he may not have fully understood." So the man repeated it all a third time, and Abū Mūsā replied, "In Heaven." He then said, "I have no other opinion than that. What do you say?" Then Ibn Masʿūd said, "Well, I would not put it quite that way." "Then what would you say?" Abū Mūsā asked. "I would say that if he is killed in the cause of God and has correctly apprehended the truth, he is in Heaven." So Abū Mūsā replied, "He has spoken truly. Do not ask me about anything else as long as this learned man is among you."

Simple acceptance and handing down of the traditions about God's attributes, and reticence concerning their interpretation, as the specialists in Ḥadīth have recommended, presupposes *maʿrifa* and experience of the meanings of the divine names and attributes. It does so by ruling out the use of mere opinion and insinuation and by repudiating attempts to posit equivalences or analogies between God and creatures. This settling into the tranquility of certitude through *maʿrifa* and through witnessing to the divine reality is the spiritual station of those who possess certitude. The further conviction that they are the characteristics of God through which He is manifest—along with whatever other limitless and countless ways He wishes—and which make evident His attributes however He wishes, without being constrained by specific features or obliged to conform to a specific image—this is the spiritual station of those among the witnesses who have drawn near to God. They know that He is simply He and need not display His otherness but manifests Himself in whatever appearance under any guise, thus ruling out any question of manner or analogy because of the absence in God of any species or substance. These are the upright and the elect among those endowed with certitude. But anyone who turns away from these (upright ones) and does not acknowledge what they have testified has turned toward (mere) acceptance and assent (to a substitute for actual experience), and settles there as in a refuge and place of repose. Beyond these (possessors of certitude) there is no laudable spiritual station and no noteworthy quality. Anyone, therefore, who pursues a rational inquiry of those matters, interpreting them according to his own opinion, ends up either asserting God's likeness to created things or denying God's attributes altogether and evacuating them of significance.

(On the benefits of "sessions of recollection" and the negative aspects of sessions dedicated to mere storytelling for entertainment's sake)

An indication of the excellence of this knowledge over other forms of knowing has come to us in the traditions transmitted from the Prophet and from the Companions and Followers. They concern the excellence of gatherings for the purpose of being mindful of God and the excellence of those who keep God in mind. These Ḥadīths refer to the knowledge of faith, *maʿrifa*, the sciences of devotional deeds, deep understanding through spiritual insight into hearts, and examining with the eye of certainty the mysteries of the unseen. They are not referring to gatherings for the purpose of recounting tales, nor are they talking about professional raconteurs, for they regard storytelling for entertainment as a religious innovation. They say, "In the days of God's Messenger and Abū Bakr and ʿUmar, they did not recount entertaining stories, until the onset of the (first) [268] civil war (36/656). But when the civil war broke out, professional storytellers appeared." When ʿAlī entered Basra, he expelled the professional storytellers from the mosque and said, "There will be no storytelling in our mosques." When he came to Ḥasan, as he was discoursing on this kind of knowledge, he listened to Ḥasan. Then he departed without expelling him. Ibn ʿUmar came to his gathering in the mosque, and he found a storyteller recounting a tale, so he sent the chief of police to him to eject him from the mosque, and he threw him out. If the storytelling had been part of the sessions dedicated to mindfulness of God and the storytellers had been religious scholars, Ibn ʿUmar would not have ejected them from the mosque, in spite of his own spiritual reticence and asceticism.

We have a saying from Ibn Shawdhāb (d.c. 144/761) from Abū 't-Tayyāḥ (d.c. 128/745), who said, "I said to Ḥasan, 'Our Imām tells stories, so men and women gather and raise their voices in supplicatory prayer and extend their hands.' Ḥasan replied, 'Raising the voice in supplicatory prayer is an innovation, and extending the hands in supplication is an innovation.'" Abū 'l-Ashhāb (d. 165/782) has communicated that Ḥasan said, "Storytelling is an innovation." Someone said to Ibn Sīrīn,[87] "If only you would tell stories to your brothers!" So he replied, "It is said that only these three discourse publicly to people: a ruler, a deputy, or an imbecile. I am neither a ruler nor a deputy, and I would hate to become the third!" A saying has come down to us from ʿAwn ibn Mūsā that Muʿāwiya ibn Qurra (d. 113/731) said, "I asked Ḥasan al-Baṣrī, 'Would you rather I visited a sick person or attended a session of a storyteller?' He replied, 'Visit your sick person.' So I said, 'Would you rather I escorted a funeral procession or attended the session of a storyteller?' 'Escort your funeral procession,' he answered. I asked, 'And if a man in need asks me for help, should I help him or attend a session of a storyteller?' He replied, 'Go after your needy person,'" thus indicating what was better than frivolous gatherings. If they had considered gatherings for the purpose of recollecting God equivalent to storytellers' sessions, and stories were recollection, Ḥasan would not have steered him away from storytelling and indicated a preference for many other deeds. Ḥasan was wont to call out to God while acknowledging the divine transcendent unity and to discourse about the science of *maʿrifa*, of certitude, and of those who recollect God.

Participation in a session of recollection increases faith, and God elevates the spiritual station of those who recollect Him above those of believers, according to the Most High's word, "Men who surrender and women who surrender, [and men who believe and women who believe]" (33:35). God places recollecting men and recollecting women in the highest of spiritual states. We have received a Ḥadīth through Abū Dharr saying, "Participation in a session of recollection is more excellent than ritual prayer of a thousand prostrations, and participation in a session of knowledge is more excellent than visiting a thousand sick persons, and participation in a session of knowledge is more excellent than witnessing a thousand funerals." Someone asked, "Messenger of God, even more excellent than reciting Qur'ān?" He replied, "Is Qur'ān recitation beneficial apart from knowledge?" One of the ancestors in faith said, "Participation in a session of recollection makes up for ten banal gatherings." ʿAṭāʾ (ibn Abī Rabāḥ) (d.c. 114/732), for his part, said, "A session of recollection makes up for seventy sessions of idle amusement." We have a tradition from Muʿādh al-Aʿlam, saying "Yūnus ibn ʿUbayd (d. 139/756) saw me while I was in the circle of the Muʿtazila, and he said, 'Come!' So I went, and he said, 'If you have no alternative (to associating with the systematic theologians), then at least avoid the circle of the storytellers.'"

Ḥasan al-Baṣrī was one of those who recollected God and his gatherings were sessions of recollection in which he met privately in his house with his brothers and his followers among the ascetics and devotees—people like Mālik ibn Dīnār, Thābit al-Bunānī,[88] Ayyūb as-Sakhtiyānī (d. 131/748), Muḥammad ibn Wāsiʿ, Farqad as-Sabakhī, and ʿAbd al-Wāḥid ibn Zayd. He said, "Come let us give forth [269] light!" He was talking to them about this discipline of the knowledge of certitude and power concerning the inner movements of hearts, depraved deeds, and the insinuations of the ego-soul. Often one of the Ḥadīth specialists would veil his head so that he was disguised among them in order to hear that. So when Ḥasan spotted him, he would say to him, "You disgraceful person, what are you doing here? We have come together privately with our brothers in order to recollect with each other."

Ḥasan is our imām in this knowledge of which we are speaking. We pursue his footsteps, follow his path, and seek illumination from his niche.[89] It is by God's leave that we have traced this teaching from imām to imām all the way back to Ḥasan. He was among the best of the Followers in spirituality, so that people said, "He kept the wisdom within for a full forty years before he ever spoke about it." He had met seventy combatants from the Battle of Badr and seen three hundred Companions. He was born two years before the end of the caliphate of ʿUmar ibn al-Khaṭṭāb, in the year 20/642. He was born in Medina, and his mother was a handmaid to Umm Salama (Hind bint Abī Umayya, d.c. 61/681), a wife of the Prophet. It is said that she gave him her breast to divert him when he cried, and her breast flowed abundantly for him. His word was like the word of God's Messenger. He saw ʿUthmān ibn ʿAffān[90] and ʿAlī ibn Abī Ṭālib, and whichever of the Ten[91] survived to his day. In other words, he saw Companions of the

Messenger of God from the period of ʿUthmān and from about the year twenty to about the year ninety (of the Islamic calendar).

The last to die among the Companions of God's Messenger were Anas ibn Mālik in Basra; Sahl ibn Saʿd as-Saʿadī (d. 88/706) in Medina; Abū 'ṭ-Ṭufayl in Mecca; Abyaḍ ibn Ḥammāl al-Maʿribī in Yemen; ʿAbd Allāh ibn Abī Awfā (d.c. 86/705) in Kufa; Abū Qirṣāfa in Syria; and Burayda al-Aslamī (d. 63/682) in Khurasan. At the turn of the first Islamic century there remained on the face of the earth, in any region of the earth, not one who had actually seen God's Messenger. Then Ḥasan (al-Baṣrī) died in the year 110/728. Abū Qatāda al-ʿAdawī used to say, "Attach yourself to this shaykh, for by God, none of the Companions of God's Messenger I have seen is more like the Companions of God's Messenger than he." They used to say, "We likened him to the Prophet Abraham the Intimate Friend of God for his gentleness, his humility, his dignified bearing, and his tranquility, such were Ḥasan's fine qualities." A woman in Basra made a vow, that if God did thus and so with her, she would weave a garment of her own yarn, and she described it, and would clothe with it the finest person in Basra. So when her vow-request was fulfilled, and she had completed what she had promised, she inquired as to who was the finest person in Basra. People said, "Ḥasan."

Ḥasan was the first of those who set out on this path of knowledge. He clarified the discourse about it and spoke about its spiritual significance; he made its lights manifest and pulled back its veil. He expounded on it in words none of them had ever heard from any of his brothers, so someone asked him, "Abū Saʿīd (i.e., Ḥasan), you discourse on this knowledge with words we have never heard from anyone but you. From whom did you get this?" He replied, "From Ḥudhayfa ibn al-Yamān." It is said: "People said to Ḥudhayfa ibn al-Yamān, 'We see you discoursing on this knowledge with words we never hear from any of the Companions of the Messenger of God. So where did you get that?' He said, 'God's Messenger has made it my specialty. People used to ask him about the good, but I would ask him about evil out of fear that I might fall into it, and I knew that the good would not outdistance me.'"[92] Once he said, "I knew that one who has no experiential knowledge of evil has none of good either." [270] And in another version, "People used to say, 'Messenger of God, what will be the fate of one who does thus and so?' They would ask him about morally positive deeds, while I would ask, 'Messenger of God, what does this or that action corrupt?' And when he saw that I asked about actions that resulted in calamity, he made this knowledge my specialty."

Ḥudhayfa was a specialist in knowledge of the hypocrites,[93] unique among the Companions in the intimate understanding of matters of hypocrisy as well as in other aspects of knowledge and the subtleties of profound comprehension and the arcane aspects of the faith. ʿUmar and ʿUthmān and the most prominent Companions of the Messenger of God used to ask Ḥudhayfa about the general and specific temptations, having recourse to him concerning the knowledge that was his specialty. They would ask him about whether there still remained any hypocrites among them whom God had mentioned (in the Qur'ān) and thereby provided information about them. Then he would inform them about their numbers, but never mentioned their names. But ʿUmar asked for a disclosure about himself, as to whether Ḥudhayfa was aware of any tinge of hypocrisy in him, and Ḥudhayfa cleared him of any doubt. ʿUmar asked him about the hallmarks of hypocrisy and the scriptural verses dealing with the hypocrite, so Ḥudhayfa informed him about that to the extent that it was appropriate and permissible for him, begging off when it came to matters on which he was not allowed to impart information and excusing himself for that. When ʿUmar was called to attend a funeral to perform the ritual prayer for it, he looked around, and if Ḥudhayfa was in attendance, he would perform the ritual prayer; but if he did not see Ḥudhayfa, he did not perform the ritual prayer for the funeral. Ḥudhayfa was known as the Master of the Secret, and when one of the Companions of the Messenger of God asked about knowledge, he would say, "You are asking me about this while the Master of the Secret is among you?"—referring to Ḥudhayfa.

We have it from Anas ibn Mālik that when he transmitted the Ḥadīth from the Prophet concerning the excellence of the session of recollection—"I would rather keep the company of people who are mindful of God from morning till sunset than free four slaves"—he turned toward Yazīd ar-Raqashī[94] and Ziyād an-Numayrī and said, "There were not formerly sessions of recollection like these sessions of yours, in which one of you recounts a story and gives an address to his companions, and you exchange Ḥadīths with each other. When we sat together, we reflected on the faith, contemplated the Qur'ān, sought a deeper understanding of the religion, and counted God's graces to us." ʿAbd Allāh ibn Rawāḥa used to say to the Companions of God's Messenger, "Come, let us be believers for an hour," so they would sit with him and he would recall for them the knowledge of God and of the divine transcendent unity and of the world to come. And after God's Messenger stood up, he would take his place. The people would gather around him, and he would focus their attention on God and His days, giving them deeper understanding of what God's Messenger had said. Often God's Messenger came to them while they were together with ʿAbd Allāh, and they would fall silent. He sat with them and instructed them to take up again what they had been doing, saying, "In this I have instructed you, and to this I have called you." In this regard we have been told about Muʿādh ibn Jabal also, who used to discourse about this knowledge.

By way of explanation we have received the Ḥadīth of Jundab, "While we were with God's Messenger we came to know the faith before we came to know the Qur'ān." So he referred to the knowledge of the faith as faith, as Ibn Rawāḥa had done, for the knowledge of faith is a characteristic of the faith. The Arabs name a thing by its characteristic even as they name it according to its source, as God's Messenger has said by way of analogy, "Come to know certitude," and as God has said, "And his (Jacob's) eyes turned white from grief" (12:84), that is, from weeping, so He named it according to its source, since grief is the source of weeping. We have a tradition from God's Messenger "He went out one day and saw two gatherings. The people in one of them called out to God [271] and petitioned Him, while those in the other sought deeper understanding of the religion and were teaching the people. So he stopped between the two and said, 'These people are making requests of God; if He chooses, He grants them, and if He chooses otherwise, he denies them. But these others are teaching the people and seeking deeper understanding of the religion, and indeed I was sent as a teacher.' Then he went toward those who sought to give the people deeper understanding of the religion and recollected God, and sat with them."

One of the ancestors in faith recounts, "I entered the mosque one day and there were two circles of instruction. The people in one of them were telling stories and offering prayers of supplication, while those in the other discoursed on knowledge and deep understanding of action. So I went to the circle of supplicatory prayer and sat with them. My eyes glazed over and I fell asleep. Then a voice as in a dream called out to me, or someone said to me, 'You have sat down with these people and have neglected the session of knowledge. Had you sat down with the latter instead, you would have found Gabriel among them on God's behalf.'"

The essence of recollectedness is the knowledge of God. Have you not heard what has been communicated from the Prophet, "The most excellent recollection is saying 'There is no deity but God'"? And God has said by way of affirmation of that, "Know that there is no deity but God" (47:19). Similarly, He has said, "Know that (the Qur'ān) is revealed with knowledge of God, and that there is no deity but God" (11:14). Therefore, the knowledge deriving from recollectedness is the knowledge of contemplation, and contemplation is a characteristic of the essence of certitude. So when the veil over the eye is removed, you contemplate the inner meanings of the divine attributes by means of their lights, and it surpasses the light of certitude, which is in turn the perfection and ultimate reality of faith. In that context you become mindful of the One who possesses the attributes, by contemplating the One recollected by the light of His attributes. Are you not aware of the word of the Most High, "Those whose eyes were veiled from the remembrance of Me" (18:101)? Anyone whose eye is unveiled for recollection of Him witnesses the One recollected. And as he recollects, he discovers the ultimate reality of knowledge, after forgetting creatures, according to the word of the Most High, "And be mindful of your Lord once you have forgotten all else" (18:24). For authentic mindfulness means forgetting all that is not He, just as the ultimate reality of faith involves unbelief in every deity other than God, according to the word of the Most High, "The one who disbelieves in false gods, believes in God" (2:256).

One of the traditionists said, "One of my brothers among the proponents of *maʿrifa* came to me and said, 'I have discovered heedlessness in my heart, and I would like you to take me to one of the sessions of recollection.' I said, 'Yes.' There is someone called a *mudhakkir* who exhorts people to remembrance, who discourses on popular types of knowledge. So we came into his presence and the people were gathered, and he had begun recounting stories and mentioning Heaven and Hell. My companion looked at me and said, 'Do you not claim that this is the recollection of God and an exhortation to remembering Him?' I replied, 'Yes, that's what we think.' So he said, 'I hear nothing but recollection of creatures. Where is the recollection of God?' For a while he continued to anticipate something of the science of *ma'rifa* that he desired, and which he had heard from his Sufi shaykhs. But since only stories and narrative accounts were forthcoming, he turned to me and said, 'Let's go. It makes no sense to keep sitting here since I find no purpose in that kind of material.' So I replied, 'I would be embarrassed to walk through the crowd, but do as you see fit.' So he got up and walked through the crowd on his way out."

(Ibn Shihāb) Zuhrī (d. 124/742) transmitted a saying from Sālim (ibn ʿAbd Allāh ibn ʿUmar, d. 106/725), that (ʿAbd Allāh) Ibn ʿUmar left the mosque and said, "It was only the storyteller that caused me to leave, and but for him I would not have departed." And Ḍamra (ibn Rabīʿa) (d. 202/818) said, "I said to (Sufyān) ath-Thawrī, 'Shall we go meet the storyteller face to face?' [272]. He replied, 'Turn your back on innovation!'" Ibn ʿAwn said, "I went in to Ibn Sīrīn and he asked me, 'What's new today?' I replied, 'The Amīr has forbidden the storytellers to tell stories.'" Tradition has come down through Abū Maʿmar (d. 224/838) that Khalaf ibn Khalīfa said, "I saw Abū 'l-Ḥakam cleaning his teeth at the door of the mosque, while a storyteller was narrating a tale in the mosque. So a man came to him and said, 'Abū 'l-Ḥakam, people can see you!' So he replied, 'What I'm doing is preferable to what they're doing—I'm observing the Sunna while they're engaging in innovation.'" Aʿmash[95] did something still more striking than that when he entered Basra as a stranger. He spied a storyteller in the congregational mosque, who was saying, "Aʿmash transmitted to us from Abū Isḥāq...(d. 129/746)" and "Aʿmash transmitted to us from Abū Wā'il...(d.c. 82/701)." Aʿmash then situated himself in the middle of the circle, lifted his arm, and began to pluck hairs from his armpit. The storyteller noticed this and said, "Shaykh, aren't you embarrassed to be doing that while we are concerned with knowledge?" So Aʿmāsh said to him, "What I'm doing is more excellent than what you are doing." Came the retort, "How could that be?" And Aʿmāsh answered, "Because I'm acting according to the Sunna whereas you are caught in a lie. I am Aʿmash, and I have transmitted to you none of what you have said." And when the people heard what Aʿmash had to say, they dismissed the storyteller, gathered around Aʿmash, and besought him, "Transmit Ḥadīths to us, Abū Muḥammad."

According to a tradition transmitted to us from Muḥammad ibn Abī Hārūn, (Ibn Ḥanbal's assistant Abū Yaʿqūb) Isḥāq (an-Naysābūrī) told him, "I was praying the ʿĪd ritual prayer[96] with Imām Aḥmad ibn Ḥanbal when a storyteller began to recount tales such as deserve to be accursed as innovation and which the Sunna mentions disparagingly. After we had completed the ritual prayer and were on the road, Abū ʿAbd Allāh (Aḥmad ibn Ḥanbal) alluded to the storyteller as he said, 'How helpful they can be for the public, even though what they pass along is generally a lie!'" I have received a tradition from Muḥammad ibn Jaʿfar[97] that Abū 'l-Ḥārith said that he heard Imām Aḥmad ibn Ḥanbal say, "The most deceitful people are the storytellers and the panhandlers." I have also heard that Aḥmad said, "How desperately the people need credible storytellers! For they make mention of the Scale of Judgment and the punishment of the grave."[98] I (the transmitter of the saying) asked, "Would you have remained at their sessions?" "No," he replied.

We have a tradition from Ḥabīb ibn Abī Thābit (d.c. 119/737) that Ziyād an-Numayrī said, "Once I came to Anas ibn Mālik while he was in the oratory, and he said to me, 'Tell a story.' 'How can I,' I asked, 'since people claim that it is an innovation?' He responded, 'Nothing that concerns the recollection of God is an innovation.' So I told a story, praying hopefully that he would approve of most of my accounts. Then I began to tell stories, and he approved of them." So they used to make stories into supplicatory prayers.

Yūsuf ibn ʿAṭīya (d. 187/803) handed on the tradition that Muḥammad ibn ʿAbd ar-Raḥmān al-Kharrāz said, "Ḥasan (al-Baṣrī) missed ʿĀmir ibn ʿAbd Allāh al-ʿAnbarī (d.c. 41/661), so he said, 'Let's go to Abū ʿAbd Allāh.' When Ḥasan came to him, ʿĀmir was in a room with his head wrapped and nothing else in the room but sand. Ḥasan said to him, 'Abū 'Abd Allāh, we have not seen you for days.' He replied, 'I was attending these sessions, and what I heard was confusing and befuddling. And I was listening to our shaykhs concerning what they knew from our Prophet that he used to say, "On the Day of Resurrection the people of purest faith will be those who reflected most in this world. The people who will laugh most in Heaven will be those who wept the most in this world. And the people whose joy will be most intense in the next life will be those whose sadness was the most persistent in this world." So I found the room that was the most conducive to my heart's freedom and in which I could best pursue for my soul what I desired.' Ḥasan said, 'He was not referring to these sessions of ours but was referring to the sessions [273] of the itinerant storytellers who confuse and befuddle and get the order of things wrong.'"

One of the religious scholars divided those who discourse publicly into three groups, categorizing them according to the places they occupied. He said, "Those who discourse are three kinds: those who sit on chairs, and these are the professional storytellers; those who have pillars to lean against, and these are the *muftīs;* and those in secluded corners, and these are the proponents of *ma'rifa.*" The study circles of those who possess knowledge of God, the proponents of the divine transcendent unity and experiential knowledge, are the sessions of recollection of God, and it is in these that people deal with the traditions. Among the Ḥadīths we find this, "When you stroll through the meadows of Paradise, feed your flocks there. Someone asked, 'What are the meadows of Paradise?' Muḥammad responded, 'The sessions of recollection of God.'" According to a Ḥadīth, "God has angels who travel the firmament—in addition to keeping account of human deeds—who, when they see sessions of recollection, call out to one another, 'Come to the object of your desire!' So they come and sit with them and the members of the sessions receive them hospitably, and the angels hear from them, 'So be mindful of God and be mindful of your own souls!'"

Wahb ibn Munabbih al-Yamānī said, "A session concerned with knowledge is dearer to me than the equivalent amount of ritual prayer. For it may be that one of them in the session will hear a word and profit from it for a whole year or even for the rest of his life." Someone asked Aḥmad ibn Ḥanbal about sessions of recollection, so he spoke of their merits and of how they appealed to him, saying, "What could be lovelier than people coming together to be mindful of God and to enumerate His blessings to them, just as the Helpers[99] said?" We have a tradition from ʿAlī, "I would have had no delight had God caused me to die as a child and given me access to the highest levels of Paradise." "Why not?" someone asked. "Because He has extended my life so that I could gain experiential knowledge of Him." Mālik ibn Dīnār said, "People depart from this world without having tasted the best it has to offer." "What is that?" someone asked. "*Maʿrifa,*" he replied, then he recited this verse:

> Experiential knowledge of the Majestic One is exaltation
> and radiance and splendor and delight.
> And in addition, those endowed with experiential knowledge know a brilliance
> and over them flows a light from the divine love.
> So blessings to the one who has known You through experience, my God!
> By God, such a person knows joy unending!

Yaḥyā ibn Muʿādh ar-Rāzī said, "There is a garden in this world, and whoever enters it has no need of Paradise and knows no loneliness." Someone asked, "What is it?" He replied, "Experiential knowledge of God." Someone else has said, "None of the following three distinctive characteristics will you find wanting in the possessor of experiential knowledge: reverence, sweetness, and intimacy." Our teacher Abū Muḥammad Sahl (at-Tustarī) said, "The religious scholars, ascetics, and devotees left this world behind with their hearts locked, and none will be opened but the hearts of the truthful and the witnesses." He then recited the Qur'ānic text, "His are the keys of the unseen, and none knows what it holds but He" (6:59)—meaning that their hearts are locked without the keys of *maʿrifa* and witnessing of the essence of the divine transcendent unity.

These sessions of recollection, therefore, were from ancient times the province of the proponents of experiential knowledge, and of the deeds of hearts and of inward knowledge. These are the ones knowledgeable about the next life and the possessors of deep religious understanding. God has said, and He is the most veracious of speakers,

"For if a group from every segment did not go out, they would devote themselves to deeper understanding of the religion, in order to warn their people, when they return from an expedition, that perhaps they would become attentive" (9:122). The mindfulness of deeper understanding is among [274] the characteristics of the heart, as is the fear which is a consequence of deeper understanding. Intellectual knowledge belongs to external learning while the knowledge of God belongs to certitude, as the Ḥadīth has it, "Certitude is the whole of faith." God has said, "None but those possessing knowledge understand them (that is, the similitudes God coins for humankind)" (29:43). He thus made understanding a characteristic of knowledge. And God's Messenger enjoined the learning of certitude, just as he enjoined the quest for knowledge. This Ḥadīth became a specific example of that. His saying "learn certitude" applies to the elect, because certitude is a station above knowledge. His saying, "The Quest for knowledge is a duty," on the other hand, applies to the general public.

In his saying "learn certitude" he enjoins the study circles of those who possess certitude, because certitude does not become evident of itself but is discovered among those who possess certitude. Muḥammad, therefore, commanded them in that way and did not say, "Learn the rational sciences," or "Acquire the knowledge of legal advisories." In ancient times they called the exoteric religious scholars *muftīs,* and that is the reason for Muḥammad's saying "Seek a *fatwā* from your heart, even if the *muftīs* have delivered a *fatwā* to you." He thus directed him[100] toward the deeper understanding of the heart and away from the legal advisories of the *muftīs*. If the heart were not possessed of deeper understanding, and esoteric knowledge did not take precedence over exoteric knowledge, he would not have urged Wābiṣa away from the sciences of the exotericists, who are the scholars of the tongue, toward esoteric knowledge, which is the science of hearts. He would thus not have been permitted to direct him to one who lacked deeper understanding or to deflect Wābiṣa from one who possessed deeper understanding to another, lesser one. This Ḥadīth has actually come down in a version attested through reiteration and embellishment, saying, "Seek an opinion from your heart, even if they give you one legal advisory and then another." This is meant especially for the person who possesses a heart, who is attentive, and who observes directly the beginning of his being a witness,[101] and who is divested of his concupiscence and ingrained habits, for deeper understanding is not a characteristic of the tongue. Have you not heard the word of the Most High, "They have hearts with which they fail to attain deeper understanding" (7:179)?

One who has a heart hears through One who hears, sees firsthand through One who witnesses, and understands through his heart that which is addressed to it. And he responds to what he has heard, and turns to God in recollectedness. In the word of the Most High, "To dedicate themselves to attaining deeper understanding of the religion" (9:122), two features of deeper understanding are evident. One of them is the warning, which is a spiritual station in calling out to God. The one who issues a warning does so only in order to instill fear; the one who instills fear can only be one who experiences fear; and the one who experiences fear is the one who possesses knowledge. The second characteristic is circumspection, which is one of the spiritual states associated with *maʿrifa* of God and involves a sense of dread before Him. The words *fiqh* and *fahm* are virtually synonymous. The Arabs say *faqihtu* interchangeably with *fahimtu* (I have understood or comprehended deeply). God has given priority to profound comprehension over discursive knowledge and wisdom, and has elevated instances of profound comprehension above legal rulings and judgements: "We endowed Solomon with profound comprehension of them" (21:79, which continues: "and to everyone We gave judgement and discursive knowledge"). God therefore equipped Solomon uniquely with the profound comprehension of Him, making him superior to his father's (David's) ability to render judgment, after He had made the two partners in judgment and discursive knowledge. Ḥasan ibn ʿAlī gave preference to religious scholars who provide correct guidance toward God, who lead people to Him, in a saying handed down to us from him in which he calls them the ones who possess knowledge and certifies their knowledge. We have also received these verses from ʿAlī:

> Glory belongs only to the proponents of knowledge, for it is they
> who lead with guidance those who seek to be guided.

And every person's weight in the scale of Judgment is what
he has done well,
while the ignorant are enemies to the people of knowledge.

If an individual is learned in a science whose object of knowledge is God, who can be more excellent and what value can one recognize in him [275] when the value of every science is recognized and the weight of every learned person is his knowledge? ʿAbd al-Wāḥid ibn Zayd, the imām of the ascetics, has made a statement about this notion, in which he sets apart those who possess knowledge of God by extolling their path over every other. We have the following verses from him:

Diverse are the paths, and the paths of God are distinct,
and those who travel the path of God are incomparable.
None has intimate knowledge of them or understands their goals,
yet they journey along steadily and purposefully.
And the people (in general) remain heedless of what the journeyers desire,
the majority of them asleep and oblivious to the way of God.

We have received a tradition that Ibn Masʿūd said, at the death of ʿUmar, "I reckon that this man took away with him nine-tenths of knowledge." Someone asked him, "And you make this statement while the Companions of God's Messenger remain alive?" He replied, "I am referring not to the knowledge that you possess, but to the knowledge of God." Ibn Masʿūd used to say, "Those who fear God are the invisible ones." He also used to say, "Those who fear God are masters, those endowed with knowledge are leaders, and participating in their sessions is worthwhile." In other words, those who fear God are the masters of the people, as God has said, "Indeed, God considers the noblest among you those who are most god-fearing" (49:13). Those who possess knowledge are the leaders of those who fear God, that is, those who stand before them and whose footsteps they follow, for the Most

High has said, "And make us a model for those who fear God" (25:74). He thereby gave priority to the knowledgeable over those who fear God, making them models for the latter. Those who fear God are their companions. He further informs us about the augmentation that comes from participation in their sessions, meaning that such participation yields an increase over participation in the sessions of those who fear God without those who possess knowledge; for while every knowledgeable person is god-fearing, not every god-fearing person possesses knowledge. In this context we have received a tradition that "those who possess religious knowledge are many, but those among the religious scholars who are wise are few. Similarly, though righteous persons are numerous, those among them who speak the full truth are few."

Someone asked Ibn al-Mubārak, "Who are the people?" "The religious scholars," he answered, "And who are the kings?" asked another. "The ascetics," said he. Someone asked, "Then who are the riffraff?" He replied, "Those who feed on their religion." And he once said in an account, "The riffraff are those who dress up, beg, and seek the opportunity to be a witness in legal cases." Farqad as-Sabakhī answered a question put to him by Ḥasan (al-Baṣrī) by saying, "Abū Saʿīd, those who possess deeper understanding disagree with you." So Ḥasan replied, "Farqad, may your mother grieve over you (for saying such a thing)! Have you yourself ever seen people of genuine understanding? One who possesses genuine understanding is the one who practices asceticism with respect to this world and who pines for the next world; who has spiritual insight into his religion and who constantly attends to the worship of his Lord; who refrains out of spiritual reticence from the private affairs of Muslims and who does not covet their possessions; and who is well-disposed toward all of them." I have cited this saying of his as a single unit, though it was originally reported in three distinct segments. These, then, are the characteristics of those who possess knowledge of God, and they are the ones endowed with experiential knowledge.

I have received a tradition in which ʿAbd Allāh ibn Aḥmad ibn Ḥanbal said, "I said to my father, 'I have discovered that you used to visit Maʿrūf (al-Karkhī).[102] Did he transmit any Ḥadīths?' He replied, 'My son, he knew the most important matter—fear of God.'" Someone asked Imām Aḥmad (ibn Ḥanbal), "How does one speak of and describe these exemplars?" He replied, "What they possessed was none other than veracity." Someone asked, "And what is veracity?" Said he, "Sincerity." "And what is sincerity?" asked another. [276] "Self-denial," he responded. "And what is self-denial?" came the query. He bowed his head in silence, then said, "Ask the ascetics. Ask Bishr ibn al-Ḥārith."

Someone related to me a charming narrative from Bishr about Manṣūr ibn ʿAmmār.[103] Manṣūr ibn ʿAmmār was one of the preachers who exhorted. The religious scholars in his day, like Bishr and Aḥmad and Abū Thawr, did not consider him learned. They thought of him as one of the storytellers, though the general public called him a learned person. I have received a tradition from Naṣr ibn ʿAlī al-Jahḍamī (d. 250/864), saying, "He made a joke one day, but overdid it. Someone asked him, 'You say this, and you are one of those who possess knowledge?' He replied, 'I have never seen one who possessed knowledge who did not joke.' Someone said to him, 'But you have seen Bishr ibn al-Ḥārith. Have you heard him jest?' 'Yes,' he answered. 'I was sitting with him one day on a side street, when Manṣūr ibn ʿAmmār came running and said, "Abū Naṣr, the amīr has commanded an assembly of those who are knowledgeable and upright. Do you think I should hide myself?" Bishr shoved him aside and said, "Make way! You will cause a passing load of thorns to fall upon us and incinerate us all."'"[104]

This, therefore, was how the religiously knowledgeable viewed the situation of the storytellers in former times, but at length the proponents of this knowledge dwindled. People became ignorant of the sessions of recollection and the sciences of certitude and pious deeds. The rare exceptions were those familiar with the life stories of the predecessors and the way of their ancestors in the faith, who used to separate sessions of recollection from those dedicated to storytelling. They distinguished between the religiously knowledgeable and those who engage in public discourse, between knowledge of the tongue and the deeper understanding of the heart, and between the knowledge of certitude and discursive knowledge. For the difference between the religiously knowledgeable person and the storyteller is that the former remains silent until someone asks a question, and, when asked, responds on the basis of sound knowledge of what God has made available and disclosed to him, articulating what God has granted him to know intimately. When silence is preferable, this individual chooses not to speak since he knows what is better. If he sees no one worthy of a response, he bides his time until he can bestow it on someone deserving of such a response, and a person thus worthy is one who has experiential knowledge of it and who has a contemplative relationship to the experience.

God said, "So inquire of those worthy of the reminder, if you do not possess knowledge" (16:43). This text embraces two concepts: One is that those worthy of the reminder (that is, the Qur'ān) are those who possess knowledge of God, as indicated by the phrase, "if you do not possess knowledge." He could not have said, "Inquire of those who have no knowledge," since they are ignorant and would only increase the ignorance of the inquirers. The second concept suggests that the religiously knowledgeable remain silent until someone inquires of them; then, when asked, they must respond to the inquiry in keeping with the Most High's saying to those who do not know, "Inquire!" It indicates that the sessions of recollection are the sessions of the religiously knowledgeable, reports of whose merits have come down to us. It indicates further, as one reflects on the matter, that the proponents of recollection are the very individuals to whom people address their questions and to whom the Qur'ānic text pertains, "[And We have made the Word come to them,] so that perhaps they might become mindful (28:51)." And when the Word just mentioned came to them, they became mindful of what the Most High had pledged, so that when they became mindful, they attained knowledge. It is in that context that God enjoins them to inquire.

Similarly, we have a tradition from God's Messenger, "It is inappropriate for the ignorant person to be satisfied with his ignorance, and it is inappropriate for the religiously knowledgeable to keep quiet about his knowledge." Hence, God said, "So inquire of those worthy of the reminder, if you do not possess knowledge" (16:43). In the same vein God's Messenger said in the Ḥadīth that has come down to us by way of the Prophet's family, "Knowledge is a treasury whose keys are questions, so ask questions, for four kinds of people benefit from that: the questioner, the one who possess knowledge, the one who listens in, and the one who loves them." [277] Ibn Masʿūd used to say, "One who renders a legal opinion every time people request one from him is a fool." And Aʿmash said, "There are some discourses whose answer is silence." Dhū 'n-Nūn al-Miṣrī said, "The beautiful question of the righteous is the key to the hearts of those endowed with experiential knowledge." The storyteller, on the other hand, is one who sets out to narrate accounts and recall tales and prophetic traditions, and is therefore known as a raconteur; that is, he traces a story from the ancestors.[105] The word of the Most High is relevant here, "She (Pharaoh's wife) said to (Moses') sister, '*quṣṣīhi*'" (28:11, from the same root as "storytelling"), that is, "Follow Moses' traces to discover his story and bring me news of him." Mālik ibn Anas said, "One of the ways in which knowledge is debased is articulating it before being asked about it." He once said, "Knowledge is debased when an individual responds to every question asked of him," referring to an abūse and denigration of knowledge. In ordinary usage people say, "Raise *(ashil)* this" or "Lower *(adhil)* this," meaning, respectively, "grant an elevated status" and "demean." In other words, "If someone discourses on knowledge before being asked about it, its light diminishes by two-thirds."

Ibrāhīm ibn Adham and others have said, "The silence of the religiously knowledgeable person is harder on Satan than his discourse, for he keeps silent out of discretion and expresses himself with knowledge. So Satan says, 'Observe this: His silence is more difficult for me than his discourse.'" ["Nothing is more difficult for Satan than a religiously learned person who speaks knowledgeably and holds his tongue out of discretion."] In this context the saying goes, "Silence is the adornment of the religiously knowledgeable person and the veil of the ignorant one." Qāsim ibn Muḥammad[106] said, "A man treats himself most nobly when he is silent about his opinion until someone asks him for it." And I am sure that is accurate. For when one discourses in response to an inquiry, he does so out of necessity, and indeed often out of duty; and neither necessity nor response to a duty arises from the passions. With regard to the Most High's word, "So inquire of the practitioners of recollectedness" (16:43; 21:7), God has made response a requirement to the extent that He has enjoined inquiry. Muḥammad said, "A person who is asked about knowledge and then keeps it hidden will have a bridle of fire placed in his mouth," thereby promising such a person chastisement.

(On the reticence of the truly knowledgeable to discourse on what they know)

Launching into discourse can result from hidden disordered cravings, and such cravings are of this world. Someone described a man to Mālik ibn Anas, and he replied, "There is nothing objectionable about him if he did not discourse on a matter before being asked about it." Another version says, "He would not have been objectionable except that he discoursed in one day on a subject that should have taken a month." In response to someone's question about the meaning of the statement "discourse arises from the passions," he said "It is that with which one begins before being asked about it." Someone described the *Abdāl,* commenting on their characteristics, "They eat out of necessity only, and they speak only under duress." They do not speak until someone has inquired about something, then they answer. One who does not discourse until being asked will not be considered vainly loquacious or one who discourses on what does not concern him. For a response after a question is like the duty of returning a greeting when the greeting "Peace be with you" is offered. And as Ibn ʿAbbās said, "I consider the rendering of an answer as compulsory as the return of a greeting." Abū Mūsā (al-Ashʿarī) and Ibn Masʿūd said, "One who is asked about something he knows should talk about it; and one who is not asked should keep silent, or else he is associated with those who feign knowledge and thus deviates from the religion." We have a tradition from Ibn ʿAbbās also, that he used to fear they would take on affectation in all things. Abū Mūsā said, "Launching into discourse without some evident necessity, or before being asked about something, and without seeing a proper context for it or finding someone who merits a response—all these conditions put an individual at risk of affectation."

In his advice to Mujāhid, Ibn ʿAbbās said, "Do not discourse about what does not concern you, for that is the most excellent course and there is nothing that will make you more secure from error. And do not discourse on what does concern you until you perceive an appropriate context, for many are the people who discourse on what is their business but do so in inappropriate contexts and get themselves into trouble." [278] We have a Ḥadīth about one of the Anṣār whose mother said to him as he was dying, "May you be happy in Heaven! You engaged in the struggle with God's Messenger and were killed in the cause of God." In response to her God's Messenger said, "How can you know for sure that he is in Heaven? Perhaps he spoke about what did not concern him or was stingy with something that was of no value to him."[107]

Anyone who manifests some aspect of knowledge without being asked about it, and makes it available to those who are not worthy of it and are ill-disposed toward it, will be interrogated about that at the final reckoning of Judgment. He will be called to account because his manifesting the knowledge was a pretense. If, on the other hand, a person is asked about a subject of knowledge and then discourses on it, he will not be held accountable with respect to those who reject it, since the knowledge became available in response to a question. In this context, the ancestors in faith who discoursed on this aspect of knowledge remained silent until asked.

Abū Muḥammad (Sahl at-Tustarī) used to say, "The religiously knowledgeable person sits and keeps quiet, elevates his heart to his Master, senses his utter neediness of His beautiful gift of divine accord, and asks that He inspire in him appropriate conduct. He discourses, therefore, on whatever anyone asks him about, insofar as his Master reveals it to him." Abū Muḥammad thus situates the possessor of knowledge in the spiritual state of his silence and of his looking toward his Lord as one in need of trust and one who waits for the object of his trust in everything He brings to pass. One of them said, "The knowledgeable person is one who, when posed a question, acts as if one of his molars is being extracted." Raqaba ibn Maṣqala (d. 129/746–47) and others have said, "One who assembles the people to tell them stories is not a knowledgeable person; for one who possesses knowledge is one who, upon being asked about knowledge, acts as if he had gotten a noseful of mustard powder." According to tradition, Aʿmash said that after Muḥammad ibn Sūqa had asked him about the Ḥadīth and Aʿmash had turned away from him without responding to him. Then Aʿmash turned to face Raqaba and said to him, "He is as much a fool as you if he surrenders his advantage to someone of my wicked disposition." So Muḥammad ibn Sūqa said to Raqaba, "Woe to you! I considered my inquiry the equivalent of a medicinal remedy: I put up with its bitterness because I had hope that it would be beneficial."

We have a tradition from ʿAlī via ʿAbd Allāh (Ibn Masʿūd), that ʿAlī came across a man who was discoursing to the people, so he said, "This man is saying, 'Get to know me.'" One of the learned ones of Khurasan passed along a tradition to us from a shaykh of his that Abū Ḥafṣ an-Naysābūrī al-Kabīr, whose stature there was equal to that of Junayd here, said, "The learned person is one who, on being asked a question about religion, becomes so distressed that if he were injured, no blood would flow because of his intense fear that he might be asked in the next life about the question posed to him in this world. He would be terrified that he would not escape the question unless he saw that he had a duty to answer, because of the dearth of truly learned people." For that reason Ibn ʿUmar declined to answer nine questions and responded to one, saying, "You want to make us a bridge you will cross over into Hell, because you will say, 'Ibn ʿUmar gave us a legal opinion on this.'"

When someone asked Ibrāhīm at-Taymī[108] about a problem, he would weep and say, "Can't you find someone else to ask, or do you really need me?" Replied (the questioner), "We importuned Ibrāhīm an-Nakhaʿī[109] to let us lean him against a column, but he declined; and when asked a question about something, he would weep and say, 'The people need me.'" Sufyān ibn ʿUyayna[110] had been in his day unequaled in various forms of knowledge because he was unique in his time. He therefore fashioned a metaphor for himself, saying in a poetic verse,

> The abodes are derelict. I am a master who has not been made a master.[111]
> It is my misfortune that I have been singled out for mastery.

Abū 'l-ʿĀliya ar-Riyāḥī (d.c. 93/711) used to discourse to two or three, but if a fourth person arrived, he would get up. Similarly, Ibrāhīm (an-Nakhaʿī), (Sufyān) ath-Thawrī, and Ibrāhīm ibn Adham used to discourse to a few people, and when the number [279] of people multiplied, they would leave. Abū Muḥammad Sahl (at-Tustarī) used to sit with from five or six to ten persons. A shaykh told me, "Junayd used to discourse before some ten persons, and the sessions' participants never reached a full twenty." I have received a tradition about our shaykh, Abū 'l-Ḥasan ibn Sālim (d.c. 356/967), that the people gathered in his mosque and sent one of their number to him to say, "Your brothers are present, and they would like to meet with you and listen to you. So if you see fit to go out to them, fine." Now the mosque was near the door to his house, but no one went in to him in his residence. So he would say to the person sent (to fetch him) after he had gone out to him, "Who are they?" The messenger would reply, "So-and-so, and so-and-so, giving their names." Then Abū 'l-Ḥasan would say, "Those people are not my companions, they are session groupies," and he would not go out, for he regarded them as generally unfit to deal specifically with the fine points of his knowledge. He therefore did not waste his time on them, and in just that way is the learned person's time of solitude most precious to him. However, when he gets together with a special group of his brothers, he prefers them to his solitude, and they are beneficiaries of that. But, if the situation does not call for it, he will not cede priority to anything else over his solitude and his spiritual moment, lest he provide a haven to those who prattle on mindlessly. Abū 'l-Ḥasan used to go out to his brothers, whom he considered worthy of the place of his knowledge, and sit with them. He would converse with them and often bring them in to him day or night. And I assure you, the discussion occurred among equals and it was a conversation among brothers. Sitting together for the sake of knowledge is what companions do, and response to a question forms the nexus of the gathering.

Proponents of knowledge regarded their knowledge as appropriate only for the elect, and the elect are few. They considered it essential and incumbent upon them not to talk about it except in the presence of those worthy of it. ʿAlī described them that way (in the Ḥadīth of Kumayl) when he said, "so that they might entrust it to their likes and implant it in the hearts of people of their kind." In that context we have traditions on the subject from our Prophet. And from Jesus, "Do not bestow wisdom on anyone unworthy of it, for you do an injustice to the knowledge; and do not withhold it from those who are worthy of it, lest you do them an injustice. Be like the gentle physician who applies medication only where there is illness." In another version, "Whoever bestows wisdom upon those unworthy of it is ignorant, while whoever withholds it from those worthy of it does an injustice. For there is an etiquette to wisdom and there are those worthy of it [and a rightness associated with those worthy of it], so deal with each as is individually appropriate." In a Ḥadīth of Jesus, "Do not hang pearls around the necks of swine."[112] To be sure, wisdom is finer than pearls, and whoever despises it is baser than a pig.

A member of this group used to say, "Half of this knowledge is keeping silent, and half of it is knowing where to impart it." An individual endowed with experiential knowledge said, "One who discourses to the people about how he acquired his knowledge and the breadth of his understanding, and addresses them without taking their limitations into account, disregards their prerogatives and does not attend to the rights of God with respect to the people." Yaḥyā ibn Muʿādh used to say, "Dip water for each person from his own stream and give each a drink with his own cup." I suggest that this means accounting for each godservant's capacity for understanding and measuring out to each in proportion to the person's learning, so that you give each a sense of well-being and each one benefits from you; otherwise, the net result is withholding knowledge because of disparate capacities in individuals. Some of our shaykhs from this group have passed along to me a tradition about Abū ʿImrān, also known as (Abū Jaʿfar) al-Muzayyin al-Kabīr al-Makkī, "I heard him talking to Abū Bakr al-Kattānī,[113] at a time when the latter was liberally imparting this knowledge, lavishing it upon all the poor. Abū ʿImrān began [280] to reprove him and forbid him to dispense knowledge so prodigally and to discourse so copiously about it. At length, Abū ʿImrān said, 'For twenty years I have asked God to make me forget this knowledge.' Abū Bakr al-Kattānī asked, 'Why?' The other responded, 'I saw the Prophet in a dream and heard him say, "Everything is sacred from God's perspective, and one of the most sacred of all things is wisdom. Whenever someone imparts it to one not worthy of it, God demands of him what is due as a result of the action; and whenever He demands that of someone, God wins the argument."'" One of the ancestors in faith used to say, "If a man leans against a pillar or loves to have people ask him questions, do not sit with him, and there is no need to inquire of him."

In the early days one did not see thirty or even twenty men in the sessions of the proponents of this knowledge, except on rare occasions and not as a rule or consistently. There were usually between four and ten, and occasionally ten. From the time of Ḥasan (al-Baṣrī) until ours, people used to assemble in the sessions of the storytellers, admonishers, and preachers. And this is also one of the differences between the two phenomena, namely, that knowledge is restricted to a few, whereas popular narratives appeal to a wide public. One of our learned ones said, "In Basra there were 120 people who discoursed on ethical admonition and preaching, but only six who discoursed on the science of experiential knowledge and certitude, and on the spiritual stations and states. Among them were Abū Muḥammad Sahl (at-Tustarī), aṣ-Ṣubayḥī, and ʿAbd ar-Raḥīm. As a saying went, "Anyone who did not profit from the silence of a religiously knowledgeable person would not profit from his discourse either." In other words, one needs to be tutored by such a person's silence, humility, and spiritual reticence, and emulate his certitude in those things, just as one is tutored by such a person's verbal communication and follows what he says. Indeed, people used to say that exoteric learning belongs to the knowledge of earthly sovereignty, whereas esoteric learning belongs to the knowledge of Lordly Dominion. What they meant was that the former pertained to knowledge of this world insofar as it was a requisite for managing mundane affairs, whereas the latter pertained to knowledge of the next world insofar as it transcended the former. This is the way people ordinarily put it, for the tongue is externally oriented, associated with earthly sovereignty, and is the storehouse of the knowledge of outward realities; while the heart is the storehouse of Lordly Dominion and the door to the knowledge of inward realities. Knowledge of inward realities is as far superior to knowledge of outward realities as Lordly Dominion is superior to earthly sovereignty, for it is a hidden and interior form of rule; and as the heart is superior to the tongue, which is evident and manifest.

(On the differences between transmittal of tradition and knowledge of external matters, and genuine knowledge)

Bishr ibn al-Ḥārith used to say, "The expressions 'We have received a tradition' and 'We have received the report' are among the gateways to this world." And he once said, "The Ḥadīth are not provisions for the next life." One of my shaykhs passed along to me a tradition from one of his shaykhs, saying, "We had some ten books bound for Bishr—about what a satchel or date basket would hold—from which he had transmitted no traditions apart from what one rarely heard from him of the odd saying." He used to say, "I have a craving to transmit Ḥadīth, and if that craving departs from me, I will transmit Ḥadīth." Then he said, "I have been struggling against my ego-soul for forty years." And he said, "When you hear a man saying, 'We have received a tradition' and 'We have received the report,' he is saying, in effect, 'Make room for me.'" [He was a possessor of knowledge who practiced self-denial.]

He and others said, "If you have a craving to transmit Ḥadīth, do not do so; but if you have no desire to transmit Ḥadīth, transmit Ḥadīth." Rābiʿa al-ʿAdawīya[114] had said previously of (Sufyān) ath-Thawrī, "What a fine man Sufyān would have been had he not been so attached to the Ḥadīth!" She also said, "The seduction of the Ḥadīth is more intense than the seduction of acquiring possessions and begetting children." And she once said, "If only he had not been attached to this world,"[115] referring to the gathering of people [281] around him to hear him transmit the Ḥadīth. Abū Sulaymān ad-Dārānī used to say, "Anyone who marries or transcribes Ḥadīth or seeks a livelihood relies on this world."

One of this group said, "Anyone who attains the sciences apart from the knowledge of God is only playing at understanding, but anyone who attains the knowledge of God has truly been brought to full comprehension." He proceeded to recite the word of the Most High, "If grace from his Lord had not reached him, he would have been cast away upon a barren (strand)" (68:49). In other words, had he not been brought to the science of *maʿrifa*, he would have been exiled in the distant land of concupiscence. The "barren strand" is distance from God, while purely intellectual knowledge is distance from the knowledge of certitude. He also commented on the profound comprehension of the word of the Most High, "Had We not established you firmly, you would have become virtually dependent on them" (17:74), by saying, "In other words, '(Had We not) established you firmly upon *maʿrifa*, you would have in effect relied on discursive knowledge.'" Sahl ibn ʿAbd Allāh (at-Tustarī) glossed the word of the Most High, "And provide me from Your presence an authority and a helper" (17:80), by saying, "Provide me a tongue with which to speak about You and to speak about none but You."

Knowledge of God, along with knowledge of the faith and knowledge of certitude, are as far superior to knowledge of statutes and legal judgments as contemplation is to hearsay. God's Messenger said, "Hearing a mere report is not like seeing." In another version, "One who merely hears a report is not like one who sees with his own eyes." ʿIyāḍ ibn Ghanm (d. 20/640) transmitted a saying from the Prophet by way of interpretation of the sūra that begins, "The competitive drive to acquire more distracts you" (102), "'The knowledge of certitude' (102:5) is equivalent to seeing with the eye." And the Ḥadīth, "The best of my community are the people who laugh because of the expansiveness of their Lord's mercy and who weep in secret for fear of His punishment. Their feet are on the ground and their hearts in the heavens, their spirits in this world and their minds in the next. They go forward in tranquility and draw near to God in measured pace," is referring to this. Now legal advisories are in the category of transmitted reports, and engaging in issuing legal advisories is equivalent to seeking to transmit traditional reports. On this point the word of the Most High, "So seek an opinion from them" (37:11), is apposite; so also, "They seek an opinion from you" (4:176)—in other words, people ask you for a report. Now the knowledge imparted through reports is subject to mere supposition and doubt, while contemplation elevates mere supposition and removes doubt, as the Most High said, "The heart did not lie as to what it saw" (53:11). He thus establishes that the heart has eyes; so the vision of the heart is certitude, and one who possesses heart is endowed with certitude.

The Prophet said, "In certitude there is sufficient wealth." In certain knowledge lies wealth equal to all other forms of knowledge, for it is the inward reality and purity of knowledge. On the other hand, possession of all other forms of knowledge does not allow one to dispense with the knowledge of certitude, because there is poverty in doubt. Moreover, the need of certitude in the knowledge of the divine transcendent unity and the knowledge of the faith is more intense than the poverty one experiences in the need for the disciplines of legal advisement and other forms of technical knowledge. As a result, the riches of certitude outstrip the self-sufficiency of the other branches of the sciences, so that in its relationship to the others this knowledge is like the opening sūra of the scripture in relation to the rest of the Qur'ān. As the saying we have received from the Prophet has it, "The opening sūra of the scripture is worth the whole of the Qur'ān, but the whole of the Qur'ān is not equal in value to the opening sūra of the Book." Such is the relationship of the knowledge of God to the knowledge of everything else. In the knowledge of God is compensation for all the sciences, but there is no substitute for the knowledge of God in the other sciences insofar as God substitutes for what is other than Him. Every form of knowledge is oriented to its own object. Certain knowledge's [282] proper object is God, so its priority is analogous to God's priority over all beside Him.

A wise person said by way of interpreting what I have just said, "If a person has experiential knowledge of God, then of what is he ignorant? And if a person is ignorant of God, then of what does he have experiential knowledge?" As for those who are knowledgeable about God, they are the heirs of the prophets, for they inherit from them guidance toward God as well as an invitation to Him and the imitation of them in the deeds of the heart. God has said, "Whose speech is more beautiful than one who invites to God and whose deeds are upright?" (41:33), and again, "Invite people to the path of your Lord with wisdom" (16:125). God therefore enjoined the Prophet to invite people to God and associated his followers with him as proxies in spiritual insight. So the Most High has said, "Say: This is my way. I call you to God in keeping with spiritual insight, I and those who follow me" (12:108). And they will gather with the prophets on resurrection day, as the Most High has said, "They are with those to whom God has been gracious, including the prophets" (4:69); and again, "And the prophets and witnesses will be brought forward" (39:69). Then He elaborated on this, "In that they were entrusted with the safekeeping of the Book of God, and they were witnesses to it" (5:44). We have reflections on this in a Ḥadīth transmitted by Muʿādh ibn Jabal, in which God's Messenger said, "The people closest in rank to prophethood are the proponents of knowledge and the proponents of spiritual striving. As for the proponents of knowledge, they guide the people to what the prophets have brought, while the proponents of *jihād* strive with their swords for what the messengers have brought."

Those who possess knowledge of this world throw in their lot with overseers and wielders of authority. One of the ancestors in faith said, "The genuinely learned ones assemble with the contingent of the prophets, but the magistrates gather with the cohort of sultans." Ismāʿīl ibn Isḥāq al-Qāḍī[116] was a learned man among the children of this world, a ranking member among the intelligent magistrates, and brother of Abū 'l-Ḥasan ibn Abī 'l-Ward, who was one of those endowed with experiential knowledge. When Ismāʿīl assumed the judgeship, Ibn Abī 'l-Ward parted company with him. Then one day, when he was required to go before Ismāʿīl to testify, Ibn Abī 'l-Ward struck the shoulder of Judge Ismāʿīl with his hand and said, "Ismāʿīl, ignorance is better than the knowledge upon which you have presided over this session!" So Ismāʿīl pulled his cloak over his face and began to weep until he had dampened the cloak. Those who possess exoteric knowledge are the ornaments of the earth and earthly sovereignty, while those who possess inward knowledge are the adornment of the heavens and Lordly Dominion. Those who are learned in external matters are the people of reports and of the tongue, but those who are learned in interior realities are the masters of hearts and of eyewitnessing.

One of the learned ones said, "When God created the tongue, He said, 'This is the stronghold of my traditional reports; if it represents me accurately, I save it.' And when God created the heart, He said, 'This is where I direct my gaze; if it is pure for Me, I will purify it.'" One of the people of old said, "The ignorant person is redeemed through knowledge, the one who possesses discursive knowledge through proof, and the one endowed with experiential knowledge through rank." One of those endowed with experiential knowledge said, "Knowledge of outward realities is judgment, but knowledge of inward realities is what passes judgment; the judgment awaits the arrival of the one who passes judgment to bring it into being."

When those knowledgeable about external matters of religion could not resolve a question of knowledge because of conflicting opinions as to which direction to take, they would ask the proponents of the knowledge of God, for they considered them closer to divine assistance and farther from concupiscence and rebelliousness. Shāfiʿī [283] was one such scholar. When he had an issue that remained problematical because of the disparity of views of the religious scholars about it, despite the homogeneity of the deductive-inferential method applied to it, he had recourse to the scholars who possessed experiential knowledge and inquired of them. He used to sit with Shaybān ar-Rāʿī (d. 158/774) like a youngster before a teacher and would ask him, "How does one act in such a situation, and what does one do in such a situation?" So someone asked him, "How is it, Abū ʿAbd Allāh, that someone like you, with your level of knowledge and deep comprehension, inquires of this Bedouin?" So he replied, "Because this man has put into practice what I know intellectually." Shafiʿi was wont to say when he was seriously ill, "O God, if it please you, give me more of it." So (Yaḥyā ibn Idrīs) Maʿāfirī wrote to him from the south of Egypt, "Abū ʿAbd Allāh, neither of us are among the people of (that is, who ought to ask for) tribulation. Let us, therefore, request of God's good pleasure what is more appropriate to us, namely, that we ask for divinely granted success and good health." Shāfiʿī wrote back, saying, "I seek forgiveness of God and turn toward Him in repentance." After that, he was wont to say, "O God, bring about my good under circumstances that I love."

Aḥmad ibn Ḥanbal and Yaḥyā ibn Maʿīn (d. 233/848) used to visit Maʿrūf ibn Fayrūz al-Karkhī, and even though he did not possess a high level of knowledge or familiarity with the Sunna, they used to ask him questions. A tradition has come down that someone asked, "Messenger of God, how should we act if we receive a command that we find neither in the Book of God nor in the Sunna of God's Messenger?" He replied, "Ask the upright and consult with them, and, apart from them, do not comply with any command." According to a saying of Muʿādh (ibn Jabal), someone asked him, "What if a matter arises for you that is in neither the Book of God nor the Sunna of God's Messenger?" He replied, "I behave according to the disposition of the upright." Someone then exclaimed, "Praise be to God who has given success to the messenger of His Messenger!" Another version reads, "I exercise my personal opinion."

We have received a tradition in which Junayd said, "I was walking along with Sarī as-Saqaṭī, and he said to me, 'When you part company with me, with whom will you sit?' So I replied, 'Ḥārith al-Muḥāsibī.' He said, 'Yes, accept his knowledge and tutelage, but leave his faulty theological responses for the theologians.'" Then Junayd said, "As I was departing, I heard him say, 'May God make you a master of Ḥadīth who is a Sufi, and not a Sufi who is a master of Ḥadīth!'" In other words, when you undertake the knowledge of the Ḥadīth and traditions and intimate knowledge of legal principles and the compilation of Ḥadīth, and thereafter practice devout asceticism, you will have arrived at the science of the Sufis and will be a Sufi who possesses experiential knowledge. But if you begin with devotion and fear of God and the spiritual state, you will divert yourself from religious knowledge and the Ḥadīth collections, so that you will wind up as one who makes ecstatic utterances or errs religiously because of your ignorance of the principles of law and the practices of the Prophet. As a result, it would be better to have recourse to exoteric knowledge and the compilation of traditions, for that is the root from which devotion and knowledge branch off; otherwise, you would have put the branch before the root. On the other hand, it has been said, "They who are heedless of the fundamentals will be prevented from arriving at the goal." The fundamentals are the compilation of Ḥadīth and knowledge of traditions and Sunnas. So if you were lulled to sleep, you would be returned to the fundamentals, for you would have lost the rank of those endowed with experiential knowledge, forfeiting the increase of faith and certitude.

Sufyān ath-Thawrī said, "When people used to seek knowledge, they acted; and when they acted, they did so with dedication; and when they were dedicated, they fled (the public eye)." Someone else said, "When the learned person flees from the people, they come looking for him; and when he goes in search of the people, [284] they run away from him." Abū Muḥammad Sahl (at-Tustarī) said, "Knowledge calls out to action if a person responds to it affirmatively; if not, the knowledge takes flight." Dhū 'n-Nūn[117] said, "Sit with those whose qualities speak to you, not with those whose tongues talk at you." Previously, Ḥasan (al-Baṣrī) had said, "Sit with those whose actions speak to you, not with those whose utterances address you." A numerous contingent used to keep company with the proponents of *maʿrifa* in order to benefit from their tutelage and observe their guidance and ethical traits, even though the latter were not acknowledged as religious scholars.

That was so because spiritual tutelage comes with deeds while overt teaching comes from what is said. [One of the most sagacious sayings I have heard on this concept is what] one of the wise has said, "One person's preaching to a thousand people by means of one action is more beneficial and efficacious than the preaching of a thousand people to one person by means of a mere word." *Sahl used to say, "Knowledge is altogether this-worldly, while action pertains to the next world; and without sincerity, action is nothing but dust in the air." He said once, "Except for the learned, the people are dead. Apart from those who act, the learned are drunk. Apart from the sincere, those who act are deluded. The sincere person lives in trepidation until his life is sealed in sincerity."

(Crucial differences between firsthand and derivative knowledge)

The truly learned do not consider learned one who is knowledgeable about someone else's knowledge or who has has merely committed to memory someone else's interpretation. They call such a person a reporter, a memorizer, a conduit, or one who hands on traditions. Abū Ḥāzim the ascetic used to say, "The truly learned have vanished, while bits of knowledge have survived in unreliable receptacles of memory." Zuhrī used to say, "So-and-so was a receptacle of knowledge," and "So-and-so passed traditions along to us, and he was a receptacle of knowledge," but he did not say, "He possessed knowledge." In that context the tradition is pertinent, "Many are the conduits of deeper understanding who do not possess deeper understanding themselves. And many are those who are the bearers of deeper understanding to those who already have more of it than they do." They used to speak of "Ḥammād the reporter,"[118] and they meant that he gave an account of tradition. The letter "h" in the word (*ar-rāwiy[ah]*, "the reporter") serves to underscore the description of his function, as in the terms *ʿallām(ah)* (the *outstanding* teacher) or *nassāb(ah)* (the *noted* genealogist). But this usage means that they regarded such an individual as abundantly learned in his own area of knowledge rather than that of someone else. That is how they regarded someone who possessed deeper understanding as a result of penetrating deeply into his own area of knowledge and heart, rather than as a result of securing a tradition from someone else. Hence the tradition, "Someone asked, 'Who are the richest people?' Muḥammad replied, 'The learned person is wealthy because of his knowledge. If someone has need of him, he offers a benefit; otherwise he is content with his knowledge apart from the people.'" That is so because every person who is learned in someone else's knowledge becomes, as it were, one who knows only by virtue of his connection with the other person, and his "connections" are the religious scholars. Every person whose excellence depends on another person's attributes derives his qualities from those who are outstanding. When such a person leaves their company and is alone, he has nothing to say, for he cannot have recourse to a knowledge of his own that sets him apart. He must, then, in reality be described as an ignorant camp-follower of the truly distinguished, and as one identified only by a knowledge of what is heard and handed down.

One who is learned in the knowledge of another is like a person who describes the spiritual states of the righteous, and who is aware of the spiritual stations of the righteous without actually experiencing any such spiritual state or station. His description of such people only returns to him as a proof against him with respect to knowledge and discourse. As for proofs of their deeds and spiritual station, on the other hand, the truly learned are way ahead. By analogy with them God has said, "Woe to you for what you describe concerning God" (21:18), and, for example, in His word, "Whenever the light illumines them, they walk in it, but when darkness descends upon them, they stand still" (2:20). Such a person does not proceed along his path with spiritual insight because of the darkness that envelops him as a result of the disparity of views of the religious scholars, nor does he have a genuine experience of it on the basis of his own spiritual state. For he cloaks his own state over with inauthentic experience, since he is only experiencing it vicariously. Someone else, therefore, is actually having the experience, and he is giving witness to what someone else has actually witnessed—the other person is the real witness.

Ḥasan (al-Baṣrī) used to say, [285] "God could not care less about one who engages in reporting tradition, but he does pay attention to the person of profound comprehension and understanding." He also said, "When a person has no understanding that imposes demands on him, a plethora of reports of Ḥadīth will be of no use to him." One of the wise (ʿAlī) has recited these verses on the meaning of that:

Knowledge is of two kinds: knowledge generated and knowledge gathered
Gathered knowledge is useless if it does not include knowledge generated
Just as the sun is useless when the eye is incapable of receiving illumination.

And Junayd used to recite:

The *ʿilm* of Sufism is a science of which no one has experiential knowledge
except one who is sagacious and intimately familiar with the truth.
One who has not witnessed it firsthand does not know it experientially.
How can one who is blind witness the brilliance of the sun?

The books and collections are more recent developments. The same is true of the practice of quoting people's sayings and individual authorities' legal advisories, seeking support in all things from such an individual's utterances and stories, and seeking deeper understanding according to his school of legal methodology. During the first and second centuries people were not familiar with all that. These systematized books appeared only after the year 120/737, and after the death of all the Companions and the most prominent Followers. It is said that the first systematic Islamic work was the book of (ʿAbd al-Mālik) Ibn Jurayj (d.c. 150/767) concerning the traditions, and the exegetical texts of Mujāhid and ʿAṭā' (ibn Abī Rabāḥ)[119] and the companions of Ibn ʿAbbās in Mecca. Then there was the book of Maʿmar ibn Rashīd as-Sanʿānī (d.c. 152/769) in Yemen, in which he gathered widely dispersed sunnas according to thematic chapters. Then came Mālik ibn

Anas's *Book of the Level Path (Kitāb al-muwaṭṭā')* in Medina, concerning religious law, followed by the *Anthology (Jāmiʿ)* of Sufyān ath-Thawrī (d. 161/777–78) concerning religious law and Ḥadīth. Then there was Ibn ʿUyayna's anthologized *Book of Gathered Versions (Kitāb al-jawāmiʿ)* concerning sunnas and thematic chapters, along with the *Book of Scriptural Commentary (Kitāb at-tafsīr)* about the terminology and science of the Qur'ān. These are among the first systematically composed books, after the death of Saʿīd ibn al-Mūsāyyib and the outstanding Followers, subsequent to the year 120 of the history of Islam.

The learned people who were the models of these religious scholars belonged to the four categories of Companions,[120] and after the death of the first generation, they were among the foremost Followers. They died out prior to the composition of books, and they were averse to writing down of Ḥadīth and people's authoring books, out of concern that they might distract them from the Qur'ān and from recollection and reflection. They said, "Keep it in memory as we have memorized it, so as not to be distracted from God by any written traces or marks." Just so did Abū Bakr the Trustworthy One and the most prominent Companions hold back from gathering the leaves of the Qur'ān into a volume, saying, "How can we do something God's Messenger did not do?" They were afraid the people would become preoccupied with the written text and rely on books. So they said, "Should we make an exception of the Qur'ān so that the people learn it from one another, acquiring it through instruction and recitation, and so that it will be their focus and concern and the object of their recollection?" Eventually, ʿUmar and the rest of the Companions advised Abū Bakr to gather the Qur'ān into [286] written volumes, because he had the firmest grasp of it. The people would thus be able to resort to the bound volume, for no one is safe from preoccupation with worldly concerns. God therefore expanded the center of Abū Bakr's being to accept that, so he gathered the Qur'ān from loose leaves into a single volume.

In that way they acquired the knowledge from one another and saw to its safekeeping. This process led to cleansing their hearts of uncertainty, emptying them of worldly concerns, strengthening their faith, purifying their certitude, elevating their zeal, amending their intention, and bolstering their determination. Then, after the year 200/815—indeed after the passing of three centuries—there appeared during the unfortunate fourth century the written works of systematic theology and the books of those who discoursed speculatively on the basis of personal opinion, rationalist methodology, and the use of analogical inference. As a result, the knowledge of the god-fearing waned, and the *maʿrifa* of those who possessed certitude vanished from the science of godliness, with its inspiration to right guidance and certitude. And in their place came others after them, in continuous succession to this age. Now in our time, matters have gone on to become thoroughly obfuscated, so that people refer to the speculative theologians as religiously knowledgeable and consider the storytellers endowed with experiential knowledge; they call reporters and transmitters of tradition learned even though they possess neither deep religious understanding nor spiritual insight in certitude.

We have received a tradition from Ibn Abī ʿAbla (d. 152/769), saying, "We used to sit with ʿAṭāʾ al-Khurāsānī (d. 135/752) after the dawn ritual prayer, and he would speak to us. But when he was detained one morning, one of the muezzins—a decent enough fellow—spoke to us about the kind of thing on which ʿAṭāʾ had discoursed. Then Rajāʾ ibn Ḥaywa (d. 112/730), who found the man's voice annoying,[121] asked, 'Who is this speaker?' The man answered, 'I am so-and-so.' Replied the first man, 'Be quiet! We are loathe to hear religious knowledge from any but those worthy of it.'" As a result people used to say, "Proponents of the knowledge of God decline to hear of this knowledge except from those worthy of it, who reject this world." They refused to hear of it from the sons of this world, asserting that such knowledge was unbefitting to them.

Know that when God discloses experiential knowledge and the knowledge of certitude to the devotee, that individual is no longer at liberty to accept the views of any religious scholar uncritically. Similarly, when the Muslims of old found themselves in this situation, their views differed from those of the people from whom they had received the religious knowledge, because of their more abundant certitude and penetrating insights. Ibn ʿAbbās said, "There is no one other than God's Messenger whose teaching one receives without some time later rejecting it." Now he had learned religious law from Zayd ibn

Thābit,[122] and recited Qur'ān with Ubayy ibn Kaʿb (d.c. 19/640), but then disagreed with Zayd concerning legal matters and with Ubayy concerning Qur'ānic readings.

One of the jurists among the ancestors in faith said, "What has come to us from God's Messenger we have received most gladly. What has come to us from the Companions, we have taken and then set aside. As for what has come to us from the Followers, they were human beings and we are human beings; they had their views and we have ours." As a result, the jurists used to abhor uncritical acceptance of authority *(taqlīd)*, saying, "No one should issue a legal advisory without being familiar with the disparity of views of the religious scholars." In other words, he should choose from among those views the one that, as far as he knows, is the most religiously prudent and promises the strongest certitude. Then, should people prefer that the religious scholar issue a legal advisory according to someone else's school of legal methodology, the scholar would not need to be familiar with the variant views, and it would be sufficient for him to be familiar with the legal teaching of the other teacher.

Hence it is said that if a servant is interrogated on the morning of Judgment Day, he will be asked, "What did you practice of what you knew?"—he will not be asked, "What did you do in accord with what someone else knew?" [287] When God said, "Those who received knowledge and faith" (30:56), He distinguished between the two and indicated that one who receives faith receives knowledge, just as one who receives beneficial knowledge receives faith. This is one of the facets of the meaning of His word "He has inscribed faith upon their hearts and affirmed them with a spirit from Him" (58:22). That is, He strengthened them with the knowledge of faith, and the knowledge of faith is His spirit. The "Him" in the phrase "a spirit from Him" has as its antecedent "the faith." The learned person, therefore, is among the proponents of deeper interpretation and of deriving meanings from the Book and the Sunna, for he has the power of making distinctions and spiritual insight and is given to contemplation and profound reflection. The ignorant, coarse, heedless person, on the other hand, should accept the authority of the religious scholars unquestioningly. In fact, the scholar whose knowledge is general has to accept the authority of the scholar whose knowledge is specialized, just as the scholar who possesses knowledge of outward matters must accept the authority of his betters—namely, those whose task is knowledge of things inward and who are the people of heart. For the Prophet directed people away from the knowledge of tongues and legal advisories and toward the science of hearts, but he did not steer the people of heart, with respect to the kind of knowledge in which they specialized, toward those who issue legal opinions. That is because when the people of heart take the legal opinions from those who dispense them, then they discover contrivance and sarcasm in their hearts. So they must obtain the advice of the heart, according to the Prophet's saying, "Ask your heart for advice," after he had said, "Even if the specialists have given you an opinion."

He said in addition, "Sin is the rancor of hearts," and again, "Let go of what ties the center of your being in knots, even though it offers you opinion after opinion." Then this intimate knowledge, too, was obliterated, so that people became ignorant of it, to the point that every person who articulates a word whose presentation eludes listeners, and whose truths are indistinguishable from his falsehoods, is known as learned. Every word deemed pleasant, embellished, and adorned, however baseless it may be, is known as knowledge, because the general public hasn't a clue about what knowledge is, and because of the dearth of *maʿrifa* among listeners as to the way the truly learned ancestors in faith were. Numerous systematic theologians these days have become a temptation for the gullible. Many a word, personal opinion, and rational conclusion whose essential reality is ignorance, the ignorant consider knowledge. They make no distinction between the speculative theologians and the religious scholars, nor do they know the difference between knowledge and speculative theology.

I have said that those who are particularly ignorant make themselves out to be learned people so that they appropriate the state of a learned person in their study circles. But the most knowledgeable person nowadays is the one with the most intimate familiarity with the manner of life of the ancients and the most knowledgeable among them concerning the ways of the ancestors in faith. The most knowledgeable person, therefore, is one who is best informed about what knowledge is and who the truly learned person is, as opposed to the student or the one who merely acts the part. Becoming intimately familiar with this is virtually a duty for those who seek knowledge, for since the Prophet said, "The quest for knowledge is a duty," it has been incumbent upon them to become aware of what knowledge is so that they can seek it; it is impossible to search for that which one cannot recognize. Consequently, it is incumbent upon them to be intimately aware of who the truly knowledgeable person is in order to seek knowledge with such an individual, since knowledge is an accident[123] and can be located only in a body and is found only among its proponents.

As someone said to ʿAlī, "You contradicted so-and-so on such-and-such a point." He replied, "The best of us is the one among us who follows this religion most assiduously." And when someone said to Saʿd, "Saʿīd ibn al-Mūsāyyib recites, 'When We abrogate a verse or set it further back,'"[124] he replied, "The Qur'ān was revealed neither to Ibn al-Mūsāyyib nor to his father." Thereafter, he recited, "or cause it to be forgotten."[125] The most learned person these days, therefore, and the one nearest to divine assistance and right guidance, is the one who follows most closely the ancestors in faith and who is in character most like the righteous forbears. No wonder we have received a tradition from God's Messenger that, when someone asked him who was the most knowledgeable person, he responded, "The one most intimately aware of the truth when uncertainty abounds." [288] One of the ancestors in faith said, "The most knowledgeable person is the one most familiar with the differences among people."

Ḥasan al-Baṣrī used to say, "Two innovations that have appeared in Islam are a man with faulty views who claims that Heaven is for those whose view is like his; and a person who lives an opulent life, who worships this world, is rapacious because of it, is satisfied with it, and considers it his goal. May they both be consigned to Hell! Be aware of how loathsome their actions render them to their Lord. When a man is born into this world between the high-roller who invites others to this world and the person inclined to innovation, God preserves him from them both. And if this individual has recourse to the upright ancestors in faith, inquires about their deeds, and gives an accurate account of their patrimony, then an immense reward is in store for him. May it be so for you all.

(Beginning of a discussion of the value of the knowledge of the ancients and the dangers of innovation)

We have received a tradition from Ibn Masʿūd, with a complete chain of transmitters, "There are two realities only: speech and guidance. The best speech is the word of God, and the best guidance is Muḥammad's guidance to God. Be on guard against innovation, for the most insidious of all things are human inventions. Every novelty is an innovation, and every innovation is a cause of error. Indeed, the time will not be long before your hearts are hardened. Truly, all that is yet to come is nigh. Indeed, what is not to come is far off." And in a sermon transmitted to us through Abān (d. 138/755) from Anas, the Prophet said, "Happy are they whose preoccupation with their own faults distracts them from the faults of the people, who are generous with the possessions they have acquired honestly, who associate with people of deep understanding and wisdom, and who keep their distance from the vile and fractious. And happy are they who humble themselves, who are of good character, whose inmost thoughts are upright, and who hold their evil tendencies aloof from the people. Happy are they who act according to what they know, who give generously from the overabundance of their wealth, who restrain themselves from talking too much, for whom the Sunna offers ample scope, and who do not preempt it for the sake of innovation."

One literary figure described our times in exquisite language as though he had witnessed it personally:

Gone with their deeds are the men worthy of emulation,
as are they who disapproved of every detestable matter,
While I am left among their successors who vouch for one another,
so that the blind urge on the blind.
Little son of mine, among human beings there lurks a beast,
in the guise of a man who hears and sees
And who is on the lookout for threats to his possessions,

but, when calamity befalls his religion, it does not faze
him.
Inquire of one with deep understanding and you will attain
perspicacity like his,
for one who makes progress in deeper understanding will
be victorious.

Ibn Masʿūd used to say, "At the end of time, good guidance will be preferable to a plethora of pious deeds." Characterizing his time as one of certitude and ours as one of doubt, he said, "You live in a time when the best of you is the one who gets things done with dispatch. But there will come a time after you when the best of them will be the one who proceeds with caution and remains undecided"—referring to the prevalence of ambiguities. Ḥudhayfa (ibn al-Yamān) said something even more astonishing than that: "What you consider acceptable today was detestable in a former time, and what you consider detestable will pass for acceptable in time to come. But you will not cease to experience goodness so long as you know the truth experientially and the truly knowledgeable person in your midst is not despised."[126] He also said, "At the end of time there will come a people among whom the knowledgeable person will have the status of a dead jackass, for they will pay him no heed. The believer among them will be despised as we despise [289] the hypocrite among us today, and the believer among them will be the most contemptible of the community."

ʿAlī said in a Ḥadīth, "A time will come upon the people in which nine-tenths of them will despise the truth. In that day none of them will be saved apart from every believer who is asleep—that is, who is silent and apathetic. They are the lamps of knowledge and the paragons of guidance, not those who go scattering seeds abroad." He is referring to those who discourse at length and put on a show with their boastful speech. And a Ḥadīth says, "A time will come upon the people when one who recognizes the truth will be saved. Someone asked, 'So what is one to do?' Came the reply, 'In that day there will be no action, and none will be saved except the person who flees with his religion from one high mountain to another.'" A Ḥadīth of Abū Hurayra says, "A time will come upon the people when the person among them who acts upon a tenth of what he is commanded will be saved." Another version reads "who acts upon a tenth of what he knows." [One of the Companions (Ḥudhayfa) said, "You are now in a time when one of you who disregards a tenth of what he knows perishes; but a time will come upon you when the person who acts upon a tenth of what he knows will be saved."] One of the successors of the Prophet said, "The most excellent knowledge at the end of time will be keeping silent and the most excellent action will be sleeping." In other words, because of the large number of hypocrites spouting off ambiguities, silence will become the knowledge of the ignorant person, and because of the numerous people engaging in questionable actions, sleep will become the devotion of the heedless. I assure you, silence and sleep are the lowest of the states of the knowledgeable person, and the loftiest of the states of the ignorant person.

Yūnus ibn ʿUbayd used to say, "Today the person intimately familiar with the Sunna has become an oddity, but still stranger than he is the person who is intimately familiar with him"—referring to the way of the ancestors in faith. He is saying that the individual who is intimately familiar with a person who has an experiential knowledge of the path of someone who has passed on is also a stranger because he is familiar with a stranger. Ḥudhayfa al-Marʿashī (d. 207/822) said, "Someone wrote to Yūsuf ibn Asbāṭ, saying, 'Obedience has vanished, along with the person intimately familiar with it.'" He also used to say, "Nobody with whom one can associate is left." And he said, "What is your view about a time in which pursuing knowledge is a form of disobedience?" Someone asked, "And how could that be?" "Because," he answered, "one could not find a proponent of knowledge." Abū 'd-Dardā' used to say, "You will continue in a good situation so long as you love the best among you, and the truth is spoken among you and recognized as such. Woe to you, should the learned person in your midst become like a sheep that has been butted by another animal with horns."[127]

People of old had sciences upon which they concurred and about which they conferred with each other, but in our age (the traces of that knowledge) have disappeared. The upright had their notions about which they inquired and ways on which they traveled, but they, too, have vanished in our time. The disciplines of certitude and experiential knowledge once had stations and states which their proponents would discuss with each other and whose masters people sought out. But their traces have, from our perspective, been obliterated due to the scarcity of seekers, the lack of people desirous of them, the loss of those who are truly learned about them, and the disappearance of those who travel their paths. These things include the science of the quest for what is permitted; the knowledge of spiritual reticence with respect to means of livelihood and social relations; the knowledge of sincerity; the knowledge of the ego-soul's negative tendencies and of the corruption of deeds; the science of hypocritical knowledge and action, [and of the distinction between hypocrisy in knowledge and in action,] and of the distinction between hypocrisy of the heart and that of the ego, and between the ego-soul's manifestation and concealment of its passions, and of the distinction between the heart's resting in God and the ego's resting in material things, and the distinction between the interior impulses of the spirit and the ego and the impulse of faith, certitude, and reason; and the science of the characteristics of the spiritual states, and of the states of the paths of the devout, and of the diversity of contemplative experiences of the mystics, and of the varied colorations of things contemplated by seekers; and the science of contraction and expansion, and of the verification of the attributes of worshipfulness, and of conforming one's character to the attributes of Lordliness, and of the differences between the spiritual stations of the knowledgeable and other [290] things I have not mentioned. For example, the knowledge of the divine transcendent unity, and intimate familiarity with the meanings of the divine attributes, and the sciences of divine disclosure through the theophany of the divine essence, and of the manifestation of actions that indicate the meanings of the hidden divine attributes, and of the disclosure of the meanings that point to the divine glance and aversion, drawing near to and distancing from God, decrease and increase, reward and punishment, election and trial. I have mentioned all of these concepts individually and delineated them as a complex of ideas and principles to call attention to their ramifications and to allude to their (possible) ambiguities, for the benefit of those who have been rendered suitable to reflect on them, who have been given the desire to consider them and who have been given a share of these sciences.

One of our learned ones said, "I am aware that the ancients had seventy forms of knowledge. They used to discuss them and learn together the kind of knowledge with which no one these days is intimately familiar. And I know of countless forms of knowledge in our time that are just so much gibberish, pretentiousness, and banality. They present and label themselves as sciences but were not recognized as such in the past. They are thus like the mirage God described when He said, 'The person desperately thirsty makes it out for water, until, when he comes to it, he discovers that it is nothing'" (24:39). Before him, Junayd had said, "This knowledge of ours, on which we used to discourse, is like a carpet that has been rolled up for twenty years, so that now we talk only about its fringes." He also said, "Over the years I used to sit with a group of people who had intense discussions about forms of knowledge of which I had no serious comprehension—I did not even know what they were. Still, I was not inclined to reject them outright, so I accepted them and came to love them without possessing any experiential knowledge of them." He also said, "I used to engage in mutual competition with my brothers with respect to many forms of knowledge not well known in our time, and no one ever asked me about them. This is a door now bolted shut and blocked."

And when our shaykh Abū Saʿīd ibn al-Aʿrābī (d. 341/952) composed *The Book of the Generations of the Ascetics (Kitāb ṭabaqāt annussāk),* he described the first people to discourse on this science and make it public, as well as those Basrans, Syrians, Khurāsānīs, and finally Baghdadis who came after him. Then he said, "The last to discourse on this was our master Junayd al-Qawārīrī (the Glass Merchant, d.c. 297/910), who had spiritual insight into it and its essential significance, as well as the ability to articulate it beautifully. After him there remained only those whose company was exasperating." In another place he said, "After Junayd there remained only people whom one is embarrassed to mention."

Our imām Abū Muḥammad Sahl used to say, "After the year 300 one is no longer allowed to discourse on this science of ours, because there has appeared a crowd who put on airs for the benefit of the public and use their discourse as a costume so that their alleged experiences of ecstasy are their garment, their finery is their speech, and their object of worship is their bellies." When someone asked Ḥudhayfa what the most intense temptation was, he replied, "Being presented with good and evil and not knowing which of the two to choose." He was referring to the plethora of ambiguities, as was Sahl when he said, "After the year 300, scarcely anyone will be able to repent, for their bread will be moldy, but they will still not be able to renounce bread." In other words, repentance starts with eating only what is permitted. We have received the tradition, "A time will come upon the people when they will stray from their religion and no longer recognize it. A man will wake up adhering to one religion and retire that night adhering to another. His situation will continue without certitude, and the understandings of most people of that time will be snatched away. And the first thing to be taken from them will be humility, then trustworthiness, and then spiritual reticence." Someone has said, "The first thing to be taken from the people will be affection."

[291] A chapter on the words and deeds with which people have only recently concerned themselves, but which were not a concern of the ancestors in faith

In ancient times, when people met each other, they would say to each other, "What's new?" and "How are you?" What they meant was, "What's the latest about how you are persevering in your spiritual struggle?" and "What's the state of your heart with respect to an increase in faith and the knowledge of certitude?" And "What's the latest on your deeds of piety on behalf of your Master?" and "What's your spiritual state in relation to matters pertaining to this world and the next?" "Have you advanced or regressed spiritually?" In other words, they would remind each other of the spiritual states of their hearts, describing actions related to their knowledge, and mention the deeds of devotion God had bestowed upon them and the marvels of profound comprehension He had revealed to them. Thus did they enumerate God's graces to them and the beauty of their gratitude, so that they experienced an increase of *maʿrifa* and deeds of piety.

One of them used to say, "Most of our knowledge and spiritual experience consists in what one of us learns from another and what one of us informs his brother about." Nowadays people are ignorant of that and thus disregard it. If someone asks them about what's new or about what's happening with them, they are referring to worldly matters and the objects of covetousness. As a result, every one complains of his Majestic Master to His lowly servant by expressing displeasure at His judgments, exonerating themselves of His decrees, and forgetting the former deeds of their own hands. In that vein the Most High has said, "Who commits greater evil than one whom We have made mindful of the signs of his Lord, but who then turns away from them and forgets the former deeds of his hands?" (18:57); and as the Most High has also said, "Indeed, the human being is ungrateful to his Lord" (100:6). In other words, people are ungrateful for His graces, so that they enumerate their misfortunes and discount their benefits. All of that is ignorance and heedlessness of God.

Other current common expressions include: "How are you this morning?" and "How are you this evening?" This is a recent development. People used to say when they met each other, "Peace be to you and the mercy of God." A Ḥadīth says, "If someone begins to address you without giving the greeting of 'Peace,' do not respond." That occurred in the time when the pestilence that people called the Plague of ʿImwās[128] brought widespread death to Syria. A man who would meet his brother in the morning would ask him, "Did you survive the night in spite of the plague?" and if he met him in the evening he would ask, "Have you made it to evening in spite of it?" For a person among them who lived through the night often did not make it till evening, and one who survived the day often did not do so till next morning. So this expression has survived to this day, but its origins have been forgotten. Those among the ancients who were aware that the usage was a recent development disliked it. We have received a Ḥadīth from Aḥmad ibn Abī 'l-Ḥawārī,[129] "A man said to Abū Bakr ibn ʿAyyāsh (d.c. 193/808), 'How are you this morning' or 'How are you this evening,' but Abū Bakr would not talk to him. He would say, 'Spare me this innovation!' So I (Aḥmad) said to one of the ancestors in faith, 'How are you this morning?' and he turned away from me, saying, 'Why the "How are you this morning"? Greet me with Peace instead.'" Abū Maʿshar (d. 170/787) passed along a tradition from Ḥasan (al-Baṣrī), "One had only to say to another, 'Peace be to you,' and, by God, hearts experienced peace. But nowadays, people say, 'How are you this morning?—

may God cause you to prosper; How are you this evening?—God protect you!' If we employ their expressions, it is innovation—there is no esteem in that. Let them be angry at us if they wish!"

Among the novel practices people began to indicate in the opening section [292] of a letter the name of the person to whom it was written. But according to the Sunna, one begins with oneself and writes "from so-and-so to so-and-so." Ibn Sīrīn said, "I was away from home, so I wrote to my father, beginning with his name. He then wrote to me, saying, 'My son, when you write to me, start the letter with your name; if you begin by putting my name before your name, I will not read your letter and I will not send you a reply.'" ʿAlā' ibn al-Ḥaḍramī (d.c. 21/641) wrote to God's Messenger beginning with his own name, writing, "From ʿAlā' ibn al-Ḥaḍramī to God's Messenger." It is said that the first to engage in the new practice was Ziyād (ibn Abīhi) (d. 53/673), but the religious scholars blamed him for that and attributed it to the novelties of the Umayyad family. This accepted custom remains in the writings of the caliphs and commanders to this day as in the past, so that they put their names first in their letters.

One of the novel practices is that upon arriving at his brother's dwelling a man says, "O servant boy," or "O serving maid," in contravention of the command of God and the injunction of His Messenger. God said, "Do not enter houses other than your own without asking and wishing peace to those who dwell in it" (24:27). The exegetes have said that social conventions include knocking on a door or clearing one's throat or making a commotion in order to announce one's presence. And God's Messenger said, "When one of you comes to the dwelling of his brother, he should give greetings of peace three times, and if permission is granted, then he may enter. Otherwise, he should go back." Every one of the ancestors in faith used to knock on his brother's door, then give the greeting of peace three times, pausing briefly after every "Peace be to you." If permission was granted, he would enter; for the owner of the dwelling might not want him to enter at that moment because of some reason or excuse, and might say to the visitor, "Peace to you as well, and the mercy of God. But I am occupied, so go away, and God bless you." So the visitor would leave without hesitation and with no hard feelings, for he would consider the owner's telling him to leave more desirable to the extent that it was preferable for him to have the hope of a future positive response and of spiritual purification—as in the Most High's word, "If someone tells you to leave, then go back, for it will purify you more" (24:28).[130] Often enough, one might turn away two or three times after the owner of the house sends him away, to try again later since that experience left no hard feelings in his heart. If this were to happen to one of the people of this age of ours, he would find it offensive and might very well not return to visit later that day.

As for the religious scholars, some people have not sought permission to visit them except in the instance of a very important and unavoidable matter. For the most part, however, out of respect for knowledge and esteem for the religious scholars, people used to wait at their doors and in their mosques, expecting them to come out at ritual prayer times. We have a tradition in which Abū ʿUbayd said, "I have never knocked on the door of a religious scholar. If I went to a scholar's dwelling, I would situate myself before his door and wait for him to come out, while I plumbed the meaning of the word of God, 'If they were patient until you came out to them, it would be better for them'" (49:5). A similar tradition has come down to us about Ibn ʿAbbās concerning the status of his knowledge and nobility. Someone once encountered him while he was leaning against the door of the dwelling of a man from the Anṣār, as the wind buffeted him. So the passerby said, "Son of the uncle of God's Messenger, why are you sitting there?" "I'm waiting for the owner of the house to come out," he replied. When the man emerged, he said, "Son of the uncle of God's Messenger, if you had sent for me I would have come to you." Ibn ʿAbbās replied, "No, it was more appropriate that I come to you." So Ibn ʿAbbās asked the man about a Ḥadīth he had in mind, one he had heard that the man had transmitted from [293] God's Messenger but which Ibn ʿAbbās himself had not heard from the Prophet.

Among novel practices as well is a person's making too extensive an inquiry concerning his brother's condition, trolling for news about him, so that his brother resents it. Salmān al-Fārisī got married, and when he had consummated the marriage, he went out to the people the next day, and a man asked him, "How are you, Abū ʿAbd Allāh?" "Fine, praise be to God," he replied. The man went on, "How are things going for you and how did last night turn out for you?" In another version, the inquirer asks, "How did things go with your wife?" Salmān became angry and asked, "Why does the likes of you ask a question in such a way that the real question is hidden, so that he is actually inquiring about private affairs? It is sufficient for the likes of you to inquire about external matters." A man asked Sulaymān ibn Mihrān al-Aʿmash in his home, "How are you, Abū Muḥammad?" He replied, "Fine." The man asked, "How are you really?" "My health is good," he answered. "How did things go last night?" the man continued. At that Sulaymān shouted, "O serving maid! Bring down the bed and the pillows!" So she brought them down, and Sulaymān said, "Spread out the bed and lie down on it while I lie by your side, so that we can show our brother how things went last night!" He used to say, "When one of them encounters his brother, he asks him about everything, including the chickens in the house. But if he asks for a dirham coin, the other man will not give it to him. It used to be that if one of the ancestors in faith encountered his brother he would say only, 'How are you?' or 'God give you good health!' And if one asked the other for half of his possessions, he would share it with him."

Another novel practice is that when a man meets his brother as he is going along the path, he says to him, "Where are you heading?" or "Where are you coming from?" That is unacceptable and not in keeping with either the Sunna or good upbringing. It verges on prying and intrusiveness, in that intrusiveness has to do with one's personal affairs and prying leads to gossip. That kind of inquiry combines the two, and no individual wants his companion to know where he's going or where he is coming from. Mujāhid and ʿAṭā' disparaged that, saying, "When you meet your brother on the way, don't ask him where he's coming from or where he's headed, for he might tell you more of the truth than you want to hear, or he might deceive you and you will have pressured him into that." They also used to disapprove of buying and selling copies of the Qur'ān, and some of them were more averse to selling them than to buying them.

People these days have innovated sciences with which the ancestors in faith were not familiar. These include the science of speculative theology and disputation, and the disciplines of analogical reasoning, investigation, and inference as applied to the Sunnas of the Messenger by employing personal opinion and reasoning. And among these is the preference for rational knowledge, individual assessment, and argument from analogy over the apparent meanings of the Qur'ān and the Ḥadīth. Other new forms of knowledge include the publicizing of allusions resulting from mystical experience, apart from either the sciences that would make them understandable or an elucidation of the distinctions among their various types. As a result, those who have heard these things have become confused, and those who have acted upon them have gone astray. Formerly, the people who were knowledgeable about this science publicized the sciences of mystical experience, while concealing the ecstatic allusion. They thus made available to the people what would be helpful to them and kept hidden what would be harmful. Since mystical experiences are spiritual states of hearts, it is preferable to conceal them. The sciences of those things, on the other hand, belong to spiritual seekers and those who act, so that making it known is their aim. They therefore made the science in general public while keeping their ecstatic experience private, for it was their secret. In that way they remained untainted by affectation and pretense, giving to those who heard them what was appropriately theirs, while deflecting from them what did not belong to them. In so doing, they did justice to the two sets of characteristics together and gave due attention to both circumstances simultaneously. Nowadays people are ignorant of this accommodation, so its opposite has become the general rule, and that is closer to being harmful and farther from being faultless. For when an individual lacks a refined sense of specific details and is not endowed with the ability to communicate articulately, he is well advised to keep quiet, for in silence there is ample breadth; if one does not discourse on the knowledge [294] of the Sunna, his silence brings him nearer to God. In this context what God has said is apposite, "When a person's resources are limited, let him expend in proportion to what God has given him. God exacts only as much as He has given" (65:7).

One of the newly accepted practices is publicizing the disciplines of *ma'rifa* as a result of disordered desire, so that in their arrogance they set themselves apart from the spiritually poor. People consider them peerless, so that they allow means of livelihood to be directed their way, in keeping with their sartorial splendor and the style to which they have become accustomed. This is among the widest doors to this world and the most dangerous for seekers of the next life, and the subtlest in its distortion of the religion.

One of the problems here is that of discoursing on the divine transcendent unity in such a way that it conflicts with the knowledge of Revealed Law. Such an approach avers that ultimate truth is at odds with knowledge, when in fact mystical truth is knowledge and one of the paths of the Revealed Law from which knowledge of the science of revelation itself derives. How, they argue, could this ultimate truth be incompatible with Revealed Law when it is that very truth that makes the Revealed Law necessary? On the contrary, the ultimate truth is a firm source of definition and a limiting factor, whereas exoteric knowledge is, in comparison, a form of dispensation and permissiveness. As a result, one who discourses on esoteric knowledge without reference to the foundations and principles of exoteric knowledge introduces corruption into the Revealed Law and sets up a barrier between the Book and the Sunna. One of the mystics has said, "I have observed these people who make ecstatic utterances, and have found them nothing but ignorant and deluded, or vulgar and dim-witted, or people whose statements are unfounded."

Another innovation is religious discourse based on diabolical insinuation and fleeting inner impulses without referring the associated inner experiences to the Book and the Sunna. However, an intimate awareness of how these experiences differ is essential, as is the rejection of those experiences to which the Book and the Sunna do not attest. For in mystical experiences there is the potential for error and delusion, just as there may be falsehood and deception in contemplative visions. In addition, they claim to love God while disavowing the divine attributes that the Sunna mentions, and that in the absence of any revealed testimony to the One whose attributes they describe. And they claim experiential knowledge without having any actual familiarity with the object of such experiential knowledge.

Another novel practice is the use of rhymed prose and departure from traditional expression in supplicatory prayer, practices rooted neither in the Book nor in traditions from God's Messenger or the Companions. On the contrary, these sources loathed excessive verbiage in supplicatory prayer and avoided departure from the collected, brief, familiar prayers of supplication that God has handed down from

His Friends. We have a tradition from God's Messenger, "Avoid rhymed prose in supplicatory prayer. It is sufficient for an individual to say, 'O God, I ask You for Paradise, and for the words and deeds that bring it nigh. And I take refuge in You from the Fire and from the words and deeds that bring it nigh.'" A tradition says, "There will come a people who will commit excesses in supplicatory prayer and in purifying themselves ritually." ʿAbd Allāh ibn Mughaffal (d.c. 57/676) heard his son offering an overblown prayer of supplication, so he said, 'My son, avoid excesses in devotional prayer.'" And God's word says, "Make supplication of your Lord humbly and privately, for He does not love those who commit excesses" (7:55). They say this refers to supplicatory prayer.

Excess in supplicatory prayer is an abandonment of the devotional prayers for forgiveness, mercy, and repentance that God has handed down from His righteous Friends—that is, familiar prayers of supplication and widely known sayings—in favor of the obstinate use of more abstruse, nontraditional, and more exacting language. A saying has it, "None of the religious scholars and Abdāl exceeded seven phrases in supplicatory prayer." In the scripture one finds corroboration of that, in that God did not hand down any one supplicatory prayer from His servants that exceeded seven requests, and those are at the end of the Sūra of the Cow (2:286). Rather, He handed down from them, scattered throughout the scripture, prayers containing two, three, four, and up to five requests at a time.

[295] One of the ancestors in faith came upon a storyteller who was offering a prayer of supplication in rhymed prose and precious language, so he said to him, "Woe to you, are you trying to be more eloquent than God? I testify that I saw Ḥabīb al-ʿAjamī (d. 156/772) offering prayer of supplication, saying no more than, 'O God, give us two excellent things: O God, let us not be ashamed on Resurrection Day. O God, prosper us in goodness.' The people wept on all sides, and we felt sure that Ḥabīb's prayer of supplication was answered and that he was blessed." Abū Yazīd al-Bisṭāmī used to say, "Ask Him with the tongue of need, not with the tongue of wisdom." One of them (Ḥasan al-Baṣrī) said, "Make supplication with the tongue of submissiveness and neediness, not with that of rhetorical style and fulsome expression."

Another novel practice is reciting the Qur'ān in turns (with varied recitations), or two people vying with one another in recitation of the same verse or the recitation of two people of two verses in one place, which leads to misappropriation and taking things from their proper place without humility or awe before the Qur'ān. On the contrary, the recitation of the Qur'ān requires a sense of reverence, sadness, and tranquility. Another such novelty is that one who recites the Qur'ān takes his recitation from two teachers. Better that he attend to the recitation of one at a time, for under these circumstances the heart becomes distracted. As someone said to Ibrāhīm (ibn Isḥāq) al-Ḥarbī (d. 285/898), "So-and-so is learning from two people." So he replied, "My goodness! It is more fitting that two students take lessons from a single teacher." Another innovation is chanting as if singing while reciting, so that people have no comprehension of what is being recited. For reciters fail to articulate words properly because they pronounce short syllables as long and long syllables as short, and they assimilate letters that should be pronounced and pronounce letters that should be assimilated,[131] thereby blurring the distinction between Qur'ān recitation and singing. No one cares about the distortion of language and its modification beyond its essential meaning. This is an innovation that one is loathe to hear. Bishr ibn al-Ḥārith (al-Ḥāfī) said, "I asked ʿAbd Allāh ibn Dāwūd al-Khuraybī, 'If I come upon a man who is reciting Qur'ān, should I sit with him?' He asked, 'As if he were singing?' 'Yes,' I answered. 'No,' he responded, 'This exposes him as an innovator.'"

A related novel practice is introducing melody into the call to prayer, a practice that is both incorrect and an example of excess. One of the muezzins said to Ibn ʿUmar, "Indeed, I love you in God." So he replied, "But I hate you in God." The man asked, "Why, Abū ʿAbd ar-Raḥmān (Ibn ʿUmar)?" "Because you make the call to prayer incorrectly and you accept compensation for it." Abū Bakr al-Ajurrī (d. 360/970) used to say, "I left Baghdad, because it was no longer possible to feel at home there. They engaged in innovations in everything, including the recitation of the Qur'ān and the call to prayer." He was referring to reciting Qur'ān in turns and with melody. He came to us in Mecca in the year 330/941.

One of the many novel practices of contemporary Muslims that is at odds with traditional values of the ancestors in faith is that they are stricter in matters in which the ancestors in faith were more lenient, while they are more lenient in matters on which the ancestors in faith took a harder line. For example, the Khawārij[132] take a hard line on minor sins and go easy when it comes to the traditions and practices of the Prophet, as well as in relation to abandoning the approach of the assembly at large, even to the point of separating themselves from it. A matter in which later generations were strict while the ancestors in faith were more lenient is that the former wrote down the various types of Ḥadīths and pursued the ones narrated by only a single transmitter, and in their approach to traditions, investigating their precise verbal formulation.

Ibn ʿAwn said, "I have come across three people who were flexible with respect to the contents of a Ḥadīth: Ibrāhīm (an-Nakhaʿī), Shaʿbī, and Ḥasan." Among the generality of religious scholars of the ancestors in faith and the Companions there was latitude concerning the sense of the Ḥadīths, even when their precise wording did not indicate it. Another novelty is dispensing with vowels and diacritical marks so that the individual reader may pursue all variants of recitation, to such an extent that it is virtually a duty to do so.

Another novel practice is refinement in the use of analogical reasoning and investigation, along with detailed study of the sciences of Arabic grammar. [296] As Ibrāhīm ibn Adham said, "We are meticulously correct in speech and utter no barbarisms, but our deeds are full of errors and lack propriety. I only wish that we committed errors in speech and were correct in action." Someone brought up the subject of Arabic linguistics[133] with Qāsim ibn al-Mukhaymara (d.c. 101/718), and he responded, "It begins with arrogance and ends with injustice." One of the ancestors in faith said, "Grammar ostracizes humility from the heart." Another of them said, "Someone who wants to show contempt for all the people need only study Arabic linguistics." (Another novel practice is that) they are stricter still in ritual purification with water, as well as in cleaning and frequently washing their garments clean of fluids that cause ritual impurity, of menstrual pollution, and of the urine of animals whose flesh one may not eat (because it is ritually impure); and in the washing away of a small quantity of blood and similar stains. The ancestors in faith used to be permissive in all these matters.

On the other hand, there are some matters about which the ancestors in faith were strict but about which people nowadays are more lax. They include the ethics of acquisition and the abdication of appropriate oversight; discourse about topics that are not one's own concern; becoming absorbed in banalities; participating actively in slander and gossip as well as listening to them; and giving credence to defamatory talk and the negative opinion of others that results from it, for that is participating in slander and gossip. All gossip tends either to exaggerate or minimize. So if a person is wicked, he becomes more wicked; if he is good, gossip takes him down a notch. People today are lax in that they look for falsehood and frivolity, keep the company of the heedless, give in to disordered cravings and bigotry, and covet this world voraciously. The ancestors in faith were more stringent in all of these matters.

Other novel practices include women entering the bath unnecessarily and men entering without being wrapped in a towel—that is an outrage! Someone asked Ibrāhīm ibn Isḥāq al-Ḥarbī if he should pray behind someone who had imbibed date wine but was not drunk. He replied, "Yes." Someone asked, "How about a man who entered the bath without a proper wrap?" "He should not perform ritual prayer behind him," he replied. That is because there are variant opinions concerning drinking date wine without becoming intoxicated, whereas everyone agrees that entering the bath not properly clad is forbidden. One of the religious scholars used to say, "One who enters the bath must be clad in two wraps, one for the face and one for the private parts (from navel to knees); otherwise he is not blameless when he enters." Ibn ʿUmar used to say, "The bath is the amenity they introduced as a novelty." One of the bath's objectionable features is that an attendant is entrusted with applying a depilatory to a Muslim man's private parts.

In their study circles it was the practice of the religious scholars to gather each of them together, sitting around with their knees drawn up together, and some of them would sit upon their heels and rest their elbows on their knees. That became the manner of sitting for everyone who discoursed on this science, particularly from the age of the Companions of God's Messenger and since the time of Ḥasan al-Baṣrī, the first to make this knowledge public and to loose tongues to speak of it, on down to the time of Abū 'l-Qāsim al-Junayd, before the use of chairs appeared. In that vein we have a tradition from God's Messenger that he used to sit in a squatting position, his arms holding his legs drawn up under his robe. Another tradition says that he used to sit on his heels and put his elbows on his knees. The first among the proponents of this science to sit on a chair was Yaḥyā ibn Muʿādh in Egypt, and Abū Ḥamza (d.c. 269/882) followed him in Baghdad, but the shaykhs censured both of them for that. That practice was not the way of the mystics who discoursed on the science of *maʿrifa* and certitude. Indeed, it was the grammarians, the linguists, and the *muftīs* who were children of this world who used to sit cross-legged. That is the way the haughty sit, but the modest way is to gather people as equals in the study circle.

[297] Discussion of the specific varieties of knowledge: those well known and ancient, and the more recent and unacceptable

Know that there are nine varieties of knowledge. Four of them are part of the Sunna and have been well known since the Companions and the Followers. Five are of more recent origin and were unknown in the early days. The four well-known types include the sciences of the faith, of the Qur'ān, of Ḥadīths and traditions, and of legal advisories and judgments. The five novel forms include grammar and prosody, the science of analogical reasoning, disputation in jurisprudence, the science of rational inquiry, and the science of defective Ḥadīths. The last involves tracing the paths of Ḥadīths, pointing out the defects of weak Ḥadīths and the unreliability of the transmitters of traditions. This is a newfangled form of knowledge, albeit one whose proponents consider valid knowledge and whose followers seek to hear from them.

They used to consider storytelling an innovation, so they forbade it and took exception to storytelling sessions. One of the religious scholars said, "Such-and-such a man would have been a fine person, if only he hadn't been a storyteller." One of this group said, "The relationship of proponents of *maʿrifa* to those who collect narratives is much like that of the jurists to the storytellers." Someone else said, "Storytellers are to the religious scholars what country folk are to city dwellers." One of the loathsome novelties is that people use religion to acquire worldly goods, taking them in exchange for righteousness, and selling knowledge in exchange for this world, while behaving hypocritically and pretentiously in public. This is so evident to those familiar with explicit religious knowledge that it is not necessary to explicate its corrupt nature. Nowadays those who have no scientific knowledge call them religious scholars. Though the ignorant know little of the ways of the ancients and lack their spiritual insight into the essential truth of religion, those who are deficient in excellence proclaim these people outstanding.

Know that discourse is divided into seven parts. One portion is knowledge, while the remaining six are nonsensical rubbish of the sort that people who do not recognize it as such and make no distinction between knowledge and ignorance will collect. The Arabs say, "For every thing that falls there is someone who will pick it up, and for every one who talks, there is one who will pass it on." The six portions include falsehood, stupidity, error, supposition, rhetorical embellishment, and diabolical insinuation, as the scholars list them. They distinguish among them just as God has laid them out in His clarification, and He has given them His Book for safekeeping and has made them witnesses to His religion and His servants. Now the seventh part of speech is very different than these six, and none of their reprehensible labels applies to it. It is traditional knowledge, consisting of the text of the Qur'ān and the Sunna or what they elucidate, or what one may extrapolate from the two sources, or whose name and meaning—whether in word or deed—one finds in them. Esoteric exegesis, when it does not diverge from the consensus, is also part of knowledge, as is deeper interpretation, provided it is contained in scripture, the generally accepted view testifies to it, and the text does not contradict it.

Ibn Masʿūd used to say, "You today are in a time in which disordered craving is subordinate to knowledge. But a time will come upon you in which knowledge will be subordinate to disordered craving." God made an identification between splendor of expression and worldly pleasure with the term *adornments,* when He said, "And for your houses, doors, and thrones on which to recline, and mere adornments" (43:34–35), and again, "(We have made an enemy for every Messenger, evil ones among humankind and the jinns, who inspire one another with) deceptively embellished discourse" (6:112). Thus the ignorant person's placing a high value on the "embellished discourse," which those who are knowledgeable about this world disguise as mindless pleasure, is like pleasure the children of this world take in embellishments that hide the essential reality of a thing. Mere adornment is that which is disguised with gold, so that it looks like gold, and the ignorant person and the child alike think it is actually gold.

Similarly, embellished speech is that [298] which is disguised as and resembles knowledge, so that the ignorant ones who listen to it will reckon it to be knowledge. For that reason God brought the two concepts together in the term "mere adornment." It has been said that "mere adornment" refers to gilding, and on that basis God likens beguiling speech to the gold whose "permanence" is fleeting. From the perspective of those who have a relationship to their Lord and the ascetical proponents of mystical truth, the essential meaning of such a ploy is negligible. For that reason, too, the prophets and authentic ones likened beguiling speech to stone and mud, and that is indeed how they regarded it.

Imām Aḥmad ibn Ḥanbal used to say, "You have abandoned knowledge and dedicated yourselves to curiosities. What little deep understanding you have. God help us!" Imām Mālik ibn Anas said, "In the past, people never used to inquire about these matters the way they do today. Religious scholars did not classify most matters as 'forbidden' or 'licit'; it is my understanding that they used the classifications 'discouraged' and 'recommended.'" Mālik was wont to waver in his responses, often answering inquiries with "I don't know. Ask somebody else." A man said to ʿAbd ar-Raḥmān ibn Mahdī (d. 198/814), "Do you not observe how so-and-so classifies issues of knowledge as 'licit' and 'forbidden' and how he preempts further discussion on them—he was referring to one of the proponents of personal judgment—and how when someone asks Mālik a question, he says 'I think…'?" Replied ʿAbd ar-Raḥmān, "Woe to you! I consider Mālik's saying 'I think…I think…' preferable to so-and-so's saying, 'I testify…I testfify.'" Hishām ibn ʿUrwa (d.c. 145/762) used to say, "Do not ask them today about the novel practices they accept, for they have a pat answer for that. Ask them instead about the Ḥadīth—they haven't a clue about that!" When Shaʿbī considered people's novel use of personal opinion and caprice, he used to say, "I once loved sitting in this mosque more than anything else. But since these proponents of personal opinion have been there, they have made participation in study circles there odious to me. I would rather sit on a garbage heap than join a study circle there." And he used to say, "Accept the Ḥadīths and traditions that have been handed down to you, and blow your nose on what they pass on to you from their newfangled personal opnion." He once said, "Piss on it."

The ancestors in faith used to prefer speechlessness and simplicity to the rational sciences. God's Messenger viewed those qualities as part of faith and associated them with shame, saying, "Shame and simplicity are two of faith's branches, whereas obscenity and the facile retort are two of the branches of hypocrisy." He also said, "The most detestable of people in God's eyes is the glib person who rolls speech around on his tongue the way cows chew the cud." He is referring to fresh herbage. In another Ḥadīth he said, "I'm talking about the inarticulateness of the tongue, not that of the heart." And he said, "God loathes your overzealous explication. " All elaboration has to do with erudition. True erudition, therefore, is the deeper understanding of the heart concerning the Lord, while the artificial erudition of the tongue expressed in facile discourse betokens the heart's inability to articulate the confession of faith and certitude.

Speechlessness of the tongue and protracted silence, to which the ancestors in faith were inclined, are today regarded as a shortcoming. The speculative theologians are not familiar with it; and the verbal expression of novelty, and the science of the hypocrites, which the ancients censured, nowadays has the status of the Sunna, so that those who articulate it are considered learned. The ethically acceptable has become reprehensible, and the reprehensible acceptable. The Sunna has become an innovation, and innovation has the weight of prophetic example. Accordingly the traditional reports figure in religious scholars' description of the end of time, as in the well-known tradition, "God detests the loud-mouthed chatterboxes." If this is a person's dominant characteristic, [299] in such a way that he shoots off his mouth and is given to rhetorical embellishment in the science of personal opinion and the application of reason, while his heart is unable to put into words the contemplative vision of certitude and the knowledge of faith, then he is on the verge of hypocrisy and far from the essential reality of faith.

Abū Sulaymān ad-Dārānī used to say, "The person who has been inspired with accomplishing something good need not act upon it until he hears of it in traditional sources, then he should give praise to God if it accords with what is in his soul." One of the mystics said, "I have never accepted a passing thought from my heart until I can rely on two solid witnesses from the scripture and the Sunna." Our Imām Abū Muḥammad (Sahl at-Tustarī) used to say, "The servant does not arrive at the essential reality of faith until these four things occur in him: the performance of duties prescribed by the Sunna; partaking of permissible foods in moderation; avoidance of things forbidden whether external or internal; and persistence in that until death." They used to reprove those who talked from before dawn until sunrise about things other than God-recollectedness, and they used to drive from the mosque people engaged in conversation, so that only those performing ritual prayer or recollecting God remained there.

The ancestors in faith used to consider of great consequence both new inventions in religion and the minute details of innovation in Islam, because of the immense place the Sunna occupied in their hearts and because of their intimate awareness of the essential reality of what was legally and ethically acceptable. ʿAbd Allāh ibn al-Mughaffal said to his son, once he had heard him recite Qur'ān behind the imām, "My son, beware of novel practices! Beware of novel practices!" Saʿd ibn Abī Waqqāṣ said to his son ʿUmar after hearing him use rhymed prose in his speech, "I find this detestable, and I will never fulfill any need of yours!" The son had come to him to ask about some need he had. God's Messenger said, "No greater evil will befall a person than a glib tongue." He said this to ʿAbd Allāh ibn Rawāḥa after he had spoken in rhymed prose and had strung three words together. And he said, "Beware of rhymed prose, Ibn Rawāḥa"—rhymed prose consists of more than two words in a row rhyming. Similiarly, a man whom Muḥammad had ordered to pay the blood money for a dead fetus asked, "How are we to pay blood money for one who neither drank nor ate, who never cried and never raised his voice? This kind of thing needs no compensation." God's Messenger said to him, "Could this be rhymed prose like that of the Bedouins?"

Tradition tells us that when Marwān introduced the pulpit[134] at the prayer place for the feast-day ritual prayer, Abū Saʿīd al-Khudrī stood before him and said, "Marwān, what is this innovation?" He replied, "It is no innovation. It is something better than you realize. The people have grown numerous, and I wanted the voice to reach them." Abū Saʿīd said, "By God, you will never bring something better than I know. I will not perform the ritual prayer behind you today!" Then he turned away and did not perform the ritual prayer with him at the feast-day prayer. Preaching the sermon upon the *minbar* during feast-day ritual prayer and during the prayer for rain is an innovation. The Prophet used to preach a sermon on both occasions on the ground, leaning on a bow or staff.

Tradition has come down to us that ʿUmar (Ibn al-Khaṭṭāb) postponed the after-sunset ritual prayer one night until a star had set, then he freed a slave. ʿUmar ibn ʿAbd al-ʿAzīz did the same, setting a slave free after the example of ʿUmar (Ibn al-Khaṭṭāb), who was his maternal grandfather. We have received a tradition that Ibn ʿUmar postponed the after-sunset ritual prayer until two stars had set, and then freed [300] two slaves. According to a Ḥadīth, "My community will hold fast to its religion so long as they do not postpone the after-sunset ritual prayer until stars are indistinguishable from one another, as the Jews do, and do not postpone the pre-dawn ritual prayer until the stars appear few in number, as the Christians do."

Sufyān ath-Thawrī and Yūsuf ibn Asbāṭ said, "Do not accept uncritically views about your religion expressed by one who has no religion." And Wakīʿ said, "I would rather commit adultery than ask an innovator about my religion." Imām Aḥmad ibn Ḥanbal had received many traditions from ʿUbayd Allāh ibn Mūsā al-ʿAbsī (d. 213/828), when something from ʿUbayd bordering on innovation came to Aḥmad's attention: People said that ʿUbayd had elevated ʿAlī over ʿUthmān, while others said he had accused Muʿāwiya of misconduct. So Aḥmad turned away (from ʿUbayd), tore to shreds everything he had gotten from him, and handed on no more Ḥadīths from him. Someone once asked, "Abū ʿAbd Allāh,[135] who is more like the ancestors in faith: Wakīʿ or ʿUbayd Allāh?" "Wakīʿ," he answered, "even if he should commit adultery." We have a tradition from Ibrāhīm al-Ḥarbī, saying, "I have garnered a variety of material from ʿAlī al-Madyanī (d. 234/849), I assure you, but I have not passed along a single iota from him." "Why so, Abū Isḥāq?" asked someone. He explained that it was because ʿAlī had performed his ritual prayer behind an innovator. He used to say, "I kept the company of the jurists, Ḥadīth specialists, and linguists for seventy years, but I never heard any of them raise these novel questions." He was referring to issues of terminology and the like. He went on, "And I have forbidden any proponent of speculative theology and dialectics to attend my study circle or ask me any questions. For I have no knowledge of speculative theology, and am not proficient at it, nor do I talk to its proponents. And even if I were familiar with any of them, I would not converse with him or respond to him concerning anything."

Zayd ibn Akhzam (d. 257/870) passed along a Ḥadīth in which Wahb ibn Jarīr (d.c. 206/821) said, "I heard Shuʿba say, 'I came to Ḥārith al-ʿUklī and asked, "What is the meaning of the saying of the Prophet, 'When one of you goes along with a funeral procession, he should not sit down until [301] the body has been lowered'?" ʿUklī answered, "Don't you think it means that if we come and they have not yet buried him, then we must remain standing?" When he said to me, "Don't you think," I disregarded the rest.'" Maḥmūd ibn Ghaylān (d.c. 239/854) handed down a tradition from Wahb as well, and from Shuʿba, saying, "I came to Minhāl ibn ʿAmr to ask him about a Ḥadīth, when I heard the sound of a lute coming from his dwelling. So I left without putting my question to him. Then after that I felt regret and said to myself, 'Why didn't I ask him? Perhaps he would not have known the answer.'"[136]

Imām Aḥmad ibn Ḥanbal parted company with Abū Thawr, Shāfiʿī's companion, because when someone asked Abū Thawr about the meaning of the Prophet's saying "Indeed God created Adam in His image," he responded that the "his" before "image" referred to Adam. So Ibn Ḥanbal became angry and said, "Woe to him! What form did Adam have prior to being created? Woe to him, for saying that God created according to a prototype. What, then, does he make of the tradition that proposes the gloss, 'God created Adam in the image of the

Merciful'?" When that came to Abū Thawr's attention, he came to Ibn Ḥanbal and excused himself and swore that he had not made that statement out of doctrinal conviction but that it had been no more than a debatable opinion that he had considered. He said to Ibn Ḥanbal, "The authentic teaching is what you expressed, and to that I give my assent."

Ibn Ḥanbal also parted company with Ḥārith al-Muḥāsibī, criticizing him on the grounds that he engaged in disputation with innovators, even though he was among the proponents of the Sunna. Ibn Ḥanbal asked Muḥāsibī, "How can you claim to refute them while repeating what they say?" "As a matter of fact," he went on, "you are inducing them into speculation and the exercise of personal opinion through what you say, so that it becomes an occasion for their rejecting the truth in favor of falsehood."[137] He also parted company with Yaḥyā ibn Maʿīn (d. 233/848) concerning one of his sayings, to wit: "If Satan were to offer me something, I would take it." Someone said to ʿAbd ar-Raḥmān ibn Mahdī, "So-and-so refuted the innovator." He then asked, "By means of the Book of God and the Sunna of God's Messenger ?" "No," replied the first man, "rather by using rationalist methods." Ibn Mahdī said, "What he did was most unfortunate—refuting an innovation with an innovation." Mālik ibn Anas said, "There is nothing in the Sunna that says you should engage in disputation about the Sunna. Rather, one simply reports on it, and if someone accepts it from you, fine; if not, then you should say no more."[138]

Other novel practices include selling and buying along the street. Those who are spiritually reticent don't buy anything from vendors who sit along the street. It is likewise unacceptable to have the windows of houses oriented out to the street and have the doorway near the shops. One of the things the spiritually reticent detest is selling to or buying from children, because they cannot own things legally and because their word is not acceptable as legal testimony. I have received a Ḥadīth from Abū Bakr al-Marwazī (d. 275/888), saying, "A shaykh of some prestige used to sit with Imām Aḥmad ibn Ḥanbal, so Aḥmad took an interest in him and held him in high esteem. But when it came to Aḥmad's attention that the shaykh had covered the outer wall of his house with clay, he banned him from sitting with him. The shaykh did not understand that and asked, 'Abū ʿAbd Allāh, has word gotten to you that I have engaged in some novel practice?' 'Yes,' he replied, 'you have covered the outer wall of your house with clay.' The shaykh asked, 'Isn't that allowed?' 'No,' responded Ibn Ḥanbal, 'because you have shaved off the space of a fingertip from the Muslims' street.' 'How should I remedy that?' he asked. Replied Ibn Ḥanbal, 'Either you should scrape off the coating of mud you have applied, or tear down the wall and move it back a finger's width, and then coat the surface with clay.' So the man tore down the wall, moved it back a finger's width, and coated the surface of it with clay. Then Abū ʿAbd Allāh again accepted him as before."

Among the things the ancestors in faith abhorred was discarding cats and dead animals in refuse heaps on the roads, so that the Muslims had to put up with the foul odors. When one of their cats died, Shurayḥ[139] and others used to bury them within their compounds. They dealt with drainage conduits in like manner, when they drained outside the house and into the streets. Imām Aḥmad ibn Ḥanbal and the proponents of spiritual reticence arranged to have their drainage conduits drain to the inside of their compounds. Ibrāhīm an-Nakhaʿī said, "The likes of you lies twice without noticing, saying, 'It is nothing at all,' or 'It is but nothing,' 'It amounts to nothing.'" He meant that people refer to something minor, which they do not describe as much, as "nothing." He considered this a grave matter, for he saw it as "lying twice."

We have received a tradition about ʿUmar in which he said to (Abū 's-Saʿdī) ʿAwāna, "I used to be sad for you because of your blindness, but now I have come to envy you for it." "How's that?" he asked. ʿUmar replied, "Abū 's-Saʿdī, you no longer see with your own eyes the innovation in Medina." Someone asked Qatāda, "Would you like to be able to see?" He answered, "Not what would be revealed to my eye now, but if I lived in the time of the Companions of God's Messenger I would like to have seen them."

We have a tradition from Faḍl ibn Mihrān, in which he says, "I said to Yaḥyā ibn Maʿīn, 'A brother of mine sits with the storytellers.' He responded, 'Forbid him.' I said, 'He won't accept it.' He replied, 'Admonish him.' I said, 'He won't accept it. Should I part company with him?' 'Yes,' he answered. Then Imām Aḥmad ibn Ḥanbal came along, and when I mentioned the matter to him, he said, 'Tell him to read the sacred text, to be mindful of God interiorly, and to seek the

Ḥadīth of God's Messenger.' 'And if he won't do it?' I asked. 'Then as God wills, for this conference we're having is already a novelty.' I asked further, 'If he won't do it, should I sever my relationship with him?' Then he laughed and said nothing."

A man asked Bishr ibn al-Ḥārith about an issue of the science of hearts, [302] so he paused and then answered him. Then the man asked him another question concerning the science of devotional deeds, but he looked at the man in silence. Then Bishr asked, "What sort of people do you sit with?" He replied, "Manṣūr ibn ʿAmmār and Ibn as-Sammāk."[140] So Bishr asked, "Aren't you ashamed to ask me about the science of hearts while you are keeping the company of storytellers?" Then he turned away from him until we said to him, "Abū Naṣr (Bishr), there's nothing wrong with him. He is one of the people of the Sunna."

They also used to abhor the ritual prayer in the royal enclosure,[141] and they considered it the first innovation newly introduced in the mosques. And they frowned upon the ornamental embellishment of mosques, such as adorning the *qibla* (the *miḥrāb*) with colors, and illuminating copies of the Qur'ān, for this is innovation. According to a tradition, "If you adorn your mosques and illuminate your copies of the Qur'ān, you will come to ruin." Another thing they condemned was a multiplicity of mosques in one locale. According to a tradition, when Anas ibn Mālik entered Basra, he saw a mosque every few paces. He said, "What is this innovation? When the mosques proliferate, those performing the ritual prayer diminish. I testify that for every full tribe there should be only a single mosque. Tribespeople would cooperate in constructing the one mosque in one of their quarters of the city." Opinions differed as to which mosque should be the place of ritual prayer when two mosques were situated in one locale. Some said in the older of the two, and Anas ibn Mālik and other Companions were inclined to that view. Anas said, "They used to bypass the newer mosques in favor of the more ancient." Ḥasan used to say, "They should perform the ritual prayer in the closer of the two."

It is said that the first innovations to be advanced are these four: tables, sieves, potash, and eating to satiety. They used to be appalled that house vessels were of material other than earthenware, and the spiritually reticent did not consider vessels made of brass and copper ritually pure. Junayd said, "Sarī as-Saqatī said to me, 'Make an effort to use in your house only vessels made of the same substance as yourself'"—in other words, made of clay. People said there was no calling to account over them.

Another thing the ancestors in faith found unacceptable was constructing a building with gypsum (plaster) and baked brick. It is said that the first person to fire clay was Hāmān, under orders from Pharaoh.[142] People say it was a building for the arrogant. They also disliked carvings and decoration on ceilings and doors and used to close their eyes to keep from seeing them. Aḥnaf ibn Qays (d.c. 72/691) was away from home for a while, and when he returned they had painted the ceiling of his quarters green and yellow. When he saw it, he left his dwelling and swore he would not enter it again until they had removed the paint and returned the room to its former condition.

Yaḥyā ibn Yamān (d.c. 189/804), a companion of (Sufyān) ath-Thawrī, said, "I was walking with Thawrī on the road, and we happened upon a door that was carved decoratively. When I looked at it, Sufyān pulled me away until I was past it. So I asked, 'What do you find objectionable about looking at this?' He replied, 'They built it so that people would look at it, and if no passerby looked at it, they would not build things that way.'" It is as though he was afraid that by looking at it, he was encouraging its construction.

A novelty that people introduced and that the ancestors in faith found detestable was luxurious apparel, such as embroidered fabric and refined Egyptian linen [for the women and the men, but it is more reprehensible and gauche for the women]. They used to say, "Luxurious apparel is the uniform of the dissolute," and "When an individual's vesture is delicate, so is his religion (fragile)." They also said, "Asceticism begins with clothing." Ibn Masʿūd said, "Clothing is most like clothing when the heart is most like the heart." Bishr ibn Marwān[143] was preaching a sermon while wearing a luxurious garment. Then Rāfiʿ ibn Khadīj (d. 74/693) began to ridicule him, saying, "Look [303] at your governor, who preaches to the people cloaked in the garb of a dandy." And when a finely dressed ʿAbd Allāh ibn ʿAmīr ibn Rabīʿa (d.c. 59/680) came to Abū Dharr to ask him about asceticism and began to discourse about it, Abū Dharr scoffed at him. Then he left him and did not converse with him. So Ibn ʿĀmīr became enraged, for he was a noble member of the Quraysh tribe, and complained to Ibn ʿUmar about Abū Dharr. Ibn ʿUmar said to him, "You went to Abū Dharr dressed like that to ask him about asceticism? You sabotaged yourself!"

According to a tradition, God's Messenger was describing how women would be at the end of time when he said, "scantily clad, with lilting and enticing gait, wearing on their heads something like the hump of a camel"—referring to veils and head wraps.[144] "They will not experience the Garden's perfume." [Luxurious garments for women are particularly objectionable and inappropriate.] Ibn ʿAbbās used to interpret the display of beauty as including luxurious clothing. Thus he glossed the word of the Most High addressed to Muḥammad's wives, "Do not display your beauty as they did of old in pre-Islamic times" (33:33), saying that in those days women wore a garment whose value was such-and-so, but which was not sufficient to conceal their nakedness and in which they were not permitted to perform the ritual prayer because it was form revealing or gossamer. It was, therefore, objectionable to wear it.

The ancestors in faith used to wear the Sunbulānī and Qaṭawānī garment, the Yemeni turban, the Egyptian garment from Maʿāfir, the Coptic garment like the veil of the Kaʿba, the Saḥūlī garment from Yemen, and white cotton garments from Ḥaḍramawt. All of these were rough and thick, with a value of between five and thirty dirhams. Then people introduced the novelty of luxurious garments of Egyptian linen and Khurāsānī cotton. God's Messenger wore a wrap four and a half measures long,[145] which cost about four or five dirhams. The cost of their undergarment was between five and twenty dirhams. According to a tradition (from Ḥudhayfa), "The Hour of Judgment will not come until the morally acceptable has become unacceptable and the unacceptable acceptable."

Ibn ʿAbbās said, "Not a year comes upon the people but that they kill a sunna and bring an innovation to life. Eventually, the sunnas will have perished and innovations alone will live." If people are not familiar with something, they say it's objectionable. If the truth is hidden and unknown, the label *objectionable* sticks to it. Likewise, when something is widespread and familiar, people call it morally acceptable. As a result, when falsehood gains ground and ignorance proliferates until it is familiar and comfortable, the label *morally acceptable* sticks to it. In that vein people say that oppression spreads until those born under its sway no longer recognize justice.

Shaʿbī used to say, "A time will come upon the people when they will mention the name of Ḥajjāj in the Friday ritual prayer."[146] And this is now long since the case, for Ḥajjāj introduced innovations for which the people took exception to him in his time. Today, however, those things are well-known sunnas and actions considered good, for which the people give thanks to God and in whose novelty they rejoice, reckoning that Ḥajjāj deserves a reward and gratitude for his efforts. They are not aware, however, that he has introduced novelties, so that even if they do not actually pronounce his name in the ritual prayer, nevertheless their use of the novelties he advanced and their acceptance of the innovation he introduced is their asking mercy for him. And asking for mercy is equivalent to the ritual prayer. In addition, he did introduce as innovations some things that were good and gave him entry to the doors of the next life.

But after him there appeared provincial administrations that introduced inappropriate novelties and made corrupt innovations, which subsequently became sunnas. As a result of that, people ought to mention the name of Ḥajjāj in their supplications, especially by contrast with what occurred after him. He introduced the novel practices of these sedan chairs and awnings [304] with which he went counter to the guidance of the ancestors in faith, in the interest of ease and comfort. By contrast, people used to set out on female riding camels and pack camels and be exposed to the sun, exhausting themselves in the cause of God. They were disheveled and coated with dust, ate and slept little, while maximizing the comfort of the camels by minimizing their labor and burden. Their recompense was that it purified their pilgrimage and kept their camels in better health. By such behavior they more closely approximated the exemplary behavior of God's Messenger. As a result of the innovations to which he introduced them, Ḥajjāj diverted them from all that. Thus they would venture out in shaded gondolas, with which they replaced the camels' pack load, lest they be unable to bear it and it become a source of injury to them. They therefore made common cause in the practice, and they joined together in the sunna that Ḥajjāj had established.

Ḥajjāj also introduced the innovation of dividing the Qur'ān into five or ten sections; of marking the beginnings of verses; and of using black, red, green, and yellow ink. He thereby introduced into the copies of the Qur'ān embellishments not of Qur'ānic origin, while the ancestors in faith used to say, "Keep the Qur'ān plain, the way God sent it down, and do not contaminate it with extraneous elements." For the religious scholars had objected to that, to such a degree that Abū Razīn (d.c. 85/704) said, "A time will come upon the people when there will arise a new generation who think that God sent down the novel practices that in reality Ḥajjāj introduced into copying the Qur'ān." May God rebuke Ḥajjāj for that! As time went by, people advanced a divergence of opinion: Some of them used to recite from a text pointed in red diacritics,[147] while others did not approve of reciting from pointed texts. Similarly, tradition has it that some of them regarded the purchasing of copies of the Qur'ān as acceptable but objected to selling it. In other words, if you yourself did not point the text, there is no problem with your reciting from what someone else has pointed.[148]

They also took exception to taking remuneration for pointing the Qur'ān on the grounds that pointing is an innovation. Abū Bakr al-Hudhalī (d. 167/783) said, "I asked Ḥasan about being compensated for pointing the text, and he replied, 'What does pointing involve?' I answered, 'Rendering the Arabic unambiguous.' So he responded, 'There is nothing wrong with rendering the Arabic clearly.'" Khālid al-Hadhdhā' (d.c. 141/758) said, "I visited Ibn Sīrīn and saw him reciting from a pointed text of the Qur'ān, even though he found the pointing objectionable." Firās ibn Yaḥyā (d. 129/746) said, "I found a grammatically pointed folio in Ḥajjāj's prison, and I was astonished at it, for it was the first pointing I had seen. So I brought it to Shaʿbī, and he said to me, 'Recite from it, but do not add the pointing with your own hand.'"

Another of Ḥajjāj's innovations was his assembling thirty Qur'ān reciters. They then counted the letters of the written text, and they tallied up its words for a month. If ʿUmar or ʿUthmān or ʿAlī had seen them doing this to the Qur'ān, namely, counting the letters and words of each chapter, they would have given them a nasty clout on the head. This is what the Companions abhorred and the way they characterized the Qur'ān reciters at the end of time, namely, that they memorized the Qur'ān's letters but neglected their meaning. Ḥajjāj was the best of the Qur'ān reciters and had memorized its letters most completely. He used to recite the whole Qur'ān every three days, but of all the people he was the least attentive to its meaning.

Ḥajjāj also introduced the innovation of removing gravel and sand from the mosques and furnishing them with reed mats. According to a tradition, Qatāda was performing the ritual prostration when a bit of reed got into his eye. Qatāda, who was already blind, said, "God curse Ḥajjāj for introducing the innovation of these reed mats that injure people making ritual prayer!" They used to prefer to make prostration on the ground and in the dust, as a sign of humility, surrender, and insignificance before God. He introduced other innovations, but I do not intend to enumerate or summarize them here, since these days they are accepted ways of behaving and familiar legal stipulations. But his and other people's novelties are countless, and anyone who is familiar with those aspects of the way of the ancients that are religiously acceptable, and with the good qualities of the upright, will regard them all as objectionable.

[305] Ibn Masʿūd said, "Abhorrent innovations keep popping up, to the point that when one of them is modified in turn, people say that the Sunna has been altered." And he ends his tradition by saying, "In that time the most astute of them will be those who are as shifty in their religion as foxes." In the days of Ḥajjāj, in the year 80/699, Anas ibn Mālik said, "I am aware of nothing today that originated during the age of God's Messenger that has not been changed, other than the confession of faith, 'There is no deity but God.'" Someone asked him, "And the ritual prayer, Abū Ḥamza?" He responded, "Do you know of anything in the ritual prayer that has not been newly introduced?" He was referring to its postponement, and the placement of the call to prayer before it, and he refers to the greeting of peace for the rulers that they combined with the beginning of the ritual prayer and declared consistent with the Sunna. When Qur'ān reciters the likes of Yazīd ar-Raqāshī, Ziyād an-Numayrī, and Farqad as-Sabakhī visited him, he would say, "How like the Companions of Muḥammad you are!" And when they expressed delight at that, he would add, "Your heads and your beards are fine," much as the poet Majnūn[149] said,

The tents are very much like their tents,
but I see that the tribe's women are not really its women.[150]

And as was related from a large number of the Companions, "If the Companions of God's Messenger were to arise and see you, they would not recognize anything you do except for the Friday congregational ritual prayer." Another version says, "except that you perform the ritual prayer together." Ḥasan has said, "I have been in the company of groups that, were you to see them, you would call them crazy; and if they were to see the best of you, they would say 'These people are disgraceful!'"[151] Abū Ḥāzim said, "I have come across Qur'ān reciters who really were Qur'ān reciters. If there were one in a hundred men who knew the Qur'ān, one could identify him by his compelling modesty, his attractive manner, and his humility, for the Qur'ān will have settled him down and made him humble. But these are not authentic Qur'ān reciters; on the contrary, they are filth!" One of the ancestors in faith characterized them in that way, saying, "We were attending a funeral but could not identify the victim of the disaster, nor did we know whom to console, so intense was the sadness of the people. One of them remained unable to do anything useful for three days after attending the funeral."

Fuḍayl (ibn ʿIyāḍ) used to caution against the Qur'ān reciters of his time, saying, "Beware the company of these Qur'ān reciters, for if you contradict them on anything, they pronounce you an unbeliever." Sufyān ath-Thawrī said, "Nothing is dearer to me than associating with a young gentleman, and nothing more loathsome to me than associating with a Qur'ān reciter." He used to say frequently, "One who does not excel at gentlemanly demeanor will not excel as a Qur'ān reciter." Bishr ibn al-Ḥārith used to say, "I would rather associate with a rogue[152] than with a Qur'ān reciter." Be wary, therefore, of associating with the Qur'ān reciters, for they transform into a blameworthy person one who is not blameworthy. And if you should skip the ritual prayer with them in the assembly, they will bear witness against you. All of that is because they overstep the boundaries in the matter and are quick to take exception in everything because ignorance has overcome them, so seldom do they sit with the religious scholars and so meager is their regard for knowledge. In addition, they are particularly susceptible to the subtle influences of ostentation and of playing to the public. So they find objectionable what is not abhorrent, and take sides petulantly and in partisan fashion over minor matters that people have already discounted. Their qualities do not include refinement of character, nor are they noted for cheery demeanor and spontaneity. They are tedious, rude to the people, stiff, and resentful of the wealthy as if the rich had devoured their sustenance and as though they worked as slaves for them. Theirs is an abundant loathing for people who are happy and buoyant, to such an extent that one might say, "The noble person who functions as a Qur'ān reciter is brought low, [306] while the humble person who functions as a Qur'ān reciter is aggrandized." Someone else said, "The common person who functions as a Qur'ān reciter increasingly commands the good and takes his neighbor to task in all things." In other words, he continually commands the good so that people will acknowledge him as good also.

As a result of that, the religious scholars reject them and the sages find fault with them, for knowledge is expansive and open, and goes hand in hand with high moral character, proper comportment, and magnanimous generosity. The knowledgeable person situates things in their proper places for people, in such a way that he neither overstates the issues nor overtaxes people's capabilities, and he ferrets out people's misgivings for them. One of the qualities of scholars is a tendency to introspection and reserve. Imām Shāfiʿī said, "Introverted disposition in relation to the people can elicit their animosity. Therefore cultivate a public demeanor between complete privacy and glad-handing."

According to a tradition, "Your wealth is not wide enough to encompass the people, so let your cheerful countenance and beautiful character surround them."[153] Another version reads, "delight and a happy face." All of this the Qur'ān reciters lack and do not understand. God has given everything a measured capacity, so that anyone who exceeds a thing's limits ruins it. One of the ancestors in faith said, "A little humility suffices for a lot of action, and a little spiritual reticence suffices for a lot of knowledge."

One of the moral qualities of the ancestors in faith that their successors have neglected is that whenever anyone spoke ill about someone with whom he was on speaking terms, or engaged in conversation with someone of whom he had spoken ill, they charged that person with hypocrisy. That was because if they spoke with someone or offered a greeting of peace, they entrusted their hearts to that person and spoke no ill of him. And if they spoke ill of someone because of his innovation or because his corruption and injustice came to light, then they would not engage in conversation with that person. When they praised someone with words, they did not then accuse him with deeds, and when they accused someone with an action, they would not then praise him with words, for that would be speaking with two tongues, self-contradictory duplicity, and playing off secrecy against openness. They used to say that the meaning of the greeting "Peace be to you" offered upon meeting someone, was "I assure you that I will not slander or criticize you." They regarded doing the opposite of this as one of the doors of hypocrisy. We have a tradition from God's Messenger, "The basest person is the two-faced one who presents one face to these people and another to those." According to another Ḥadīth, "For anyone who speaks with two tongues in this world, two tongues of fire will be fashioned on Judgment Day."

One of them used to say, "No one has ever been mentioned in my presence but that I imagine him to be sitting with me. That way I will say in his absence only what he ought to hear." Someone else said, "No one has ever been mentioned in my presence but that I had an image of his likeness within myself, so that I said about him everything I would have liked him to say about me."[154] These, then, are the qualities of the Muslims that make the people safe in their hands and hearts. If one of them speaks ill of another in his presence, he pauses to reflect on his own situation. If he detects a similar evil in himself, shame prevents him from speaking against his brother and he keeps quiet. If, on the other hand, that is not the case, he praises God and has compassion on his brother, overcome with gratitude to his Master for forgiving him. This was the way of the ancestors in faith.

One of the Books of God says, "How amazing is a person who is well spoken of in spite of there being no good in him! How can such a one rejoice (at what people say)? And how rare is a person of whom ill is spoken and who actually is evil. How can such a one be angry (at what people say)? Still more amazing the person who loves himself on the basis of certainty (about what he knows of himself from personal experience) while detesting people purely on the basis of conjecture about them." One facet of the way of the ancestors in faith is their stern reaction to the love of flattery and the search for praise, to the point that [307] one of them said, "Whoever loves flattery and loathes blame is a hypocrite." ʿUmar said to a man, "Who is the master of your clan?" "I am," he replied. Said ʿUmar, "If you were, you wouldn't have said so." Muḥammad ibn Kaʿb (d.c. 118/736) once wrote down his kinship name, al-Quraẓī. Someone said to him, "Say instead, al-Anṣārī," and he replied, "I am loathe to present to God something I have not done."[155]

(Sufyān) ath-Thawrī said, "If someone were to say to you, 'What a despicable individual you are!' and you became irate, then you would indeed be a despicable person." Someone else said, "You will not cease to have good in you so long as you do not take credit for the good in yourself." Someone asked one of the religious scholars, "What is the telltale sign of a hypocrite?" He replied, "A hypocrite is one whose heart rejoices when praised for something for which the person cannot honestly take credit." Sufyān (ath-Thawrī) used to say, "When you see someone who loves to have all the people love him and detests having even one person mention something negative about him, know that he is a hypocrite." This pertains to God's description of the hypocrites in the word of the Most High, "You will find others who want you and their people to put faith in them" (4:91). It thus behooves those who trust in the people of the Sunna to fear the innovators. This is one of the things that led the Qur'ān reciters, whom the religious scholars censure, into error the way the night steals over the day.

It may be that a deluded, ignorant person will interpret in a distorted fashion the Ḥadīth that has come down, "When someone praises the believer, the faith in his own heart grows," misconstruing its meaning. But Muḥammad said, "the faith grows," not "the believer increases," for the growth of faith is its increase, and its increase occurs as a result of fear and anxiety, over the divine wiles hidden in it and the enticement of it.[156] Herein lies the path of those who possess experiential knowledge in that the lofty faith rises to the loftiest believer. The individual might well rejoice in that before his Master and attribute that faith to his Lord who has entrusted it to him. The individual thus refers the product back to its Maker and contemplates in the creation the One who created it. That thereby becomes praise for the Maker and a description of the Creator, while the individual neither looks upon himself nor marvels at his own qualities. These are the pathways that have been obliterated and whose travelers—apart from those who have received your Lord's compassion—have been cut off.

A chapter on the superiority of this science [of faith and certitude] over the other disciplines, along with a caution against erroneous interpretation of it, and a clarification of what I have been discussing

Know that a hypocrite, an innovator, or a polytheist who learns and teaches might learn by heart and transmit any one of the disciplines, should he or she desire and be motivated to do so, for the sciences are a product of intellect and the fruit of reason. But the knowledge of faith and certitude is the exception, for the manifestation resulting from contemplating it, and the ability to discourse on its inner realities, come only to the believer possessed of certitude. For that manifestation is an increase of faith and the essential spiritual reality of knowledge and faith. It is among the signs of God and His pledge of unveiling His power and grandeur. But the signs of God are not available to the corrupt nor His pledge to the unrighteous. No one who swerves from the truth bears witness to His grandeur and power, nor are they found in the utterances of idle chatterers. For through such deficiencies the signs of God and His manifest decree are taken lightly, His power and proofs are diminished; doubt infiltrates the certitude that is the pilgrim's goal of the sincere and the remnant among God's servants; and falsehood is mistaken for the truth that is the attribute of the veracious, who are the guides to Him and the people God loves. And this is the most telling indicator of the excellence of the knowledge of *maʿrifa* over the other sciences. God said, "Is it not a sign to them that the religious scholars [308] of the children of Israel knew it?" (26:197). And the Most High said, "Indeed these are clear signs in the inmost beings of those to whom knowledge has been granted" (29:49). And He said, "Indeed, in that there are signs for those who pay attention to the evidence" (15:75). And, "We have made the signs clear to those who possess certitude" (2:118). And again, "So that we make it clear to the people who possess knowledge" (6:105).

These are the people who are knowledgeable of God and who speak from God. He has secured for them a portion from Him and a place in His presence. But that is not for those who are not worthy or deserving of what are, in fact, signs of God, His clear proofs, witnesses, and penetrating insights that disclose His Path and bring to light His elucidation—as when the Most High says, "Then We indeed provide an elucidation of it" (75:19). Then the Most High said, "He created the human person and taught him the elucidation" (55:3–4); in addition, there is His word, "Assisting the believers is your duty" (30:47); along with the Most High's word, "And they were indeed deserving and worthy of it" (48:26). So they assist by means of the assistance He gives them, and they are proven true to the degree that He brings them to their full potential, and they give witness to Him on the grounds of what He witnesses to them about Himself. They thus become examples for the god-fearing and a signpost of guidance.

One of the proponents of *maʿrifa* said, "One who does not contemplate this knowledge is not free of polytheism or hypocrisy, for he is devoid of the knowledge of certitude; and in one who is devoid of certitude, the subtle indicators of doubt are evident." One of the mystics said, "I fear an evil end for the person who has no share in this knowledge. And the least portion of it is accepting its authenticity and acknowledging its practitioners." Someone else said, "None of this knowledge will be revealed to anyone disposed toward either innovation or arrogance." A group of its proponents said, "No one who is in love with this world or is addicted to caprice will come to a full realization of this knowledge." Abū Muḥammad Sahl (at-Tustarī) said, "The lightest punishment in store for one who despises this knowledge is that he will never be endowed with any of it."

They are in agreement that it is the knowledge of the veracious ones, and that one who has a share in it is among those who draw near to God above the rank of the Companions of the Right Hand. Know that the knowledge of the divine transcendent unity and the *maʿrifa* of the divine attributes are different from the other sciences. The divergence of views in the exoteric sciences is a mercy, whereas divergence of views in the science of the divine transcendent unity is error and innovation. Being mistaken in outward matters is forgivable and is often a good thing if it involves appropriate striving.[157] Error in the science of the divine transcendent unity and in witnessing to certitude, on the other hand, is infidelity. Moreover, God has not made the realization of the essential truth of knowledge in the quest for exoteric learning incumbent upon His servants. It is, however, incumbent upon them in the quest for conformity with God's view of the divine transcendent unity.

Whoever introduces the slightest innovation will have his innovation work against him and he will be accountable for it. Such a person will not be a proof of God for His servants, nor will he bring beneficial rain to his region. On the contrary, such a person becomes identified with this world as one of those who crave it, and is neither a guide to God, nor one who invites to the religion, nor a model for the god-fearing. In that vein a tradition says, "The learned are the heirs of the Messengers to the degree that they do not engage in worldly activities. So, if they actively engage this world, you must guard your religion from them." A widespread tradition says, "Whoever introduces a novelty that is not part of our religion is to be rejected." A sparsely attested tradition says, "Whoever misleads my community is liable to the curse of God and the angels and all the people." Someone asked, "Messenger of God, what constitutes misleading your community?" He replied, "Introducing an innovation into Islam and imposing it upon the people."[158]

We have received a tradition in which someone asks Jesus, "Who represents the most dangerous threat of temptation to the people?" He answered, "The religious scholar who commits an error, for when such a person slips the whole world slips with him." Our Prophet Muḥammad has passed down to us a comment on the meaning of that, saying, "What I fear most for my community are the religious scholar's error [309] and the debate of hypocrites concerning the Qur'ān." One of the ancestors in faith used to say, "A religious scholar who errs is like a ship that sinks, for many people drown with him; and like an eclipse of the sun, when the people shout, 'O you heedless ones, go to the ritual prayer!'" In other words, this is a sign that makes the generality of people anxious.

Ibn ʿAbbās used to say, "Woe to the scholar because of his following, and woe to the scholar's followers because of the scholar! For when the scholar makes a mistake, a segment of the population follow him in it, and the error makes its way to the horizons." I know of no one who causes a more colossal injury than one who introduces an innovation into the religion of God and who says things God has not permitted concerning the scripture of God and the science of *maʿrifa*. Such a person inflicts such great damage because he disregards the sunnas of God's Messenger that are God's proof to all His creation and the way of those servants of His who are His Friends [or: those who are brought near to Him], thereby leading the servants of God astray.

Comparing a person who introduces innovation into the religion, confiding in authorities other than the scripture and the Sunna, and who has departed from the path of the believers with one who ever seeks increase in worldly affairs and gives free rein to capricious cravings is like comparing one who tyrannizes the people by attacking their lives and property with one who does injustice to himself by committing sins that are between him and his Lord. For the injustices of god-servants are most serious and comprise a register that one cannot disregard.[159] In that category, misrepresenting the religion is the most egregious because it includes injustices with ultimate consequences, namely, cutting off the paths of the believers and effacing the Revealed Law of the Messengers.

Another analogy is that such a person is like one who is guilty of sin but refuses to acknowledge his sinfulness, and who justifies himself to those who sin and who acknowledge their sinfulness and ask forgiveness. These latter are nearer to forgiveness and have greater hope of mercy than the former. Likewise, there is the person who offers excuses for shortcomings or being entirely remiss in deeds and who is not honest with himself, but who nevertheless manifests the inner reality of knowledge and gives good counsel concerning God and His Messenger in the way he elucidates His scripture and discusses his Sunna. Such a person is nearer to a beautiful life-conclusion and more deserving of a successful outcome than the person who uses his authority in the religion of God to introduce into the community innovations that are not in accordance with the scripture and the Sunna. This is tantamount to turning the religious community topsy-turvy and substituting another Revealed Law, for hypocrisy is born in the heart of this individual so that he ends up in hypocrisy.

The person who introduces innovation into the religious community and departs from the path of the authorities compared to the one who does evil to himself with sins is comparable to a person who rebels against the king in the heart of his realm and conspires against him in his sovereignty by overthrowing it, refusing to obey his commands and minimizing the right citizens owe him. One of the sages has said, "There are three things a king ought not forgive: overthrowing the political regime by his subjects; performing deeds that weaken the sovereignty; or undermining one of the king's sacrosanct decrees."

We have received a tradition from the Prophet, "God has an angel who calls out each day, 'Whoever contradicts the Sunna of God's Messenger will not enjoy the benefit of his intercession.'" ʿAlī said, "Being content with one's own opinion is the partner of blindness." And God said, "And who is more veracious than God?" (4:122); and "Who does greater injustice than the one who conjures up a lie about God to mislead the people without their knowing it?" (6:144). Then the Most High said, "(After beginning the verse with a clause very similar to the foregoing)...or who says, 'I have received a prophetic revelation' when nothing has been revealed to him; or who says, 'There has been revealed to me the likes of [310] what God has sent down'" (6:93). God has thus equated lying by uttering a calumny against God with a human being's comparing his qualities to God's and likening his own state to Lordliness. After this egregiously objectionable stance comes repudiating the truth of those who are its proponents and rejecting it as though it were a lie. The Most High has also established an equivalence between declaring the truth a lie, and inventing a lie against the Creator, in His word, "And who does a greater injustice than the person who invents a lie against God or who declares the truth a lie when it comes to him?" (29:68). In a similar vein, the Most High has said, "So who does a greater injustice than the person who invents a lie against God and declares veracity a lie when it comes to him?" (39:32). In the same vein, but by contrast, He established an equivalence between the person who tells the truth and the one who affirms its veracity, when the Most High said, "And the one who brings forth veracity and the one who attests to its veracity—these are the god-fearing" (39:33). God's Messenger said, "The one who possesses knowledge and the one who seeks knowledge are two partners in knowledge." On this subject, Jesus said, "The one who listens is the partner of the speaker."

On the other hand, God has created this faction of those endowed with knowledge of God in order to censure all the factions who produce ecstatic utterances, and the innovators, those who are ignorant of the religion and who deviate from the path of the believers. He has done so by that which He has shown them of certain knowledge and by the testimony of God's Messenger to their knowledge and appropriation, in his saying, "They preserve this knowledge from every disparity that results from those who renounce it, and they protect it from the tampering of the extremists, the false assumptions of the heedless, and the errant interpretations of the ignorant." The extremists are those who make ecstatic utterances, for they overstep knowledge and efface its forms so that they render it amorphous. The heedless are those who introduce innovations with their inflated rhetoric, for they engage in idle disputation in order to refute the truth thereby, fabricate lies with their pretenses, and introduce innovations based on opinion and whim. And the ignorant are those who disavow the marvels of knowledge and are deceived by the superficial understanding they possess. We have received a tradition on this from the Prophet: "There is a type of knowledge that is like a concealed form, which none know but those who possess *maʿrifa* of God. So when they articulate it, the only ones who don't understand it are those who are deluded about God. Do not despise a religious scholar to whom God has given knowledge, for God does not think little of him when He gives it to him."

Anyone who interprets the Ḥadīth according to personal opinion or rational methods, or gives expression to what the ancestors in faith did not teach or discuss before him, is a mindless pretender. Those endowed with knowledge of God respond to the rational sciences by means of the knowledge of certainty, and to science based on personal opinion by means of the knowledge of the Sunna. People of knowledge corroborate the Ḥadīth scholars and shore up the Ḥadīth transmitters.

They analyze the Ḥadīth the transmitters hand on and provide glosses on the Ḥadīths they narrate in ways not accessible to the transmitters themselves, ways that have not been disclosed to the narrators. God has disclosed this to the truly knowledgeable by casting a light into their hearts. He has thereby granted them eloquence, for they speak from God of that which they narrate from Him. "That is a grace of God that He bestows on whom He will" (5:54; 57:21); "And We have appointed examples from among them, offering guidance to Our command, so long as they kept patience and were responsive to Our signs" (32:34).

One of the religious scholars said, "Keeping silent about what the ancestors in faith talked about is estrangement, and discoursing on what the ancestors in faith said nothing about is affectation." Another said, "The truth is heavy: The person who circumvents it does evil; the person who is unable to handle it is weak; and the person who [311] upholds it experiences sufficiency." And ʿAlī said, "Keep to the midmost way, the one to which the loftiest persons return and to which those who proceed along it will be raised."[160]

It was the customary behavior of the ancestors in faith not to give a hearing to an innovator, for such a person is objectionable, and not to refute him with disputation and speculation, because that is an innovation. Instead, they marshaled reports of the Ḥadīths and argued by means of the traditions. If the innovator was receptive, then he was your brother in God, and it was incumbent upon you to befriend him. Otherwise, if he rejected it and became contentious, his very contentiousness was his own loss; he became known by his innovation, the truth of his enmity was evident, [and he was left alone for the sake of God]. This is a road traveled in this time of ours only by those who recognize that it is excellent and that it was the path of the ancestors in faith.

I have received a tradition about Iblīs, that when he had sent his minions out in the time of the Companions and they returned to him exhausted, he asked them, "What's the matter?" They replied, "We've never seen the likes of these people; we couldn't get to them at all, and they badgered us." So he responded, "You have no control over them, for they were Companions of their Prophet, and they witnessed their Lord's revelation. But there will come after them a people from whom you will be able to get what you need." When the Followers came along, Iblīs sent his minions to them, but they returned to him dejected and crestfallen. So he asked, "What's wrong?" They answered, "We've never seen anything as remarkable as these people. We couldn't get to them at all, and even after a little sinning, when the day was over they would begin to seek forgiveness, thus exchanging their evil deeds for good ones." So Iblīs said, "You couldn't get anything out of these people because of the soundness of their acknowledgment of the divine transcendent unity and of their adherence to the Sunna of their Prophet. But after these there will come a people that will delight you. They will be your plaything, and you will lead them around at will by the nose-rein of their passions. If they ask for forgiveness, they will not be forgiven, and they will not repent, so that their evil deeds will replace their good ones." Then, after the first century there came a people among whom wanton passions were widespread. They found innovation attractive, so that they considered it permissible and accepted it as religion. They did not ask forgiveness for it, nor did they repent before God, and thus the devils gained power over them and led them where they would.

Ibn ʿAbbās said, "Error tastes sweet to the hearts of those in error." God said, "They consider their religion a game and a pastime" (6:70). And the Most High said, "What of the person beguiled by the evil of his deeds so that he regards it as good?" (35:8), just as the Most High said, "What of the person who receives a clear indicator from his Lord and to whom a witness from Him recites?" (11:17).

Knowledge, therefore, is the way the righteous ancestors in faith lived, in whose tracks people follow, as well as of those who followed their guidance after them. They are the Companions, the people of tranquility and God's good pleasure, then their Followers in the perfection of their spirituality among the practitioners of asceticism and self-denial. And the truly learned person is the one who calls the people to a spiritual state like his own, until they become like him. When they observe him, then, they practice a detachment from this world like his detachment in it, as Dhū 'n-Nūn used to say, "Sit with one whose action speaks to you, not one whose tongue talks at you." Ḥasan said before him, "Preach to the people with your deeds, not with your words." Abū Muḥammad Sahl (at-Tustarī) said, "Knowledge calls people to action; if someone answers it, fine, and if not, it moves on." We have a tradition about this from God's Messenger in which someone asked him, "Which [312] of our colleagues is the best?" He replied, "The one whose view causes you to be mindful of God, whose discourse increases your knowledge, and whose deeds put you in mind of the next life." The worst of them, on the other hand, is the one who seeks people's worldly interests to the point of becoming like them, and who, when the people see him, they are happy with their own spiritual state. That is so because such a person invites people to himself rather than to his Master, and because he is covetous toward them while they practice asceticism (in relation to him).

The learned ones are thus the heirs of the prophets; they are those who are spiritually reticent in the religion of God and who practice asceticism with respect to the vanities of this world. They speak with the knowledge of certitude and power rather than the knowledge of personal opinion and caprice, and they keep silent about ambiguities and matters of opinion. From the perspective of the learned ones whose testimony comes from God, the latter vain notions will stand against neither the opinion of any speaker nor the word of a mindless windbag, all the way to Resurrection Day. ʿAbd Allāh ibn ʿUmar handed down an apposite saying of the Prophet, "This community's first people will prosper in asceticism and certitude, while its last will be lost in stinginess and vain hope." According to a tradition, "Yūsuf ibn Asbāṭ wrote to Ḥudhayfa al-Marʿashī, 'What do you think about a person who could no longer find anyone with whom he could recollect God without becoming a sinner and having his mutual recollection with that person constitute disobedience, because he could not find anyone worthy of it?' I asked Yūsuf, 'Abū Muḥammad, do you know who they are?' He replied, 'No, they are hidden from us.'"

It is said that the Abdāl are dispersed over all parts of the earth and seek to be hidden from the eyes of the multitude, for they cannot bear to look at the religious scholars of this age, nor do they have the patience to listen to their discourse. The Abdāl regard these scholars as utterly ignorant of God, even though they themselves, and the ignorant, consider them endowed with genuine knowledge. They are thus proponents of ignorance who do not know they are ignorant. Sahl was describing them when he said, "One of the most egregious sins is being ignorant of one's own ignorance." Observing the common throng and listening to the discourse of the heedless is less tedious for the Abdāl (than listening to scholars), for they do not lack that where they are on the outskirts of populated areas. That is because the common throng do not adulterate the religion, nor do they deceive the believers. And they do not claim to be learned, for they seek to learn and are aware of their ignorance. They are thus nearer God's mercy, further from His wrath.

Abū Muḥammad (Sahl at-Tustarī) also used to say, "Hardness of heart resulting from ignorance of knowledge is more serious than hardness resulting from disobedience; the one who is ignorant of knowledge is negligent and makes claims, whereas the one who acts sinfully is aware of that through knowledge." He is saying, in effect, "That is because knowledge is a remedy by which diseases are cured, in that it forestalls the corruption of actions by correcting them. Ignorance, on the other hand, is a malady that corrupts deeds that were once healthy, in that it replaces good actions with evil ones." What a difference there is between that which brings the corrupt to righteousness and that which corrupts what was righteous! God said, "God does not prosper the actions of those who foster corruption" (10:81). And the Most High has said, "We will not disregard the reward of those who bring healing" (7:170). This, then, is one of the most telling indications of the superiority of the deficient learned person over the devoted ascetic. Know that the godservant who is at odds with people with respect to every detail of their spiritual states separates himself from them all and is on familiar terms with none of them. And if he is at variance with the majority of their spiritual states, he is cut off from most of them. And if he distances himself with respect to some of their affairs while others of his own states are consistent with theirs, he mingles with the good people and keeps his distance from the evil people.

[313] A chapter on the various aspects of traditional accounts, with an explanation of the Path of Right Guidance and a discussion of permissiveness and latitude in passing on and reporting traditions

All of the traditions of the Prophet that I have been discussing in this book, as well as those from the Companions and the Followers and their followers, I have set down from memory, narrating them according to their sense. The exceptions are a few lengthy reports that were easily accessible and chanced to become available to me, and those I have transmitted from their sources. In the case of traditions unfamiliar to me, and of which I had no deeper understanding or with which I was not actively concerned, I have relied on God's granting me good success and the power of His support for whatever accuracy and elucidation and authentication there is here. As for the errors, haste, and caprice in my treatment, the inattentiveness and heedlessness are my fault, while the work of Satan is the cause of the hastiness and forgetfulness. In that vein we have a tradition from Ibn Masʿūd concerning a case that he decided according to his personal opinion, and what I have to say is in accord with his view. We have received a Ḥadīth from God's Messenger saying, "Elucidation and verification are from God, while hastiness and forgetfulness are from Satan." In other words, the latter clause means through Satan's interference and the paucity of divine assistance. In general, I have not considered in detail the exact wordings of the reports; on the other hand, I have reproduced the sense in every instance. For I do not consider it necessary to take note of the precise wordings when you adduce the sense, provided you have come to know the inflection of a word and the range of meanings, taking care to avoid any tampering or modification between two variant expressions.[161]

Most of the Companions permitted the quoting of a Ḥadīth according to its sense without reproducing the wording exactly. They included ʿAlī, Ibn ʿAbbās, Anas ibn Mālik, Abū 'd-Dardā', Wāthila ibn al-Asqaʿ (d.c. 83/702), and Abū Hurayra. That was the case with most of the Followers, including the Imām of Imāms Ḥasan al-Baṣrī, then

Shaʿbī, and ʿAmr ibn Dīnār (d. 126/743), Ibrāhīm an-Nakhaʿī, Mujāhid, and ʿIkrima (d.c. 107/725). That has been handed down to us from them in the books of their life stories in variously worded reports. Ibn Sīrīn said, "I have heard a Ḥadīth from ten transmitters, with a single sense but variant wordings." For that reason the Companions differed in the transmission of Ḥadīths from God's Messenger. Some of them transmitted them intact; others adduced the sense; and others preferred an abbreviated version. And still others even interchanged two wordings and regarded that as permissible, so long as that did not miss the point. None, however, committed an outright fabrication, and all of them made authenticity their intent, so that the sense and intent of what they had heard was not subverted. These are the circumstances in which they allowed latitude. They used to say, "It is the one who tells a lie deliberately who bears the responsibility."

We have received a tradition from ʿImrān ibn Muslim, "A man said to Ḥasan (al-Baṣrī), 'Abū Saʿīd, when you transmit a Ḥadīth, you reproduce it more beautifully and with more elegant refinement and more classical pronunciation than we do when we transmit it.' He replied, 'So long as you get the sense right, there's no harm in that.'" Naḍr ibn Shumayl (d.c. 203/819) said, "Hushaym's (ibn Bashīr, d. 183/799) Arabic was inelegant, so I have cloaked his Ḥadīths for you in a lovely veil." In other words, he filled out Hushaym's expression by adding the proper vowel sounds, for Naḍr was a linguist. I, for my part, interject in every item I have transmitted [314] "as has been said," or "words to that effect," or "like this," or "with this sense." Ibn Masʿūd said something like that in his Ḥadīths, and Sulaymān at-Taymī (d. 143/761) used to say that in every Ḥadīth he transmitted.

Sufyān (ath-Thawrī) used to say, "When you see a man focusing intently on the wording of a Ḥadīth in a session, you can be sure he is saying, 'Take notice of me.'" A man began to ask Yaḥyā ibn Saʿīd al-Qaṭṭān (d. 198/813) about the precise wording of an expression in the Ḥadīth, so Yaḥyā replied, "Sir, we can hold in our hands nothing more sublime than the Book of God. It is permissible to recite a word according to any of seven readings, so don't approach it so rigidly." Traditions that have been transmitted to us include some handed down from the Followers[162] and some reports from the followers of the Followers. Among them are some whose chain of transmission has prompted discussion, and often enough, a tradition from the Followers or their followers is more reliable than one whose chain can be traced all the way back to the Prophet, since the custodians of tradition transmitted it.

Guidelines for that spiritual reticence have come to us in the form of several issues.[163] First, we are not certain of a given tradition's falsehood. Second, we have a reason for that spiritual reticence, and it is that we have transmitted and heard the tradition. So if we have erred with respect to what God considers the essential truth, we are free of that burden. As the Jews[164] said, "We bear witness only to what we know and cannot be on guard against matters unseen" when Joseph instructed his brothers to return to their father, Jacob, and say "Your son has committed theft" (12:81).[165] In so doing, they were in error with respect to the ultimate spiritual reality as God sees it, but they were exonerated with respect to the evidence, in that they were eyewitnesses when the gold cup was removed from their brother's traveling sack.

Third, weak traditions are not contradictory to the scripture and the Sunna in such a way that we are bound to reject them. On the contrary, such traditions contain material that points to the sacred sources. Fourth, we are devoted godservants when we uphold a positive opinion of the traditions—indeed, we are forbidden to proliferate suspicion, and we are guilty of sin if we entertain negative views. Fifth, one cannot arrive at the essential truth of that except by way of direct observation, and we are unavoidably obligated to accept without questioning and give our assent to and maintain a positive view of the transmitter. So doing, our hearts will be tranquil about the traditions, our skin will become supple,[166] and we will see that what the traditions have brought is true. In addition, we must acknowledge that our ancestors in faith were superior to us. If we are not to instigate a lie against God's Messenger or the Followers, we can hardly take the view that they who rank above us perpetrated lies.

On the other hand, weak Ḥadīths with sound chains of transmission have indeed come down to us. By the same token it is appropriate that we cite sound Ḥadīths with weak chains of transmission, for it is likely that they will have been transmitted in a reliable fashion, even though we ourselves have not been granted full knowledge of the matter. Alternatively, some transmitters whom some of the Ḥadīth specialists classify as weak others classify as strong. A transmitter, moreover, whom one of the Ḥadīth specialists deprecates and considers blameworthy, another specialist holds in high regard and praises. As a result, there is a divergence of opinions about the transmitter, so that a Ḥadīth of his will not be rejected on the basis of a single citation, absent another tradition that supersedes it or is similar to it.

In addition, it may be that scholars of Ḥadīth classify some transmitters as weak and their Ḥadīths as defective, while the jurists and those who possess knowledge of God see no reason to find them defective or unreliable. Suppose, for example, that a transmitter is unknown because he is rarely attested to as a trusted authority, or has few traditions attributed to him because he has few followers. Another possibility is that a transmitter may be unique in his wording or in his memorization of a Ḥadīth, or in that no other trustworthy transmitter had reported a particular Ḥadīth. Still another possibility is that a transmitter has not cited the Ḥadīth verbatim or was not concerned with studying and memorizing it. One of the memorizers (of Ḥadīth), by contrast, might speak audaciously and recklessly. He might engage in excessive criticism and inflated rhetoric, even though his interlocutor is superior to him and, in the opinion of those who possess knowledge of God, is of a higher rank. As a result, the criticism boomerangs on the critic.

It may also happen that one [315] observes the transmitter wearing a garment, or hears him say something, that the jurists do not consider harmful to his credibility even though some Qur'ān reciters among those who transmit Ḥadīths might fault him for it. Some of those who might impugn his credibility are Ḥadīth specialists, whereas he is one of those who are knowledgeable about the next life and a proponent of *maʿrifa* of God who espouses methods divergent from those of some of the Ḥadīth specialists in transmitting Ḥadīths. As a result, when he engages in Ḥadīth transmission according to his own method, the Ḥadīth specialists constitute no proof against him. On the contrary, he stands as a proof against them, for his own colleagues among the religious scholars regard him as equal to the very Ḥadīth specialists who have impugned his credibility in that they espouse a method other than his.

One of the learned ones said, "A Ḥadīth indeed stands as a testimony that allows ample scope for positive construction, but also allows one to accept a unique witness to it"—that is, under special circumstances such as the testimony of a midwife and the like. Imām Aḥmad ibn Ḥanbal passed along to us an interpretation of that. He explained that so long as neither the scripture nor the Sunna contradicts a Ḥadīth, even if they do not direcly support it, and so long as its interpretation does not depart from the consensus of the community, then one is obliged to accept it and act upon what the Prophet has said. And how else is one to act other than as one has been taught? In my view an inaccurate Ḥadīth bears the marks of personal judgment and analogical reasoning, and this is the approach of Imām Abū ʿAbd Allāh Aḥmad ibn Ḥanbal. When a Ḥadīth has been passed back and forth for two eras, or has been transmitted through three generations, or has made the rounds through a single era without having that era's religious scholars pronounce it objectionable, then it has become generally accepted. As such, no generation of Muslims can declare it objectionable, so that the matter is settled and proven, even if there is some discussion about its chain of transmitters. All of that assumes that the Ḥadīth in question does not contradict the scripture and the authoritative collections of Ḥadīth, or the consensus of the community, and that the testimony of veracious authorities turns up no mendacity on the part of those who transmitted it.

Waqīʿ ibn al-Jarrāḥ (d.c. 196/812) said, "Let no one say, 'This Ḥadīth is worthless,' for the Ḥadīth are more numerous than (what any one individual can master)." According to Abū Dāwūd (as-Sijistānī), Abū Zurʿa ar-Rāzī (d. 268/881) said, "God's Messenger was taken from twenty thousand living persons every one of whom transmitted something from him, whether in the form of a single Ḥadīth or a word or something they had seen. As a result, the Ḥadīth of God's Messenger are too numerous to count." A man referred to a Ḥadīth in the presence of Zuhrī, saying, "We've never heard this one." So Zuhrī inquired, "Have you heard all of the Ḥadīths of God's Messenger ?" "No," the man answered. "How about two-thirds of them?" asked Zuhrī. "No," replied the man. "Half, perhaps?" was the next question, but the man said nothing. So Zuhrī said, "Add this one to the half of them you've already heard."[167]

Imām Aḥmad ibn Ḥanbal said, "Yazīd ibn Hārūn used to take dictation from a man whom he knew to be an inaccurate source, and that is how he became an astute Ḥadīth scholar." Ishāq ibn Rahūya (d. 238/853) said, "Someone asked Imām Aḥmad ibn Ḥanbal, 'Do you think we should take down only the best parts of these beneficial things that also contain objectionable material?' He answered, 'What is objectionable will always be objectionable.' Someone asked, 'What about inaccurate reports?' He replied, 'One needs them now and then.'" It was as if he did not consider it detrimental to record them. According to Abū Bakr al-Marwazī (d. 275/888), Ibn Ḥanbal said, "We need Ḥadīths even from inaccurate reporters." One of the hallmarks of his method with respect to the latitude of Ḥadīths is that he put forth all of his Ḥadīths that he reported in the *Musnad,* from which our shaykhs have passed them along to us through Ibn Ḥanbal's son ʿAbd Allāh, without taking special note of the sound material there. As a result, it contains numerous Ḥadīths that the critics know are inaccurate, and, indeed, Ibn Ḥanbal himself had a clearer knowledge of their inaccuracy than the critics. Even so, he published them in his *Musnad,* because he wanted to underscore the fully supported traditions. It was not his intent to establish the soundness of the chains of transmission, so he considered it permissible to transmit them as he had heard them. He ceased to transmit Ḥadīths to the people in the year 228/842 [316] and died in the year 241/855. During that period no one heard any reports from him but his son, ʿAbd Allāh, and then, for a short interval also Ibn Māniʿ, after the intercession of his grandfather Aḥmad ibn Māniʿ (d. 244/859).

According to a Ḥadīth transmitted to us from him, that is Imām Aḥmad (Ibn Ḥanbal), "ʿAbd ar-Raḥmān (ibn Mahdī) pronounced a Ḥadīth unacceptable, then after a while he came out to us and said, 'It is sound. I found it.' He said, 'As far as Wakīʿ is concerned, he did not declare any Ḥadīth objectionable, but, when asked about one, he would say "I did not memorize it."'" We have received a Ḥadīth from the son of the sister of ʿAbd ar-Raḥmān ibn Mahdī, saying, "My uncle would scratch out Ḥadīths and then proceed to call them sound, and I recited them with him. When I observed, 'But you scratched them out!' he would say, 'Yes, but then I reconsidered, and when I have declared them inaccurate, I have in effect maligned the good reputation of the one who transmitted them. So when he sits knee-to-knee with me before God and asks, "Why did you impugn my good name? Have you seen me or heard me speak?" I will have no rejoinder.'" This was the approach of the spiritually reticent among the ancestors in faith. One of them used to say, "We quit the sessions of Shuʿba because he used to lead us into gossip, for his discourse tended toward pronouncing on the inaccuracy of Ḥadīth transmitters." Concerning the practice of declaring Ḥadīth transmitters imprecise, one of them said, "When your intention is sincere, that is, when you are focused on God and the religion, it is neither in your favor nor against you."

These specific issues that I have been discussing are the principles of intimate familiarity with the Ḥadīth. It is a knowledge for those worthy of it, and a path on which they journey. Then a people appeared who were neither endowed with a knowledge in which they specialized, nor characterized by a spiritual relationship to knowledge, nor dedicated to a demanding piety that set them apart. So they fashioned for themselves a knowledge that kept them busy, and they provided a distraction for those who listened to them. They composed books and began to discourse on deficiencies of the transmitters of traditions and the continuing succession of scholarly error. When (the pseudo-scholars) saw themselves discredited (in the act of narrating Ḥadīths), they opened a path for the innovators leading to the rejection of the Ḥadīths and traditions and the preference of personal opinion and rational methods over (the traditions). They also eagerly desired analogical reasoning and speculation when they became aware of (the rational scholars') renunciation of the Sunna and traditions, as in this time of yours. And the Ḥadīths about longing for the next life and self-denial in this world, about dread at the threat of God, about the merits of pious deeds, and about the superiority of the Companions, ought to be received and accepted in every situation, whether imperfect in their chains of transmission or traceable all the way back to the Prophet, and neither second-guessed nor rejected. The same goes for Ḥadīths about the terrors of the Day of Resurrection and the description of its cataclysm and calamities. No one should despise them on the basis of rational inquiry but should instead receive them with assent and surrender, for that is how the ancestors in faith behaved. *ʿIlm* leads to none other than that, and its principles rest on that.

We have received a tradition that says, "If an individual receives a grace from God or His Messenger and acts upon it, God gives him a reward for that even if it is something that has not actually been said." And according to another tradition, "If someone relates the truth from me, I say it even if I never actually said it. But if someone relates a lie about me, I do not speak lies."

With regard to all that I have laid out in this book, I say, God is most knowledgeable and wise. His knowledge is foremost and the inner truths of all forms of knowledge He knows. All matters return to Him. What God wills, comes to be, and it is from Him we seek aid. There is no power except in God. This, then, is the end of the Book of Knowledge, with its analysis of the disciplines, its description of the way of the ancestors in faith, and its presentation of the innovations introduced subsequently.

4

ʿAlī ibn ʿUthmān Hujwīrī: *The Revelation of Realities Veiled (Kashf al-maḥjūb)*

In this first major Sufi work in Persian, Hujwīrī sets his whole discussion of the spiritual life on the foundation of ʿilm. *Then, as he maps out the path toward the upper reaches of mystical attainment, he discusses* maʿrifa *as the first of a series of veils to be lifted for the seeker. Hujwīrī often quotes the Arabic of famous authorities and then glosses in Persian: I have indicated those texts with an asterisk (*) but have not included his gloss except when it amounts to significantly more than a simple, literal rendering of the Arabic original.*[1]

Chapter 1: Affirming *ʿIlm*

[11] God describes possessors of knowledge with the words, "Indeed, those among His servants who possess knowledge fear God" (35:28). And the Prophet said, "The quest for knowledge is required of every Muslim." He also said, "Seek knowledge even as far as China." But the expanse of acquired knowledge is vast and life is brief. People are therefore not required to pursue all the branches of learning, such as astronomy and medicine and mathematics and the fine arts, and the like, except insofar as any one of these branches of learning is relevant to the fulfillment of the Revealed Law. For example, astronomy provides knowledge of time for night prayer; medicine, of possible impediments;[2] and numerical calculation augments knowledge of inheritance

law and the proper interval for a divorced woman to refrain from remarrying.[3] In other words, acquired knowledge is religiously enjoined to the degree that correct action depends on it. God censured those who acquire worthless knowledge when He said, "They learned what hurt them, not what benefited them" (2:102). And the Messenger referred to this when he said, "I seek refuge with You from useless knowledge." Understand that a little knowledge can yield a great deal of action, and knowledge and action must always be connected, as the Prophet said, "The devotee who lacks understanding of religious law is like a donkey bound to a millstone."* Devotees without understanding of religious law are like donkeys working a mill, because the jackass continually [12] retraces its steps and never gets anywhere.

A group among the common folk rate knowledge above action; others rank action over knowledge. Both sides are mistaken, for there can be no action without knowledge of action. Only when action is conjoined with knowledge does it merit compensation. For example, ritual prayer performed without knowledge of the principles of purification and ablution, along with an awareness of the *qibla* direction and of how to form one's intention—the pillars of ritual prayer—would not be ritual prayer as such.[4] Therefore, since action and knowledge of action are intimately connected, how can the ignorant person consider knowledge separate from action? And as for those who rank knowledge over action, that is equally absurd, because knowledge apart from action is not really knowledge. ["As God says, 'One faction of those who had been given the Book of God threw it behind their backs as though they did not know' (2:101), thereby denying the designation 'knowledgeable' to those who know without acting on what they know."] That is so because learning, memorizing, and retaining in memory are also all actions for which a person will reap the ultimate reward.

But if such a person did not join that knowledge to deeds and the accomplishment of actions, no reward would be forthcoming. These are views held by two groups of people. One of them associates knowledge with lofty reputation, for they are unable to express it in action and arrive at the full realization of knowledge. The other separates action from knowledge because they have neither knowledge nor action. Thus, one ignorant person says that talk *(qāl)* is not necessary whereas a spiritual condition *(ḥāl)* is, while another ignorant one claims that knowledge is necessary and action is superfluous.

A story is told of how Ibrāhīm ibn Adham said, "I saw a rock along the path and on that stone was written, 'Turn me over and read.' I turned it over and saw that on it was written 'You do not take action on what you know, so why go looking for what you do not know?'"* (Adding in gloss: It is impossible to look for what you do not know.) [13] In other words, be attentive to what you know so that you will know the blessings of the unknown as well. Anas ibn Malīk said, "The main concern of the learned is knowledge, that of fools is relating traditions." That is how the ignorant are distinguished from the learned. One who seeks status and worldly power through knowledge is not a learned person, for the quest for status and worldly power is a preoccupation of the ignorant. No rank among the levels of spiritual attainment equals or surpasses that of knowledge, for in none of them can one become aware of the subtle mysteries of God. *ʿIlm* is thus the essence of all the spiritual stations and is consistent with the evidence of experience and high degrees of spiritual attainment.

Understand that *ʿilm* is of two kinds: the one is the knowledge of God and the other that of human beings. As for human knowledge, it is of no consequence in comparison with God's knowledge, for that is an attribute of God and thus subsists in Him whose attributes are without end. Our knowledge, on the other hand, is an attribute of ours and thus subsists in us, whose attributes are finite. According to God's words, "We have passed on to you only a little knowledge" (17:85), and in general, knowledge is a praiseworthy characteristic. *Knowledge* can be defined as "comprehension and elucidation of the thing known," but the best definition of *ʿilm* is "an attribute by which the Eternal becomes a knower." God has said, "And God comprehends the unbelievers" (2:19), and again, "And God is knowledgeable of all things" (2:282). His knowledge is one through which He knows all things both existent and nonexistent. Human beings have no part in this knowledge, for it is indivisible and inseparable from God. The indication of His knowledge is in the way He plans His acts, for action necessitates knowledge in the agent. God's knowledge reaches into the deepest secrets and encompasses all that is apparent. A seeker must act always while contemplating God, since he knows that God is aware of him and his every act.

A story is told of how an important citizen of Basra entered one of his gardens when he caught sight of [14] the gardener's lovely wife. He sent the man on an errand and told the woman, "Close the gate." "I have closed every gate," she replied, "but there is one I am unable to close." The man asked, "Which gate is that?" She answered, "The gate that stands between us and God." At that the man felt ashamed and sought forgiveness.

Ḥātim al-Aṣamm[5] said, "Of all things knowable in this world, I have selected four as worthy objects of knowledge and dismissed the rest." Someone asked, "Which four?" He answered, "First, I know that I have responsibilities to God that I alone can fulfill and have occupied myself with that. Second, I know that my sustenance has been apportioned to me and that my coveting more will not augment it, so I have given up seeking an increase. Third, I know that there is one stalking me—namely, Death—whom I cannot outrun, so I am preparing myself for him. Fourth, I know that God is scrutinizing me so that I feel shame before Him and cease to do what is inappropriate." When the servant knows that God is observing, he will not do something that would cause him shame before God on the last day.

ʿIlm must encompass God's commands and the experiential knowledge of Him. Required of the servant is knowledge of the spiritual moment[6] and of the external and internal aspects[7] of the religious law that are directly related to time. This includes two parts, one relating to principles and the other to practice.[8] The external aspect of the part concerning principles involves articulating the profession of faith, while its internal aspect involves the full realization of experiential knowledge. The external aspect of the part relevant to practice has to do with proper devotional acts, while the internal aspect concerns formulating a sound intention. Observance of one without the other of these aspects is impossible. Divorced from the internal aspect, the external aspect of ultimate reality is hypocrisy, [15] while the internal aspect of ultimate reality divorced from the external is heresy. The external meaning of the Revealed Law without the internal is incomplete, just as spirituality without its outward consequences is useless.

There are three pillars of the knowledge of ultimate reality: first, knowledge of the essence and oneness of God, along with the repudiation of likening anything to His pure essence; second, knowledge of the divine attributes and decrees; third, knowledge of God's deeds and wisdom. Knowledge of the Revealed Law also has three foundations: first, the Qur'ān; second, the Sunna; third, the consensus of the community. Proof of knowledge lies in the affirmation of the essence and pure attributes and deeds of God, according to God's words, "Therefore know that there is no god but God" (47:19); and again, "Know therefore that God is your protector" (8:40); and "Do you not see how your Lord lengthens the shadows?" (25:45); and "Do they not observe how the camels have been fashioned?" (88:17). There are many other texts like these that refer to observing God's deeds and holiness. As for knowledge of the deeds of the Agent through His attributes, the Prophet has said, "When a person knows that God is his Lord and that I am his Prophet, God forbids that person's flesh and blood to the Fire." The condition for knowledge of the essence of God is that the individual must have attained the use of reason and be past puberty, and must also acknowledge that God is in essence an eternally existent being, is unlimited and undefinable, is not conditioned by place or direction, does not cause evil through His essence, is unlike any of His creatures, has no female consort and no offspring, and is the fashioner and preserver of everything that the imagination can picture or mind can conceive, as in the words, "There is nothing like unto Him and He is the all-hearing and all-seeing" (42:11).

As for knowledge of the divine attributes, one must understand that God's qualities exist within Him but are neither identical with Him nor individual parts of Him but subsist in Him and through Him eternally. These include knowledge, power, life, will, [16] hearing, sight, speech, among others, as in the Most High's words, "Truly He is knowledgeable of what is in the inmost beings" (8:43); and "God is powerful over all things" (59:6); and "He is the living one, there is no other God but He" (40:65); and "He is the all-hearing, the all-seeing" (42:11); and "He does what He wishes" (11:107); and (His words are) "the words of the Truth" (6:73). Knowledge based on the affirmation of God's deeds means understanding that the Most High and Holy One is the creator of human beings and of their actions, who brought the world from nothingness into existence by His action and is the disposer of good and evil and creator of all that profits and harms, as, in His words, "God is the creator of every thing" (13:16).

The indicator of your affirmation of the requirements of the Revealed Law is that you understand that it is from God that the Messengers have come to us with evidentiary miracles that contravene customary understandings, that our Messenger Muḥammad the Chosen One is an authentic messenger to whom many evidentiary miracles were granted, and that the news he has brought us about the unseen and visible worlds alike is entirely true. The first pillar of the Revealed Law is the scripture, according to God's word, "Among its verses are those of firm meaning" (3:7). Second comes the Sunna, according to the Most High's word, "So take what the Messenger gives you and refrain from what he forbids for you" (59:7). Third is the consensus of the community, in accord with the Ḥadīth, "My community will not concur on an error, and it is incumbent upon you to act with the great majority." All told, the requirements of the ultimate reality are many, and if any person wanted to encompass them all, he or she would not be able to do so, for there is no end to the subtle mysteries of God.

There is a heretical faction—may God curse it—known as the Sophists, who hold that one cannot know anything and that even knowledge itself is nonexistent. To them I say, "Is your contention that nothing can be known, correct or not?" If they say, "It is correct," they affirm the existence of knowledge. If they say, "It is not," then it is ridiculous [17] to argue against a false assertion, and anyone who agrees with them is not wise. A heretical faction that has links to this Path of Sufism likewise claims that nothing can be accurately known, and that therefore its repudiation of our knowledge is more perfect than the affirmation of it. Its position derives from foolishness, error, and ignorance, for the repudiation of knowledge can only come from either knowledge or ignorance. However, since knowledge cannot deny knowledge nor be its own opposite, it is impossible for knowledge to repudiate knowledge. Therefore, repudiation of knowledge comes from reprehensible ignorance, and ignorance is analogous to falsehood and unbelief, since truth and ignorance have nothing in common.

This view is inimical to the common agreement of shaykhs. However, since people have heard of this opinion and subscribed to it, they say that it is the opinion and the way of acting of Sufis in general. They have therefore persisted to the point that their belief has become hopelessly confused, failing to discern truth from falsehood. I, for my part, commend to God the whole matter of their wandering in error. Should religious faith seize them, they would practice Sufism better than they do. They would treat it more justly, and have a better opinion of the Friends of God, paying greater attention to their own unresolved business. Even if certain heretical groups associate themselves with the spiritually liberated for the purpose of cloaking their own vileness with the beauty of the Sufis and living in the shadow of their glory, why should people infer that they are of the same persuasion, concluding that it is acceptable to look down on them and consider them disreputable?

[According to one author,] someone who [18] made a conceited show of learning and dedicated adherence to the Sunna of the Messenger, but who in reality was one of Satan's helpers who disputed the way of proceeding of the imāms, came among us Sufis and said, "Of the twelve heretical factions, one is in the midst of those who call themselves Sufis." I answered, "If one (heretical) faction is theirs (that is, the Sufis'), the eleven others are yours; and the Sufis can police their own ranks against one more ably than you can defend yourselves against eleven." All of this is the result of the religious lassitude of this age and the calamities that are currently manifesting themselves. God, however, continues to conceal His Friends from the rabble and to keep them sequestered from the generality of humankind. That supreme spiritual guide and Sun of the Seekers, ʿAlī ibn Bundār aṣ-Ṣayrafī (d. 359/969–70), put it well when he said, "The corruption of human hearts matches that of the age and its people."

In the next section I deal with some of the Sufis' sayings, in the hope of catching the attention of those among this group who remain unconvinced but toward whom God remains solicitous. Success, however, belongs to God alone.

Muḥammad ibn al-Faḍl al-Balkhī[9] says, "There are three types of *ʿilm:* knowledge from God; knowledge with God; and knowledge of God." Knowledge of God means knowledge that involves the experiential awareness of God by which His [Prophets and] Friends know Him. They have access to this tutelage and intimate familiarity with Him not through normal channels of human experience, since such means are not directly connected to God. The individual's knowledge does not effect the experiential connection to God; rather, God grants experiential knowledge through His guidance and way signs. Knowledge from God is knowledge of the Revealed Law that He has enjoined and required of His servants. Knowledge with God is the knowledge of the stations of God's Path and an elucidation of the levels of the Friends of God. *Maʿrifa* cannot be complete apart from acknowledgment of the Revealed Law [19], but the practice of the Revealed Law is not mature apart from the manifestation of the spiritual stations.

Abū ʿAlī Thaqafī says, "*ʿIlm* is the life of the heart over against the death of ignorance, and the light of the eye of certainty over against the darkness of infidelity."* The heart of everyone who lacks the knowledge of the intimate awareness of God is dead in its ignorance, and the heart of everyone uncommitted to the Revealed Law suffers the illness of failure to know. The hearts of unbelievers are dead because they know not God, and the hearts of the heedless are sick because they know not His sacred injunctions.

Abū Bakr Warrāq of Tirmidh says, "One who is content with debating questions of knowledge apart from asceticism is engaging in religiously wayward thinking *(zandaqa)*, and one who is content with knowledge of the law apart from spiritual reticence becomes corrupt."* Everyone who settles for defining the knowledge of the affirmation of God's transcendent unity and does not pay attention to its opposite becomes a *zindīq;* and everyone who settles for knowledge of the Revealed Law and *fiqh* without spiritual reticence becomes corrupt. In other words, assertion of the divine unity and transcendence apart from religious action and spiritual struggle is tantamount to predestination. Therefore, one who attests to the divine unity and transcendence should affirm God's omnipotence while acting as one who exercises moral choice, thereby standing between divine power and human free will. This is the gist of what that spiritual guide meant when he said, "Assertion of the divine unity and transcendence is beneath predestination but above free will." Thus, anyone who considers the affirmation sufficient without religious action is a *zindīq*, for action is a requirement for the fulfillment of religious law and fear of God. Whoever becomes preoccupied with lax interpretation and is infatuated with anthropomorphism, and circumvents the teaching of those authorized to interpret the law in order to ease his own burden, falls into corruption. All of these are manifestations of heedlessness.

Yaḥyā ibn Muʿādh of Rayy said appropriately, "Eschew the company of three types of people: heedless religious scholars, hypocritical mendicants, and ignorant pseudo-Sufis." The heedless religious scholars are those who have made this world their hearts' *qibla* and [20] chosen the path of ease, bowing before sultans. They have turned royal audience halls into their places of circumambulation and have made the adulation of other people into their *miḥrābs*.[10] In their vanity they are beguiled into congratulating themselves on their theological disputation, criticizing the authorities and masters and overwhelming the religious leaders with the opinions they pile up. They are so preoccupied that if you were to weigh the two worlds on a scale, it would not attract their attention! They have made ire and envy their teaching. In the final analysis, none of this is genuine knowledge, for knowledge is a characteristic rejected by the likes of these in their ignorance.

As for the hypocritical mendicants,[11] they praise whatever anyone else does in accord with their preference, even if it is foolish, and condemn whatever anyone else does in contradiction to their whim, even if it is authentic. They cultivate people's favor with their religious behavior and hypocrisy in accord with the people's folly.

Finally, the ignorant Sufi pretenders are those who have never sought the companionship of a spiritual guide, nor learned proper demeanor from an influential Sufi, nor tasted the rebuke of time. Still they blindly don the blue (Sufi) garb, thrusting themselves into the midst of the Sufis, and cavalierly set out on the path of levity in their company. Such a person's lack of understanding makes him think that they are all like himself, and the path of true and false becomes confused for him. Let the seeker, therefore, be mindful and advised to steer clear of the company of these three groups to which that successful one (Yaḥyā ibn Muʿādh) referred; the gist of his comment was that they are all false in their claims and incomplete in their practice.

Abū Yazīd Bisṭāmī says, "I gave myself over to spiritual struggle for thirty years, but I found nothing [21] more difficult than the pursuit of knowledge."* Walking on fire is, on the whole, more congenial to human nature than conformity to knowledge. A foolish heart would sooner cross the bridge that spans Hellfire's chasm a thousand times than engage a single matter of knowledge. A corrupt person would prefer to camp out in Hell rather than practice a single thing learned. Therefore, you must seek comprehensive knowledge, even though, when compared to God's knowledge, that amounts to ignorance. You must have sufficient understanding to realize that you lack knowledge. In other words, human beings are capable only of human knowledge, but humanity is the heaviest veil between a human being and God. A poet says in this connection:

Inability to attain understanding is itself understanding,
But getting stuck on the paths of the righteous is idolatry.

A person who refuses to learn and holds fast to his ignorance is an idolater, but when an individual does learn and approaches the perfection of knowledge, the inner meaning becomes apparent. That person realizes that his knowledge is but a lack of capacity to know what destiny awaits him: knowing the names of things does not change their reality. The person's incapacity to attain knowledge is therefore itself the attainment of knowledge, and God's is the greatest knowledge of all.

Chapter 15: Drawing Back the First Veil: Experiential Knowledge of God

[341] God has said, "And they do not measure God's expansiveness accurately" (6:91). The Prophet said, "If you knew God experientially, you would walk on the seas, and mountains would disappear at your bidding." *Maʿrifa* of God [342] is of two kinds: one is discursive *(ʿilmī)* and the other affective *(ḥālī)*. Discursive *maʿrifa* is the basis of every good thing in this world and the next; knowledge of God is the most important condition in all spiritual moments and states. God

has said, "I did not create jinns and human beings except to serve Me" (51:56), that is, so that they would know Me experientially.* Most people, however, ignore this state of affairs, except those whom God has chosen and led forth from the darkness of this world, and whose hearts He himself has brought to life with His own presence, according to the word of the Most High, "He made for him a light by which he might walk among the people" (6:122)—alluding to a life "like one in profound darkness" (6:122 cont.), by which he meant Abū Jahl.[12]

Maʿrifa is the life of the heart through God, and the innermost being's refusal to attend to anything but God. Each individual's value is in experiential knowledge, and whoever lacks experiential knowledge is worthless. Religious scholars and jurists and others call sound conceptual knowledge about God *maʿrifa,* but the Sufi shaykhs reserve the term *maʿrifa* to refer to affective integrity in relation to God. It follows that they consider *maʿrifa* superior to *ʿilm,* since affective integrity presupposes sound discursive knowledge. Sound conceptual knowledge is not affective integrity, so that one cannot possess experiential knowledge without sound conceptual knowledge of God. But one can possess discursive knowledge without possessing experiential knowledge. Members of these two groups who have been unaware of the aforementioned two types of "knowledge" have become embroiled in unprofitable debate, one faction repudiating the views of the other.

Let me now unveil the mystery of this situation in a way that both factions, God willing, might find helpful.

Understand that there is considerable divergence of views concerning the experiential knowledge of God and sound traditional knowledge of Him. The Muʿtazila claim that *maʿrifa* of God is intellectual [343] and that it is proper only to a rational individual. Such a claim is flimsy, given that insane persons within the Abode of Islam are judged to possess *maʿrifa,* and that children who have not attained the age of reason are judged to possess faith. If, therefore, *maʿrifa* were an intellectual quality, people like these could not be judged to possess *maʿrifa* since they lack rationality, nor could unbelievers be judged guilty of unbelief if they possessed reason. If rationality were the cause of *maʿrifa,* one would have to conclude that every rational person possessed *maʿrifa* and that everyone lacking rationality was ignorant of God, but that is clearly absurd.

One faction claims that the cause of *maʿrifa* of God is demonstrative argument, and that only those who engage in deductive reasoning attain *maʿrifa*. This argument's weakness is that Iblīs witnessed many divine signs, including Heaven and Hell, and the divine Throne and Footstool, but these did not bring about *maʿrifa* in him. As the Most High said, "Even if We were to send them angels and the dead were to speak to them, and We were to bring together all things before them, they would not believe except as God willed" (6:111).* If the vision of divine signs and demonstrative proof of them were the cause of *maʿrifa*, then, in the above scriptural verse, God would have pointed to that, rather than to His own will, as the cause of *maʿrifa*.

Sunni Muslims regard soundness of intellect and the vision of divine signs as a means to *maʿrifa* but not its cause; that cause is none other than God's favor, kindness, and will. Lacking the divine favor, the intellect is blind, for by itself intellect is ignorant even of itself and cannot know the reality of other intellects. Since it does not know even itself, how [344] can it know something other than itself? Without divine favor, demonstrative proof and reflection on the vision of divine signs are all inaccurate, for whimsical people and sundry heretical factions rely on demonstrative proof but most of them do not possess *maʿrifa*.

As for those privy to the divine favor, however, all their spiritual movements are indications of *maʿrifa*. When they pursue demonstrative proof, they are searching, and when they leave demonstrative proof aside, they are surrendering to God. But with respect to sound *maʿrifa*, surrender to God does not take precedence over searching. Abandoning the quest is not an acceptable principle, and surrender to God is a principle in which no anxiety is appropriate, but the spiritual reality of these two is not *maʿrifa*. Understand that in the final analysis there is no center-expanding[13] guide for the individual except God in the face of all that the wrongdoers say. Neither intellect nor rational proofs are capable of guiding the individual, and there is no demonstrative proof clearer than the fact that God has said, "For if they were brought back, they would surely revert to what had been forbidden them" (6:28). That is,* if the unbelievers were brought back into this world, they would still act on the basis of their infidelity.

When someone asked ʿAlī, Commander of the Faithful, about experiential knowledge, he replied, "I gained experiential knowledge of God through God, and of that which is other than God through the light of God."* God fashioned the body and entrusted its life to the soul; He fashioned the heart and entrusted its life to Himself. Therefore, since neither intellect nor human judgment have the power to give life to the body, neither can they give life to the heart, as God has said, "or one who was dead and whom We brought back to life…" (6:122). He has thus entrusted all life to Himself, as when He continued in the same verse, "and for whom We have made a light by which he might walk among humankind." In other words, "I am the creator of the light that illumines the faithful one." He also said, "What of the one whose spiritual center God has expanded toward surrender and so toward receiving light from his Lord?" (39:22). He has taken charge of the unfolding of the heart Himself, and [345] its closure as well, as He has said, "God seals their hearts and their hearing" (2:7), and, again, "Pay no heed to any person whose heart we have allowed to stint in remembering Us" (18:28).

It follows, thus, that since it is He who contracts and expands, seals and amplifies the heart, it would be impossible for the heart to recognize any other guide than Him. For all that is not God is a cause or a means, and anything that proceeds from cause and means cannot show the way apart from the providence of the One who creates the means—without God's favor it is a veil and a highway robber rather than a guide.[14] The Most High has said, "But God has made the faith dear to you and has made it attractive to your hearts" (49:7). He has thus associated beautification and endearment with Himself, and the requirement of the reverential fear that is essential to intimate knowledge is from Him. They who are so obliged, since they are under the obligation, cannot choose (either) to reject it or undertake it. As a result, in the absence of God's tutelage, human beings' share of *maʿrifa* of Him will be none other than their incapacity to know Him.

Abū 'l-Ḥasan Nūrī says, "There is no guide to God apart from Him, for one seeks knowledge in the performance of service."* Apart from God, hearts have no guide to *maʿrifa*; let them seek knowledge to render service, not the soundness of *maʿrifa*. No creature has the capability of taking anyone else to God. People who use demonstrative proofs are no more rational than Abū Ṭālib,[15] nor was there a guide greater than Muḥammad. Even so, since it was the foreordained lot of

Abū Ṭālib to come to an unfortunate end, Muḥammad's guidance was of no use to him.

In demonstrative proof one first turns away from God, since demonstrative proof requires one to focus on something else; but the essence of intimate knowledge is turning away from all that is not God. Ordinarily one searches for objects of knowledge through demonstrative proof, but intimate knowledge of God goes against the grain. As a result, intimate knowledge of God is impossible apart from endless intellectual perplexity. One does not receive the divine favor by a process of human acquisition. Without God's graces and kindnesses [346] the individual has no guidance—that comes from revelations to hearts and from the treasuries of the unseen realms. Everything other than God is created in time. It stands to reason that while a contingent being might come to its own kind, it cannot arrive at the ontological status of its own Creator. For a being that "acquires" another must be of a higher order than the one acquired, so that the one acquired is overcome. The marvel here is not that evidence of an act leads the intellect to affirm the existence of the agent, but that by the light of God the heart denies its own existence. In the former instance, the resulting realization is discursive, in the latter, affective.

The faction that considers intellect to be the cause of *maʿrifa* should ask itself what aspect of *maʿrifa* it is that reason establishes in the heart, since whatever reason affirms, *maʿrifa* can only deny. In other words, God is the opposite of whatever image of Him reason constructs in the heart. And if the image of God that reason fashions is different from God's reality, how can intellect attain *maʿrifa* through demonstrative proof? Since reason and imagination are of the same genus, and since the affirmation of genus negates *maʿrifa*, any affirmation [of the existence of God] from demonstrative proof amounts to anthropomorphism and any denial of God amounts to a denial of divine attributes.[16] It is impossible for intellect to transcend these two opposite principles, both of which are sheer ignorance from the perspective of *maʿrifa*, since those who adhere to either of these views do not proclaim God's transcendent unity.

Once intellect has reached its limit, and the [347] hearts of God's Friends have no remedy other than their quest, they take repose in the courtyard of helplessness, bereft of resources. But they become restless in their repose, raising their hands in a plea for help as they seek a balm for their hearts. When they have exhausted their own power to continue the quest, the power of God becomes their power. In other words, they find the way from Him to Him, experience relief from the anguish of separation, and find rest in the garden of intimacy, nestled in perfect refreshment and joy. When intellect saw that the hearts had achieved their desire, it searched in vain for mastery and did not find it. Intellect was left behind and became perplexed, and in its perplexity and agitation it lost its power to act. At that point God clothed the intellect in the garb of service and said to it, "When you relied on your own resources, your attempts to do so kept you behind a veil; but when your resources vanished, you were left behind, and in your being left behind you arrived at the goal."

Nearness to God is therefore the heart's portion, while that of the intellect is service. God supplies the individual infused knowledge of God by His tutelage and instruction, so that the individual knows God through Him rather than as a result of human faculties. This is a knowledge in which the existence of the human being is merely borrowed, so that for the existence of one endowed with intimate knowledge, narcissism is a betrayal, and the individual's remembrance of God is incessant, his labor unstinting, and his experiential knowledge becomes a spiritual condition rather than a mere claim.

Yet another faction claims that *maʿrifa* is a matter of inspiration. Again, this is not possible, because experiential knowledge is based on the ability to distinguish falsehood from truth, whereas those who appeal to inspiration do not provide a sound criterion for distinguishing wrong from right. Suppose one person claimed, "I know by inspiration that God does not occupy a place," while another argued, "Inspiration tells me that God does have a place." One of these two contradictory claims [348] must be true and the other false, but both appeal to inspiration. One needs to distinguish between truth and falsehood with respect to these two claims, and that requires evidence. Thus, the argument for inspiration is folly. This is a view espoused by Brahmans and inspirationists, and I have known some people who have taken the position to extremes while associating their work with the views of religious people. These people, however, are entirely in error and their opinions are at odds with (all) rational people, unbelievers and Muslims alike. As a result, if ten proponents of inspiration put forth ten contradictory opinions concerning the same issue, all are equally mistaken and not one gets it right. If someone were to say that anything at odds with the Revealed Law is not inspiration, I would respond that the view was inherently mistaken and ill-conceived. For if one evaluates and affirms inspiration in relation to Revealed Law, then intimate knowledge derives from the Revealed Law, prophethood, and divine guidance rather than from inspiration. Consequently, the issue of inspiration in relation to *maʿrifa* is moot.

Another group has claimed that *maʿrifa* of God is necessary.[17] That, too, is impossible, for it would imply that rational human beings would have to be in agreement on what they know. But we observe that certain reasonable people willfully deny and disavow the truth by holding teachings of anthropomorphism or denial of divine attributes, proving that intimate knowledge is not innate. In addition, if intimate knowledge of God were innate, the concept of religious duty would be meaningless. For obligation in *maʿrifa* in relation to things known as necessary, such as the self, the heavens and the earth, day and night, pain and pleasure, and the like, is an absurdity; no rational person can doubt [349] these things, for there is great need to know them, and even one who preferred not to know them would be incapable of doing so. There is, however, a faction of would-be Sufis who, reflecting on the soundness of their certitude, claim, "We know God innately." Since they have not the slightest doubt in their hearts, they call their certitude necessity. They are not mistaken about the meaning of their claim, but their mode of expression is faulty. Knowledge of that which is necessary cannot be the sole possession of an elite but belongs to all rational beings. Moreover, innate knowledge would be evident in the hearts of lovers without a secondary cause, while discursive knowledge of God, as well as intimate knowledge of Him, must be a result of some cause.

However, the master Abū ʿAlī Daqqāq[18] and Shaykh Abū Sahl [Suʿlūkī] (d. 369/980) and his father, who was an authoritative teacher at Nishapur, hold that the inception of *maʿrifa* is based on demonstrative proof but that its end is intuitive, just as one initially acquires a knowledge of devotional actions, a knowledge that eventually becomes necessary. Some Sunni Muslims put it this way: "Don't you see that in Paradise knowledge of God becomes necessary, so that what is necessary there should be necessary here as well? In this world, too, when the prophets were in the spiritual state in which they heard God's word, whether directly or when an angel mediated the revelation, they knew necessarily." To that I respond that those who dwell in Paradise know God necessarily because no religious duty applies in Paradise, and the prophets are preserved from punishment and safe from separation. The one who has necessary knowledge about Him has no fear of being cut off. The superiority of faith and experiential knowledge is in their hiddenness, for when these things become visible, faith becomes common knowledge; and when something becomes visible, free choice [350] departs and the roots of Revealed Law are disturbed. Even the law of apostasy becomes pointless, so that Balʿam[19] or Barṣīṣā[20] or Iblīs are not precisely guilty of unbelief, since it is agreed that they had experiential knowledge of God. Regarding Iblīs, for example, God has informed us about the situation of his banishment and reproach, with the words spoken by Iblīs, "Then, by Your might, I will lead them all astray" (38:82). Indeed, his saying "by your might" and his hearing God's response imply a degree of experiential knowledge.

One who possesses experiential knowledge, while he remains in that condition, is safe from being separated from God. Separation results from the cessation of *maʿrifa*, whereas one cannot conceive of the loss of necessary *ʿilm*. For the majority of people this question is fraught with difficulty. The crux of the matter is that if one is to steer clear of the danger, one must understand that, apart from God's ceaseless informing and guidance, human beings have no *ʿilm* or *maʿrifa* of Him. It is appropriate that individuals' certitude in experiential knowledge may wax and wane, but the principle of experiential knowledge itself is not subject to increase or diminishment, for a change in either direction would amount to a diminishment.

Uncritical acceptance of authority must not characterize one's knowledge of God. One must know God through the attributes of His perfection, a knowledge incomplete except by the goodness of God's providence and the assurance of His favor. For the guidance of minds belongs entirely to God, and they are wholly under His disposition. As God chooses, He can either make one of His deeds a source of guidance with which to point the way to Himself or use the same deed as a veil that thwarts access to Him. Jesus, for example, was a source of guidance to some people through *maʿrifa*, while for others he was a hindrance to intimate knowledge: The first said, "He is God's servant," and the second, "He is God's son." Some people, similarly, have taken idols and moon and sun as guides to God, while for others these proved to be false leads.[21]

If sources of guidance such as these were the cause of intimate knowledge, it would follow that every one guided by them would possess intimate knowledge, but that is clearly not the case. God chooses individuals and [351] transforms things into their guides so that by means of those things people come to Him and know Him. But a source of guidance is a means only and not a cause, and no one means has any priority over another with respect to God, who brings all means into existence. Those who possess intimate knowledge, who swear by a particular means, are guilty of dualistic thinking. Acknowledgment of anything other than the object of intimate knowledge is idolatry, (according to the divine words), "Those whom God leads astray have none to guide them" (7:186). If according to the Preserved Tablet, indeed, according to God's preference and foreknowledge, an individual is destined to misery, how can any evidence or demonstrative proof provide guidance? According to an Arabic saying, "The *maʿrifa* of one who turns to attend to what is other than God is dualism *(zunnār)*." Such an individual is annihilated and overwhelmed in the wrathful power of God, so how can anything other than God be His witness?

Ordinarily one apprehends proof more readily, and marvels are more apparent, by day. But if evidence were the cause of intimate knowledge of God, and evidences are more easily apprehended and wonders more accessible by day, how is it that when Abraham emerged from the cave by day, he saw nothing, but when he came out at night, "he beheld a star" (6:76)? Therefore, God shows the way to whatever servant He chooses and in whatever way He chooses, and opens for him the door of experiential knowledge. The servant thus arrives at a level in which the essence of *maʿrifa* seems alien and its qualities become harmful to him. *Maʿrifa* itself becomes a veil over the One Known and turns into a vain pretense. Dhū 'n-Nūn of Egypt says, "Be careful not to make a pretense of experiential knowledge." [An unidentified poetic verse says:

> Mystics make a pretense of experiential knowledge.
> I sidle up to ignorance—that is my experiential knowledge.]

Take care, therefore, not to make a pretense of experiential knowledge, or you will be destroyed. Adhere instead to the meaning of *maʿrifa* so that you will find salvation. When an individual is ennobled by a revelation of God's grandeur, his very being becomes a burden and all his personal characteristics become occasions of misfortune.

An individual who is God's, [352] and to whom God belongs, remains unassociated with anything in creation and the two worlds. The central reality of experiential knowledge is understanding that the dominion belongs to God. Once an individual realizes that God has disposition of all possessions, why would he continue dealing with creatures to the point where he becomes veiled by them or by himself? Veils result from ignorance, so that, when ignorance vanishes, veils are obliterated and experiential knowledge sees life here in terms of the life to come. And God knows best.

Shaykhs have made many veiled references to the meaning of *maʿrifa*, and, God willing, I will mention some of those for the reader's benefit. ʿAbd Allāh Mubārak says, "*Maʿrifa* means not being astonished at anything."* The object of astonishment is a deed that exceeds the capability of the agent, but the Most High and Most Holy One (the agent) is omnipotent, so the one who possesses experiential knowledge cannot be astonished at what God does. If astonishment were to occur, it should be at the fact that God so elevates a handful of dust that it is capable of receiving His commandments and so ennobles a drop of blood that it speaks of intimate friendship and experiential knowledge of God, seeks the vision of God, and becomes intent on nearness and union with Him. Dhū 'n-Nūn the Egyptian says, "The inner reality of *maʿrifa* is human access to mysteries through the imparting of the subtlest of lights."* In other words, by His light, God adorns the servant's heart with favor and removes all troubles from it, to the point that in the servant's heart created earthly beings are of less weight than a mustard seed. The contemplation of mysteries, whether hidden or manifest, does not overpower [353] him; and once God has brought this about, the merest glance becomes a contemplation.

Shiblī says, "*Maʿrifa* is ceaseless perplexity." There are two kinds of perplexity: one at God's existence and the other at God's attribute. Perplexity over God's existence is idolatry and unbelief, while perplexity over God's attribute is experiential knowledge; one who possesses experiential knowledge can have no shred of doubt about God's existence, while God's qualities elude the intellect altogether. What remains here is certitude concerning the being of God and perplexity concerning His manner of being, about which someone said, "O Guide of the perplexed, increase my perplexity." On the one hand, he affirmed experiential knowledge of the divine existence and the perfection of the divine attributes, while acknowledging that God is the desire of creation and the one who answers their prayers and gives perplexity to the perplexed. On the other, he asked for greater perplexity, thereby acknowledging that with respect to the object of its quest, the intellect is stymied between confusion and idolatry.

This is a subtle observation, recognizing, as it does, the possibility that experiential knowledge of God's existence necessitates confusion about one's own existence; a human being who knows God recognizes that he is wholly in thrall to God's power. Since both his being and nonbeing arise from God, and both his rest and movement depend on God's power, he becomes astonished, saying, "If all that I am rests with God, who am I and for what purpose do I exist?" It was in reference to this that the Prophet said, "An individual endowed with intimate self-knowledge knows his Lord intimately."* One who understands his own annihilation understands God's perdurance. As a result of annihilation, intellect and human attributes vanish. And if the intellect cannot comprehend the essence of a thing, it cannot arrive at experiential knowledge of it except through perplexity.

Abū Yazīd said, "*Maʿrifa* means understanding that both the motion and repose of human beings depend on God."* And no one exercises control over God's dominion without God's permission: An essence is an essence through Him; an effect is an effect through Him; [354] an attribute is an attribute through Him; and it is He who gives motion and repose. None has the capability of motion or repose, or can perform any action unless God creates the possibility and instills in the human heart the desire. Human acts are secondary; God is the primary agent. Describing the person endowed with experiential knowledge, Muḥammad ibn Wāsiʿ says, "One who knows God intimately says little and is ceaselessly astonished."* For only that which falls within the limits and principles of human expression can be expressed, and expression is fundamentally limited. Since, in this case, that which one would like to talk about is unlimited and cannot be confined within the boundaries of human language, how can one affirm it? If, therefore, there is no way to express it in human language, what option remains for the servant other than ceaseless astonishment?

Shiblī says, "The essence of experiential knowledge is the inability to attain it"; *that is, apart from the very incapacity to know the central reality of a thing, the servant has no inkling. It follows, therefore, that once a servant arrives at experiential knowledge, claiming personal credit would be inappropriate. Incapacity implies ongoing quest, but as long as the seeker continues to depend on his own resources and qualities, "incapacity" does not aptly describe him. When these resources and qualities leave the servant, then his condition is annihilation rather than incapacity. A faction of charlatans who affirm human qualities and the ongoing responsibility for sound judgment, as well as God's eternal standard of proof, nevertheless identify *maʿrifa* entirely with powerlessness, claiming that human beings lack the capacity to achieve anything. This view is erroneous and harmful. I say to them, "In quest of what object have you become incapacitated? You manifest neither of the two indicators of powerlessness, namely, the annihilation of the means of seeking, and the appearance of the divine manifestation of transcendence." Where human faculties are annihilated, [355] expression fails. Verbal expression ceases in its inability to speak of incapacity, for speaking about incapacity is not incapacity. And where the manifestation of divine transcendence occurs, there is no indication and powers of discrimination are out of the question.

Since that is the case, the incapacitated individual is unaware, either of being incapacitated, or that one would call his condition helplessness. Helplessness is other than God, and affirming *maʿrifa* of what is other than God is not *maʿrifa*. As long as the heart has room for anything other than God, and as long as the would-be possessor of experiential knowledge talks about other than God, that person does not yet truly possess experiential knowledge. Abū Ḥafṣ Ḥaddād says, "Since I gained experiential knowledge of God, neither truth nor falsehood has entered my heart."* When desire and passion arise in the heart, the individual turns to the heart, so that the heart can offer guidance to the ego-soul, where falsehood resides. But when a person discovers evidence of experiential knowledge, he likewise has recourse to the heart so that it can guide him to the spirit, the wellspring of truth and spiritual reality.

When the heart is occupied by anything other than God, and the one who seeks experiential knowledge has recourse to the heart, that individual ends up in ignorance of God. All human beings seek evidence of experiential knowledge from the heart, and they seek passion and desire from the heart as well; that is why they do not attain what they desire. Apart from God there is no repose so long as they go on seeking the truth from the heart. When an indication of evidence is required, they must return to God; this is the difference between a servant who has recourse to the heart and one who has recourse to God. Abū Bakr Wāsiṭī says, "One endowed with experiential knowledge of God is isolated, in fact, he is mute and totally subdued."* And the Prophet said, "I cannot praise you adequately." [356] While he was in a state of absence from God, he said, "I am the most eloquent among Arabs and non-Arabs." When he was taken from absence to presence, he said, "My tongue is incapable of praising You adequately, for I have gone from speech to speechlessness, from a spiritual state to being without a spiritual state. You are the one who is You. My speech is either from me or from You. If I spoke on my own, I would be veiled by my own speech. If I spoke through You, the apparent accomplishment of realizing proximity to You would in reality be a flaw. So I won't speak." Came the reply [to the first saying], "O Muḥammad, if you do not speak, We will speak. 'By your life' (15:72), if you do not speak in praise of Me, then all of you will be My praise. Since you do not consider yourself among those who praise Us, We have made every part of the universe your representative, so that they praise Me in your stead." And in God is success; God is our portion and the best of Friends.

5

Abū 'l-Qāsim al-Qushayrī: *The Treatise on Sufism (Ar-Risālat al-qushayrīya)*

Qushayrī's most famous work is a remarkable combination of hagiography and mystical theory. Roughly the first quarter of the book consists of over eighty short lives of famous Sufis. Section two analyzes several dozen technical terms commonly used by early Sufi authors, sometimes singly, sometimes in pairs or triads of terms typically used together.[1] *In the third section Qushayrī continues his conceptual analysis but shifts the focus slightly, with typically longer (up to five pages) essays on some four dozen terms that refer to major experiential aspects of the Sufi path. These do not precisely outline a progressive program, but they do in general represent an upward series of stages and states that Qushayrī regarded as critical indices of spiritual development. Most important here, Qushayrī situates* ma'rifa *well down the list, after chapters on acknowledgment of God's transcendent unity* (tawḥīd) *and spiritual states that accompany one's departure from this world, and before those on love* (maḥabba) *and longing* (shawq).[2]

Chapter on the *Ma'rifa* of God

[342] God has said, "They cannot assess God's scope accurately" (6:91). Qur'ānic exegetes have interpreted the verse to mean, "They have not known God experientially with a truly intimate knowledge."[3]

The Prophet said,[4] "What undergirds a house is its foundation, and what undergirds the religion is experiential knowledge of God, along with certitude and circumspect intelligence." ʿĀ'isha asked, "You who are worthy of my father and mother in ransom, what is circumspect intelligence?" He replied, "Stopping short of rebelling against God while being intent on obeying God."

As religious scholars generally use the term, *maʿrifa* is synonymous with *ʿilm,* so that every variety of *ʿilm* is a form of *maʿrifa,* and all *maʿrifa* belongs to the category of *ʿilm.* Therefore, everyone who possesses *ʿilm* about God possesses *maʿrifa,* and vice versa. According to the Sufis, however, *maʿrifa* is characteristic of an individual who is intimately familiar with God through His names and attributes, and whose actions toward God are entirely authentic, whose character has been rid of destructive tendencies and faults, who awaits God's pleasure, and whose heart is held endlessly in reserve for God. Such a person enjoys a beautiful closeness to God, and God in turn accommodates Himself to all the individual's spiritual states. The individual is liberated from the ego-soul's machinations, the heart no longer given to notions that distract it toward what is not God. Such a person finds human company uncongenial, is free of the ego-soul's noxious qualities, is no longer under the sway of things or values of this world, carries on the most secret of intimate conversations with God incessantly, is sure from moment to moment of returning to God, and becomes apprised through God's intimate communication as to what God has in store. And when all these conditions are present, this individual is known as one endowed with experiential knowledge, and the corresponding spiritual state is that of experiential knowledge. In general, the level of *maʿrifa* will be commensurate with the degree to which the individual has parted company with the ego-soul.

Shaykhs who have discoursed on experiential knowledge have done so in terms of their own experience and have alluded to individual ecstatic experience related to a particular mystical moment. [343] I heard my teacher Abū ʿAlī ad-Daqqāq say, "Among the characteristics of experiential knowledge of God is arrival at awe in God's presence, so that as one's experiential knowledge increases, so does one's awe." I heard him say further, "A concomitant of experiential knowledge is tranquility of heart, much as traditional knowledge brings contentment;

as one's experiential knowledge increases, so does one's tranquility." Shiblī said,[5] "There is no attachment for one endowed with intimate knowledge, no complaint for a lover, no claim for a servant on the master, no respite for one who fears God, and no eluding God for anyone." Shiblī said,[6] when someone asked him about *ma'rifa,* "The first of it is God, and the rest of it is endless."

Abū Ḥafṣ (al-Ḥaddād) said,[7] "Since I have known God experientially neither truth nor falsehood has entered my heart." What Abū Ḥafṣ has said here is a bit problematical, but the gist of it seems to be this: Sufis believe that experiential knowledge presupposes that the godservant, possessed by the remembrance of God, has taken leave of the ego-soul and neither takes account of nor has recourse to anything other than God. An intelligent person appeals to his heart, with its reflective and recollective capabilities with respect to matters of concern to him or a spiritual state he might find himself in. Similarly, the mystic appeals to his Lord, and when an individual is totally absorbed with his Lord, he does not refer the issue to his heart. For that matter, how can any concern enter the heart of a person who has no heart? Herein lies the difference between a person who lives through his heart and one who lives through his Lord. Someone asked Abū Yazīd about experiential knowledge, and he replied, citing the Qur'ān, "When kings invade a country, they plunder it and reduce its most noble people to its basest" (27:34). And it is to this that Abū Ḥafṣ is alluding.

Abū Yazīd said, "Human beings experience spiritual states, but the mystic does not, for the latter's individual characteristics are obliterated. The person's individuality has been transplanted into the individuality of another, and his features have departed and been replaced by those of another." Wāsiṭī said, "*Ma'rifa* is weak so long as the godservant depends on, and is in need of, God." Wāsiṭī means here that need and dependence are among the characteristics of a godservant's sobriety and residual individuality, for they are attributes of the person. One endowed with experiential knowledge, on the other hand, disappears in that experiential knowledge. How, then, could such a person's *ma'rifa* be intact so long as the individual is totally invested in God's existence or absorbed in attending to God? For such a person has not arrived at existence, coopted as he is by what he perceives to be his own attributes. Wāsiṭī has, therefore, observed further, "One who knows God intimately is isolated, in fact, he is speechless and totally subdued." Muḥammad said, [344] "I cannot praise you adequately."[8] These comments refer to characteristics of individuals whose goal is remote, but individuals who have set their sights lower than that have discoursed at length about experiential knowledge as well.

Aḥmad ibn ʿĀṣim al-Anṭākī (d. 220/835) said,[9] "The more perfect one's experiential knowledge of God, the greater one's fear of God." One of the Sufis has said, "One who knows God intimately finds his own ongoing perdurance painful, so that, for all its breadth, this world becomes too small for him." A saying has it, "One who knows God experientially finds living carefree and life itself lovely; everything that exists holds him in awe, the fear of created beings departs from him, and he relates intimately to God." According to another saying, "When a person knows God experientially, covetousness wanes, so that he lives between self-denial and hedonism." Again, "*Maʿrifa* entails shame, on the one hand, and magnifying God, on the other, much the way acknowledgment of God's transcendent unity presupposes contentment and surrender."

Ruwaym[10] said, "*Maʿrifa* is a mirror for the mystic, for when he looks into it, his Master reveals Himself to him." Dhū 'n-Nūn of Egypt said, "The spirits of the prophets raced on the open field of experiential knowledge, but the spirit of our Prophet arrived before the spirits of the other prophets at the garden of union." He also said, "The mystic's relationships are like the relationships of God, in that, emulating God's behavior, he tolerates and is patient with you." Someone asked Ibn Yazdānyār, "At what point does the contemplative witness God?" He replied, "When the witnesser appears and the objects of witnessing vanish, the senses fail and sincerity becomes irrelevant." Ḥusayn ibn Manṣūr (al-Ḥallāj) said, "When the godservant has arrived at the station of experiential knowledge, God reveals to him through his every passing spiritual impulse, and protects his inmost being from incursion by stray thoughts of what is not God." He said further, "One who knows God experientially is characteristically unconcerned with either this world or the next." Sahl ibn ʿAbd Allāh (at-Tustarī) said, "The pinnacle of experiential knowledge involves two things: amazement and astonishment."

Dhū 'n-Nūn of Egypt said,[11] "Those who know God most intimately are they whose astonishment at him is the most intense." [345] A man said to Junayd,[12] "Some of the mystics say that refraining from external activities is part of devotion and piety." Junayd replied, "This is an opinion of people who argue that one should discount actions—a large mistake, in my view. Thieves and adulterers enjoy a better spiritual state than those who say that, for those who know God experientially get their deeds from God and return to God through them. Should I live a thousand years, I would not diminish my deeds of devotion by the merest particle."

Someone asked Abū Yazīd (al-Bisṭāmī), "How did you achieve this intimate awareness?" He replied, "With a famished belly and a bare body." Abū Ya'qūb an-Nahrajūrī (d. 330/941–42) said, "I asked Abū Ya'qūb as-Sūsī (late third/ninth century), 'Does the mystic feel regret over any thing other than God?' He responded, 'And does he take notice of anything other than God over which he might experience regret?' So I (Nahrajūrī) asked, 'Then with which eye does the mystic regard things?' He answered, 'With the eye of annihilation and finitude.'"

Abū Yazīd (al-Bisṭāmī) said, "The mystic flies, the ascetic walks." A saying has it that "while the mystic's eye weeps, his heart laughs." Said Junayd, "A mystic has not truly attained experiential knowledge until he becomes like the earth, on which walk the devout as well as the sinner; like the clouds that overshadow everything; and like the rain that waters what it loves as well as what it does not." Yaḥyā ibn Mu'ādh said, "The mystic departs this world without doing as much as he ought in two areas: weeping over his ego-soul and praising his Lord." Abū Yazīd said, "Individuals attain experiential knowledge by divesting themselves of what belongs to them and investing themselves in what belongs to God."

Yūsuf ibn 'Alī said,[13] "A mystic has no genuine experiential knowledge until, if someone gave him the likes of the kingdom of Solomon, it would not distract him for an instant." Ibn 'Aṭā' said,[14] "*Ma'rifa* rests on three pillars: awe, shame, and intimacy." Someone asked Dhū 'n-Nūn al-Miṣrī,[15] "By what means did you come to experiential knowledge of your Lord?" He replied, "I know my Lord intimately through my Lord, and were it not for my Lord, I would have no experiential knowledge of my Lord." According to a saying, "One imitates a religious scholar, but one receives guidance from a mystic." Shiblī said, "One who possesses experiential knowledge notices nothing other than God, expresses himself with the speech of none other than God, and knows of none who can protect him other than God."

[346] It is said: "The mystic experiences intimacy through the recollection of God, so God causes him to feel lonely in the midst of God's creatures; he needs God, so God reduces his need of His creatures; and he humbles himself before God, so God exalts him above His creation." Abū 'ṭ-Ṭayyib as-Sāmarrī said, "*Maʿrifa* is the Truth's arising like the sun over the inmost being in uninterrupted illumination." Someone has said, "The mystic transcends his words, while the religious scholar falls short of his." Abū Sulaymān ad-Dārānī said, "God reveals to the mystic during sleep things He does not reveal to others even while they perform the ritual prayer." Junayd observed, "The mystic is one who speaks the truth from his inmost being even when he says nothing." Dhū 'n-Nūn said, "There is a punishment for every created thing; for the mystic, it is being disconnected from the remembrance of God."

Ruwaym observed,[16] "The hypocrisy of those endowed with intimate knowledge is more excellent than the sincerity of beginners on the spiritual path." Abū Bakr al-Warrāq said, "Most useful is the mystic's silence, while his speech is most pleasing and delightful." Said Dhū 'n-Nūn, "The ascetics may be the kings of the next life, but by contrast to the mystics they are destitute." Someone asked Junayd about the individual endowed with experiential knowledge and he replied, "The color of water is that of its container"—in other words, the mystic's condition depends on his mystical moment. When someone asked Abū Yazīd about the mystic, he answered, "In dreams he sees only God; while awake, only God; he conforms himself to none but God, and to God alone does he look expectantly."

Someone asked a shaykh,[17] "How did you come to know God experientially?" He answered, "Through a light flash that sparks from the tongue of a person removed from accustomed modes of perception, and through an articulation that flows from the tongue of a person who is as good as dead." He alludes here to an apparent experience of ecstasy and discloses an arcane mystery: The individual is himself in relation to what he divulges but not himself in relation to what he leaves ambiguous. Then the shaykh recited these verses:

> You have spoken without utterance, and that is the real communication, for
> Whether in human language or made plain wordlessly, speech is yours.
> Once concealed, you came into view so that I might be hidden;
> You flashed lightning before me and I became articulate.

Someone asked Abū Turāb (an-Nakhshabī) to describe a mystic, and he said,[18] "One whom nothing can sully, and through whom every thing becomes pure." According to Muḥammad ibn al-Ḥusayn, Abū ʿUthmān al-Maghribī[19] said, "The individual endowed with experiential knowledge is one for whom the lights of knowledge are resplendent, facilitating his vision of wonders of the unseen world." I heard my teacher Abū ʿAlī ad-Daqqāq say, "The person endowed with experiential knowledge is engulfed in the seas of full realization, according to one Sufi's saying, '*Maʿrifa* is rolling swells that raise and lower.'" [347] Someone asked Yaḥyā ibn Muʿādh to describe a mystic, so he responded, "An individual who even in the midst of created things distances himself from them." And another time he answered the question by saying, "One whose very existence is separation."

According to Dhū 'n-Nūn, "Distinguishing features of the mystic are these three: the light of his experiential knowledge does not wash out the light of his spiritual reticence; he gives no credence to any aspect of inward knowledge that would run afoul of an outward statute; and the largesse of God's graces to him does not impel him to pull back the veils over the inner sanctum of God." Someone has said, "One who described experiential knowledge to the children of the next world would not be a true mystic; how much the less were he to do so among the children of this world!" Abū Saʿīd al-Kharrāz observed, "*Maʿrifa* is the result of a tearful eye and a commitment to self-discipline." Someone asked Junayd[20] about a comment of Dhū 'n-Nūn describing the mystic as "one who was here and then left," and Junayd replied, "The current spiritual state of one endowed with experiential knowledge does not restrict him to one state, nor does his current spiritual resting place veil him from resettling into others. He is therefore present to the inhabitants of every place as if he were one of them, participating in life much as they live it, and speaking in a way they will understand and find helpful."

Muḥammad ibn al-Faḍl said,[21] "*Maʿrifa* is the heart's life with God." Someone asked[22] Abū Saʿīd al-Kharrāz, "Does the person endowed with experiential knowledge come to a spiritual state in which his tears are permanently dried up?" He replied, "Yes, for weeping is appropriate to the spiritual circumstances of their journey toward God. Then, when they stop to rest in the spiritual realities of proximity to God and savor the taste of arrival, by God's kindness, then tears cease."

6

ʿAbd Allāh Anṣārī: *The Hundred Fields (Ṣad maydān): Resting Places of the Wayfarers (Manāzil as-sāʾirīn)*

Here, from Anṣārī's two short pedagogical texts, are brief descriptions, first of ʿilm *and then of* maʿrifa. *They are set side by side to give a sense of how he developed his understanding of the two concepts in the period between the Persian and the Arabic works in question. In the Persian text, Anṣārī locates* ʿilm *at number seventy-one, just after, and arising out of, solitude. He begins by quoting the Qur'ān and then describes the "field" in greater detail.*

"And only those who possess knowledge understand the parables" (29:43). *ʿIlm* is knowledge and it has three divisions: knowledge deriving from inferential deduction, knowledge deriving from instruction, and knowledge deriving from the divine presence. As for knowledge deriving from inferential deduction, it is the fruit of intellects, the consequence of experience, and it assists in discrimination, for human beings are ennobled by that in distinctive levels. Knowledge deriving from instruction results when human beings receive a message delivered from God and learn from teachers by means of pedagogy. Those endowed with that knowledge are rare in the two worlds. Finally, knowledge deriving from the divine presence is of three kinds: one form of knowledge is wisdom concerning God's creative work, and one gains familiarity with it through divine signs; the second form is knowledge of spiritual reality in the course of devotional dealings with God as found in certain signs; and the third is knowledge of God's judgment received from God through the vision of the unseen world. The last is the prerogative of Khiḍr.[1]

In Resting Places, ʿilm *is located, and therefore functions, differently. In the sixth of his ten clusters of "resting places," called "the Valleys," Anṣārī places* ʿilm *second among the ten (that is, number fifty-two), after spirituality and before wisdom, insight, discernment, awe, inspiration, repose, tranquility, and preoccupation. His Arabic description of* ʿilm *begins with a sacred text that alludes to Khiḍr, "And whom We had endowed with* ʿilm *from our (divine) presence" (18:65) and continues:*

ʿIlm rests upon proof and removes ignorance. It consists of three levels: The first level is clear, obvious knowledge arising either from direct eyewitnessing or an authentic disclosure or a genuine experience of long standing. The second level is a covert knowledge that germinates in pure mysteries from inviolate seeds, thanks to the water of sincere spiritual exercises. It manifests itself in the true breathings of the people of lofty aspiration, in times of spiritual freedom, in attentive ears. It is a knowledge that makes present that which is absent, renders absent the one who witnesses, and points toward union. And the third level is a knowledge from the divine presence, (a knowledge) whose corroboration is its being found, the perception of which is the direct experience of it, whose description is its judgment; and there is no veil between it and the unseen.[2]

In the Persian Fields, *Anṣārī places* maʿrifa(t) *in seventy-fifth place, arising out of wisdom. Again, he begins with a Qur'ānic text and expands:*

"You will see their eyes overflow with tears because of the experiential knowledge they have received from God" (5:86). *Maʿrifa* is a form of knowledge of which there are three doors and three levels, as follows: The first of its doors is knowledge of the divine existence and unity, and the divinity's dissimilarity to anything else. The second is knowledge of the divine omnipotence, omniscience, and largesse. And the third is knowledge of good deeds, friendship, and intimacy. *Maʿrifa* of the first sort is the door to the edifice of Islam; that of the second, to the edifice of faith; and that of the third, to the edifice of sincerity. The road toward the first door consists in the vision of the Creator's arrangement of the disclosure and concealment of the fabrications of human beings. The way to the second door consists in observing the wisdom of the Creator in such a way as to recognize other prominent examples of that wisdom. And the way to the third door consists in observing the graciousness of the Master in acknowledging good works and disregarding offenses. This last door is the field of those endowed with experiential knowledge, the alchemy of lovers. It is the path of the elect, the path by which the heart is adorned, by which joy is enhanced and affection expanded.[3]

> *In the fuller treatment of the Arabic* Resting Places, *Anṣārī sets* maʿrifa *in first place in the tenth cluster, that of "final destinations." It is followed by annihilation, perdurance, full realization, concealment, finding, casting aside, isolation, union (or pure focus), and acknowledging the divine transcendent unity. He begins with a fuller citation of the same Qur'ānic verse and then proceeds to his analysis of the tripartite significance of the concept.*

"When they hear what has been sent down to the Messenger, you will see their eyes overflow with tears because of their intimate experience of the truth" (5:86). *Maʿrifa* is the comprehension of the essence of a thing as it is. It has three levels and human beings are divided into three categories in relation to it. The first level is intimate knowledge of the divine attributes and characteristics whose names were made available through the Prophetic office. Evidences of it are manifest in creation through the spiritual insight afforded by the light that supersedes mystery, and through the goodness of the life of the intellect in sowing the seeds of thought, and the life of the heart through the propriety of its distinguishing between magnifying God and undivided attention. This is ordinary *maʿrifa* apart from which the bonds of certitude cannot be tied together, and it rests on three foundations. The first of them is the affirmation of a divine attribute according to its name without positing anthropomorphism; second, the negation of anthropomorphism without denying the divine attributes; and third, despair of attaining its full reality or of seeking its inner interpretation.

The second level is intimate knowledge of the divine essence, together with the elimination of a distinction between divine attributes and essence. It germinates in the knowledge of union, waxes luxuriant in the field of annihilation, attains completeness in the knowledge of abiding, and arrives at the lofty status of the essence of union. It rests on three foundations: the sending of the divine attributes in the form of testimonies; the sending of means in the form of the various stages of the path; and the sending of explanations of the way markers. This is the *maʿrifa* of the elect, by which one becomes familiar with the horizon of the ultimate spiritual reality.

The third level is *maʿrifa* that is immersed in unalloyed communication of experiential knowledge. Deductive inference cannot attain it, nor does evidence point to it, nor can any method realize it fully. It rests on three foundations: contemplation of proximity to God; transcending knowledge; and the realization of union. This is the intimate knowledge of the elect of the elect.[4]

> *In his next "resting place," that of annihilation, Anṣārī explains that the first annihilation is that of* maʿrifa *in that which is known* (maʿrūf), *and he glosses that as "annihilation with respect to* ʿilm."[5]

7

Abū Ḥāmid Muḥammad al-Ghazālī: *The Elaboration of the Marvels of the Heart (Kitāb sharḥ ʿajāʾib al-qalb):* *Book 21* of the *Revitalization of the Religious Disciplines (Iḥyāʾ ʿulūm ad-dīn)*

Book 21 of the forty major divisions of Ghazālī's Revitalization of the Religious Disciplines, *called "The Elaboration of the Marvels of the Heart," sets forth the essentials of the imām's psychology and of the epistemology that undergirds his mystical theology. In fifteen "clarifications" or expositions* (bayān), *Ghazālī begins with a broader contextual description of the principal internal or spiritual human faculties—ego-soul* (nafs), *spirit* (rūḥ), *intellect* (ʿaql), *and heart* (qalb). *Recalling the concerns of earlier authors, such as Sarrāj and Kalābādhī, to distinguish Sufi usage from that of the other religious disciplines, Ghazālī observes that religious scholars generally possess only a truncated understanding of the full significance of these terms, in that they typically think of them only in their outward meanings. His purpose here is to point out both outward and inward aspects of these faculties, emphasizing the centrality of the latter for spiritual development.*

Moving quickly to focus on the heart, whose mount is the body and whose provision for the journey is ʿilm, *Ghazālī devotes sections two and three to a more detailed description of the functions of the heart as the inner battleground of the human struggle. Heart is assisted by its "soldiers," the internal powers of appetite or desire (including, for example, irascibility and other aspects of motivation), the capability of acquisition or taking action on what it desires or fears, and perception* (idrāk). *In sections 4 and 5, Ghazālī focuses still more sharply on the distinctively human qualities of the heart, particularly on the two characteristics that distinguish humans from animals: knowledge and will. In Clarification 4 he observes that* ʿilm *in this context refers to knowledge of truths about both this world and the next that transcend mere sense-awareness.*

All mature human beings gain knowledge from experience, but there is in addition a more advanced level of learning whose source is beyond ordinary experience, and that includes varieties of divine inspiration and revelation available only to the most advanced (such as Prophets and Friends of God). Most human beings can arrive at an inward ʿilm *that encompasses their present and past spiritual states but does not extend forward. And the highest form of knowledge available to most people is that of God's attributes. Then, in section five, Ghazālī sums up the balance of the positive and negative potential of the heart as represented by its predatory, animal, diabolical, and divine qualities, symbolized respectively by the pig, dog, devil, and wise person.*

What follows here are the key epistemological sections (6, 7, 9, and 10) of Book 21 not currently available in McCarthy's, or any other, English translation.[1] *Ever the consummate pedagogue, Ghazālī says he will make use of images to communicate a subject that most people would otherwise find too daunting.*

[14] Clarification 6: The likeness of the heart, particularly in relation to the religious disciplines

Know that the dwelling place of *ʿilm* is the heart. I am referring to the subtle faculty that governs all the limbs, and which all of the members obey and serve. Its relationship to the true natures of things known is like that of a mirror to evanescent images. Just as the evanescent image and the likeness of this image are imprinted upon the mirror and appear there, so everything known has a true nature whose image is imprinted upon the mirror of the heart and becomes visible there. And just as the mirror is a distinct item, and the images of persons are a separate item, and the occurrence of their likeness upon the mirror still another, so that it is a question of three distinct items, so the three in this instance are, specifically, the heart, the true natures of things, and the occurrence of those true natures in the heart and their presence there. The term *knower* is a reference to the heart in which the likeness of the true natures of things dwell, while *that which is known* refers to the true natures of things, and *knowledge* refers to the occurrence of the likenesses in the mirror.

Just as in the act of grasping, that which does the grasping is like the hand, and that which is grasped is like the sword, and the "reception" that characterizes the relationship between sword and hand resulting from the hand's taking the sword is known as grasping—so the heart's reception of the likeness of the thing known is called knowledge. Now the true nature of a thing exists, as does the heart, even when knowledge is not in progress, for knowledge refers to the occurrence of the truth in the heart. Similarly, both the sword and the hand exist independently even when one does not speak of the occurrence of grasping and seizing when there is no sword in the hand. One must note that "grasping" refers to the presence of the sword itself in the hand, whereas that which is known does not itself enter into the heart. So, for example, fire itself does not enter into the heart of one who knows fire; instead, what enters there is its definition and the true nature of it that is congruent with its image. The creation of its likeness in the mirror, therefore, is fundamental, for the individual person as such does not enter into the mirror—only the likeness that is congruent with the person does so. That is how the presence in the heart of a likeness congruent with the true nature of the thing known is called *ʿilm.*

There are five conditions under which an image is not revealed in a mirror:

[15] First, deficiency in its reflective capability when it is raw iron, before it is rounded, trimmed, and burnished.

Second, the presence of a blemish, rust, or tarnish, even if it is perfectly shaped.

Third, its being deflected away from facing the image and toward something else, as when the image is behind the mirror.

Fourth, the interposition of a veil between the mirror and the image.

And fifth, ignorance with respect to where the desired image is, so that one becomes unable to orient the mirror directly toward the image.

The heart, too, functions as a mirror subject to all of these limitations, in that the essential nature of the Truth is revealed in it, even though hearts may at times be devoid of knowledge, for the following five reasons:

First, an inherent deficiency, as in the instance of the heart of a child to which things known are not revealed because of its undeveloped state.

Second, the tarnish of sins and the imperfections that have accumulated on the face of the heart as a result of a multitude of cravings, robbing the heart of its purity and clarity, so that the efflorescence of the truth in it is foreclosed by its darkness and its accretion of blemishes. The Prophet alludes to that when he says, "When a person yields to sin, understanding withdraws from him never to return." In other words, tarnish settles on the individual's heart and its traces do not disappear. Suppose that it is the individual's intention to pursue (understanding) with some positive action by which to rub off (the tarnish). If, at that point, he brings a good act to bear upon it that is not offset by an evil act, then there will surely be an increase of illumination in the heart. But when an evil act takes precedence, the benefit of a good deed is canceled out but the heart reverts thereby to the condition in which it was prior to the evil act. As a result, light does not increase in the heart. This is an obvious deterioration and diminishment for which there is no remedy. But cannot the mirror that has been sullied then be polished by burnishing, the way one is polished by burnishing to increase its clarity beyond its former sullied condition? It is, then, the concern for obedience to God and turning away from the importunities of the passions that clarifies and purifies the heart. On that point God has said, "Those who struggle on Our behalf We will surely guide to Our ways" (29:69), and the Prophet said, "To anyone who acts upon what he knows, God bequeaths as an inheritance knowledge of what he had not known."

Third, the heart might be deflected from the direction of the spiritual reality that one seeks, so even if the heart of an obedient and upright person is pure, the effulgence of the Truth might not shine forth in it since it is not seeking the Truth and its mirror is not oriented in the requisite direction. Indeed, anxiety over fulfilling specific necessary bodily deeds or securing means of livelihood often intrudes. The individual does not turn his thoughts toward full attentiveness to the Lordly presence and the hidden divine truths. Only the minutiae of the deleterious actions and secret faults of the ego-self upon which the individual reflects are revealed to the individual as he is reflecting upon them, or the exigencies of making a livelihood when he is reflecting on them. Now if preoccupation with actions and the details of ordinary compliance with life's demands can restrict disclosure of the Truth's effulgence, how do you think a person who turns his concern toward worldly cravings and pleasures and attachments could but miss out on disclosure of the truth?

Fourth, there is the veil. It may be that an obedient heart that is victorious over its cravings and has dedicated its thoughts exclusively to one aspect of the ultimate reality still experiences no revelation because it is veiled from it by adherence to immature views arising from unquestioning acceptance of authority and concern for good repute. That condition may intervene between the individual and the reality of the Truth, so that the incongruity of what he has latched onto from the outward meanings afforded by uncritical assent prevents disclosure in his heart. This is, in addition, a great veil that veils countless speculative theologians and partisans of the various schools of legal methodology. Indeed, many upright individuals who reflect on the realms of heaven and earth are veiled by varieties of adherence to uncritical assent that congeal in their souls and take deep root in their hearts, so that a veil comes between them and the perception of realities.

Fifth comes ignorance with respect to the source of discovery of that which one seeks. The person who seeks *ʿilm* cannot attain knowledge [16] of the unknown except through mindfulness of the disciplines that together bear upon that which he seeks, to such an extent that he reflects on them and coordinates them internally with a specific ordering that religious scholars recognize from their perspective. When that occurs, the individual hits upon the direction of the object of the quest, so that its spiritual reality is manifest to his heart. But one cannot avail oneself of the desired forms of knowledge, which are not innate, except through the matrix of the sum total of the sciences. In fact, one cannot attain any knowledge except by linking together as a pair two previously known specific bits of knowledge. On the basis of their pairing, one attains a third bit of knowledge, much the way a brood of young animals comes about as a result of the conjoining of the male and female of the species. Then, just as when one wishes to produce a mare and cannot do so from a jackass or a camel or a human being, but only from the specific stock of the male and female horse, and that only with the specific conjoining of the two, so every cognition has two specific sources that are meant to be paired and from whose conjunction the desired beneficial knowledge comes about.

Ignorance as to the nature of the conjunction of these sources is an obstacle to knowledge. I have already alluded to an analogy to this in relation to ignorance of the direction in which the image lies. The analogy is this: Suppose the individual wants to see a reflection of the back of his head in the mirror. If he raises the mirror opposite his face, it is not oriented toward the back of his head, and as a result he does not see the back of his head in it. If he then raises it behind and opposite the back of his head, he has turned the mirror away from his eye so that he does not see the mirror or the image of the back of his head in it. The individual must therefore have someone else hold a mirror up behind the back of his head, while the first mirror is in front where the individual can see it. By maintaining a juxtaposition of the two mirrors, then, the image of the back of his head is imprinted upon the mirror oriented toward the back of his head. Then the image in this rear mirror is transferred to the other mirror that is before the eye, and the eye perceives the image of the back of the head. Similarly, therefore, in the course of availing oneself of the sciences there are wondrous paths along which there are deviations and detours even stranger than what I have mentioned occur on the mirror. People capable of discerning a way beyond these deviations are scarcely to be found anywhere on earth. These then are the causes that prevent hearts from the intimate knowledge of the true natures of things.

On the other hand, every heart is naturally disposed to experiential knowledge of spiritual realities, for it is a divine exalted charge that distinguishes (humankind) from the other elements of the universe through this uniqueness and nobility. The word of God alludes to this, "We did offer the trust to the heavens and the earth and the mountains, but they declined to bear it, for they feared it, but the human being undertook it" (33:72). This indicates that human beings possess a unique characteristic that distinguishes them from the heavens and the earth and the mountains, that renders them capable of undertaking the trust of God. This trust is experiential knowledge and the acknowledgment of the divine transcendent unity, and the heart of every human being is prepared for undertaking the trust and inherently capable of it. However, the conditions I have been discussing impede it from assuming its burdens and attaining the full realization of it. It was on this account that Muḥammad said, "Everyone begotten is born with a natural inclination, though his parents make him a Jew or a Christian or Magian." And the words of God's Messenger, "If the devils did not swarm about the hearts of the children of Adam, they would look toward the kingdom of the heavens," are alluding to one of these conditions that stand as a veil between human hearts and the kingdom of heaven.

Another allusion to this is a tradition we have received from Ibn ʿUmar: Someone asked God's Messenger, "O Messenger of God, where is God—on earth or in heaven?" He replied, "In the hearts of his faithful servants." And in a sacred Ḥadīth, God said, "Neither the earth nor the heavens are wide enough for Me, but there is room for Me in the gentle, meek heart of my faithful servant." And according to a report, someone asked, "O Messenger of God, who is the best person?" He answered, "Every believer whose heart is swept clean." Someone asked, "And what is it that sweeps the heart clean?" He answered, "It is the piety and purity in which there is neither deceit nor injustice nor betrayal nor envy." It was in this connection that ʿUmar said, "My heart sees my Lord," for he had lifted the veil through piety. And when [17] the veil has been lifted between an individual and God, the image of the King and the Dominion is manifest in that person's heart, so that he sees a Garden so expansive that it contains Heaven and earth. The whole of it is wider than the heavens and the earth because "Heaven and earth" is an expression for the realm of earthly sovereignty and witnessing through the senses. Even if the breadth of its limits were to exceed all bounds, it would still come to an end after all. But the realm of Lordly Dominion comprises mysteries, hidden from the sight of eyes, that are reserved for the perception of the inward vision and to which there is no end. How fortunate the heart that receives even a fleeting glimpse of that realm, though it is, in itself and in relation to the knowledge of God, limitless!

If you took it in all at one time, you would call the combination of the realm of the earthly sovereignty and the Lordly Dominion the Lordly Presence: The Lordly Presence encompasses all existent things since nothing exists apart from God and His actions. His kingdom and His servants are the results of His actions, and what is manifest to the heart from that, is, according to the Sufis, the Garden, and, according to the people of Truth, a means of realizing the Garden. The breadth of His kingdom in the Garden is commensurate with the breadth of experiential knowledge of Him and is proportionate to what is manifest to the individual concerning God and His attributes and deeds. To be sure, the desired result of deeds of obedience and the actions of all the bodily limbs is the purification, cleansing, and polishing of the heart: "One who purifies it is successful" (91:9). The desired result of its purification is the descent of the lights of faith into it, by which I mean the illumination of the light of experiential knowledge. That is the goal according to the words of the Most High, "When God desires to guide a person, He expands the center of that person's being toward surrender *(islām)*" (6:125) and "Does not a person, the center of whose being God has expanded, have the light of his Lord?" (39:22).

How wonderful is this manifestation and this faith! It has three degrees: The first degree is the faith of the generality of people, the faith of simple uncritical acceptance of authority. The second is the faith of the speculative theologians. It is alloyed with a variety of deductive inference, and it represents a level close to that of the faith of the generality of people. The third is the faith of those endowed with experiential knowledge, and it involves contemplating with the light of certitude. Let me explain these degrees to you by means of a three-part analogy with how one ascertains that Zayd is inside a house.

The first is that someone whose veracity you have checked out—and you neither know him to be guilty of mendacity nor doubt what he says—passes along to you news about Zayd. So your heart is confident about him and trusts his report on the basis of hearing alone. This belief is based purely on uncritical acceptance of authority and is like the faith of the generality of people: When they arrive at the age of discrimination they hear from their fathers and mothers about the existence of God and His knowledge, will, power, and other attributes, and the sending of the messengers, and their veracity, and what God revealed to them. They accept what they hear, depend upon it, and have confidence in it. It never occurs to them to disagree with what they have been told because of their respect for their fathers, mothers, and teachers. This faith is the means of salvation in the next life. Its proponents are among the foremost ranks of the Companions of the Right Hand, but they are not among those who draw near to God because their faith does not encompass the revelation, inward vision, and expansion of the center of one's being through the light of certitude.

Error is possible in connection with what one hears from anyone, even when it is a question of numerous individuals' adherence to creedal statements. So the hearts of the Jews and Christians as well were confident in what they heard from their fathers and mothers, but their belief in that to which they assented was erroneous because their parents had passed along erroneous belief to them. The Muslims hold to the truth, not as a result of their study of it, but because the word of truth was delivered to them.

The second degree is that you hear Zayd's speech and his voice from inside of the house, but from behind a wall. On that basis, then, you infer his existence in the house. Your faith, verification, and certitude as to his existence in the house are in this instance stronger than your verification on the basis of hearsay alone. If, therefore, someone were to tell you he was in the house, and then you heard his voice, your certitude would be increased because voices lead the one who hears the voice to infer the shape and image as if one actually witnessed the image. So your heart makes the judgment that this is the voice of that person. This faith is allied to evidence, but here also one can be led into error. [18] If the voice is similar to another voice, it could be mimicry employed as a ruse, but it has not occurred to the listener that he has any grounds for suspicion, nor does he suspect that this involves a deliberate deception and ruse.

The third degree is that you enter the house and look at Zayd with your own eyes and witness him directly. This is authentic experiential knowledge and certain witnessing, and it is similar to the experiential knowledge of those who draw near to God and those who attest to the truth because they believe on the basis of contemplative vision. On the one hand, their faith is consistent with the faith of the generality of people and of the speculative theologians, but on the other, they are different by virtue of the superiority of the evident proof by which they elude the possibility of error.

In addition, they differ with respect to both the scope of their knowledge and the levels of disclosure. As for the levels of disclosure, an analogy would be that the individual sees Zayd in the house from close proximity and in the courtyard of the house as the sun illumines it, so that his perception of Zayd is complete. Suppose that, by contrast, another individual perceives Zayd in a room or from a distance or later in the evening. The form resembles Zayd in such a way that the viewer is certain that it is Zayd, but the fine details and hidden features of his image are not visible. With regard to disparity as to the scope of knowledge, the first individual sees Zayd and ʿAmr and Bakr and others in the house, while the other individual sees only Zayd. Thus the experiential knowledge of the first person most definitely increases in proportion to the number of things known. This, then, is the spiritual state of the heart in relation to the varieties of knowledge, and God knows best what is correct.

[18] Clarification 7: The state of the heart in relationship to the divisions of the scientific disciplines—rational, religious, secular, and otherworldly

Know that, as already indicated, the heart is naturally disposed to receive the true natures of things known, but the kinds of knowledge that abide in the heart are divided into the rational and the divinely revealed. The rational is further divided into the necessary and the acquired, and the acquired still further differentiated into the this-worldly and the otherworldly. By rational knowledge I mean that which the natural disposition of the intellect calls for and which is not found in uncritical acceptance of authority and hearsay. In its necessary aspect the individual does not perceive whence or how it has come about, as when an individual knows that one person cannot exist in two places and that a single thing cannot be simultaneously new and old, or existent and nonexistent. Does not the individual, from childhood on, find himself naturally endowed with these forms of knowledge without perceiving when or whence they came to him? I mean that he perceives no proximate cause for them, otherwise it would not be hidden from him that it is God who created him and guides him.

As for acquired forms of knowledge, they are derived from instruction and deductive inference, and both of the two aspects are called intellectual understanding. ʿAlī said,

> I saw the intellect as of two kinds:
>   the imprinted and the learned.
> The learned is of no use
>   if it is not imprinted,
> Just as the sun is worthless
>   when the eye is incapable of receiving illumination.

The first aspect of intellect is what the Prophet had in mind when he said to ʿAlī, "God fashioned no creature more noble than the intellect." He was referring to the second when he said to ʿAlī, "If the people approach God through all manner of piety, you draw near through your intellect," for drawing near to God is not possible through innate disposition or necessary forms of knowledge but through acquired knowledge.

Thus the heart functions much as does the eye, and the natural disposition of the intellect in the heart functions much as does the power of vision in the eye. The power of vision is a subtle faculty of which the blind person is bereft but which is present in the sighted person, even if the eyes are closed or night has descended. The knowledge that arises from that power in the heart functions much as does the perceptive power of sight in the eye and its vision [19] of the essences of things.

The lagging of knowledge behind the eye of the intellect during the period of childhood on up to the age of discrimination or maturity is like the lagging of actual vision behind sight until the moment of the sun's rising and the flooding of its light upon the things to which the power of sight is directed. The pen with which God inscribes the varieties of knowledge upon the folios of hearts functions much like the disk of the sun. However, knowledge does not arise in the heart of a child prior to the age of discrimination because the tablet of the heart is not ready to receive knowledge itself. *Pen* is an expression for one of God's creatures that He made a means for the arising, like the sun, of the inscription of knowledge upon the hearts of human beings. God said, "He who taught by the Pen, taught the human being what he knew not" (96:4–5). The Pen of God is not like a created pen, just as one cannot describe God as one describes His creation; His Pen is not made of reed or wood, even as the Most High himself is not composed of substance and accident.

Thus the comparison between inner spiritual insight and outward vision is appropriate from this perspective, except that there is no comparison between the two with respect to nobility. Inner spiritual insight is the eye of the soul, a perceptive faculty that is like the rider of a horse—the body. The rider's blindness is more harmful to the rider than the blindness of the horse, but there is no connection between the deficit of the one and that of the other. God made reference to the comparison between inward spiritual insight and outward vision when He said, "And the heart did not lie as to what it saw" (53:11), referring to the heart's perception as "vision." Likewise, with His words, "And we gave Abraham a vision of the kingdoms of heaven and earth" (6:75), He was not referring to outward vision, for that was not conferred on Abraham specifically in order for him to display gratitude. For that reason God called the opposite of perceiving Him blindness, so He said, "It is not their eyes, but their hearts in the center of their being that are blind" (22:46). And the Most High said, "Those who are blind here will be blind in the next life and the most errant from the path" (17:72). This, then, clarifies rational knowledge.

As for the varieties of religious knowledge, they are gained along the way of unquestioning acceptance from the Prophets, and that begins with instruction in the Book of God and the Sunna of His Messenger. Profound comprehension of the meanings of these two sources goes beyond hearing and comprises the heart's perfection and its freedom from illness and disease. The varieties of rational knowledge, therefore, are not sufficient for the health of the heart, though it does have need of them. Just so, the intellect is not adequate to ensure the continued soundness of the body's operations. That requires a specialized awareness of healing remedies and medicines by way of instruction from physicians, since the intellect does not naturally lead one to them. But full comprehension of such instruction upon hearing it is not possible except through the intellect, so the intellect cannot dispense with hearing and hearing cannot get along without the intellect. It is thus ignorant folly either to appeal to simple acquiescence to authority detached from the intellect, or assert the sole sufficiency of intellect apart from the lights of the Qur'ān. You must be careful, therefore, not to opt solely for one of the two elements but must, rather, combine the two principles.

The varieties of rational knowledge are like forms of nourishment, and the varieties of divinely revealed knowledge like remedies; the person who is ill must seek nourishment when the medical treatment is over. In the same way, treatments of the maladies of hearts cannot be designed except with the medicaments available from the divinely Revealed Law, namely, daily doses of worship and the deeds in which the prophets engaged for the welfare of hearts. Anyone who does not treat his ailing heart with the regimen of divinely ordained worship, relying instead entirely on the various forms of rational knowledge, will need to have recourse to worship the way a sick person needs nourishment. The notion that the varieties of rational knowledge are contradictory to the varieties of divinely revealed knowledge, and that there is no possibility of combining the two, is a notion that originates from blindness in the eye of spiritual insight, and from that we take refuge in God.

One who makes such an assertion may well think that some divinely revealed knowledge is at odds with other aspects of knowledge and thus may be unable to integrate them. Considering that incompatible with religion, the individual becomes confused about it and slips away gradually and imperceptibly. That is only because the individual's personal incapacity appears to him as a religious conflict and a source of confusion. Such an individual is like the blind person who enters someone's house, knocks over some household vessels, and says, "What's going on with these vessels left in the way—why were they not returned to their places?" The householder replies, "These vessels are in their places! It is your blindness that keeps you from knowing where you're going. The wonder is that you haven't blamed your stumbling on your blindness, but have instead blamed it on someone else's negligence!" This then is the relationship of religious knowledge to rational knowledge.

[20] The rational disciplines are divided into this-worldly and otherworldly types. As for the former, it includes, for example, the science of medicine, mathematics, engineering, astronomy, as well as the other professions and trades. The otherworldly forms of knowledge include, for example, knowledge of the heart's spiritual states and of deleterious actions, and the knowledge of God and His attributes and deeds, as I have laid out in the Book of Knowledge. These two kinds of knowledge are incompatible with each other in the sense that when one turns his attention to the former of them until he becomes absorbed in it, his spiritual insight into the latter is largely diminished. For that reason ʿAlī coined three analogies for this world and the next when he said, "They are like the two pans of a balance scale, like the east and the west, and like two wives: When the one is content, the other is resentful."

For that reason you will observe that those astute in worldly matters and in the disciplines of medicine, calculation, engineering, and philosophy are ignorant in otherworldly matters. Those, on the other hand, who are shrewd in the fine points of the sciences of the next life are largely ignorant of the secular sciences, for the power of the intellect is not sufficient to integrate a mastery of the two matters, so that one of them militates against completeness in the second. On this point the Prophet said, "Indeed, most of the residents of Paradise are uneducated," that is, untutored in this-worldly matters.

In one of his exhortations, Ḥasan (al-Baṣrī) said, "We have encountered folk whom, if you saw them, you would call crazy; and if they encountered you, they would call you devils." Whenever you hear from them a strange religious matter that those who are educated in the other sciences repudiate, do not let their disavowal seduce you away from accepting the strange matter, for it is inconceivable that a traveler bound for the east should arrive in the west. That is the way the issue of this world and the next goes, and about that the Most High said, "Those who do not hope in meeting Us and who are content with the life of this world and take comfort in it..." (10:7).[2] And the Most High said, "They know only the externals of the life of this world and are heedless of the next" (30:7). And He said, "Keep clear of those who turn away from our Reminder, intent only on the life of this world. That far only does knowledge reach them" (53:29–30). None will succeed in integrating the perfection of spiritual insight into both secular and religious well-being except those whom God has grounded in the direction of His servants in their earthly lives and their eternal destiny. They are the prophets who are confirmed by the holy spirit and who draw upon the divine power that can achieve all things and falls short of nothing. And as for the hearts of the rest of humankind, when they rely on affairs of this world, they turn their attention away from the next life and fail to reach their consummation in it.

Clarification 8 [20–22], translated by Richard McCarthy,[3] *analyzes the distinction between inspiration* (ilhām—*which Ghazālī defines as learning not dependent on proof, but which simply "falls into" the heart effortlessly from unknown sources) and instruction (*taʿallum—*which Ghazālī defines as a path to knowledge that requires inference and effort), and between Sufi epistemology and the acquisition of reason-based knowledge. The crucial difference underlying the disparity between the two modes of knowing lies in the* *diversity of the sources of knowledge and the possibility of ascertaining the reasons why the heart finds itself "knowing" certain things. Hence, for example, one who receives knowledge by* ilhām *is unaware of its source, whereas the prophet who receives "revelation" knows that it comes from God. Inspiration involves the graced (rather than effortful) removal of a veil between the mirror of the heart and the mirror of the Preserved Tablet. Sufis prefer this to learning by instruction and strive to maximize their predisposition to receive it as and when God chooses to bestow it.*

Clarification 9 [22–25]: Explaining the difference between the two situations[4] using an analogy with sensation

Understand that the marvels of the heart extend beyond the perceptions of the senses, for the heart itself also goes beyond sense perception. The only way to comprehend the attainment of what one does not perceive sensibly is by comparison with sensation. We can clarify the matter of weak perceptive faculties with two analogies.

First, suppose we needed a pool excavated in the ground and designed to contain water from the rivers above it that flow into it. One would probably need to excavate the pool very deeply and remove dirt from it the better to ensure a supply of pure water. The water would then flow from the depths of the pool, and that water would be the purest and most continuously supplied, as well as the most plentiful and abundant. Now the heart is like the pool, knowledge is like the water, and the five senses are like the rivers. It may be that the varieties of knowledge are conveyed freely to the heart through the medium of the rivers of the senses, that is, from direct experience, until the heart is filled with knowledge. But these rivers might also be dammed by separation and solitude, so that the vision is turned downward and becomes intent on the depths of the heart in order to purify it, thereby lifting various layers of veils from it until it overflows, allowing a torrent of knowledge to flow from within the heart.

Suppose one were to object, "But how can knowledge flow out from the heart itself when it is empty of it?" Understand that this is one of the most marvelous mysteries of the heart. But one cannot discuss it in the context of the knowledge of external relations; rather, one can discuss it only to the extent that the inner natures of things are inscribed on the Preserved Tablet and even in the hearts of the angels who have drawn near to God. Just as the architect makes a drawing of the structure of a house on a blank page and then brings it out into reality in accordance with this prototype, so the Creator of heaven and earth inscribed the prototype of the universe from beginning to end on the Preserved Tablet and then brought it forth into existence in accordance with this exemplar. The universe that emerges into existence in the image of the prototype gives rise to yet another image that is the object of sensation [23] and imagination.

If the individual who gazes upon heaven and earth then closes his eyes, he sees the image of heaven and earth in his imagination as though he were still actually looking at them. Even if heaven and earth were to go out of existence and the individual stayed as he was, he would discover the image of heaven and earth within himself as though he were witnessing and gazing upon them. Then traces proceed from his imagination to the heart so that true natures of the things that entered by the senses and imagination settle there in the heart. That which arises in the imagination accords with the actual universe as it is, emerging from the individual's imagination and heart. And the actual universe is in accord with the prototype that exists on the Preserved Tablet.

It is as though the universe had four levels of existence. Its existence in the Preserved Tablet is prior to its physical existence; after that comes its existence in reality, and after its existence in reality comes its existence in imagination—I refer to the existence of its image in the imagination—and after its existence in imagination comes its intellectual existence, by which I mean the existence of its image in the heart.

Some of these levels of existence are spiritual and others physical, and some of the spiritual levels are more intensely spiritual than others. This is a gracious gift of the divine wisdom, that He has arranged that the pupil of your eye, although small in size, receives on itself the imprint of the image of the universe of heaven and earth in all its expansive breadth. Then, from its existence in the senses He brings about its existence in the imagination, and from there its existence in the heart, so that you always perceive only what comes to you. Therefore, if He did not create a likeness of the whole universe within your being, you would have no information with which to elucidate your own existence. Praised be the One, therefore, who devised these marvels in hearts and eyes and then blinded hearts and eyes from perceiving them, so that most creatures are ignorant of their selves and of their marvels.

To return to the focus of my topic: I say that the heart imagines that the true nature of the universe settles in it, and the universe's image is sometimes a result of sensation and sometimes derived from the Preserved Tablet. This happens much the way the eye imagines that the image of the sun has settled in it, sometimes as a result of gazing at the sun and sometimes as a result of gazing at water that receives the sun and makes a copy of its image. Whenever the veil is lifted between the heart and the Preserved Tablet, the heart sees things upon it and knowledge breaks forth into it from the Tablet. The result is that the heart has no need of sensory input, and that is analogous to water's bursting forth from the depths of the earth. And whenever one occupies oneself with the products of imagination that arise from sensible objects, this veils the individual from reading the Preserved Tablet much the way that water contained in rivers is prevented from flowing forth upon the earth. So when a person gazes upon water that produces a copy of the image of the sun, he is not gazing at the sun itself.

There is, then, a door to the heart that opens to the realm of Lordly Dominion, which is the Preserved Tablet and the realm of the angels, as well as a door opened to the five senses, which gives access to the realm of earthly sovereignty and experience. In addition, the realm of experience and earthly sovereignty resembles the realm of Lordly Dominion through a kind of imitation.

The opening of the door of the heart to sensory input is not hidden from you. As for the opening of its inward door toward the realm of Lordly Dominion and of reading the Preserved Tablet, you come to know that with certain knowledge by contemplating the marvels of vision and the heart's cognizance during sleep, concerning what will be in the future or what has been in the past, without input from the senses.

Nevertheless, that door opens to anyone who single-mindedly recollects God, as the Prophet said, "The single-minded are in the lead." Someone asked him, "And who are the single-minded, O Messenger of God?" He replied, "Those whose remembrance of God is pure He unburdens of the heavy load of recollection so that they come light to the Resurrection." Then by way of describing them further, Muḥammad quoted God as saying, "Then I will turn My face toward them and ask, 'Do you see before My face anyone who knows what I desire to give him?' Then the Most High said, 'The first thing I will give them is to cast the light into their hearts so that they are informed about Me as I am informed about them.'" Access to this information is the door, and the difference between the kinds of knowledge of the Friends of God and the Prophets, on the one hand, and those of the religious scholars and sages, on the other, is [24] that the knowledge of the former comes from within the heart through the door opened into the realm of Lordly Dominion, whereas the knowledge of wisdom comes through the doors of the senses opened onto the realm of the earthly sovereignty. The marvels of the realm of the heart and its oscillation between the realms of experiential witnessing and of the unseen cannot be thoroughly examined in the context of the science of deeds. This analogy, then, will teach you the difference between the modes of entry to the two realms.

The second analogy will familiarize you with the difference between two kinds of action, that is, the deeds of the religious scholars and the deeds of the Friends of God. Religious scholars work on the acquisition of the varieties of knowledge themselves and on procuring them for the heart. Sufi Friends of God, on the other hand, work solely on the clarification, cleansing, purification, and burnishing of the heart. A story is told of how some Chinese and Greeks competed with each other before a certain king on the grounds of the excellence of their creation of a painting and an image. The king decided to submit to them a description that the Chinese would depict on one side, and the Greeks on the other, and to hang a curtain between the two sides to prevent either group from spying on the other, and he did so. The Greeks mixed marvelous pigments without limit, while the Chinese proceeded without paint and busied themselves polishing and burnishing their wall. When the Greeks had finished, the Chinese called out that they, too, were finished. The king was surprised at what they said and that the Chinese had completed their painting without paint. Someone asked, "How did you accomplish that without paint?" They answered, "Never mind. Just raise the curtain." So they lifted it, and there on the Chinese wall shimmered the marvels of the Greek creation but even brighter and more sparkling, for it had become like a brilliant mirror highly burnished, and the more it was polished the more beautiful it became.

Just so the Friends of God are concerned with cleaning, shining, purifying, and clarifying the heart until the resplendence of the truth gleams upon it with the utmost illumination, as in the work of the Chinese. The concern of the sages and religious scholars, on the other hand, is acquiring and depicting the varieties of knowledge and instilling a likeness of them upon the heart, as the Greeks did. Whatever the case, the heart of the believer does not die, and his knowledge is not obliterated when he dies, nor is the heart's clarity blurred. Ḥasan (al-Baṣrī) alluded to this when he said, "Earth does not swallow up the dwelling place of faith; rather, it becomes a means and a source of nearness to God."

The knowledge and clarity and inclination to receive knowledge itself that transpire in the heart are essential to the heart, and none can be happy except through *ʿilm* and *maʿrifa*. Some types of happiness are loftier than others, as in the case of a person who is rich only in possessions. One who possesses a gold dirham is rich, as is the owner of overflowing storehouses. Similarly, the levels of those who are happy differ with respect to disparity of experiential knowledge and faith, just as the levels of the wealthy differ in relation to the scarcity or abundance of possessions. Now the benefits are lights, and believers run to meet God only with the aid of their lights, as God said, "Their light runs before them and by their right hands" (57:12). Tradition has it that "some of them are given light like a mountain and some of them less, until the last of them is a man who is given light on the big toe of his two feet, so that at one moment it shines and at another it goes out, and when it shines his two feet proceed, but when it goes out he stands still. Their progress along the path is proportionate to their light, and among these people are some who move along like the blink of an eye, others who progress like lightning, some like clouds, others like falling stars, some as fast as a horse charging across its field. The individual who is given light on his big toe creeps on his face and hands and feet, putting one hand down and extending the other, and the Fire laps at his sides, and he does not cease until he is safe (from the Fire)."

In this respect the disparity among people with regard to faith is apparent. If the faith of Abū Bakr were weighed against the faith of learned ones other than the Prophets and Messengers, his would weigh more. This is also the gist of someone's observation, "If the light of the sun were compared with the light of all lanterns, it would surpass them." Even so, the light of some among the masses of people would be like the light of a lamp, while the light of others would be like that of candle. The light of the faith of the authentic ones is like the moon and stars, while the faith of the prophets is like the sun. Just as the image of the horizons in the full breadth of their expansiveness is revealed in the light of the sun, while only a small corner of a house is revealed by the light of a lamp, so diverse are the degrees of the expansion of the center of one's being with realizations [25] and disclosure of the expanse of Lordly Dominion for the hearts of those endowed with experiential knowledge. Concerning that point the tradition has come down to us, "On the day of resurrection it will be said, 'Bring out of the Fire anyone who has an atom's weight of faith in his heart—or even a half or a fourth of a barleycorn or atom's weight.'"

That range of degrees of faith indicates that these varying capacities for faith do not forestall entry into the Fire. It is thus understood that when the weight of a person's faith increases, that person will not enter the Fire, since, if a person did enter it, the matter of his escaping would take precedence. It is understood that if one with an atom's weight of faith in his heart should enter the Fire, he would not remain there forever. In this context the Prophet said, "The individual believer is a thousand times better than anything else." He is referring to the excellence of the heart of the person endowed with experiential knowledge of God, the One who bestows certitude, indicating that such a heart is better than a thousand hearts of the generality of people. The Most High has said, "And you are superior if you are believers" (3:139), giving preference to believers over most Muslims, referring to the believer who possesses experiential knowledge devoid of uncritical imitation. And God said, "God will elevate in rank those of you who believe and who are given knowledge" (58:11), referring there, with the phrase "those who believe," to those who are truthful apart from knowledge and distinguishing them from those who are given knowledge. That indicates that the term "the believer" is synonymous with "one who follows authority uncritically" if the person's assent is not the result of spiritual insight and divine disclosure.

Ibn ʿAbbās commented on the words of the Most High, "in rank...and those who are given knowledge" (58:11), by saying that God elevates the possessor of knowledge above the believer by seven hundred ranks between each two levels, as He has elevated heaven above earth. And the Prophet said, "Most of the people of the Garden are untutored and (yet) are above those endowed with insight" and "One endowed with knowledge is superior to the devotee as I am superior to the nearest man among my Companions." One narrative has, "as the moon on the Night of Badr is superior to the rest of the stars." These citations thus make clear to you the disparity in the ranks of the people of the Garden with respect to the differences in their hearts and their experiential knowledge. Therefore the day of resurrection is the day of deception, since great fraud and depravity are excluded from the mercy of God, and the one excluded will see lofty ranks above his own rank; he will gaze at them the way a wealthy person who has ten dirhams gazes upon the wealthy person who owns the earth from the east to the west. Both of them are wealthy, but what an immense gap between them! And what an enormous defrauding of one who has forfeited his portion of that, "for in the next life there are immense differences in rank and huge disparities in excellence" (17:21).

Clarification 10: Testimonies of the Revealed Law concerning the soundness of the path of the Sufis with respect to the acquisition of *maʿrifa* other than through instruction and the accustomed path

Understand that one to whom something has been disclosed, even if it is a matter of minor significance on the path of inspiration and descends into the heart from an unknown source, becomes endowed with experiential knowledge through the integrity of the Path. And one who does not perceive that at all on his own must have faith in it. For the level of experiential knowledge in such matters is extremely rare, as the testimonies of the Revealed Law and experience and anecdotal evidence will attest.

As for the testimonies, there is the word of the Most High, "And those who struggle on Our behalf, We will surely guide them to Our ways" (29:69). All wisdom that arises from the heart as a result of assiduous devotion comes not from instruction, but belongs to the path of divine disclosure and inspiration. The Prophet said, "To one who acts on what he knows, God will bequeath as an inheritance a knowledge of what he did not know [26] and will give him success in what he does so that he deserves Paradise. But one who does not act upon what he knows will be lost in what he knows and will not be successful in what he does, so that he deserves Hell." And God has said, "For those who fear God, He makes a way out" of dilemmas and doubts, "and provides sustenance for them from unanticipated sources" (65:2–3). That is, He instructs them in knowledge without need of conventional instruction and supplies them with understanding independent of ordinary experience.

And God has said, "Oh, you who believe, if you fear God, He will create for you the power of discrimination" (8:29), a "criterion" that is called a light by which one can distinguish between truth and falsehood and by which one can escape from doubts. For that reason Muḥammad used to pray often, requesting the light, saying, "O God, give me light and increase light in me, make light for me in my heart and light in my grave, light in my hearing and light in my sight until it speaks in my hair and in my humanity and in my flesh and blood and bones." Someone asked Muḥammad about the word "expanded" in the words of God, "Is the one the center of whose being God has expanded to be receptive to Islam so that he benefits from the light of his Lord…?" (39:22). So he replied, "It is a widening, so that when God infuses the light into the heart, the center of the individual's being becomes more spacious and is amplified." Muḥammad said on behalf of Ibn ʿAbbās, "O God, give him *fiqh* in religious matters and teach him the interpretation of inner meanings."

ʿAlī said, "We know of nothing that the Prophet concealed from us, but that God gives a servant *fahm* of His Book, and this is not by way of ordinary instruction." An exegete observes in a commentary on the Most High's word, "He gives wisdom to whom He wishes" (2:269), that it refers to the profound comprehension of God's Book. And God said, "So we gave Solomon *fahm* of it" (21:79), specifying what the words "profound comprehension" disclose. Abū 'd-Dardā' used to say, "Believers are those who see with the light of God what is behind a gossamer veil, and God infuses it into their hearts that God is the truth and causes it to flow on their tongues." And one of the ancestors in faith said, "Even the believer's mere supposition is perspicacity." The Prophet said, "Beware the discernment of the believer, for he sees with the light of God." Alluding to that are the words of the Most High, "In that are signs for those who know how to interpret the traces" (15:75), as also His words, "We have made the signs clear to any people who hold the faith surely" (2:118).

Ḥasan transmitted from God's Messenger that he said, "*ʿIlm* is of two kinds, and inward knowledge in the heart—that is the *ʿilm* that is truly beneficial." Someone asked one of the religious scholars what inward knowledge is, and he replied, "It is one of God's mysteries that God infuses into the hearts of those He loves most, and neither angel nor human being can gain insight into it." And the Prophet has said, "If there are in my community (even) two Ḥadīth transmitters, two teachers, or two speakers, surely ʿUmar is one of them."

Ibn ʿAbbās recited, "Never have We sent [27] before you a messenger or a prophet [or a speaker]" (22:52),[5] referring to the authentic ones. The speaker is the one inspired, and the one inspired is the one who has received a divine disclosure in the depths of his heart, in the sense of something that enters from outside rather than something that results from external sensory input.

The Qur'ān makes it clear that fear of God is the key of guidance and divine disclosure, and that is knowledge independent of instruction. God has said, "What God has created in heaven and earth are signs for the god-fearing" (10:6); and the Most High further specified those people by saying, "This is a clarification for the people, and guidance and admonition for the god-fearing" (3:138). Abū Yazīd (al-Bisṭāmī) and others used to say, "The learned person is not the one who memorizes from a book, and who, when he forgets what he had memorized, becomes ignorant; the learned person is the one who receives his knowledge from his Lord whenever He wishes, without memorizing and without studying. And this is the Lordly knowledge as indicated in the word of the Most High, 'And We have taught him (Khiḍr) a knowledge from Our presence'" (18:65). Though all knowledge is from the divine presence, nevertheless some of it occurs through the medium of human instruction; that is not called knowledge from God's presence. Knowledge from God's presence is that which is revealed in the depths of the heart without an identifiable secondary cause. These, then, are the testimonies of tradition, and if one gathered together all of the relevant examples of verses, reports, and traditions, they would be beyond counting.

As for actual contemplative vision, that belongs to the category of experience, and that would likewise exceed our reckoning. That was familiar to the Companions and the Followers and their successors. Abū Bakr the Truthful One said to ʿĀ'isha when he was at the point of death, "These two are your brothers and your sisters." His wife was pregnant and gave birth to a daughter, and he already knew before the birth that it was a daughter. ʿUmar said in the course of his Friday sermon, "O Sāriya! The mountain!" when it was divinely disclosed to him that the enemy was approaching, so (ʿUmar) warned (Sāriya the military commander) as a result of (ʿUmar's) *maʿrifa* of that situation. Thus the communication of (ʿUmar's) voice to (Sāriya) was one of the great marvels.[6]

Anas ibn Mālik said, "As I was going to visit ʿUthmān, I encountered a woman along the way. I gave her a sidelong glance, and then I took a good look at her beauty. When I went in to ʿUthmān he said, "One of you has come to visit me with the vestiges of adultery evident in his eyes. Do you not know that adultery of the eyes is a look you need to repent of or for which I must reprimand you?" So I asked, "Is there Revelation after the Prophet?" "No," he replied, "but there is vision and proof and discernment and authenticity." Abū Saʿīd al-Kharrāz said, "I entered the mosque of the sanctuary in Mecca, and I saw a beggar wearing two patched frocks, so I said to myself, 'This one and his kind are everywhere among the people.' So he called out to me and said (quoting the Qur'ān), 'God knows what is within yourselves, so be wary of

Him' (2:235). So I asked forgiveness of God in secret, and the man called out to me, 'He it is who accepts repentance from His servants' (42:25). Then he was gone from me and I saw him no more."

Zakariyā ibn Dāwūḍ said, "Abū 'l-ʿAbbās ibn Masrūq (d.c. 298/910) went to visit Abū 'l-Faḍl al-Hāshimī—who was ill and had a family and had no obvious means of support—and said, 'When I left I said to myself, How does this man eat?' So (Abū 'l-Faḍl) called out to me, "O Abū 'l-ʿAbbās, reject this worldly concern, for God's are hidden kindnesses."'" And Aḥmad an-Naqīb said, "I went to visit Shiblī, and he said charmingly, 'O Aḥmad.' I replied, 'What's new?' He answered, 'I was sitting and it occurred to me that you're a cheapskate.' I replied, 'I am not a cheapskate.' Then as I was letting go of my irritation, he said, 'But you *are* a cheapskate.' So I retorted, 'This day had scarcely begun but that I handed something over to the first poor person who encountered me.' But my pique was not complete until a companion of Mu'nis the servant, who had fifty dinars, came to visit me. He said, 'I give this to you for your use.' So I stood and took the money and left, and there before me with a poor blind person was a barber shaving the man's head, so I approached him and gave him the dinars. Then he (the poor person) said, "Give it to the barber." So I replied, "Even though it is such a sum?" He said, "Didn't we tell you that you are a cheapskate?" So I gave it to the barber and the barber said, "We made a deal when this poor person sat down with me that I would not charge him a fee." So I tossed the money into the Tigris River and said, "No one elevates you but that God humbles him."'"

Ḥamza ibn ʿAbd Allāh al-ʿAlawī said, "I went to visit Abū 'l-Khayr at-Tīnātī (d. 349/960–61), and I decided privately that I would greet him [28] but would not eat food in his house. So, when I left his presence, he caught up with me. He was carrying all sorts of food, and said, "Young man, eat, for you have passed the time limit of your decision not to eat." Now this Abū 'l-Khayr at-Tīnātī was famous for working wonders. Ibrāhīm ar-Raqqī (d. 342/953–54) said, "I intended to greet him (Tīnātī), so I attended the evening ritual prayer. The recitation of the opening sūra of the Qur'ān was almost finished, and I said to myself, 'My journey has been in vain (because I was late).' Then after the final greeting, I went out for purification. A lion was following me, so I hurried to Abū 'l-Khayr and said, 'A lion is coming after me,' so he went out and called to the lion, 'Didn't I tell you not to harass my guests?' The lion then went his way, and I performed my purification. When I came back he said to me, 'You were preoccupied with external standards and you were afraid of the lion; I was preoccupied with internal standards, so the lion was afraid of me.'"

Countless stories are told about the perspicacity of the shaykhs and their being aware of people's beliefs and thoughts. Indeed, their narratives about visions of Khiḍr and inquiries of him, about hearing the voice of an unseen speaker, and about the various kinds of marvels are beyond reckoning. Narrative accounts are of no avail to the unbeliever to the extent that such an individual has no personal experience of things like this. Whoever refuses to acknowledge the principle, disavows its implications, and the conclusive evidence that no one can refute consists of two matters: First, the wonders of authentic visionary experience disclose the unseen, and if that occurs during sleep, then it is also possible in the waking state. For sleep does not differ from the waking state except with respect to the suspension of sensation and the lack of engagement with the objects of sensation. How many people are awake but with eyes cast down, neither hearing nor seeing because of their self-absorption!

Second, there is the manner in which God's Messenger was informed about the unseen world and questions of reception of the Qur'ān when it was made known to him. If that happened to the Prophet, it happened to others to the extent that *prophet* is a term for an individual to whom the ultimate truths of things are disclosed, and who is concerned with the welfare of humankind. It is possible that an individual could experience disclosures of the ultimate truths and not be occupied with the welfare of humankind, but then such a person is not called a prophet, but a Friend of God. When a person believes in the prophets and has a sound, authentic visionary experience, it follows necessarily that one must conclude that the heart has two doors: a door to the outside that is the senses, and a door to the Lordly Dominion within the heart that is the door of inspiration, of infusing into the spirit, and of prophetic revelation. Though it is entirely impossible for the more proximate of the two doors to give access to the varieties of knowledge through instruction and the pursuit of ordinary means, it is, nevertheless, conceivable that spiritual struggle might provide a path to that. This, then, points to the spiritual reality I have been discussing in terms of the wonder that holds the heart between the realm of experience and the realm of Lordly Dominion. As for the means of the disclosure of the matter in a dream through similitudes that require interpretation, that is how the angels deliver similitudes to the prophets and Friends of God, namely, by means of various images, and that too is among the marvels of the heart. This is not appropriate subject matter except through the knowledge of divine disclosure, so I will discuss the matter no further, since what I have said is sufficient prompting toward spiritual struggle and the quest for divine disclosure.

One of those who disclose has said, "The recording angel appeared to me and asked me to dictate to him some of my secret recollection of my contemplation of the divine transcendent unity. He said, 'What deed shall we record for you? We would like to improve your standing through an action by which you would draw near to God.' So I asked, 'Are the two of you recording legal duties?' The two said, 'Yes.' I said, 'That's enough for you two.'" This indicates that even the exalted recorders are not acquainted with the mysteries of the heart, even though they are familiar with external actions. One of those endowed with experiential knowledge said, "I asked one of the Abdāl about a matter of the experience of certitude, so he turned toward his left and asked, 'What do you say, God be merciful to you?' Then he turned over toward his right, and asked, 'What do you say, God be merciful to you?' Then he oriented himself toward his center and asked, 'What do you say, God be merciful to you?' His response was the strangest answer I have ever heard, so I asked him about his turning, and he said, 'I didn't have a ready reply to the question, so I asked the companion on the left and he replied, "I don't know"; so I asked the companion on the right, who is more knowledgeable, and he answered, "I don't know"; so I looked into my heart and asked it, and it informed me how I should answer you, and indeed, it is more knowledgeable than the other two.'" And this was the meaning of (the Prophet's) saying, "If there are two Ḥadīth specialists in my Community, ʿUmar is one of them."

[29] Tradition reports that God says, "Whatever arises in the heart of a servant, so that I see devotion overcoming him with remembrance of Me, I see to his governance and I become his companion and

confidant and intimate friend." And Abū Sulaymān ad-Dārānī said, "The heart dwells beneath an elaborate dome around which are closed doors, so which door does the heart's action open for it? The opening of one of the doors of the heart looks toward the Lordly Dominion and the sublime assembly. That door opens through inner struggle, spiritual reticence, and turning away from worldly cravings." On this subject ʿUmar wrote to the commanders of the army, "Take to heart what you hear from those who are obedient, for authentic matters are manifest to them." One of the learned ones said, "The hand of God is over the mouths of the wise, so that they utter only the truth that God desires." Another said, "One might say that God provides the lowly with the apex of insight into some of His mysteries."

In Clarifications 11 through 15 Ghazālī focuses on the range of problems with which the ever mutable heart must deal. These include, most of all, the temptations and insinuations that the devil manages to introduce through the heart's many openings. The heart that does not struggle to fend off these suggestions is blameworthy, but the heart can also hope for forgiveness. Likewise, Ghazālī discusses the question of whether the deliberate recollection of God renders the heart impervious to diabolical influences. He concludes that, because its state changes so rapidly, no heart can hope to be free of temptation for long. This conclusion sets the stage for his consideration of the process of "training" the heart as the foundation of advanced Islamic ethics (in Book 22).

8

Ibn al-ʿArīf: *The Beauties of Spiritual Sessions (Maḥāsin al-majālis)*

We begin with Ibn al-ʿArīf's brief introductory section on maʿrifa *as the first stage of the advanced spiritual path. Then, later in the treatise, he sets* maʿrifa *within a larger context: knowledge as a fundamental need, and advanced mystical knowledge as a marvel bestowed on the servant hereafter. These two aspects of knowledge function as a set of bookends, so to speak, on either side of* maʿrifa, *itself one stage on the path of the seeker.*[1]

Chapter 1: *Maʿrifa*

[75] *Maʿrifa* is my (pilgrim) goal and *ʿilm* is my proof. The religious scholar asks me for demonstrative argument, but one endowed with *maʿrifa* accepts guidance from me. Religious scholars become attached to me, while mystics become attached through me. Worshipers look for actions, spiritual seekers for spiritual states, and mystics for movements of the spirit. God is beyond all that, and the only connection between Him [76] and the devotees is divine favor, while the only causes are the divine decrees. God has no "present moment" but eternity. What remains for human beings is blindness and deceit, so that they regard their deeds as cause for recompense, their spiritual states as intended to conjure up saintly wonders, and movements of the spirit as meant to produce union with God. The Truth,

however, is evident only when the personal attributes of individuality disappear, so that the mystical allusion is a call from the distant summit and a disclosure of a specific instruction to the servant.[2]

Discursive knowledge is to hearts what the search for secondary causes is to mysteries; everything that is not God is a veil over them. If not for the darkness of created reality, the light of mystery would be manifest, and but for the ego-soul's seduction there would be no veils over mystery. If not for distractions, spiritual realities would be unveiled, and if not for the search for causes, amazing powers would be evident. If not for human affectation, there would be pure experiential knowledge, and were it not for cupidity, love would take root. If not for the wayward glance toward passing delights, spirits would yearn for God, and were it not for the godservant's distance, he would witness the Lord. [76] When the veils are pulled aside with the disruption of secondary causes, and the barriers are lifted through the severing of attachments, then it will be as (Ḥallāj) said:

Now that which has long been a secret is disclosed to you,
and dawn has broken over the darkness in which you have dwelt.
It is your own heart that has veiled the mystery in its depths,
and if you had not surrendered yourself, the mystery's seal would not have been impressed on it.
But if you empty your heart, He will dwell therein and pitch His
tent in the very midst of the closely guarded revelation.
And a conversation you would never tire of hearing would ensue,
one whose rhymed prose and embellished verse alike would delight us.

Chapter 13: The Wider Contexts of Mystical Knowledge

This chapter lists maʿrifa *as the twenty-second of the marvels of the next life. Here Ibn al-ʿArīf lays out his brief characterizations of each of the forty marvels. Then, linking faith with experiential knowledge, he turns to an explicitly epistemological contextualization of everything he has been discussing, placing* maʿrifa *in the wider contexts of mystical knowledge in general.*

[101] Twenty-two: Steadfastness in experiential knowledge and faith, from which come fear of God and confusion as well as tears and sadness. God has said, "God will firmly establish those who believe, with the unshakable word in this life as well as the next" (14:27).

[103] And what impels us to seek to know all of that? After all, our Lord says, "No one knows what delights are kept in secret for them" (32:17), and God's Messenger has said, "He has created there in Paradise what eye has not seen nor ear heard, nor human heart imagined." Concerning the words of the Most High, "The sea of ink would run out before the words of my Lord were finished" (18:109), the exegete has observed that these are the words that He will say in Paradise to the inhabitants of the Garden as a way of being gracious to them and ennobling them. How could a person in this condition of ours attain even a thousandth of a thousandth of their condition, human as we are? And how could creaturely knowledge embrace Him? Indeed, spiritual aspirations fall short and intellects get nowhere close to Him. Appropriately so, for such understanding is a gift of the All-powerful, All-knowing in accord with His enormous bounty and commensurate with His timeless largesse. I pursue the matter in order that those who labor will work toward the likes of this, and that those who strive dedicate their efforts wholly to this tremendous goal, since they know that their efforts are meager indeed by contrast with that which they need, for which they search and to which they have turned their attention.

Understand that, on the whole, there are four things essential to the servant: First, *ʿilm* of the essence of God as the one, the eternal; second, knowledge of God's attributes, namely, life, *ʿilm,* will, power, [104] hearing, seeing, speech—which has no letters and no sound—and His perceptions; third, in recognition of His perfect being, denial of any divine deficiencies or maladies along with affirmation of His beautiful names; finally, the essential deeds associated with this knowledge to the extent that it is a required legal duty and is characterized by sincerity and fear of God.

In other words, the servant first acquires *ʿilm* of the path, persuaded of the need for investigation, without which he is blind. Then he either acts upon what he knows conceptually or is veiled from authentic knowledge. Then, he either acts entirely out of genuine motives or he is deceiving himself. Finally, either he lives in ceaseless fear of God and scrupulous attention to his faults until security from them descends upon him, or he becomes arrogant. Dhū 'n-Nūn was right when he said, "Apart from the religious scholars, all human beings are dead; apart from the religious scholars who put their knowledge into action, all of them are dead too; and except for the productive scholars who are sincere, all of them are deluded; and all those who are sincere are in serious danger."

These four types are very peculiar, it seems to me. The first is intelligent but knows nothing. Has he no concern for insight into his situation? Does he not understand what awaits him at death? Let him examine these clues, heed these signs and warnings, experience discomfort at these passing spiritual impulses and suggestions, and keep the ego-soul in check. God has said, "Have they not reflected...on the kingdoms of the heavens and the earth and everything God has created?" (7:184–85). And again, "Do these people not think they will be raised up on an awful day?" (83:4–5).

As for the second, the learned person who does not act on what he knows, does he not bear in mind the tremendous terrors and severe punishments he knows await him? This is a serious message from which you turn away!

The third, the learned person who acts but who lacks sincerity, should meditate on the Most High's words, "Let any who hope to meet their Lord do good works and serve no other Lord" (18:110).

And fourth, the one who is sincere but lacks fear of God, does that person not take stock of how God treats His chosen ones and Friends who stand between God and His creatures, even to the point of saying to the best of His creatures, Muḥammad, [105] "We have revealed to you and to those who preceded you…" (39:65).[3] When Muḥammad came to the point of saying "Sūrat Hūd and its sisters have turned my hair white," he was referring to "Remain steadfast as you were enjoined" (11:112).

9

Abū Ḥafṣ ʿUmar as-Suhrawardī: *The Benefits of Intimate Knowledge (ʿAwārif al-maʿārif)*

Here are Suhrawardī's first three chapters, dealing, respectively, with the origins of the Sufi disciplines; the superiority of the Sufis in "keen attentiveness," a prerequisite to knowledge; and the superiority of the disciplines of the Sufis. They form the foundation of the entire work and function as a defense against claims that the Sufis devalued the fundamentals of Islamic tradition. Like Makkī and several other authors, Suhrawardī combines various genres, interweaving exegesis and narrative with extensive citation of paradigmatic Sufi figures.[1]

Chapter 1: [55] On the origins of the disciplines of the Sufis

In the month of Shawwāl of the year 560/1165, our shaykh, Shaykh al-Islām Abū 'n-Najīb ʿAbd al-Qāhir ibn ʿAbd Allāh ibn Muḥammad as-Suhrawardī, dictated to us the following account of his recollection, saying: God's Messenger said,[2] "I and the message with which God has sent me are like a man who came to a people and said, 'O my people, I have seen the army with my own eyes, and I am the naked herald. Run for your lives! Save yourselves!' A group of his people obeyed him and set out under cover of night at a comfortable pace and were saved. Some of the people dismissed his warning and spent the night in their place, so that the army came upon them at dawn, slaughtered and annihilated them. That is an analogy with, respectively, those who obey me and follow the message I have brought, and those who rebel against me and reject the message I have brought from God." [The expression "annihilated them" means "it (the army) uprooted them," and derived from this is the calamity that results in the destruction of a crop's yield.]

And Muḥammad said, "The guidance and knowledge with which God has sent me are like an abundant rain that showered the earth. Some of the earth received the water, so that it sprouted grass and abundant herbage. Some of the earth had cisterns that gathered the water, so that God benefited the people with it, and they drank and irrigated and planted. Another portion of the earth was low flatlands that did not collect water and sprouted no verdure. So it is, respectively, with those who possess deeper understanding in the religion of God, to whom the message with which God has sent me is beneficial, so that they know and teach and act, and with those who pay no heed to that and do not accept the guidance with which God sent me."

God has prepared the purest hearts and truest souls to receive what God's Messenger has brought. Variation in purity and clarity is evident in the disparity of profit and utility. Some hearts are like the good earth that sprouts grass and herbage in abundance, and these are they who benefit from knowledge interiorly and are guided, and whose knowledge and guidance orients them to the straight path of following God's Messenger. Other hearts are like cisterns—that is, pools, from the plural of *ikhādha,* an enclosure or reservoir in which water collects. The souls of the ascetical learned individuals among the Sufis and the shaykhs are clear and their hearts pure. As a result they reap especially great benefits and become cisterns. Masrūq[3] said, "I have associated with the Companions of God's Messenger and have found them to be like cisterns. Their hearts are attentive so that they become most receptive to the forms of knowledge by virtue of the pure profound comprehension bestowed on them."

ʿAbd Allāh ibn al-Ḥasan reported to me,[4] "When [56] this verse was revealed, 'that attentive ears absorb (the Qur'ān's reminder)' (69:12), God's Messenger said to ʿAlī, 'I have asked God to make your ear attentive, O ʿAlī.' ʿAlī said, 'I have forgotten nothing since then, and I have not been able to forget.'" Abū Bakr al-Wāsiṭī referred to "ears receptive to mysteries from God." He also said, "(ears) that are receptive in their mines (i.e., their innermost capacities), but without actually experiencing anything (outwardly), so that they are empty of anything other than (God)." Temperamental restlessness is thus none other than a type of ignorance.

The hearts of the Sufis are attentive, for they discipline themselves in this world after becoming firmly grounded in reverential fear. Their souls are cleansed by reverential fear, and their hearts are purified by self-denial. When, through fully realized renunciation, their preoccupation with this world has vanished, the pores of their inner selves are opened and the ears of their hearts hear. Their renunciation of this world assists them in that.

The exegetical specialists, the authorities in Ḥadīth studies, and the legal scholars of Islam master a knowledge of the Book and the Sunna. From those two sources they derive legal requirements and refer newly realized circumstances to principles derived from the source texts, and God protects the religion through them. Specialists in exegesis are intimately familiar with the field of scriptural interpretation and the science of symbolic exegesis, with the ways of the Arabs in speech, the fine points of syntax and inflection, and with the principles of narrative storytelling and the differences in the variant Qur'ānic readings. They have composed books on these things, and through them the Qur'ānic sciences have been made accessible to the community of Muslims.

The authorities on Ḥadīth have distinguished between "sound" and "good" traditions and have made a specialization of the knowledge of transmitters and their names. They have critiqued Ḥadīths on the basis of unreliability and credibility so as to distinguish clearly the healthy from the sick and to separate the crooked from the straight. Through them the method of transmission and the chains of transmitters have been preserved as a way of safeguarding the Sunna. Specialists in jurisprudence are dedicated to drawing out legal requirements and elaborating on questions, knowing legal explanation, referring new cases to the original cases through common legal causes, and including new conditions within the principles of the source texts. From the knowledge of religious law and legal requirements the disciplines of the principles of jurisprudence and of variant opinions branch off. From the knowledge of variant views the science of dialectic branches off, and the discipline of the principles of jurisprudence requires some knowledge of the principles of religion. Part of their discipline is the knowledge of the rules of inheritance, and from that, knowledge of arithmetic and algebra, among others, is needed.

Thus the Revealed Law has been set in order and confirmed, the Hanifite[5] religion has been set straight, and the prophetic guidance and law of the Chosen One (Muḥammad) has been set forth in principle and ramification. So the soil of the hearts of the religious scholars has sprouted grass and herbage as a result of the waters of life it has absorbed in the form of guidance and knowledge. God has said, "From the heavens He has sent water down so that the river beds flow in their fullness" (13:17). Ibn ʿAbbās commented, "The water is knowledge, and the river beds are hearts." Abū Bakr al-Wāsiṭī said, "God created a pure pearl and beheld it with the eye of majesty. It melted away out of shame in His presence so that it flowed, and God said, 'From the heavens He has sent water down so that the river beds flow in their fullness'" (13:17). The purity of hearts is a result of that water's coming to them. Ibn ʿAṭā' said, "From the heavens He has sent water down. This is a similitude God has coined for the godservant: When the torrent flows through the water courses, no impurity remains in the water-courses but that the water washes it away. As a result, when the light that God has apportioned for the servant flows in his soul, there remains in it neither heedlessness nor darkness." "From the heavens he has sent water down" refers to the allotted portion of light, and "so that the river beds flow in their fullness" means that the lights flow in the hearts according to God's apportioning from pre-eternity. "But the scum vanishes like loathsome waste" (13:17) so that hearts wax luminous with no residue of roughness. "While what profits humankind abides on the earth" (13:17 continues); in other words, inane falsehoods disappear and the spiritual realities remain.

Someone else said, "'From the heavens He has sent down the water' of varieties of blessings, so that every heart took its portion and share." And "the river beds" of the hearts of the specialists in exegesis, Ḥadīth, and jurisprudence "flow in their fullness." And the "the river beds" of the hearts of the Sufis among the religious scholars who renounce this world and who hold fast to the spiritual realities of reverential fear "flow in their fullness." The person within whom resides the pollution of love of this world, in the form of possessions and prestige and lust for rank and high standing—the river bed of that person's heart likewise "flows according to its capacity." That person garners a goodly bit of useful knowledge but does not share in the spiritual realities of knowledge. The watercourse of the heart of a person who renounces this world broadens so that it flows with the waters of knowledge that accumulate, and it becomes a cistern.

Someone said to Ḥasan al-Baṣrī, "Those who possess deeper understanding say thus-and-so." He replied, "And have you ever seen a person who possesses deeper understanding *(faqīh)*? For the *faqīh* is one who renounces this world." The Sufis have claimed for themselves a portion of academic study, and that learning through study has brought them to act according to what they know. When they act according to what they know, [57] this action has brought them knowledge of hereditary transmission. So, on the one hand, they are with the other religious scholars in their disciplines, while on the other, they distinguish themselves from them with respect to additional disciplines, namely, the sciences of hereditary transmission. And knowledge by hereditary transmission is deep religious understanding. God has said, "From every cohort among them let a contingent set out to devote themselves to in-depth study of the religion, so that they might warn their people when they return to them" (9:122). The warning therefore arises from the profound comprehension. The warning results in the revitalization of those being warned by means of the water of knowledge, and revitalization through knowledge is the role of the *faqīh*. Therefore religious *fiqh* has become among the most perfect and loftiest of religious specializations. The one who possesses this knowledge is the god-fearing person who renounces this world and who, by reason of his knowledge, arrives at the status of warner.

The wellspring of knowledge and guidance is first and foremost God's Messenger. Guidance and knowledge came upon him from God so that it quenched his thirst both outwardly and inwardly. From his outward imbibing the religion became manifest. The term *religion,* which means "compliance and humble surrender," derives from a root meaning "lowly." Everything that humbles itself is lowly, and religion implies that individual persons humble themselves before their Lord. God has said, "He (God) has ordained for you the religion He enjoined upon Noah, and that which We have revealed to you and enjoined upon Abraham and Moses and Jesus, that you abide by the religion and make no distinctions concerning it" (42:13). For as a result of divisiveness in religion a withering overcomes the members so that the bloom of knowledge fades from them. The heart's imbibing makes possible an outward freshness by adorning the members with spiritual and material surrender.

In its imbibing through knowledge the heart is like an ocean. The heart of God's Messenger, therefore, became a surging ocean through knowledge and guidance, some of which then flowed from the ocean of his heart to his lower self so that the freshness of knowledge and its quenching of thirst were manifest to his noble soul. The base qualities and characteristics of his lower self were thereby transformed [and invested with the exemplary qualities that belong to the heart], whence a stream flowed to the members and they grew lush and verdant. And when his luxuriance was complete and the moistness full, God sent him to humankind. He devoted himself to the *umma* with a heart brimming with the waters of knowledge. The streams of profound comprehension received him so that in every stream a portion and measure flowed from his ocean. Now, that portion coming to the intellect is deep religious understanding. ʿAbd Allāh ibn ʿUmar reports that God's Messenger said, "Nothing comprises more excellent worship of God than deep religious understanding. Indeed, a single person endowed with *fiqh* is harder on Satan than a thousand devotees. All things have their mainstays, and the mainstay of this religion is *fiqh.*"

Our shaykh, Shaykh al-Islām Abū 'n-Najīb, dictated to us,[6] "I heard Muʿāwiya say in an address, 'I heard God's Messenger say, "On the person for whom God desires good things He confers deeper religious understanding. As for me, I merely divide things up, but it is God who bestows.'"'"

When the water of knowledge comes to the understanding, the heart's vision clears so that it perceives the true and the false, and the difference between right guidance and error becomes clear to it. When God's Messenger recited to the Bedouin,[7] "Anyone who does even so little as an atom's weight of good will see it at judgment, and anyone who does even so much as an atom's weight of evil will see it then" (99:7–8), the Bedouin replied, "Enough, enough!" Said God's Messenger, "The man has deep understanding."

ʿAbd Allāh ibn ʿAbbās recounted that Muḥammad said, "The most excellent form of worship is deeper religious understanding." And God has made *fiqh* an attribute of the heart. So He has said, "They have hearts with which they do not understand deeply" (7:179). Therefore, when they understand deeply, they know; and when they know, they act accordingly; and when they act, they possess experiential knowledge; and when they possess experiential knowledge, they are guided. The greater a person's comprehension the more quickly his soul assents, the greater his adherence to the tenets of the religion, and the more ample his share in the light of certitude. Thus, knowledge is an integral reality granted by God to hearts, while experiential knowledge is the ability to discern all of that, and guidance is the heart's discovery of that. Therefore, when the Prophet said, "The guidance and knowledge with which God has sent me are like...," he was indicating that the prophetic heart had experienced knowledge and was therefore guiding and guided. His knowledge includes a congenital inheritance from Adam, the father of humanity, in that he knew all the names (2:31) of created things, and the names are the signs of things. God, therefore, ennobled Adam with knowledge, and has said, "He taught the human being that which he had not known" (96:5). Thus as a result of the knowledge and the wisdom instilled in him, Adam was endowed with profound comprehension, [58] sagacity and experiential knowledge, kindliness and grace, love and hatred, joy and sorrow, equanimity and indignation, and intellectual acuity.

Then God decreed that Adam put all of that to use, creating spiritual insight for his heart so that he was led toward God by the light

God had granted him. So the Prophet was sent to the community with the light bestowed on him as his unique inheritance. And it is said that when God addressed the heavens and the earth with the words, "'Come forward either willingly or reluctantly.' The two of them replied: 'We come forward willingly'" (41:11); it was the place of the Kaʿba that spoke from the earth and answered, and from the heavens it was that which lies parallel to the Kaʿba.[8] ʿAbd Allāh ibn ʿAbbās said, "The clay of God's Messenger is from the navel of the earth in Mecca." One of the learned has said, "This indicates that what came from the earth by way of response is a tiny particle of Muḥammad the Chosen." Beginning from the place of the Kaʿba the earth spread out, so that God's Messenger himself became the origin of creation, and created beings are secondary to him. This is the import of his saying, "I was a prophet when Adam was between water and clay," or, as a variant has it, "between the spirit and the body." It is said, "He was called *ummī* (unlettered) because Mecca is the Mother *(umm)* of cities and that tiny particle of him is the Mother of creation." A person's plot of earth is his burial ground, which would mean that his burial place would be in Mecca whence came the earth of his body. But it is said that "when the water was agitated, it cast the foam off in all directions," and in that way, the essence of the Prophet fell upon what corresponds to his plot of earth in Medina. God's Messenger was both a Meccan and a Medinan whose longing was for Mecca and whose earth was in Medina.

An allusion to what I have mentioned concerning the "tiny particle" of God's Messenger is what God has said, "And when your Lord took from the children of Adam, out of their backs, their progeny and made them witness concerning themselves, asking them, 'Am I not your Lord?' they replied 'Yes'" (7:172). As the Ḥadīth has it, "God rubbed the back of Adam and collected his progeny out of it in the form of tiny particles. He extracted the tiny particles from the pores of Adam's hair, and the tiny particles came out the way sweat exudes." Some say one of the angels did the rubbing, and Muḥammad, in the Ḥadīth, attributed the action to the One who caused the action. According to others, the meaning of the saying that He "rubbed" is that He took their reckoning, just as the earth is reckoned by way of surveying it.[9] That took place in Baṭn Nuʿmān, a river bed near ʿArafa, between Mecca and aṭ-Ṭā'if. When God addressed the tiny particles, they replied with a "Yes." God recorded the covenant on parchment and had the angels witness it, and made Adam swallow the Black Stone. The tiny particle of God's Messenger, therefore, is what replied from the earth. Knowledge and guidance were kneaded into him, and he was sent with the knowledge and guidance that were his inheritance and prerogative.

It is said that when God sent Gabriel and Michael to collect a handful of earth, it refused; so God sent 'Azrā'īl, who collected a handful of earth. But Iblīs had trampled the earth with his feet, so that some earth lay between his feet and some in the place under his feet. The ego-soul was fashioned from that which the foot of Iblīs had touched, so that it became the refuge of evil. Iblīs's foot did not cover part of the earth, and from this dust the Prophets and Friends of God originated. The tiny particle of God's Messenger was in a portion of 'Azrā'īl's handful upon which God gazed and where the foot of Iblīs had not stepped. As a result Muḥammad did not receive a share of ignorance but instead came to be devoid of ignorance and received an abundant share of knowledge.

God therefore sent him with guidance and knowledge that were transferred from his heart to the hearts of his people and from his soul to their souls. The result is an affinity with Muḥammad through the root purity of the primal clay, and an intimacy through the original mutual familiarity. The more intimate with Muḥammad each person is, through the connection of the purity of the primal clay, the more ample his or her share in receiving what the Prophet has brought. It is the hearts of the Sufis that are the nearest in intimacy, so that they gather an ample share of knowledge and their inner beings become cisterns. They learn and they teach, like cisterns that facilitate irrigation and planting. They unite the utility of formal study and inherited knowledge by means of meticulous adherence to the fundamental demands of reverential awe. And when the souls have been purified, the polishing effect of reverential awe burnishes the mirrors of their hearts, so that the images of things are manifest in them according to their actual form and essence. This world's ugliness becomes clearly apparent, so that they reject it, and the world to come appears in its beauty, so that they seek it. When they renounce this world, the tributaries of the sciences flow profusely into their inner beings and knowledge gained through inquiry comes together with inherited knowledge.

Know that every lofty spiritual state that I attribute to the Sufis in this book is the spiritual state of one who is close to God, and the Sufi is one who is close to God. The term *sūfi* is not in the Qur'ān, for the word *sūfi* was omitted and was coined in reference to the one who is close to God, as I will explain in the appropriate chapter. [59] But neither in the eastern nor the western quarters of the realms of Islam is this term common for those close to God. The term is, however, common to those who copy them in externals. How numerous have been those close to God in the western lands and the region of Turkestan and Transoxiana who, because they did not assume the outward trappings of the Sufis, were not called Sufis! But there is no quibbling over terminology. One need only know that by the term *sūfi* I mean those who are close to God. The Sufi shaykhs named in biographical anthologies and similar works were all on the path of those who drew near to God, and their disciplines are the sciences of the spiritual states of those who are near to God. One who strives for the station of those among all the devout who are near God is known as a Sufi-striver, insofar as that person has not fully realized the spiritual state of the Sufis. One who has fully achieved their spiritual state has become a Sufi. Aside from these two groups there are those who set themselves apart by means of external accouterments and associate with Sufis, and they are copycats. "But above every one endowed with knowledge there is an All-knowing One" (12:76).

[60] Chapter 2: On the Superiority of the Sufis in Keen Attentiveness

God's Messenger said,[10] "May God make radiant a man who has heard a Ḥadīth from us and has committed it to memory in order to pass it along. Many are they who convey deep understanding to one who understands more deeply than they themselves do. And many are they who convey deep understanding without themselves being actually endowed with deep understanding!"

The foundation of every good thing is keen attentiveness, as God has said, "Had God discerned any good in them, He would have made them listen" (8:23). One of the Sufis has said, "The sign of goodness in listening is that the godservant hears through the annihilation of his characteristics and attributes, so that he listens to the Truth by means of the truth." Another of them said, "Had God determined that they were worthy of hearing, He would have opened their ears for attentiveness." If demonic insinuation takes hold of a person and the prattle of the ego-soul overcomes him inwardly, that person is incapable of keen attentiveness.

When the Sufis and the people near God understand that the word of God is His prophetic messages and His addresses to His servants, they see that every verse of God's word is a sea among the oceans of knowledge that encompass both the outward and inward, manifest and hidden aspects of knowledge. They perceive the word as one of the gates of the Garden of Paradise, in view of the warning it provides and of the deeds to which God's word calls them. They regard the speech of God's Messenger, which "he does not articulate of his own accord" and is "none other than a prophetic inspiration revealed" (53:3–4), as coming from God, and they must be attentive to it. The Sufis therefore consider readiness to listen attentively of the highest importance, and they regard keen attentiveness as knocking on the door of the realm of Lordly Dominion and invoking the descent of blessing from the realm of longing and fear. They consider satanic insinuations as so much smoke rising from the fire of the soul that incites to evil,[11] and as a deep gloom gathered from Satan's whispered insinuations. They believe that the mundane pleasures and worldly spoils that are dependent upon disordered craving and the cause of ruin, are like the wood that increases a fire's blaze and redoubles the heart's anguish. Thus they reject this world and renounce it.

When, therefore, the wood is no longer supplied to the fire of the ego-soul, so that its flames subside and its smoke dissipates, their inmost beings and hearts become witnesses to the sources of knowledge, so that they make their wellsprings ready for drinking by the purity of profound comprehension. And when they become aware, they hear. God has said, "Therein is a reminder for those who have a heart or who listen and are aware" (50:37). Shiblī said, "The Qur'ān's summons is for the person whose heart is present to God and does not lose its focus on Him for even an instant." Yaḥyā ibn Muʿādh ar-Rāzī said, "There are two kinds of heart: One is the heart that is so totally preoccupied with this world that when some matter of devotional duty arises, the individual does not know what he is doing because of his heart's fixation on this world. The other is the heart so full of the spiritual states of the next world that when some this-worldly matter arises, the individual does not know what he is doing because of his heart's journeying to the other world. Mark well the difference between the blessing, in the latter instance, of well-founded understanding, and in the former, the curse of ephemeral distractions that holds you back from obedience." Another of the Sufis glossed the Qur'ānic text, by saying, "'For those who have a heart' free of negative tendencies and infirmities...." Ḥusayn ibn Manṣūr (al-Ḥallāj) said, "'those who have a heart' in which there is no thought but awareness of the Lord...," and he recited (this verse of poetry):[61]

> I announce to you the death of hearts on which, for so long,
> the clouds of prophetic revelation unleashed endless
> oceans of wisdom.

Ibn ʿAṭā' said the verse means, "When a heart regards God with the eye of exaltation, it melts before Him and is devoted to Him apart from all else." Wāsiṭī said, "In other words, it 'serves as a reminder' (50:37) for a chosen group, not for the rest of humanity. 'For those who have a heart' means in pre-eternity, and they are the ones of whom God said, 'Or those who were dead and whom We brought back to life'" (6:122). Wāsiṭī also said, "Witnessing causes perplexity, while concealment brings understanding; for when God manifests Himself to something, it humbles itself before Him and surrenders." What Wāsiṭī has said is applicable only to a particular group, but this Qur'ānic verse passes a different kind of judgment on some other people, namely, those whose spiritual status is characterized by fixity, for whom contemplative witnessing and profound comprehension are united: The locus of profound comprehension is where conversation and mutual communication occur, namely, in the heart's hearing; and contemplative witnessing occurs in the heart's vision. Both hearing and vision have their own conditions and function.

When a person is in a state of intoxication, his hearing is swallowed up in his vision. But when a person is in a state of sobriety and steadiness, his hearing is not swallowed up in his vision because he is in control of his condition. He therefore understands by means of an existential receptivity prepared to comprehend speech. That is because profound comprehension is where inspiration originates, and hearing and inspiration require an existential receptivity. This existential reality, however, is a gift that arises from a second creation for the individual who stands firm in the station of sobriety. For the person who has progressed from the passing away of annihilation to the dwelling place of survival, it is not the existential reality that comes to naught in the glow of the light of contemplative witnessing.

Ibn Samʿūn[12] said, "'Therein is a reminder for those who have a heart' that knows experientially the proper comportment of service. The heart's proper comportment consists of three things: When the heart has tasted the food of worshipfulness, it is liberated from the bondage of lust. A person who keeps his lust at a distance discovers one third of proper comportment. One who still feels the need of the proper comportment that he has not found even after being occupied with what he has found has discovered another third of proper comportment. And the final third is the heart's being filled by the One who bestows bounty to one whose fidelity is abundant. [So, then, one has discovered the whole of proper comportment]."

Muḥammad ibn ʿAlī (al-Bāqir, d. 114/732) said, "Death of the heart results from the cravings of the ego-soul. Whenever it rejects lust, it gains a proportional share of life." Hearing therefore belongs to the living, not to the dead. God has said, "Surely you cannot make the dead hear" (27:80). Sahl ibn ʿAbd Allāh (at-Tustarī) said, "The heart is delicate, and sinful passing inclinations leave an impression on it, so that even a little becomes significant." God has said, "When a person is not open to the remembrance of the Merciful, we appoint Satan to be his confidant" (43:36). The heart is incessantly active and does not slacken, while the ego-soul is ever vigilant and does not slumber. So let the godservant strive to be attentive to God, for otherwise he will be attending to Satan and the ego-soul. Every thing that bars the door of attentiveness arises from a movement of the ego-soul, and through its initiatives Satan finds a way in. The saying has come down to us, "Had the Satans not swarmed about the hearts of the children of Adam, they would have been able to gaze into the kingdom of the heavens."

Ḥusayn said, "The inner vision of the spiritually insightful, and the experiential knowledge of the mystics, and the light of those learned in Lordly matters, and the paths of the successful ones who have gone before us, and pre-eternity and post-eternity and all that is not eternal that comes between these two—are 'for those who have a heart or who listen attentively'" (50:37). Ibn ʿAṭā' said, "The heart is that which regards God intently and contemplates Him and is neither momentarily nor intermittently unaware of Him, so that it not only hears through Him, but hears from Him, not only contemplates through Him but contemplates Him. For when the heart regards God with a view to the unapproachable majesty, it quakes in terror; but when it looks upon Him with a view to the intimate attractiveness, then it becomes tranquil and calm."

One of the Sufis said, "The text 'For those who have a heart' that is spiritually insightful, means being capable of 'peeling off one's shell' with God and of establishing a unique relationship with Him, until one has taken leave of this world and humanity and the ego-soul and is not involved with other than God and is dependent on none but Him." When the heart of the Sufi is freed of the husk of created things, it listens attentively and its vision witnesses. It therefore hears what is audible, sees what is visible, and witnesses what is there to contemplate, because it has been purified for God and gathered into God's presence. [62] All things are with God and the individual is with Him. As a result, the heart hears, sees, and witnesses, but it sees and hears things according to their totality and does not hear and view them in their particularity. For the totality is apprehended according to the capacity of the eye of witnessing, while the particularities are not apprehended because of the narrowness of existential receptivity. It is God who knows both the universal and the particular.

One of the wise coined a parable of the disparity of attentiveness among human beings when he said, "A sower went out with his seed. He filled his hand with it and some of it fell on the open path. Before long the birds alighted on it and snatched it. Some of the seed fell on the *ṣafwān*—smooth stones—covered by a thin layer of damp soil. It germinated until its roots reached the stones, but finding no chance for further growth there, it withered. Still other seed fell on good earth where thorns were growing. It germinated, but when it began to grow the thorns choked it, so that it weakened and became entangled with the thorns. And some of the seed fell on good soil that was neither on the open path, nor stony, nor did it have thorns growing on it. The seed germinated, grew, and flourished. Now, the sower is like the wise person and the seed is like the true word. What fell on the open path is like the person who hears the word but does not want to hear it, so that Satan soon plunders it from his heart and he forgets it. What fell on the stony ground is like the person who strives to listen to the word and finds it appealing, but then the word comes to a heart that lacks the resolve to act on it, so that the word is eradicated from his heart. What fell on good ground where thorns were growing is like the individual who hears the word and intends to act on it. But when cravings beset him and prevent him from moving forward in implementing his intention, he abandons the action he had intended because of the victory of lust, as the seed is overwhelmed by the thorns. And what fell on good soil is like the person listening carefully who intends to act on what he hears. He comprehends it and acts accordingly, and keeps his lustful cravings at bay."[13]

This individual who steers clear of lustful cravings and pursues the paths of guidance is the Sufi. There is a sweetness in lustful desire, and when the ego-soul imbibes the sweetness of passionate craving, it becomes addicted to it and delights in it. That delight in lustful craving is what chokes off growth like thorns. But the sweetness of pure love alights upon the heart of the Sufi, and pure love is the attachment of the spirit to the divine presence. Through the power of the spirit's being drawn to the divine presence at love's beckoning, the spirit makes the heart and the ego-soul follow along. The sweetness of love for the divine presence overcomes the sweetness of lustful desire. For the sweetness of lust is like an inferior tree lacking substantial foundation that is uprooted at ground level, since it cannot rise above the ego-soul. But the sweetness of pure love is like a good tree whose roots are firm and whose branches reach to the heavens. Because it is founded on the spirit, its branches extend to God and its roots into the earth of the soul. When a person hears the word of the Qur'ān or a saying of God's Messenger, he imbibes it in spirit, heart, and soul so that he gives his all for it, saying:

> I smell an aroma from you that I do not recognize,
> It seems to me that one with deep red lips has unrolled
> her (perfumed) sleeves to you.

The melody of the word pervades and encloses him so that every hair of him becomes an ear, and every atom of him the ability to see. He thus hears the all through the all and sees the all through the all, and he says:

> If I look intently at You, I am all eyes;
> Should I bring You to mind, I am all hearts.

God has said, "Announce good tidings to My servants, those who attend to the word and follow the best of it, those whom God guides. It is they who possess understanding" (39:17–18). One of them has said, "There are a hundred portions of spiritual perception and intellectual understanding: ninety-nine belong to the Prophet and one to all the rest of the believers. And the portion belonging to all the other believers has twenty-one parts. All the believers are equal in one of them, namely, the confession that there is no god but God and that Muḥammad is God's Messenger. In the twenty remaining parts the believers differ among themselves with respect to the scope of the substance of their faith." It has been said, "In this verse is a manifestation of the excellence of God's Messenger"; in other words, "the best" is that which he has brought. For when, before the creation of the world, he found himself in the company of fixity and allied with a state of abiding, the lights in all the spiritual states appeared upon him. His was the best speech; his, too, preeminence in all of the spiritual stations. Do you not note [63] his saying, "We who are the last are the foremost"? It refers to the last in being and the foremost in the first verbal communication in excellence in the place of holiness.

The Most High has said, "Oh, you who believe! Respond to God and the Messenger when he invites you to that which gives you life" (8:24). Junayd said, "They breathe the life-giving breath of that to which he has invited them. Therefore they hasten to eradicate the associations that distract them from God. They attack with their souls the embrace of timidity, and they choke down the bitter pill of long-suffering. They are sincere in their dealings with God and strive for the best demeanor in their every approach to Him. They attach little importance to calamities but are intimately acquainted with the value of what they seek. They restrain their attention from turning toward recollection of any but their Master, so that they live the life eternal through the Living One who ever was and ever will be." Wāsiṭī said, "The life of the heart and soul depends on their being clear of every ill effect in word and deed." One of them said (glossing 8:24), "'Respond to God' in your innermost being, 'and to the Messenger' through your outward actions."

The life of souls comes from following the Messenger, and the life of hearts from contemplating one's faults, and that means diffidence before God when one's limitations are evident. Ibn ʿAṭā' said, "In this Qur'ānic verse 'responding' means four things: first, the response of acknowledging God's transcendent unity; second, the response of acknowledging God's reality; third, the response of surrender; and fourth, the response of striving to be close to God." "Responding," therefore, has to do with listening, and listening derives from profound comprehension. Profound comprehension has to do with experiential knowledge of the meaning of what has been said, and experiential knowledge of what has been said has to do with intimate awareness and knowledge of the One speaking. But the range of modes of comprehension is limitless because the range of meanings of what has been said in this scriptural text is limitless.

God has said, "Say: If the sea were ink with which to write the words of my Lord, the sea would run out before the words of my Lord were exhausted" (18:109). In every text of the Qur'ān, God's words are such that the sea would be exhausted but the words would not. The whole of God's speech is but a single word when one looks at the reality of the acknowledgment of the divine transcendent unity, and each individual word is as if all words combined when one considers the breadth of the eternal knowledge of God.

The Prophet said,[14] "Not a verse of the Qur'ān has been revealed but that it had both an outward and an inward meaning. Every letter has a fundamental sense[15] and every fundamental sense has an apex of insight."[16] ʿAlī ibn Zayd said, "So I inquired, 'O Abū Saʿīd (Ḥasan al-Baṣrī), what is the apex of insight?' He replied, 'A group of people will appear who will act upon it.'" Abū ʿUbayd said, "I have concluded that this saying of Ḥasan (al-Baṣrī) relates to the saying of ʿAbd Allāh ibn Masʿūd, then Abū ʿUbayd quoted[17] ʿAbd Allāh ibn Masʿūd as saying, "Not a letter or verse (of scripture) but some (particular) group of people has made a cause of action—or, that some group will (sooner or later) make a cause for action." So, the apex of insight is the place of ascent to which one ascends from experiential knowledge of what one knows discursively. (In other words,) the apex of insight is the profound comprehension that results from God's opening of every heart with the light He provides.

People disagree as to the significance of the "outward" and "inward" meanings. Some say, "The outward is the verbal expression of the Qur'ān, while the inward is its interpretation." Others say, "The outward is the apparent form of a narrative through which God informs us about His displeasure with a people and His punishment of them. So the outward is that account about them, while its inward aspect is the admonition and its announcement to those among the Muslim community who recite and listen to the text." Still others say, "The outward refers to the revelation, to which people must respond in faith, while its inward aspect refers to the requirement of acting upon it." Again, some say, "The outward refers to the scripture's being recited just as it was sent down, as the Most High has said, 'Recite the Qur'ān in a measured chant' (73:4). And its inward dimension consists in reflection and meditation on it, as God has said, 'A Book, blessing-laden, that We have sent down to you so that they might reflect on its verses and that those possessed with insight might meditate'" (38:29).

It has been said that the Ḥadīth, "For every letter there is a fundamental sense," means that in recitation one does not take liberties with the written text, which is the exemplary version established by ʿUthmān; and in exegesis, one does not go beyond that which has been heard and handed down." A distinction between *tafsīr* and *ta'wīl* is that *tafsīr* involves the scientific knowledge of the revelation of the verse, its principle theme, its narrative, and the circumstances under which it was revealed. In this it is off-limits for people [64] to comment on the text beyond what hearing and tradition supply. As for *ta'wīl*, it orients the scriptural verse toward a possible meaning, so long as the possible meaning that the interpreter sees there is consistent with the Book and the Sunna. *Ta'wīl*, therefore, varies in relation to disparity of spiritual state of the one engaging in symbolical interpretation, as I have mentioned, according to the purity of understanding, the degree of experiential knowledge, and the level of proximity to God.

Abū 'd-Dardā' has said, "A human being does not arrive at deeper understanding until he sees that the Qur'ān has many dimensions." How astonishing is the saying of ʿAbd Allāh ibn Masʿūd, "There is not a scriptural verse that some group will not make a cause of action!" This comment urges every seeker of serious intent to purify the sources from which the word springs and to comprehend profoundly in his heart its rarified meanings and the hidden recesses of its mysteries. The Sufi who has fully renounced the world and de-husked the heart from what is not God, finds an apex of insight in every verse. For that Sufi every occasion of recitation is a new apex of insight and an unfolding of profound comprehension. Every instance of profound comprehension, in turn, implies new action for him, for profound comprehension summons one to action. Action in turn brings about purity of understanding and refined insight into the meanings of the divine communication. From knowledge, therefore, comes action, and knowledge and action reinforce each other in the individual.

But this action, from the outset, is the action of hearts, and the action of hearts is not the action of the body. Because of their subtlety and inaccessibility the deeds of hearts are like forms of knowing, for they are the spirit's intentions and inmost thoughts and cajoleries, the heart's courtesies, and the inmost being's private whisperings. Whenever Sufis engage in one of these actions, one of the escutcheons of knowledge rises for them, and they come upon the apex of insight of a new profound comprehension of the scriptural verse. My inmost being is full of the conviction that the apex of insight is not to be found in dwelling upon the purity of profound comprehension of the refined meaning and obscure secret of the verse. Rather, the apex of insight arises in connection with each verse upon the experience of the one who is speaking it, for the verse is the repository of one of the divine characteristics and attributes. In this way the divine manifestations are renewed for the individual through the recitation and aural reception of the verses, so each verse becomes a mirror that communicates to him God's sublime grandeur.

It is reported that Jaʿfar aṣ-Ṣādiq[18] said, "God has been manifest to His servants in His speech, but they did not see." From this perspective every verse has an apex of insight. As for the field of fundamental sense, it is the semantic field of the word, whereas the apex of insight[19] is an ascent from the speech to the contemplation of the speaker. It is also reported that Jaʿfar fell into a swoon while performing the ritual prayer. Someone asked him about that, and he answered, "I continued repeating the verse until I heard it from the One who spoke it."

When the [light of the] forelock of God's transcendent unity appears within the Sufi's field of vision, he "gives ear" (50:37) while attending to the divine promise and threat. With his heart prescinding from what is not God, he becomes a witness in the very presence of God. Then he sees his tongue or the tongue of another during recitation as like the Bush of Moses, in that God caused him to hear His address from it, "Behold I am God" (28:30). If his hearing is from God and his attentiveness is oriented toward God, his hearing becomes his seeing and his seeing his hearing. His knowledge becomes his action and his action his knowledge; his last becomes his first and his first his last. That means that God addressed the seed of humankind yet unborn, saying, "Am I not your Lord?" (7:172), and they heard the summons to the ultimate purity. Then the seeds wriggle ceaselessly in the loins and are conveyed into the wombs. God said, "(He) who sees you when you stand (in ritual prayer) and (sees) your movement among those who prostrate themselves" (26:218–19). That refers to your seed's wriggling in the loins of the people of prostration among your forefathers, the prophets. So the seed continued to be passed along until it emerged in their bodies. Through the divine wisdom they were veiled from seeing the divine power, and through the realm of what can be seen they were veiled from the realm of the unseen, and their darkness gathered through their constant movement in the unfolding phases of creation.[20]

When, therefore, God wants a servant to have keen attentiveness in order to make of him a pure Sufi, He leads the individual unceasingly through the degrees of purification and adornment, until he is delivered [from the confinement of the world of wisdom] into the expansiveness of divine power. Then will the veils of wisdom be withdrawn from his penetrating spiritual vision so that his hearing of "Am I not your Lord?" becomes a revelation and an eyewitnessing, and his acknowledgment of the divine transcendent unity and experiential knowledge become an illustration and proof, and the darkness of creation's unfolding phases gradually give way for him in the shimmering flash of lights. One of the Sufis has said, "I recall the divine address, 'Am I not your Lord?'" (7:172), thereby alluding to this spiritual state. For when the Sufi has fully realized this quality, his mystical moment becomes eternal, his personal witnessing endless, and his hearing uninterrupted and ever renewed. He thus hears the word of God and the word of His messenger with perfect acuity.

Sufyān ibn ʿUyayna said, "Knowledge starts with attentiveness, followed by profound comprehension, followed by safeguarding in memory, followed by action, and, finally, by dissemination." Someone has said, "Learn keen attentiveness as well as you learn eloquence." [65] And it has been said, "Keen attentiveness involves waiting for the speaker to complete what he has to say, along with minimal attention to one's response, communicating an openness with one's facial expression, looking directly at the speaker, and focused receptivity." God said to His Prophet, "Hasten not with the Qur'ān before its revelation to you is final. (Say, rather, My Lord, increase me in knowledge.)" (20:114); and again, "Do not make your tongue move with it in order to hasten (the revelation)" (75:16). This is God's instructing His Messenger in keen attentiveness. Someone has said that this means, "Do not dictate the revelation to the Companions until you have interiorized its meanings so that you become the first to benefit from its mysteries and wonders." Someone has said, "When Gabriel came down and made a revelation to him, the Messenger continued to recite Qur'ān for fear that he might let it slip away and forget it. God therefore restrained him by saying, 'Do not anticipate its recitation before Gabriel has finished delivering it to you.'"

It is sometimes the case, therefore, that the study of the religious disciplines and the traditions of God's Messenger is the equivalent of hearing. One who investigates the religious sciences and traditions, and the life stories and hagiographical narratives of the devout, as well as the various aphorisms and parables [that contain deliverance from the punishments of the next world], must behave in all those endeavors with keen attentiveness born of self-discipline and reverential fear. Just as he derives "the best" (39:18) from all that he hears, so he gleans the best of everything in his study.

Proper comportment in study means, among other things, that when the godservant wishes to investigate some aspect of the Ḥadīth and religious science, he must know that such study may motivate the ego-soul, with its meager patience, to recollection, recitation, and action. One ought, therefore, to seek refreshment in study much the way one relaxes by socializing and conversing with people. In that process the perceptive person should monitor himself and ought not take such pleasure in reading as to let it consume all his time. When he decides to study a book or some aspect of religious science, he should not rush into it without prior personal examination, heartfelt penitence, and turning to God, seeking confirmation from the mercy of Allāh. For God sometimes supplies through study that which augments one's spiritual state. Should the individual ask for divine guidance,[21] well and good. God will open for him the door of profound comprehension; and bringing one to profound comprehension is a gift of God above and beyond that which is evident in the formalities of religious knowledge. Religious knowledge has both an outward form and an inward secret that is profound comprehension. God spoke of the nobility of profound comprehension when He said, "We gave Solomon profound comprehension of it, and to all We gave wisdom and knowledge" (21:79). He thus alluded to profound comprehension by referring to it pointedly and distinguishing it from wisdom and knowledge.

God has said, "God causes whomever He will to hear" (35:22). If God brings about hearing, He does so at times through the mediation of the tongue and at times by way of the elucidation He provides through the study of books. Therefore, that which God opens up through the study of books is like God's providing what He does from what the godservant hears through the blessing of keen attentiveness, so that he takes account of his spiritual state in that situation and appropriates the knowledge and behavior pertinent to it. This is one of the greatest of the doors to goodness, and one of the most helpful of the deeds of the shaykhs and Sufis and self-disciplined, devout religious scholars for opening the doors of mercy and for receiving an increase of everything [useful for travelers to the hereafter].

[66] Chapter 3: On the excellence of the disciplines of the Sufis with reference to specific examples

Our shaykh, Shaykh al-Islām Abū 'n-Najīb as-Suhrawardī said (citing a Ḥadīth):[22] "A man asked the Prophet about evil, and he replied, 'Do not ask me about evil. Ask me about the good,' and he said it three times. Then he said, 'The most evil of the evil are the wicked learned ones, and the best of the best are the good learned ones.'" Those who possess knowledge are the guides of the community and the pillars of the religion, lanterns dispelling the darkness of natural ignorance, the chief leaders of Islam's council, mines of the wisdom of the Book and the Sunna, God's trusted ones in the midst of His creation, the physicians of godservants, the critical minds of the Hanifite religious community, and the bearers of the divine trust. They are, therefore, of all humankind most bound by the realities of reverential fear, of all godservants the most in need of renunciation of this world. For they need it for themselves and for others, so that if they go bad, others do too; and if they are righteous, so will others be.

Sufyān ibn ʿUyayna said, "The most ignorant of people are those who refuse to put their knowledge into action, while the most knowledgeable are those who act on what they know, and the most excellent are those most humble before God." This is a sound observation that makes it clear that the knowledgeable person who does not act on his knowledge is, in reality, not a learned person. Therefore, do not let such a person's glibness, air of superiority, affected cleverness, and skill in debating and dialectic deceive you. Such an individual is ignorant and not knowledgeable, unless God should turn again to him with the blessing of knowledge. Knowledge on the path of Islam does not bring to ruin those who possess it, and there is hope that the knowledgeable individual will return through the blessing of knowledge.

Knowledge is a religious duty and a supererogatory virtue. As for the duty, it is what the individual must know in order to fulfill the essential religious requirements. Supererogatory virtue, on the other hand, goes beyond what is required in that the person acquires a virtue in the soul that is consonant with the Book and the Sunna. And all knowledge that does not accord with the Book and the Sunna and with that which follows from those two sources, and either assists in the comprehension of them or rests directly upon them, whatever it might be, is not a virtue but a sham through which the individual only increases in shame and depravity, both in this world and the next. Ignorance of the knowledge that is a duty is not permissible, as our shaykh, Shaykh al-Islām Abū Najīb indicated by handing on to us[23] that God's Messenger said, "Seek knowledge, even as far as China. Thus, the quest for knowledge is a duty for every Muslim."

Scholars are of varying opinions concerning the knowledge that is a duty. Some of them have said that it is the quest for the knowledge of sincerity and intimate awareness of the destructive tendencies of the ego-soul and of that which vitiates action. That is because sincerity has been enjoined just as action has been enjoined. God has said, "They have been commanded nothing but to worship God in sincerity" (98:5). Therefore sincerity is commanded, but the ego-soul is deceptive [67], and its seductions, machinations, and covert lusts reduce to rubble the edifice of the sincerity that has been enjoined. Knowledge of that is thus a duty insofar as sincerity is a duty. In other words, that without which the godservant cannot arrive at the duty is itself a duty.

One of them has said, "Experiential knowledge and discernment of momentary spiritual inclinations is a duty, for those movements of the spirit are the root, origin, and evolution of action. Thus can one know the difference between the urging of the angel and the urging of Satan. An action is only as religiously sound as its instigation. Knowledge of that is therefore a duty, so that the godservant's actions are sound." Another of them has said, "It is the quest for knowledge of the mystical moment." Sahl ʿAbd Allāh (at-Tustarī) said, "It is the quest for knowledge of the spiritual state," that is, the terms of the spiritual state that characterizes a person's relationship with God in this life and the next. Someone has also said, "It is the quest for the knowledge of what is legally permissible, to the extent that it is a duty to eat only what is permissible." It has been handed down that, "The quest for the permissible is a duty beyond duty," and, as a result, knowledge of that is also a duty, to the extent that (the permissible) is itself a duty.

Someone also said, "It is the quest for inward knowledge," through which the godservant grows in certitude. And this is the knowledge that one gains through companionship and by keeping company with devout learned persons possessed of certitude, and with ascetics close to God whom God has appointed as His troops. He urges the seekers on toward them and strengthens them by their example and provides guidance to them. Those are the heirs of the knowledge of the Prophet, and from them people learn the knowledge of certitude. Someone has said, "It is the knowledge of selling and buying, of marriage and divorce. When one chooses to become involved in one of those things, one must seek out knowledge of it." Another has said, "It may be that a godservant wishes to do something but does not know what God requires of him in that case. But it would not be fitting that he act on his own opinion, since he does not know his rights and duties in that matter. He therefore has recourse to a religious scholar and asks him about it, so that he might offer an insightful response and so that the inquirer might not simply act on the basis of personal opinion." One who lacks this knowledge must seek it out. Someone has said, "Quest for the knowledge of God's transcendent unity is a duty." Some say that the approach to this quest should be speculative thinking and marshaling evidence, while others say tradition is the way to approach it.

Someone said, "A godservant is at peace when he experiences inner integrity and a high level of surrender and obedience in Islam, and when no doubt occurs in his mind. Should he entertain some vain concern in the center of his being, or experience anxiety as a result of something that runs counter to religious doctrine or plagues him with specious doubts that threaten to lead him into theological innovation or error, then he must seek to resolve his doubts by recourse to religious specialists and those who can afford him an understanding of the correct approach."

Shaykh Abū Ṭālib al-Makkī has said, "This is the knowledge of the five religious duties upon which Islam is founded, for they have been required of Muslims. Since performance of those things is a duty, knowledge of their performance becomes a duty." Abū Ṭālib also mentions that the knowledge of the divine transcendent unity is part of that, since the first of the five duties is the dual affirmation of faith. Sincerity, too, is part of that, since it is one of the essentials of Islam, and the knowledge of sincerity is crucial to the integrity of Islam. God's Messenger explained in a Ḥadīth that this knowledge is a duty for every Muslim, which means that ignorance of it is not permissible for any Muslim, whereas the sayings mentioned above deal largely with matters of which a Muslim is permitted to be ignorant. That is because, as you already understand, such a person does not possess knowledge of the passing spiritual impulses, or the knowledge of the spiritual state, or the knowledge of all the aspects of what is permitted, or the certain knowledge that one acquires from those knowledgeable about the next world. Most Muslims have no knowledge of these things, and if these matters were required of them, most people would not be capable of handling them except such as God wills.

From among these sayings my own preference is for those of Shaykh Abū Ṭālib al-Makkī, and that of the one who said, "Knowledge of selling and buying and of marriage and divorce is incumbent upon a person who wants to engage in these things." And I am certain that knowledge of these things is a duty for the Muslim, and similarly what Shaykh Abū Ṭālib has said on the subject. I have a comprehensive definition of the religiously enjoined quest for knowledge—but God knows best—namely, that the knowledge whose quest is a duty for every Muslim is knowledge of the command and the prohibition. What is "commanded" means that whose performance is subject to reward and whose omission results in punishment, while the term "prohibited" means that whose omission results in reward and whose performance results in punishment. Among things commanded and things prohibited are some (such as faith or murder) that are always critical for the godservant [68] in the legal judgment of Islam, and some (such as ritual prayer or fasting) to which command and prohibition apply according to circumstance. Therefore, the knowledge of that which is at all times incumbent according to Islāmic legal judgment is in no way optional for Muslims. On the other hand, the knowledge of things whose commanding and forbidding is related to context is a duty from which no Muslim is in any way exempt when the specific situation requires it. This definition (of knowledge that is a duty) is broader than all the aspects already mentioned. And God is most knowledgeable.

The Sufi shaykhs and those endowed with knowledge of the next life who renounce this world bent all their efforts to the quest for the knowledge that is a duty, until they had an intimate awareness of it and carried out the command and the prohibition, discharging that responsibility thanks to the success God grants. So when they have stood firm in that, following after God's Messenger as God enjoined him to stand firm with the words, "Therefore stand firm as you have been commanded, along with those who turn to God with you" (11:112), then God opens for them the doors of those forms of knowledge I have been discussing.

One of them said, "Who could manage to do the likes of what this (Qur'ānic) injunction to standing firm enjoins, except one who has enjoyed the support of potent experiences of contemplation, lights of explication, and veracious traditions by way of an immense divine grace and confirmation, as the Most High said (to Muḥammad), 'And if We had not confirmed you…' (17:74), and, moreover, has sustained in the moment of contemplation and (God's) oral address? The person is Muḥammad adorned with the station of nearness to God and communication on the carpet of intimacy, and was thereafter addressed with His word, 'Therefore stand firm as you have been commanded' (11:112). But for these conditions, he would not have been able to manage the steadfastness that was enjoined upon him."

Someone asked Abū Ḥafṣ (al-Ḥaddād), "Which deed is the most excellent?" He replied, "Steadfastness, for the Prophet said, 'Be steadfast and you will not be held to account.'" Commenting on God's word, "Be steadfast as you have been enjoined" (11:112), Jaʿfar aṣ-Ṣādiq said, "In other words, experience your need of God with firm resolve." One of the devout ones saw God's Messenger in a dream and said, "I said, 'O Messenger of God it has been reported that you said "Sūrat Hūd (11) [and its 'sisters'] turned my hair white."' He replied, 'That's right.'" The dreamer went on, "So I asked him, 'What was it that turned your hair white? Was it the stories of the prophets and the destruction of the nations?' 'No,' he replied, 'it was God's word, "Be steadfast as you have been enjoined."'" Just as the Prophet was addressed with this injunction after the preceding visions and charged with the full realization of steadfastness, so has God bestowed upon those endowed with knowledge who discipline themselves for the next life, and upon the Sufi shaykhs who are near to God, a share and portion thereof. Then He has inspired them to carry out steadfastness as it is strictly required. They, in turn, have realized that steadfastness is the most excellent thing one can seek and the noblest thing for which one can hope.

Abū ʿAlī al-Juzjānī said, "Be a seeker of steadfastness, not a seeker of ephemeral marvels, for while your ego-soul frenetically seeks out the spectacular, your Lord looks for steadfastness from you." What he has pointed out is a major principle in this matter and a mystery whose full realization many spiritual travelers and seekers neglect. That is because those who strive spiritually and seek to serve God have heard the life stories of pious persons of times past and of the miraculous deeds and extraordinary capabilities bestowed upon them. Their ego-souls, therefore, ceaselessly pant after that sort of thing and love to have things of that kind provided to them. More than one of them has had the ongoing experience of a heart broken from anxiety over the soundness of his deeds, since none of that (in the way of marvels) was disclosed to him. Had they known the mystery of that matter, it would have been of little consequence to them.

One must know that God sometimes opens a door to that (reality) for some sincere spiritual strivers. The wisdom in this matter is that he grows in certainty in the experience of extraordinary capabilities and the evidence of divine power, so that his determination to renounce this world and avoid the enticements of lust waxes strong. God discloses to some godservants a pure certainty and lifts the veil from the individual's heart. One to whom the pure certainty is revealed is thereby spared the need for the vision of extraordinary capabilities, for the desired result of those things is the achievement of certainty, yet certainty has already arrived. If, however, something of that kind were revealed to this individual endowed with pure certainty, his certainty would not increase because of it. For the wisdom does not require disclosure of (divine) power through extraordinary capabilities to this individual, since he does not need it. The wisdom does, however, require the disclosure of that to the other insofar as he has need of it. This second person is therefore more complete and apt than the first, to the extent that he is supplied the point of that (miracle), namely, pure certainty unmediated by the vision of (divine) power; for there is a negative aspect in it, and that is pride, so he is spared problems of that kind. Therefore the path of the righteous person is to require steadfastness of the ego-soul, for that is wholly marvelous. Then, if along his path the individual encounters something of that sort, well and good, but if he should not encounter it, he doesn't care and loses nothing as a result. He does, however, suffer a loss if he violates the requirement of steadfastness. One needs to know this, for it is a major principle of seekers.

Those renunciants endowed with knowledge, the Sufi shaykhs, and those placed in proximity to God, insofar as they are graced with fulfilling the duty of steadfastness, [69] are sustained with the other forms of knowledge that, as I have mentioned, the ancestors have considered a duty. In this category are the knowledge of the spiritual state, knowledge of spiritual stewardship, knowledge of momentary spiritual impulses—and I will analyze the knowledge of momentary spiritual impulses in a later chapter, God willing—knowledge of certitude, knowledge of sincerity, knowledge of the ego-soul and intimate awareness of its behavior—and the knowledge of the ego-soul and intimate familiarity with it is among the rarest disciplines of the Sufis. The most firmly established of the people traveling the path of those who draw near to God and the Sufis are those most firmly established in the intimate knowledge of the ego-soul. Also in this category is the discipline of the experiential knowledge of the divisions of this world and of the reality of the subtle details of disordered craving and of the hidden passions of the ego-soul and its ravenous appetites and evil ways. So also the knowledge of necessity requiring the ego-soul to rest in necessary things—in speech, action, clothing, shoes, food, and sleep; and the experiential knowledge of the realities of repentance, the knowledge of covert sinfulness, and the experiential awareness of evil deeds—which are the good acts of the pious, and requiring the ego-soul to omit what doesn't concern it, and the demand of the inner part (of one's being) to combat (first) the barrage of rebellious spiritual impulses and then superfluous inclinations.

Then there is the discipline of self-scrutiny and the knowledge of what is harmful in self-scrutiny; and the discipline of examining one's conscience and introspection; the knowledge of the realities of trust in God and of the trusting person's failings in trustfulness and of what diminishes trust and of what does not diminish trustfulness, and of the difference between necessary trust in relation to faith, and the special trust proper to the people of experiential knowledge; and the knowledge of contentment and of the sins of the station of contentment; the knowledge of asceticism and the definition of what its practice requires, as well as what detracts from its spiritual reality, the experiential knowledge of the renunciation of self-denial, and the experiential knowledge of a third level of asceticism after the renunciation of renunciation; the knowledge of compunction and of taking refuge in God; and the experiential knowledge of appropriate moments for supplicatory prayer and of a time more suited to refrain from supplicatory prayer; the knowledge of love and of the difference between the ordinary love of God that is explained as obedience to the command and pure love of God. (Here Suhrawardī makes an aside:) Some this-worldly scholars repudiate the claim of those endowed with knowledge of the next life to the pure love of God—just as they reject the notion of contentment, saying "It's nothing but patience!" (He then returns to his enumeration, with the sciences of:) the division of pure love into love of the essence and the love of the attributes; and of the distinction among the love of the heart, the love of the spirit, the love of the intellect, and the love of the ego-soul; and of the distinction between the station of the lover and the beloved, the seeker and the sought.

In addition, there are the disciplines of contemplation, such as the knowledge of awe and intimacy, contraction and expansion, and of the difference between anxiety and the spiritual desolation of contraction, on the one hand, and between natural enthusiasm and the spiritual consolation of expansion, on the other. There is, further, the knowledge of annihilation and survival and of the distinction of the spiritual states of annihilation, on the one hand, and knowledge of being veiled and divine self-manifestation, of simplicity and complexity, of light flashes, breakthroughs of insight, and clear manifestations, and of sobriety and intoxication, and so on, on the other.

Given adequate time I would have discussed and expounded on these matters for several volumes, but life is short and time precious. And but for a share of inattentiveness (to God),[24] there would have been too little time to do even this much. Nevertheless, this brief survey encompasses a credible sample of the Sufi disciplines, and I hope that the bountiful God will render it useful and consider it to my credit rather than my discredit. All of these are disciplines, among others, in accord with which those ascetics endowed with knowledge of the next life labor and in which they are successful. On the other hand, covetous this-worldly scholars have no access to them, for these are disciplines one needs to "taste." Merely speculating on them does not remotely approach actually tasting and experiencing, just as a mere description does not suffice for a knowledge of the nature of sugar's sweetness; only one who has tasted it has experiential knowledge of it.

What tells you about nobility of the science of the Sufis and the ascetic scholars is that all other sciences can be attained in tandem with love of the world and failure to satisfy reverential fear. Sometimes love of this world is even an aid to their acquisition, for preoccupation with these sciences is difficult. Ego-souls gravitate naturally to the love of fame and adulation. When they sense that it is possible to achieve this by attaining knowledge, they are willing to tolerate hardships, sleepless nights, patience through separation and journeys and the difficulty of finding pleasures and amenities. But the disciplines of these (Sufi) folk are not consistent with the love of this world. They become accessible only to the degree that one avoids disordered attachment, and one can study them only in the school of fear of God. God has said, "Fear God and God will teach you" (2:282), thereby making knowledge the heritage of the fear of God. Disciplines other than those of these Sufis are no doubt easy to gain without that fear of God. Thus, knowledge is a virtue of those knowledgeable of the next life to the extent that its veil is removed only for those endowed with insight, and those endowed with insight are none other than those who renounce this world.

One of the jurists has said, "If a man were to bequeath his possessions to the most intelligent of persons, they would revert to the renunciants, because they are the most intelligent of people." Sahl ibn ʿAbd Allāh at-Tustarī said, "Understanding has a thousand names, and every one of those names has a thousand names, and the beginning of every one of its names is rejection of this world."

[70] Abū ʿAbd Allāh (Ibrāhīm) al-Khawwāṣ, a companion of Ḥātim, passed along a tradition to us,[25] "I traveled to Rayy with Abū ʿAbd ar-Raḥmān Ḥātim al-Aṣamm. Three hundred and twenty men

who wanted to make the Ḥajj accompanied him. They wore wool and coarse garments but had neither traveling bag nor food. So in Rayy we visited the dwelling of a merchant who was religiously strict and loved the ascetics, and he welcomed us as guests that night. When morning came, he said to Ḥātim, "ʿAbū ʿAbd ar-Raḥmān, are you currently obligated? I want to visit a local *faqīh* who is ill.' Said Ḥātim, 'If you have a sick *faqīh* here, then visiting the *faqīh* would be a virtuous deed, and, indeed, seeing a faqih is a worshipful act, so I'll go along with you.' Now the sick man was Muḥammad ibn Muqātil (d. 236/850), the magistrate of Rayy. The host said, 'Come with us, Abū ʿAbd ar-Raḥmān,' and they came to the gate, and it was lofty and palatial. So Ḥātim spent a moment in thought, saying to himself, 'A scholar's residence of such quality?' Then they were granted permission to enter. Inside, the house was spacious and grand and exuded an air of elegance with its wall hangings and staff of servants. Again Ḥātim remained pensive.

They then went into the sitting room where the jurist was, and there he was reclining on a soft carpet, while at his head was a servant with a fly-whisk. The man from Rayy sat down and questioned the jurist, while Ḥātim stood. So when Ibn Muqātil motioned to him to have a seat, Ḥātim said, 'I will not sit.' Asked Ibn Muqātil, 'Perhaps there is something you need?' 'Yes,' Ḥātim replied. 'And what is it?' asked Ibn Muqātil. 'I have a question to ask you,' he answered. 'Ask me,' said Ibn Muqātil. Ḥātim said, 'All right, then, sit up straight so that I can ask you the question.' So the jurist ordered his servants to prop him up, and Ḥātim said to him, 'Where did you come by this knowledge of yours?' He replied, 'Trustworthy transmitters passed it along to me.' Ḥātim asked, 'From whom?' 'From the Companions of God's Messenger,' he replied. 'From whom?' he inquired further. Said Ibn Muqātil, 'From God's Messenger.' 'And from where did God's Messenger get it?' Ḥātim pressed on. 'From Gabriel,' he responded. Said Ḥātim, 'And where did Gabriel get it?' He said, 'From God.' 'And concerning what matters did Gabriel pass along from God to God's Messenger and God's Messenger pass along to his Companions and his Companions pass along to the trustworthy transmitters that the trustworthy transmitters passed along to you? Have you heard in this knowledge that the one who is the commander in his house or whose grandeur is the greatest will have the most extensive place of repose with God?' 'No,' he replied. So Ḥātim asked, 'Then how have you heard?' Said the jurist, 'I have heard that one who renounces this world and yearns for the next life and who loves the poor and puts his next life first is the one who will have the most extensive place of repose with God.' Ḥātim responded, 'Then on whom do you model yourself? The Prophet and his Companions and the pious ones? Or Pharaoh and Nimrod, the first people to build with mortar and baked brick? O wicked scholars! The ignorant person who seeks this world and yearns for it looks at people like you and says, "With the scholar living in these conditions, I could hardly be more evil than he!"' Ḥātim left his company, and Ibn Muqātil's illness took a turn for the worse.

"What had taken place between Ḥātim and Ibn Muqātil came to the attention of the people of Rayy, so they said to Ḥātim, 'O Abū ʿAbd ar-Raḥmān, there is a scholar in Qazwin even more grandiose than this man'—they were referring to Ṭanāfisī (d. 204/819–20). So he traveled there purposefully, went in to him and said, 'God be compassionate to you! I am a Persian who would like you teach me the first fundamental of my religion, and the preparation for my ritual prayer, that is, how I should perform ablutions for the ritual prayer.' 'Yes,' the man replied, 'gladly. Young man (that is, a servant), bring a basin full of water.' So he brought a basin of water. Then Ṭanāfisī sat down [and performed the triple ablution, and said, 'There. Now you perform the ablution.'] So Ḥātim sat down and performed the triple ablution until he came to the cleansing of the two arms up to the elbows, and that he performed four times. So Ṭanāfisī said to him, 'Hey, you've overdone this.' Ḥātim asked, 'How so?' Replied the other man, 'You cleansed your arms four times.' Ḥātim responded, 'God be praised! With a handful of water I have gone too far, while you with your staff of servants have not!' Then Ṭanāfisī realized that this lesson was what Ḥātim had intended for him, and that he had no intention of taking instruction from him. So he went into the house and did not meet the public for forty days.

"The merchants of Rayy and Qazwīn wrote to the merchants of Baghdad about what had transpired between him and Ibn Muqātil and Ṭanāfisī. So when Ḥātim went to Baghdad, the people of Baghdad gathered around him and said to him, 'Abū ʿAbd ar-Raḥmān, you are a Persian who speaks flawed Arabic, and yet no one can speak with you without your rendering him speechless.' He replied, 'I have three special characteristics by which I surpass my adversaries.' 'And what are they?' they asked. Said he, 'I rejoice when my opponent is correct, I'm sad when he makes an error, and I take care not to behave foolishly toward him.' Word of that got to Aḥmad ibn Ḥanbal, so he went to Ḥātim and said, 'Praised be God! How intelligent he is!' So when Ibn Ḥanbal and companions went to Ḥātim, they said, 'Abū ʿAbd ar-Raḥmān, what will save a person from this world?' Ḥātim replied, 'Abū ʿAbd Allāh (Ibn Ḥanbal), one is not safe from this world until one possesses four qualities.' 'What are they, Abū ʿAbd ar-Raḥmān?' he asked. Ḥātim responded, 'Forgive the people their ignorance; safeguard them from your own ignorance; bestow on them what you have; and do not covet what is theirs. Given that state of affairs, you are safe.' Then he traveled back to Medina."

God said, "Only the learned among God's servants fear God" (35:28). By using the word "only" He has ruled out knowledge on the part of those who do not fear [71] God, just as when one says, "Only a citizen of Baghdad entered the house," thereby ruling out entry into the house by someone not a citizen of Baghdad. Thus it is evident to those endowed with knowledge of the next life that the only path to participation in experiential knowledge and the spiritual stations of nearness to God is through renunciation and fear of God. Abū Yazīd (al-Bisṭāmī) said to his companions, "Yesterday I kept trying until dawn to say, 'There is no deity but God,' but I couldn't manage it." "Why not?" someone asked. He replied, "I was recalling a word that I had said in my youth, but then I was struck by how awful that word was and that prevented me from (affirming God's oneness). I would be astonished if an individual could recollect God while preoccupied with one of his own foibles." Thus is the godservant "firmly rooted in knowledge" through pure fear of God and perfect renunciation.

Wāsiṭī said, "'Those firmly rooted in knowledge' (3:7, 4:162) are the ones who have rooted their spirits in the unseen of the unseen in the secret of secrets, so that He has made them intimately familiar with that of which they have experiential knowledge. They plunge into the ocean of knowledge through profound comprehension in quest of an increase of it, so that the treasures of profound comprehension and the marvels of divine communication stored away beneath every letter of the divine word are unveiled for them, and they speak with wisdom."

One of them said, "The one who is firmly rooted is the one who experiences a breakthrough of insight into the meaning of God's communication." Kharrāz said, "Those firmly rooted in knowledge are they whose command of all the disciplines is so complete that they know them experientially and that they have experienced a breakthrough of insight into the totality of creaturely spiritual longings." This saying of Abū Saʿīd (al-Kharrāz) does not mean that one who is firmly rooted in knowledge must gain perfect mastery of all of the subdisciplines, for ʿUmar ibn al-Khaṭṭāb was therefore definitely one of those firmly rooted in knowledge, and even he was not entirely certain of the meaning of the Most High's words, *"wa-fākihat^an wa-abb^an"* (80:31). He asked, "What is *al-abb*?" Then he said, "This is nothing but a verbal affectation." This hesitation concerning the meaning of the word *al-abb* has been attributed to Abū Bakr as well. Surely, then, that was Abū Saʿīd's full meaning when he said, "They experience a breakthrough of insight into all the spiritual longings of creatures." That is because when some access to the Preserved Tablet descends upon one who fears God truly and engages in true renunciation of this world, whose inner being is pure and who has burnished the mirror of his heart, that person perceives through his inward purity the foundations and principles of all forms of knowledge. This individual thus comes to know the highest accomplishments of the scholars in their disciplines, as well as the benefits of every form of knowledge.

The various subdisciplines of knowledge have become differentiated as a result of (varying methods of) instruction and application, so that one's general knowledge does not spare one having to avail himself of (the expertise) of those who specialize in the subdisciplines. The souls of these (latter) individuals are filled and preoccupied with the (knowledge of) the subdisciplines, and they have limited themselves to a specialization, to the exclusion of comprehensive (knowledge). Once they have partaken of the essential principles and fundamentals of the religion on the basis of the Revealed Law, the souls of the learned renunciants advance toward God and are completely focused on Him. Their spirits arrive at the station of proximity to Him, so that their spirits infuse their hearts with lights through which their hearts are made ready to attain (the various forms of) knowledge. Their spirits thereby rise up beyond the limits of the attainment of knowledge by reason of their total engagement with the Eternal Knower and are no longer separated from such being as is apt for a capacity to hold knowledge. Their hearts, by virtue of their nearness to their souls, become receptacles of being that are compatible with the being of knowledge thanks to an existential relationship. The (forms of) knowledge have an affinity with them in relation to the differentiation of the disciplines as a result of their being in contact with the Preserved Tablet—their being differentiated means merely that they are inscribed on the Preserved Tablet. The separation of hearts from the station of the spirits results from their being drawn to the ego-souls, so that between the two separated entities there occurs a relationship of cooperation necessitating a mutual affinity. In that way the individual attains the (various) disciplines and the lordly (possessor of knowledge) becomes firmly rooted in knowledge.[26]

God revealed in one of the scriptures sent down, "O children of Israel, do not say, 'knowledge is in the heavens—who will bring it down? Or in the depths of the earth—who will bring it up? Or across the seas—who will cross over and bring it?' Knowledge has been instilled in your hearts. Comport yourselves before Me in the manner of those who are spirit-guided and emulate the moral qualities of the authentic ones. I will make knowledge arise from your hearts until it envelops you and immerses you."[27] Behaving according to the comportment of those who are spirit-guided consists in deterring ego-souls from indulging their natural propensities and in subduing them by uncontaminated knowledge in every word and deed. That is feasible only for those who know, are near to God, and are led along the path to the presence of God, and are thus guarded by God for God.

Our shaykh, Abū 'n-Najīb ʿAbd al-Qādir as-Suhrawardī handed down to us the authorized tradition,[28] [72]"It has reached me that Shaddād ibn Aws entered a dwelling and said, 'Bring us the tablecloth so that we can play with it.' But people took exception to that, so he said, 'Aside from this, I have not uttered a word since I became a Muslim that I did not control and rein in. So don't hold it against me.'" This is what behaving in the manner of those who are spirit-guided is like.

It is written in the gospel (non-canonical), "Do not seek knowledge of what you do not know, as long as you are not putting into action what you already know." According to a report, "God's Messenger said, 'Satan will often get the better of you (Or: steal from you) when it comes to knowledge.'[29] We asked, 'O Messenger of God, how does he get the better of us through knowledge?' He replied, 'He says, "Seek knowledge and take no action until you know," so the individual goes on talking about knowledge and procrastinating until he dies without taking action.'" Ibn Masʿūd said, "Knowledge does not consist in transmitting copious traditions; on the contrary, knowledge is fear." Ḥasan (al-Baṣrī) said, "God could hardly care less about the person invested in acquired knowledge and its transmission. He is, rather, interested in the person who is endowed with profound comprehension and understanding."

The hereditary disciplines, therefore, are derived from learning acquired through study. The disciplines acquired through study are like pure milk that is palatable to those who drink it, whereas the inherited disciplines are like the cream derived from the milk; without the milk there could be no cream, but the cream is the rich substance desired from the milk. The watery substance in the milk is a body in which the rich substance of the spirit rests, while watery substance supports it. God said, "From water We made everything that lives" (21:30), and again, "Or someone who was dead and whom We brought back to life" (6:122)—that is, a person dead in unbelief whom We brought back to life in Islam. Revivification in Islam is the first vitality and the first principle; Islam has its disciplines, and they are the forms of knowledge that undergird Islam. Islam, understood as pure assent, comes after faith, but the faith branches out after the realization of Islam, on various levels, such as the knowledge of certitude, the essence of certitude, and the truth of certitude. People also speak of affirmation of the divine transcendent unity, experiential knowledge, and contemplative vision. Each of the branches of faith has its ramifications in the disciplines, so the disciplines of Islam are the disciplines of the tongue, whereas the disciplines of faith are the disciplines of hearts.

In addition, the disciplines of hearts have both restricted and general characters. As for the general character, it is the knowledge of certitude that one can attain through speculative thought and inference, and learned persons, both this-worldly and otherworldly, have a share in it. But the restricted character is unique to otherworldly learned people, and it is the divine tranquility that descends "into the hearts of believers so that they might add faith to their faith" (48:4). The term *faith* in its restricted sense encompasses all of these levels, but not in its general sense. So, from the perspective of its restricted sense, certitude in its various levels is part of faith; and with respect to its general sense, certitude goes beyond faith. Contemplation is a unique feature of certitude, and it is the essence of certitude, whereas a specific feature within the essence of certitude is the truth of certitude. The truth of certitude is, therefore, above contemplation, and the home country and abode of the truth of certitude is the next life. In this world only a passing glimpse of it is available to those worthy of it. It is among the rarest bits of the knowledge of God one can find, for it is no less than ecstatic experience.

There is thus a connection between the knowledge of the Sufis and the learned renunciants, and the knowledge of this-worldly learned individuals who attain certitude by way of speculative thought and deductive inference. It is like the connection I discussed between inherited knowledge and knowledge acquired through study. The latter knowledge is like the milk because it is the certitude and the faith that are fundamentals, whereas the knowledge of God that the Sufis possess is a part of contemplation. And the essence of certitude and the truth of certitude are like the cream derived from the milk. The excellence of faith, therefore, is based on the excellence of knowledge, and the gravity of one's actions is proportionate to one's share of knowledge. According to a tradition of Muḥammad, "The learned person is superior to the devotee as I am superior to my community." He is not referring here to the knowledge of buying and selling and of divorce and freeing a slave; the reference is rather to the knowledge of God and the power of certitude.

It is possible that a godservant might become knowledgeable about God and endowed with perfect certitude without having a knowledge of the collective duties. Indeed the Companions of God's Messenger were more knowledgeable than the Followers [in the realities of certitude and the fine points of *maʿrifa*], but some among the learned Followers were better grounded in the knowledge of legal advisory and (divine) injunctions than some among them (that is, the Companions). Tradition has it that ʿAbd Allāh ibn ʿUmar used to say when someone asked him a question, "Ask Saʿīd ibn al-Musayyib," while ʿAbd Allāh ibn ʿAbbās was wont to say, "Ask Jābir ibn ʿAbd Allāh. If the people of Basra acquiesce in his legal advisories, that will be sufficient for them." Anas ibn Mālik used to say, "Ask our Master Ḥasan. He remembered whereas we forgot."

The Companions therefore used to [73] refer people to them (the Followers) in questions of the discipline of legal advisory and statutes, but the Companions taught the people the realities of certitude and the refined points of experiential knowledge. The Companions had a stronger foundation in those matters than the Followers, because the freshness of the prophetic revelation that had been sent down had an impact on the Companions and they were filled to overflowing with the luxuriance of knowledge both comprehensive and specialized. One group among them schooled themselves in both the comprehensive and the specialized aspects of knowledge, another in the comprehensive without the specialized, while another focused on the specialized without the comprehensive. The comprehensive aspect is the root of knowledge, and its gist is acquired through the purification of hearts, the power of penetrating insight, and perfect receptivity, and it is reserved to the select few.

God said to His Prophet, "Invite people to the cause of your Lord with wisdom and beautiful exhortation, and debate them with the finest of arguments" (16:125), and again, "Proclaim: This is my way, to invite to God on the basis of spiritual insight" (12:108). There are passersby on this road, and there are hearts receptive to this invitation. Some of them are recalcitrant, impervious souls mired in the crudeness of their natural proclivities, whom God softens with the fire of admonition, exhortation, and warning. Others among them are pure souls made of good soil, harmonious with their hearts and close to them. When an individual ego-soul bullies its heart, the Prophet invites it "with an exhortation," and when an individual's heart holds the ascendancy over its ego-soul, the Prophet invites it "with wisdom." Pious individuals respond to the invitation couched in exhortation, which invites by calling to mind Heaven and Hell. Those who are near to God, on the other hand, respond to the invitation couched in wisdom, which invites by alluding to the bestowal of proximity, with pure experiential knowledge, and by pointing to the acknowledgment of the divine transcendent unity. When those who have arrived in God's proximity experience the divine allusions and the tutelage of the Lord, their spirits and hearts and souls respond. In that way their verbal acquiescence becomes the response of their souls, their following through deeds becomes the response of their hearts, and their realization of the spiritual states becomes the response of their spirits. Sufis therefore respond totally, whereas others respond only partially.

ʿUmar said, "May God be compassionate to Suhayb (ibn Sinān, d. 38/659), for had he not feared God, he would not have rebelled against Him." In other words, if his safety from the Fire had been assured ahead of time, pure experiential knowledge of God's sublime command would have brought him directly to the full accomplishment of what is required of a godservant by way of realizing what he knew experientially of the divine majesty.[30] The response of the Sufis to the invitation, therefore, is the response of the lover to the Beloved, experienced as delightful and easy-going, whereas that of others is the response of one who suffers and struggles. And the effect of this response appears with time in the accomplishment of the realities of steadfastness and servanthood.

God said, "For the person who is generous and fears God, and who attests to what is best, We will surely smooth his way to salvation" (92:5–7). One of them interpreted these verses by saying, "'One who is generous' to this world and the next and sees them as nothing, and who 'fears' foolish talk and evil acts, and who 'attests to what is best' has adhered to the quest for the high degree of nearness to God" (cf. 34:37). According to tradition, this verse was revealed in connection with Abū Bakr the Authentic One. One might also interpret the phrase "is generous" in relation to unflagging persistence in deeds; and the phrase "and fears" as referring to fear of demonic insinuations and the suggestions of the ego-soul; and the phrase "attests to what is best" as meaning that he applies himself to inward matters through maintaining his ways of desiring mystical visions free of the interference and clutter of ordinary existence; and the phrase "We will surely smooth his way to salvation" as "We will open for him the door of facility in action, daily life, and relationships." As for the phrases in the next three verses,[31] "But as for one who is stingy" in deeds and "believes he is not in need" in that his spiritual states are ample enough, and "who lies about what is best" because his spiritual insight does not travel abroad and penetrate into the unseen world, "We will surely smooth his way to hardship" means "We will shut before him the door of facility in deeds."

One of them said, "When God desires evil for a godservant, He closes before him the door of action and opens for him the door of indolence." But when the souls, hearts, and spirits of the Sufis respond to the invitation both outwardly and inwardly, their share of knowledge is more extensive and their portion of experiential knowledge more complete, so that their deeds are purer and more excellent. A man came to Muʿādh (ibn Jabal) and said, "Explain to me two kinds of people: One of them dedicates himself assiduously to acts of worship, multiplies good deeds, and minimizes sins, but he is weak in certitude and overcome with doubt." Muʿādh responded, "His doubts certainly negate his deeds." The man went on, "Now tell me about a man whose deeds are few, whose certitude is strong, but whose sins are nevertheless numerous." Muʿādh kept silent, so the man said, "By God, if the first man's doubts negate his deeds of piety, surely this man's certitude negates all of his sins!" Muʿādh took him by the hand and said, "I have never seen anyone endowed with deeper understanding than this man." [74] Luqmān said by way of advice to his son, "My son, action apart from certitude is impossible. A man can act only in proportion to his certitude, and one who acts will not act inadequately unless his certitude is insufficient."

Certitude is the most excellent aspect of knowledge, for it calls for action most insistently; and that which calls most insistently for action, calls most insistently for deeds of worship; and that which calls most insistently for deeds of worship, calls most insistently for the accomplishment of what the Lord has a right to demand. The Sufis, and the truly knowledgeable renunciants, possess the complete share of certitude and knowledge of God, and in that lies their superiority and the superiority of their knowledge.

Now then, let me illustrate a case by which the observer might come to a clearer understanding of the superiority over others of the learned renunciant endowed with experiential knowledge of the proclivities of his ego-soul. Suppose that a learned person enters a study circle and sits down, choosing for himself a place to sit that he considers appropriate to his status and learning. Then one of his peers enters and sits in a higher place than his, so that the first learned person feels crowded and the world turns dark before him: He would attack the interloper if he could. This response is an obstacle that gets in his way and a disease that afflicts him. But he is not aware that this is a hidden infirmity and a malady for which he needs a cure, and he does not reflect on the source of this illness. If only he knew that this was the ego-soul bestirred and overcome by its ignorance, and that its ignorance was a result of its arrogance, and that its arrogance was a result of his ego-soul's belief that it is better than another! The individual's conviction that he is greater than another is arrogance, and manifesting that in action is grandiosity, and grandiosity means acting out the feeling of being snubbed.

The learned, self-disciplined Sufi, on the other hand, does not set himself apart in any way from Muslims, and he does not think of himself as holding a place of distinction in which he is set apart in a study circle. If this individual were predestined to be afflicted with this kind of situation, so that he were to feel snubbed when another person took precedence over him and were elevated above him, he would identify it as a manifestation of the ego-soul. He would recognize that this is a disease, and that if he were to give in to it by paying attention to the ego-soul and its sense of constraint, that would become a sin of his spiritual condition. He would thus forthwith lift up his malady to God and complain to Him of his ego-soul's manifestation and make an effort to turn the situation around by rooting out the ego-soul's sense of conspicuousness. He would raise his heart to God, seeking relief from the ego-soul. His preoccupation with seeking to remedy the disease of the ego-soul would keep him from obsessing about the person who sat in a higher place. He might often turn toward the one who sat above him, in increased humility and brokenness, in order to expiate his actual sins and to heal the malady he was experiencing. This, then, clarifies the distinction between the two people.

As a result, when the observer considers and examines the condition of his ego-soul in this station, he will recognize that his ego-soul is, like the generality of people's souls, looking to make a mark on this world. But what a difference there is between this person and another who has no knowledge! Were we to multiply illustrations of such cases, which give proof of the superiority of the renunciants and the deficiency of the covetous, it would induce boredom. At any rate, this is a primer on the Sufi disciplines, so what do you think of the gems of their disciplines and the heights of their spiritual states? [And it is God who establishes what is correct.]

Abbreviations in Notes and Bibliography

EI[1]	*Encyclopedia of Islam.* First edition. Edited by M. Houtsma et al. Leiden: Brill, 1913-36.
EI[2]	*Encyclopedia of Islam.* Second edition. Edited by C. E. Bosworth et al. Leiden: Brill, 1986–1999.
EIr	*Encyclopedia Iranica.* Edited by Ehsan Yarshater. London: Routledge & Kegan Paul; Costa Mesa, Calif.: Mazda, 1985– .
EIM	Sells, *Early Islamic Mysticism.*
EIPM	*Essays on Islamic Piety and Mysticism.* Edited by O'Kane and Radtke.
EO	Massignon, *Essay on the Origins of the Technical Language of Islamic Mysticism.*
ER	*Encyclopedia of Religion.* Edited by Mircea Eliade et al. New York: Macmillan, 1987.
GQ	Gramlich, Makkī's *Qūt al-qulūb (Die Nahrung der Herzen).*
GA	Gramlich, Suhrawardī's *ʿAwārif al-maʿārif (Die Gaben der Erkentnisse).*
GR	Gramlich, Qushayrī's *Risāla (Das Sendschreiben al-Qushayris über das Sufitum).*
GL	Gramlich, Sarraj's *Kitāb al-lumaʿ (Schlaglichter über das Sufitum)*
HS1, 2, 3	L. Lewisohn, *The Heritage of Sufism,* vols. 1, 2, and 3.
KT	Rosenthal, *Knowledge Triumphant.*

MDI	Schimmel, *Mystical Dimensions of Islam.*
OEMIW	*Oxford Encyclopedia of the Modern Islamic World.* Edited by John Esposito. New York: Oxford University Press, 1995.
SDG	Chittick, *The Self-Disclosure of God.*
SEI	*Shorter Encyclopedia of Islam.* Edited by H. A. R. Gibb and J. H. Kramers. Leiden: Brill, 1961.
SPK	Chittick, *The Sufi Path of Knowledge.*

Notes

Introduction

1. In Toshihiko Izutsu, "Mysticism and the Linguistic Problem of Equivocation in the Thought of ʿAyn al-Quḍāt Hamadānī," *Studia Islamica* 31 (1970), 156, citing Wittgenstein's *Philosophical Investigations* 78, p. 36.

2. For broader theological and other aspects of the discussion of the meanings and interrelationships of *ʿilm* and *maʿrifa,* see *KT* 97–154, 194–341.

3. In this section I summarize and supplement *KT* 1–40.

4. For a further discussion of "*kitāb* as *ʿilm,*" and on related vocabulary and semantic field of *ʿilm* in Qur'ān, see Daniel Madigan, *The Qur'ān's Self-Image: Writing and Authority in Islam's Scripture* (Princeton, N.J.: Princeton University Press, 2001), 113–17, 149–51; see also Toshihiko Izutsu, *God and Man in the Qur'ān* (Tokyo: Keio University 1964), 49–50, 59–63.

5. For a useful overview of this general topic, see John Burton, *An Introduction to the Ḥadīth* (Edinburgh: Edinburgh University Press, 1994).

6. *KT* 71; see also 71–94 for further analysis of chapters/books on knowledge in the major Ḥadīth collections.

7. See James Robson, trans., *Mishkāt al-maṣābīḥ,* 2 vols. (Lahore: Sh. Muhammad Ashraf, 1975), 50–63.

8. See further Jane D. McAuliffe, "Text and Textuality: Q. 3:7 as a Point of Intersection," in *Literary Structures of Religious Meaning in the Qur'ān,* ed. Issa J. Boullata (Richmond, Surrey: Curzon, 2000), 56–76.

9. Harris Birkeland, "Opposition against Koran Interpretation," in *The Qur'ān: Formative Interpretation,* ed. Andrew Rippin (Brookfield, Vt.: Ashgate, 1999), 65–69; see also Jane D. McAuliffe, "Ibn al-Jawzī's Exegetical Propaedeutic: Introduction and Translation," *Journal of Comparative Poetics* 8 (1988), 101–13, and "Qur'ānic Hermeneutics: The Views of al-Ṭabarī and Ibn Kathīr," in *Approaches to the History of the Interpretation of the Qur'ān,* ed. Andrew Rippin (Oxford: Oxford University Press, 1988), 46–62.

10. *Sunan ibn Mājah* (Beirut: Dar al-maʿrifa, 1996), *as-Sunna,* 224.

11. *KT* 165.

12. I am incorporating in this section also material from *KT* 155–93.

13. See further Schimmel, *MDI* 42–46; Arberry, "Dhū 'l-Nūn," *SEI* 77.

14. On this and other early theological schools, see *EIM* 304–20.

15. Rosenthal, *KT* 178, also indicates that in this work Muḥāsibī often uses *ʿilm* and *maʿrifa* as "practical synonyms," and that the former term can refer to "the fullness of knowledge of any given subject," while the latter "often expresses acquaintance, awareness, a first realization of or knowledge about something."

16. I have relied on the following for background on Muḥāsibī: Rosenthal, *KT* 177–79; Smith, *Muḥāsibī (A.D. 781–857): An Early Mystic of Baghdad* (Amsterdam: Philo Press, 1974), 44–45, 53, 57, 98–110; Massignon, "Al-Muḥāsibī," *SEI* 410; Josef van Ess, *Die Gedankenwelt des Ḥārith al-Muḥāsibī* (Bonn: Selbstverlag des Orientalischen Seminars der Universität Bonn, 1961), 70–81; Massignon, *EO* 161–71. For a translation of texts on his "moral psychology," see *EIM* 171–95.

17. My principal sources here, in addition to A. J. Arberry, *The Book of Truthfulness (Kitāb aṣ-ṣidq)* (London: Humphrey Milford/Oxford University Press, 1937), include Massignon, *EO*, 203–5; Rosenthal, *KT* 167–68, 170–72; and W. Madelung, *EI*[2] 4:1083–84.

18. Arabic text in Arberry, *The Book of Truthfulness,* 11–17, 45–47.

19. According to *KT* 167, however, Kharrāz expresses a different view in his *Rasa'il:* "(Kharrāz)...also claimed that the knowledge *(ʿilm)* of God was something wider and deeper than the gnosis (or knowledge about, *maʿrifah*) of God, although both were infinite. The knowledge of God leads to the cognition of gnosis *(maʿrifat al-maʿrifah)* at the time of the passing of the (mere) knowledge of gnosis *(ʿilm al-maʿrifa).*"

20. My translation from Arberry's Arabic text of *Kitāb aṣ-Ṣidq*, 69–70; Arberry trans. 56–57. See p. 151 for similar tradition regarding David.

21. My translation from Arberry's Arabic text 73; Arberry trans. 59.

22. My translation from Aberry's Arabic text 77–78; see Arberry trans. 62–63.

23. Here I rely on *KT* 179–81; Bernd Radtke, *Al-Ḥakīm at-Tirmidhī: ein islamischer Theosoph des 3./9. Jahrhunderts* (Freiburg: Klaus Schwarz, 1980), esp. 74–82 *(ʿilm)* and 96–99 *(maʿrifa)*; Massignon, *EO* 192–99.

24. Cited in *KT* 179.

25. Translating from Radtke's German rendering of Tirmidhī, 128.

26. Louis Massignon, *The Passion of Al-Ḥallāj: Mystic and Martyr of Islam,* trans. Herbert Mason (Princeton, N.J.: Princeton University Press, 1982), 3:4–5.

27. Ibid., 20.

28. Ibid., 289–92, 321–34. Arabic text in Paul Nwyia, ed., *Hallāg: Kitāb Al-Ṭawāsīn* (Beirut: Imprimerie Catholique, 1972), 194–95; and L. Massignon, ed. *Kitāb aṭ-ṭawāsīn* (Paris: P. Geuthner, 1913). The latter includes both the Arabic of Ḥallāj and the Persian translation and commentary of Rūzbihān Baqlī (d. 606/1209), a major Persian Sufi. For other relevant views of Rūzbihān, see Henry Corbin, ed. and trans., *Commentaire sur les paradoxes des Soufis* (Paris: Adrien-Maisonneuve, 1966).

29. A. J. Arberry, ed. and trans., *The Mawāqif and Mukhāṭabāt of Muḥammad ibn ʿAbdi 'l-Jabbār al-Niffarī.* (London: Luzac & Co., 1935), summarizing and

paraphrasing here from 14–24, 33–45, 50–52, 72–77, 93–101, 111–15, 142–43, 177–79, and occasionally retranslating from pertinent Arabic texts provided at the back of that volume. For a new translation of selections of Niffarī, see *EIM* 281–301, where Sells includes "Standing 59: On the reality of *maʿrifa*."

30. W. Chittick translates the term as "overview" in his *The Self-Disclosure of God: Principle's of Ibn ʿArabī's Cosmology* (Albany, N.Y.: SUNY, 1998), 219. This is a term of considerable importance for later Sufis, such as Suhrawardī, and will be discussed below.

31. Translated in *EIM* 196–211.

32. Hamid Algar gives the year 391/1000 as the date of his death ("Introduction," in B. von Schlegell, trans., *Principles of Sufism* [Berkeley, Calif.: Mizan Press, 1990], xi).

33. See A. J. Wensinck, *The Muslim Creed* (New York: Barnes and Noble, 1966) for specific details on this and other early creedal statements.

34. For further details, see A. J. Arberry, *The Doctrine of the Sufis* (Cambridge: Cambridge University Press, 1978 reprint), ix–xviii.

35. See also G.-C. Anawati and Louis Gardet, *Mystique Musulmane* (Paris: J. Vrin, 1961), 129–45, on the knowledge of God, with special focus on Kalābādhī.

36. For the following summary of his life, I rely on GQ 1:11–23; Louis Massignon, "Sālimīya," EI[1] 7:115; and W. Mohd. Azam, "Abū Ṭālib Al-Makkī: A Traditional Sufi," *Hamdard Islamicus* 22:3 (1999), 71–79.

37. Among which he included (1) the Jahmīya, (2) the Rāfiḍīya, (3) the Naẓẓāmīya, (4) the Muʿtazila, and (5) the Murjī'a.

38. Or: "because of God's lack of need for the success *(tawfīq)* that *maʿrifa* presupposes"—an obscure phrase that may mean that *maʿrifa* implies process and extraordinary experience that God alone can bring to fulfillment in a human being, whereas God's *ʿilm* is eternally complete and timeless and not subject to being brought to completion.

39. For further details about Qushayrī's life, see H. Halm, "Al-Kushayrī," EI[2] 5:526–27.

40. Ḥamīd Algar, "Introduction," in *Principles of Sufism by Al-Qushayrī,* trans. Barbara R. Von Schlegell (Berkeley, Calif.: Mizan Press, 1990), iv–v.

41. Ibid.

42. I have inserted relevant Arabic terms in brackets into the translation by Fritz Meier, in his "Qushayrī's *Tartīb al-sulūk": Essays on Islamic Piety and Mysticism by Fritz Meier,* trans. and ed. John O'Kane and Bernd Radtke (Leiden: Brill, 1999), 111 [Arabic text], 124–25. See also Qassim al-Samarrai, *The Theme of Ascension in Mystical Writings* (Baghdad: National Print. and Pub. Co., 1968), 179–82.

43. From the Persian text of S. de Laugier de Beaurecueil, *Khwāja ʿAbd Allāh Anṣārī* (Beirut: Imprimerie Catholique, 1965), 259.

44. For further details, see Richard McCarthy, trans., *Freedom and Fulfillment* (Boston: Twayne, 1980), ix–lx, and translation of Ghazālī's "autobiography," 61–114; also W. M. Watt, "Al-Ghazālī," EI^2 2:1038–41.

45. Ghazālī, *The Book of Knowledge,* trans. Nabih Amin Faris, rev. (Lahore: Sh. Muḥammad Ashraf, 1966), 106.

46. Summarized from Faris's translation of *The Book of Knowledge.*

47. Farid Jabre, *La notion de la Maʿrifa chez Ghazālī* (Beirut: L'institute de lettres orientales, 1958), 16. See also his *La notion de certitude selon Ghazālī dans ses origines psychologiques et historiques* (Paris: J. Vrin, 1958). For other aspects of Ghazālī's epistemology, see, for example, Victor Chelhot, "*Al-Qisṭās al-mustaqīm* et la connaissance rationnelle chez Ghazālī," *Bulletin d'Etudes Orientales* 15 (1955–57), 7–98.

48. Foreword to "Marvels of the Heart," Dār al-kutub al-ʿilmīya edition, 3:3–4. See also Ghazālī's treatment of *maʿrifa* in relation to love later in the *Iḥyā',* 4:325–40.

49. Richard McCarthy, S.J., translated sections one through five, and eight, as Appendix 5 in *Freedom and Fulfillment,* 363–82. My further comments are based on the text of the Beirut: Dār al-kutub al-ʿilmīya edition, n.d., 3:14–29.

50. A traditional tripartite cosmological structure ranks the *ʿālam al-jabarūt,* the Realm of Absolute Deity, to which human beings have no direct access, above that of Lordly Dominion.

51. See the translation by William Shepard in John Renard, ed., *Windows on the House of Islam* (Berkeley and Los Angeles: University of California Press, 1998), 355–59.

52. Ghazālī, *Treatise on (Knowledge) from God,* trans. Margaret Smith, *Journal of the Royal Asiatic Society* (London, 1938), Part 2 (April), 177–200, Part 3 (July), 353–74.

53. B. Halff, "Le *Maḥāsin al-majālis* d'Ibn al-ʿArīf et l'oeuvre du soufi hanbalite al-Anṣārī," *Révue des Études Islamiques* 39:2 (1972), 321–35.

54. Further see Claude Addas, "Andalusi Mysticism and the Rise of Ibn ʿArabī," in Salma Khadra Jayyusi, ed., *The Legacy of Muslim Spain,* 2 vols. (Leiden: Brill, 2000), 909–33.

55. See G. Böwering, "ʿAyn-al-Qoẓāt Hamadhānī," *EIr* 3:140–43; L. Lewisohn, "In Quest of Annihilation: Imaginalization and Mystical Death in the *Tamhīdāt* of ʿAyn al-Quḍāt Hamadhānī," in ed. L. Lewisohn, *The Heritage of Sufism* (Oxford: Oneworld, 1999), 1:285–336.

56. Izutsu, "Mysticism and the Linguistic Problem of Equivocation in the Thought of ʿAyn al-Qudāt Hamadānī," 154.

57. Thanks to Leonard Lewisohn for advice on the subject and for allowing me to summarize and quote his translation of selections of Hamadhānī's *Tamhīdāt.*

58. From Persian text of Major J. Stephenson, ed. and trans., *The First Book of the Ḥadīqatu 'l-Ḥaqīqat or the Enclosed Garden of the Truth* (New York: Samuel Weiser, 1972), 3–4.

59. Afkham Darbandi and Dick Davis, trans. *Farīd ud-Dīn Aṭṭār: The Conference of the Birds* (New York: Penguin, 1984), 179ff.; Farīd ad-Dīn ʿAṭṭār, *Mantīq aṭ-ṭayr,* ed. Muḥammad Javād Mashkūr (Tehran: 1353/1974), 231ff.

60. See John Renard, *All the King's Falcons: Rūmī on Prophets and Revelation* (Albany, N.Y.: SUNY, 1994); M. Esteʿlami, "The Concept of Knowledge in Rūmī's *Mathnawī,*" in *Classical Persian Sufism: From Its Origins to Rūmī,* ed. Leonard Lewisohn (London: KNP, 1993), 401–8.

61. For translated texts on knowledge see, for example, *SPK* 147–70, 212–30; *SDG* 150–55, 245–50, 277–79, 315–17, 345–49. See also Souad Ḥakīm, "Knowledge of God in Ibn ʿArabī," in *Muḥyiddīn Ibn ʿArabī: A Commemorative Volume,* ed. S. Hirtenstein and M. Tiernan (Rockport, Mass.: Element, 1993), 264–90.

62. For a complete listing of his Sufi connections, see GA 1–9.

63. Gerhard Böwering, *The Mystical Vision of Existence in Classical Islam: The Qur'ānic Hermeneutics of the Sufi Sahl At-Tustarī (d. 283/896)* (Berlin: de Gruyter, 1980), 138–42. Böwering suggests (140) that *ḥadd* may originally have referred to a celestial body's "descendant" or limit, while the *maṭlaʿ* referred to the body's "ascendant." See also John Wansbrough, *Qur'ānic Studies: Sources and Methods of Scriptural Interpretation* (Oxford: Oxford University Press, 1977), 242–44.

64. See, for example, Valerie J. Hoffman, *Sufis, Mystics, and Saints in Modern Egypt* (Columbia, S.C.: University of South Carolina Press, 1995), 218–25. For personal reflections on the theme of knowledge in the experience individual spiritual direction, see Michaela Özelsel, *Forty Days: The Diary of a Traditional Solitary Sufi Retreat* (Brattleboro, Vt.: Threshold Books, 1996); and Frances Trix, *Spiritual Discourse: Learning with an Islamic Master* (Philadelphia: University of Pennsylvania Press, 1993).

65. Syed Muḥammad Naguib al-Attas, *The Mysticism of Ḥamza Fanṣūrī* (Kuala Lumpur: University of Malaya, 1970).

66. G. W. J. Drewes and L. F. Brakel, *The Poems of Ḥamza Fanṣūrī* (Dordrecht: Foris Publications, 1986), 47, 51, 53, 61, 65, 79.

67. Jean-Louis Michon, *Le Soufi Marocain Aḥmad Ibn ʿAjība et son Miʿrāj: glossaire de la mystique musulman* (Paris: Librairie Philosophique J. Vrin, 1973), 193, 264.

68. J.-L. Michon, "L'autobiographie *(fahrasa)* du soufi marocain Aḥmad Ibn ʿAgība," Parts 1–4, *Arabica* 15 (1968), 225–69; 16 (1969), 25–64, 113–54, 225–68; citing pt. 4, 225–48.

69. Jaʿfar Sajjādī, *Farhang-i lughāt va isṭilāḥāt va taʿbīrāt-i ʿirfānī* (Tehran: Kitābkhāna Ṭahourī, 1350/1971), 439–43.

1. Abū Naṣr as-Sarrāj

1. Texts translated from *Kitāb al-lumaʿ fi'l-taṣawwuf,* ed. R. A. Nicholson, E. J. W. Gibb Memorial Series 22 (London: Luzac & Company Ltd., 1963). With permission of Aris and Phillips.

2. The upper-case use of the words *Companions* and *Followers* refers, respectively, to the first and second generations of Muslims, that is, those who actually lived in the presence of Muḥammad, and their immediate descendants.

3. See S. Murata and W. Chittick, *The Vision of Islam* (New York: Paragon, 1994) for an introduction to Islam structured on this famous Ḥadīth.

4. The plural of *Sunna,* with lower case "s," can indicate either individual sayings of Muḥammad or specific practices that came to have the force of long-standing tradition or positive law.

5. Referring to the theological principle that God's revelation is necessarily progressive and incremental, and the corresponding hermeneutical principle according to which scholars must determine which scriptural verses must be understood as superseding, and therefore abrogating, others.

6. Qur'ān, Sunna, *ijmāʿ,* and *qiyās* are the so-called four roots of religious law, fundamental elements in the legal methodologies of all the Islamic schools *(madhāhib)* of religious law.

7. In Arabic, respectively, *muqāyasa, mushākala, mujānasa, muqārana,* possibly grammatical or logical terms that Sarrāj is using to indicate the precision and specificity of the discipline of the jurists.

8. Continuing: "so that they might warn their people on their return, that they might protect themselves" (9:122). Pickthall's translation suggests that, in this text that referred originally to sending only a part of the community out to fight, it is those who stay behind who are to study the religion carefully (*The Meaning of the Glorious Koran* [New York: Mentor, 1953], 156).

9. I.e., the spiritual condition in which one advanced on the Path becomes "as he was before he came into being."

10. Uways ibn ʿĀmir ibn Jaz' ibn Malik al-Qaranī (d.c. 37/657) never met Muḥammad, but the Prophet held this Yemeni up as an example of lofty spiritual qualities.

11. *Yaktuwūna,* here translated "branded," can also mean "cauterized." Cauterization is not in itself forbidden as a medical treatment, but the point here seems to be that under some circumstances people engaged in the practice of branding for religiously objectionable reasons.

12. See, for example, Abū Saʿīd al-Kharrāz's use of this Ḥadīth in A. J. Arberry, trans., *The Book of Truthfulness* (London: Oxford University Press, 1937), 28; and Ghazālī's citation in David B. Burrell, trans., *Faith in Divine Unity and Trust in Divine Providence* (Louisville, Ky.: Fons Vitae, 2001), 6.

13. Abū Saʿīd ibn Abi ʻl-Ḥasan Yasar al-Ḥasan al-Baṣrī (d. 110/728) was one of the Followers best known for his asceticism and most often cited in Sufi texts.

14. The "vow of abstinence," *ẓihar,* literally "back," from the pre-Islamic practice of divorce in which the husband tells the wife she is "like my mother's back" to him.

15. Ḥudhayfa ibn al-Yamān (d. 36/656–57) was an early convert and transmitter of Ḥadīths dealing especially with hypocrisy and eschatology.

16. ʿUmar ibn al-Khaṭṭāb (d. 23/644) was the second Caliph (r. 13/634–23/644). In other words, Ḥudhayfa's erudition in the subject was so highly regarded that no less than the man who would become the second Caliph was willing to rely on Ḥudhayfa's knowledge, even insofar as it might implicate him.

17. ʿAlī ibn Abī Ṭālib (d. 40/661) was Muḥammad's cousin and son-in-law, husband of Faṭima and father of the two Shīʿī martyrs Ḥasan and Ḥusayn, and the fourth Caliph, according to Sunni reckoning.

18. See Sells, *EIM* 281–301, for a discussion of Niffarī's idiosyncratic development of the term "standing."

19. Abū Saʿīd Aḥmad ibn ʿĪsā al-Kharrāz of Baghdad (d. 277/890–91) was the author of an early treatise called *The Book of Authenticity (Kitāb aṣ-ṣiḍq),* in which he analyzed various spiritual states and laid out the conditions for authenticity in each (see Introduction above).

20. ʿAskar ibn Ḥusayn Abū Turāb an-Nakhshabī (d. 245/859) was one of the leading Khurāsānī teachers and was noted for his observations on knowledge.

21. Abū ʻl-ʿAbbās ibn Muḥammad Aḥmad ibn ʿAṭāʾ (d. 309/921–22 or 311/923–24) was a close friend of the martyr-mystic Ḥallāj.

22. Abū Bakr (d. 13/634) was a preeminent Companion and Muḥammad's father-in-law and first Caliph, known for his uprightness and thus called aṣ-Ṣiddīq, the Authentic One.

23. Abū Bakr ibn Jahdar ash-Shiblī (d. 334/945–46), a Māliki legal specialist, was a disciple of Junayd of Baghdad, a friend of Ḥallāj, teacher of Naṣrābādhī.

24. Commonly known as Bāyezīd, Abū Yazīd ibn ʿĪsā al-Bisṭāmī (d. 261/874–75), a Central Asian and one of the most often quoted Sufis, a prototype of the "intoxicated" Sufi noted for his ecstatic utterance, "Glory be to me!"

25. Abū ʻl-Qāsim ibn Muḥammad al-Junayd (d. 298/910–11) was the archtypical "sober" Sufi, regarded as the leader of the Baghdadi school, though he was born in Iran. A Shāfiʿī legal scholar, he taught the doctrine of "second sobriety," namely, the importance of returning to a heightened level of spiritual sobriety after ecstatic experience.

26. Yaḥyā ibn Muʿādh ar-Rāzī (d. 258/872) was an Iranian Sufi known for his preaching and influential in the forming of the Nishapur school of Sufism in Khurasan, among whom Abū ʿUthmān al-Ḥīrī (d. 298/910) was a major figure.

27. I.e., an individual who joins the ranks of possessors of experiential knowledge of God disappears as an individual personality.

28. Abū 'l-Ḥusayn an-Nūrī (d. 295/907) was a friend of Junayd and disciple of Sarī as-Saqaṭī (d.c. 251/865), noted especially for his emphasis on love of God and early analysis of "stations of the heart."

29. Abū Bakr Muḥammad al-Wāsiṭī (d.c. 320/932) was a legal specialist who came from Farghana in Central Asia and became a member of the Baghdadi school of Sufism.

30. Abū Sulaymān ʿAbd ar-Raḥmān ad-Dārānī (d. either 205/820 or 215/830—probably the latter) was a noted ascetic of Syria influenced by the school of Ḥasan al-Baṣrī.

31. ʿAbd Allāh Ibn ʿAbbās (d. 68/687) was a Companion and cousin of Muḥammad, best known as an authoritative transmitter of Ḥadīths and Qur'ānic exegete.

32. An Ashʿarī theological expression indicating reticence to inquire about what one cannot know fully concerning the mystery of God.

33. These attributes are all items specified in various early Islamic creeds, and Sarrāj is careful to mention them here so that the reader will have no reason to suspect that Sufis have departed from the mainstream teaching.

34. Here the operative concepts are *tashbīh,* anthropomorphism, and its opposite, *taʿṭīl,* namely, claiming that the divine attributes are not one with the divine essence.

35. Literally, "makes a Hijra," thus symbolically imitating Muḥammad in his fully god-trusting departure from Mecca in 622.

36. Yūsuf ibn al-Ḥusayn ar-Rāzī (d. 304/916), an associate of Abū Turāb an-Nakhshabī in the Iranian city of Rayy, was an expert on sincerity.

37. Samnūn (alternately spelled Sumnūn) al-Muḥibb (the Lover) ibn Ḥamza al-Khawwāṣ (d.c. 298/910) was a Baghdadi mystic and friend of Nūrī who ranked love above experiential knowledge.

38. Abū Ḥafṣ an-Naysābūrī al-Ḥaddād (d.c. 265/878–79) was a noted ascetic of Nishapur in Khurasan whose sometimes extreme behavior was linked to his association groups identified as Malāmatī, those who "brought blame on themselves" through their practice of self-denial.

39. Conversation, *kalām:* Moses was known as *Kalīm Allāh,* "who conversed with God."

40. *Risāla,* the technical term used to distinguish the mission of certain prophets whose mission extends beyond "prophethood" *(nubūwa)* in that they are sent to all people and are given a scripture.

41. The full text of the two verses reads, "So they found one of Our servants to whom We had given mercy from Ourselves and to whom We had taught knowledge from within Us. Moses said to the servant, Shall I follow you so that you might teach me right guidance from what you have been taught?" The servant then warned Moses that he would not be patient enough to bear with him (18:67).

42. Sarrāj has conflated sections of several Ḥadīths here, the last part being from a saying in which Muḥammad wishes that God had originally created him as a

tree whose fruit, once felled, would be eaten. The suggestion may be that he would then not have suffered the consequence of a knowledge too hard to bear.

43. Muwarriq ibn Mushamrij al-ʿIjlī (d. 105/723 or 108/726) was a Basran traditionist.

44. Abū Dharr al-Ghifarī (d.c. 32/652) was an early convert to Islam and Ḥadīth transmitter known for his asceticism and spiritual poverty.

45. The intended point is apparently that while the Qur'ān refers to knowledge the Prophet is required to communicate, the Ḥadīth refers to knowledge given to him privately.

46. ʿUmar ibn al-Khaṭṭāb was as well a father-in-law of Muḥammad.

47. An abridged excerpt of a saying of ʿAlī in an extended conversation with Kumayl recorded in Muḥammad ibn al-Ḥusayn ash-Sharīf ar-Raḍī, *Nahj-ul-balāgha,* ed. Muḥammad ʿAbduh (Cairo: n.d.), 4:587–89; cf. same work by unnamed translator (Elmhurst, N.Y.: Tahrike Tarsile Quran, 1977), 290.

48. *Shaṭḥ* is sometimes translated "theopathic/ecstatic utterance," from a root that suggests an overflowing or superabundance, as when flour overflows a sieve during the process of sifting.

49. For M. Sells's translation of chapters 123 through 127, see *EIM* 212–31.

2. Abū Bakr al-Kalābādhī

1. Translated from *At-taʿarruf li-madhhab ahl at-taṣawwuf,* ed. Mahmūd Amīn an-Nawawī (Cairo: Maktabat al-Kulliyāt al-Azharīya, 1969).

2. *Min jihat al-ithbāt*—a note in the Arabic edition reads: That is, in terms of faith in Him and in His existence by means of infused knowledge of Him through the traces in His creation, [as the Qur'ān says] "and they will not encompass it/Him with discursive knowledge" (20:110). Arberry translates the phrase as "postulation."

3. These two are, respectively, based on acquaintance and familiarity *(taʿarruf),* and communication of information *(taʿrīf).*

4. Individuals whose *maʿrifa* derives from these two sources are reminiscent of the classic distinction between two types of individual seekers: the *majdhūb,* who is "drawn" to God immediately or directly, and the *sālik,* who "journeys" along the more protracted path of gradual realization of God through the traces of His creation. See, e.g., Ibn ʿAbbād of Ronda, *Letters on the Sufi Path,* trans. John Renard (Mahwah, N.J.: Paulist Press, 1986), 25–26.

5. Muḥammad ibn Wāsiʿ al-Azdī (d. either 123/740–41 or 127/744–45) was an ascetic active in the Muslim conquest of Central Asia, said to have had significant connections with Ḥasan al-Baṣrī, and is most famous for the saying cited here.

6. Followed by similar references to the sky, mountains, and the earth.

7. Massignon has "Here is the transfiguring explication of the divine fires, flaming (in me)/Brilliant, like the eastern side of a pearl, irrefutable" *(Passion of*

Al-Ḥallāj: Mystic and Martyr of Islam, trans. Herbert Mason, 3 vols. [Princeton, N.J.: Princeton University Press, 1982], 3:62).

8. Literally, "knower and known," *ʿārif* and *maʿrūf,* an unusual explanation, since although God is often called *al-ʿālim,* God is not generally identified as *al-ʿārif.*

9. Muḥammad Sahl ibn ʿAbd Allāh at-Tustarī (d. 283/896), student of Sufyān ath-Thawrī and teacher of Ḥallāj; his Qur'ānic commentary was a watershed of mystical exegesis (see Gerhard Böwering, *The Mystical Vision of Existence in Classical Islam* [Berlin: Walter de Gruyter, 1980]).

10. Abū Bakr Muḥammad ibn ʿUmar al-Balkhī at-Tirmidhī al-Ḥakīm al-Warrāq (d. either 280/893 or 295/908) was a Central Asian Sufi who specialized in ascetical discipline and wrote *The Book of the Learned and the Seeker of Knowledge.*

11. Abū Bakr Muḥammad ibn Mūsā al-Wāsiṭī, a.k.a. Ibn al-Farghānī (d.c. 320/932) was a student of Junayd and Nūrī and acknowledged by some as a major theorist of Sufism.

12. Arberry glosses *rasm* (here "outlines") as "unreal impress," and *wasm* as "divine impress," 134.

13. Possibly Abū Bakr al-Ḥusayn ibn ʿAlī ibn Yazdānyār al-Urmawī (fourth/tenth century).

14. Ubayy ibn Kaʿb (d.c. 19/640), of the Medinan tribe of Khazraj, was a Companion.

15. Al-Ḥāritha, or Ḥārith, ibn Mālik al-Anṣārī (d. 2/624) was a Companion who died at the Battle of Badr.

16. Some commentators identify al-Aʿrāf as the bridge over heaven and hell, and the men there as angels or past prophets. Others regard them as souls balanced precariously between good and evil, heaven and hell, but who yet hope in divine mercy.

17. The last few words, at least, are those of Junayd, and the whole text refers to great Sufis who, even though possessed of experiential knowledge, remained hard to identify, some even born to royalty but refusing to be associated with it.

3. Abū Ṭālib al-Makkī

1. Translated from *Qūt al-qulūb,* 2 vols. (Beirut: Dār al-kutub al-ʿilmīya, 1997).

2. GQ 4:57 suggests that he may be identical with an ʿAbd ar-Raḥīm ad-Daybūlī, but gives no further identification.

3. Mālik ibn Dīnār an-Nājī (d. 131/748–49), a Qur'ānic scribe of the ascetical school of Ḥasan al-Baṣrī.

4. Farqad as-Sabakhī, rather than as-Sinjī as in the printed versions (d. 131/748–49), an ascetic of Basra.

5. ʿAbd al-Wāḥid ibn Zayd (d. after 160/767, possibly 177/793) was a Basran ascetic who emphasized the importance of keeping vigil and fasting in solitude.

6. Ibrāhīm ibn Adham (d. 161/778), from the Afghan city of Balkh, was said to have undergone a radical renunciation of royal wealth in his conversion to Islam, a story bearing interesting similarities to that of the Buddha.

7. Yūsuf ibn Asbāṭ ash-Shaybānī (d. either 195/810, 196/811, or 199/814), cited many times by Makkī, was an associate of Bishr al-Ḥāfī.

8. Wuhayb ibn al-Ward al-Makkī (d. 153/770) was an ascetical Ḥadīth specialist with whom Ibn al-Mubārak studied.

9. (Abū Ṣāliḥ) Shuʿayb ibn Ḥarb al-Madā'in al-Baghdādī (d. 197/812–13) [rather than Ḥabīb ibn Ḥarb, as in printed version].

10. Sufyān ath-Thawrī (d. 161/777) of Kufa was an oft-cited transmitter of Ḥadīth.

11. Abū Ḥanīfa (d. 150/767) of Kufa was the founding figure of one of the four surviving Sunni legal schools, the Ḥanafī, currently dominant in Turkey and parts of India.

12. Ibn al-Mubārak (d. 181/797) was a noted legal specialist of the Mālikī and (no longer extant) Awzāʿī schools.

13. Abū Thawr Ibrāhīm ibn Khālid al-Kalbī (d. 240/854), whose law school Junayd followed. The now-defunct school declined after the fourth/tenth century.

14. Abū ʿAbd Allāh al-Ḥārith ibn Asad al-Muḥāsibī (d. 243/857) was a major contributor to early Islamic mystical theology. See Sells, *EIM* 171–95, for a translation of selections on his psychology.

15. In the former case, the requirement is known as *farḍ kifāya,* that is, a requirement binding on the community as a whole to see to it that a "sufficient number" of them act on the matter, and in the latter, *farḍ ʿayn,* a duty encumbent upon every single Muslim, regardless of specific role or status within the community.

16. ʿAbd Allāh ibn ʿUmar (d. 73/693) was a Companion often cited for his complete dedication to the Prophet.

17. Anas ibn Mālik (d. 91–93/709–12) was a Companion (who knew the Prophet only as a very young boy) noted for transmitting well over a hundred Ḥadīths.

18. ʿAbd Allāh ibn Masʿūd (d. 32/653), one of the earliest converts to Islam, was celebrated as a prime source of exegesis as well as law.

19. Mālik ibn Anas (d. 179/795) was an early legal scholar of Medina after whom the Sunni school of legal method called the Mālikī was named.

20. Aḥmad ibn Ḥanbal (d. 241/855) was a traditionist after whom the Ḥanbalī Sunni legal school, currently dominant in Saudi Arabia, was named.

21. Fuḍayl ibn ʿIyāḍ (d. 178/803) was an early Khurāsānī Sufi, who, according to legend, had been a notorious highway robber; he was noted for his asceticism.

22. Bishr ibn al-Ḥārith "al-Ḥāfī" (The Barefoot) (d. 227/841) was a colorful associate of Fuḍayl, and, as his nickname suggests, a hardcore ascetic.

23. ʿAbd ar-Raḥmān ibn Abī Laylā (d.c. 83/702) was one of the Helpers of the Aws tribe in Medina.

24. A Ḥadīth like this one is associated with the early transmitter Ḥudhayfa ibn al-Yamān, who specialized in Ḥadīths on hypocrisy.

25. For historical background of Makkī's views on this subject, see *Ibn al-Jawzī's Kitāb al-quṣṣāṣ wa'l-mudhakkirīn,* ed. and trans. Merlin L. Swartz (Beirut: Dār al-Machreq, 1986), and Jonathan Berkey, *Popular Preaching and Religious Authority in the Medieval Islamic Near East* (Seattle: University of Washington Press, 2001).

26. Abū Hurayra (d.c. 58/677), dubbed Father of the Kitten because of his love of cats, became a Muslim late in Muḥammad's life and transmitted some thirty-five hundred Ḥadīths. He is identified among the "companions of the bench" *(aṣḥāb aṣ-ṣuffa),* so called because they were the devout poor who gather on a bench outside Muḥammad's residence in Medina.

27. *Ṣadaqa,* non-mandatory almsgiving, beyond the required "pillar" called *zakāt.*

28. Punning on the sounds of *riwāya,* transmission of Ḥadīths, and *riʿāya,* taking care, protecting, responsible custody.

29. Battle of Badr (Ramaḍān 2/623), in which the badly outnumbered Muslims were victorious against the Meccan Quraysh; i.e., even the great second successor of the Prophet would have consulted with the generation revered for having supported the early community through its most difficult times.

30. Muʿāwiya ibn Abī Sufyān (d. 60/680) was the first Umayyad Caliph, ruling in Damascus (41/661–60/680) where he had previously served as governor.

31. A "client" *(mawlā)* is a non-Arab convert to Islam who has been granted the equivalent of honorary membership in a sponsoring Arab tribe.

32. Ma'mūn (d. 218/833) was an ʿAbbāsid Caliph most noted for his imposition of an inquisition *(miḥna)* whose litmus test was adherence to the doctrine of the createdness of the Qur'ān. That was a crucial item in the creed of the rational theologians called the Muʿtazila, whose views Ma'mūn had elevated to the level of a state creed.

33. Muʿādh ibn Jabal (d.c. 18/639) was noted for his expertise in legal matters and is cited often by Makkī in this section.

34. ʿUmar ibn ʿAbd al-ʿAzīz ibn Marwān, also known as ʿUmar II, ruled as Umayyad Caliph (r. 99/717–101/720) and was noted for his intense piety.

35. Salama ibn Dīnār Abū Ḥāzim al-Madanī (d. 140/757) and Rabīʿa al-Madanī (d. 136/753) were ascetics of Medinan origin.

36. Banū Marwān, a term sometimes rendered as "Marwānids," refers to the Umayyad rulers descended from the "counter-caliph Marwān" (claim to rule 64/684–65/685), among whom was ʿUmar II.

37. Luqmān is a Qur'ānic figure after whom Sūra 31, much of which is framed as the sage's advice to his son, is named.

38. A proof text in which Makkī keys in on the terms *yaqīn* and *wajadtu*—terms he now uses in a mystical sense, clearly engaging in symbolic exegesis.

39. The full narration has Muḥammad describe a night vision (framed as a dream) in which God appears to him and asks him whether he knows what is a source of argument in highest council of angels (perhaps an allusion to Q 38:69). When he answers "No," God places His hand between Muḥammad's shoulders so that the Prophet feels a chill in his breast. At that point Muḥammad "knew all that was in heaven and on earth" (GQ 435).

40. *Malakūt*, a term that refers to the invisible world as opposed to the realm of *mulk,* earthly sovereignty.

41. "Companions of the Right Hand" is a Qur'ānic expression (56:27–40) for those who will enjoy the delights of Paradise.

42. Literally, "is a *mujtahid,*" a term sometimes applied to a legal scholar who is vested with the authority to exercise independent judgment in jurisprudence.

43. ʿĀmir ibn Sharāḥīl ibn ʿAbd ash-Shaʿbī (d. 103/721) was a leading traditionist of Kufa.

44. Muḥammad ibn al-Ḥanafīya (d. 81/700), youngest son of ʿAlī's second wife, became the focus of his own legendary bravery in avenging the martyrdom of his half-brother Ḥusayn.

45. In the Battle of the Camel (36/656), ʿAlī defeated the rebel forces of Ṭalḥa and Zubayr. It was so named because fighting ceased when it reached ʿĀ'isha, who was being conveyed by camel and was there in support of the rebels.

46. ʿAlī ibn al-Ḥusayn (d. 94/712), also known as Zayn al-ʿĀbidīn (Adornment of the Devotees), was grandson of ʿAlī and the fourth Shīʿī Imām.

47. Muḥammad ibn Idrīs ash-Shāfiʿī (150/767–205/820) was a student of Mālik in Medina; the Shāfiʿī Sunni legal school is named after him.

48. Abū ʿAbd Allāh al-Mahdī (r. 158/775–169/785), an Abbāsid Caliph and father of the celebrated Hārūn ar-Rashīd.

49. ʿAbd Allāh ibn Rawāḥa (d. 8/629) was a Medinan convert celebrated for bravery in battle.

50. This is a reference to the Qur'ānic statement, "The Jews say Ezra (ʿUzayr) is the son of God, while the Christians say the Messiah is the son of God" (9:30).

51. Referring, with a variant text, to Deuteronomy 30:11–14.

52. Wahb ibn Munabbih al-Yamānī (d.c. 110/728) was devout jurist during the caliphate of ʿUmar II.

53. Ḍaḥḥāk ibn Muzāhim (d. 105/723) was an exegete and Ḥadīth scholar of Balkh (now in Afghanistan) often cited as a transmitter.

54. Abū Yūsuf (d. 182/798) was the chief magistrate of Baghdad and among Iraqi jurists was second only to Abū Ḥanīfa in influence and authority.

55. Abū Saʿīd al-Khudrī (d.c. 74/693) was a Medinan Companion to whom a high volume of Ḥadīth transmission has been attributed.

56. Saʿd ibn Abī Waqqās (d. 55/675) was an important early military leader who founded the Iraqi garrison town of Kufa.

57. "...will be successful," the verse continues. GQ 1:447 translates the verse, "The scale that will weigh on that day is the Truth."

58. "Days of God" refers to times during which people experience God's mercy and blessings in a heightened manner.

59. Literally, "confusion, ambiguity" *(iltibās)*. Makkī is extending, through plays on words, the metaphor of God's conferring a hue, using language of vesture (from the root *labasa*).

60. Perhaps analogous to a type of "tax shelter" tactic, whereby one can sidestep the requirement of holding wealth for a full year in order to avoid *zakāt.*

61. Kaʿb al-Aḥbār (d.c. 32/652) was a Yemeni rabbi who converted to Islam not long after Muḥammad's death.

62. Islamic law provides for "permitted exceptions" *(rukhaṣ)* in extenuating circumstances, such as not fasting during Ramaḍān if one is traveling.

63. The word Abū Ṭālib used here to refer to dead bones comes, ironically, from a root that means "to be grand or magnificent."

64. *Zāwiyas* is a term that eventually came to refer to the small residences or oratories in which Sufi shaykhs held sessions with their disciples.

65. Ayyūb as-Sakhtiyānī (d. 131/748) was a noted traditionist and student of Anas ibn Mālik.

66. Ibrāhīm al-Khawwāṣ (d.c. 290/903) was an Iraqi ascetic who emphasized the need for total trust in God.

67. Mujāhid ibn Jabr al-Makkī (d. 104/722) was considered the preeminent exegete among the Followers and was a specialist in *asbāb an-nuzūl,* the "circumstances of the revelation."

68. *Abdāl* are the "substitutes," a class of seventy persons in the Sufi cosmological hierarchy, among whom are numbered the "veracious ones" *(ṣiddīqūn)*—the chief of whom is called the *quṭb* (axis or pole)—and the four *awtād* ("pegs"). Whenever one of them dies, his role is assumed by another, hence the name.

69. Continuing: "If you are banished, we will go out with you...." He is using here an example of people who exemplify values quite opposed to those of the prophets and their spiritual kin but exhibit qualities of fraternal affinity nonetheless.

70. In full, the verse reads: "Those who obey God and the Messenger, they are with those upon whom God has bestowed His grace, the prophets, the perfectly truthful, the witnesses, and the upright. And what good friends they are."

71. Or: "in God's presence." In between the text continues: "and in what He has revealed to them, in humility before God. They will not trade God's verses/signs for a paltry price."

72. *Sayyid* ("master, lord") and *Sharīf* ("noble person") both refer to an individual descended from Muḥammad through his daughter Fāṭima and her husband ʿAlī, with the Moroccan and Jordanian royal lines claiming this lineage today.

73. Shaqīq ibn Ibrāhīm al-Balkhī (d. 194/809), a leading figure in Khurāsānī Sufism and follower of Ibrāhīm ibn Adham, taught the need for radical trust and spiritual hunger.

74. Jābir ibn ʿAbd Allāh (d.c. 78/697), a Medinan convert and Helper to whom numerous Ḥadīths are attributed.

75. GQ 1:467 notes that two of his four mss. place the Ḥadīth before the saying of ʿAbd Allāh ibn Masʿūd.

76. I.e., a person whom God has gratified or delighted, using terms reminiscent of a traditional text describing how two angels descended upon the child Muḥammad, opened up his breast, and cleansed it with snow; and a Qur'ānic text that refers to God's "expanding the center" of Muḥammad's being—an action often interpreted metaphorically as God's enlightening Muḥammad and sealing his intimate relationship with him (94:1).

77. In this difficult passage Makkī seems to be suggesting that good guidance is very hard to find, and that one must be very careful to whom one goes for answers to the most important questions. Makkī gives only the first four types immediately, returning to the fifth later.

78. Full name Abū Bakr Muḥammad ibn Muslim ibn ʿUbayd Allāh ibn ʿAbd Allāh ibn Shihāb az-Zuhrī (d. 124/742).

79. Qatāda ibn Diʿāma (d.c. 117/735) was a Basran exegete and colleague of Ḥasan.

80. Saʿīd ibn Jubayr (d. 95/713) was a major traditionist and legal scholar among the Followers.

81. I am unable to find an equivalent Torah citation; Sirach 38 seems to come closest.

82. Salmān al-Fārisī (d. 36/657), a Persian Companion known for his asceticism whom the Sufis regard as a model of attachment to Muḥammad.

83. Abū 'd-Dardā' (d. 32/652) was a Medinan Companion who occupied himself with collecting texts of the Qur'ān and was one of the "people of the bench." Madā'in was the former Sasanian Persian imperial capital on the Tigris in Iraq, southeast of Baghdad, where Salmān had been an early Muslim administrator (see M. Streck, "Al-Madā', in"EI^2 5:945–46).

84. Jābir ibn Zayd al-Azdī (d. 93/711 or 103/721–22) was a Kharajite exegete and traditionist from Basra, and a transmission link between Ibn ʿAbbās and Qatāda.

85. Saʿīd ibn al-Musayyib (d. 94/713) was an ascetic and important jurist among the Followers in Medina.

86. Abū Mūsā al-Ashʿarī (d. 42/662–63), military commander under ʿUmar, who later negotiated for ʿAlī in his battle with Muʿāwiya in 37/657 at Siffin.

87. Muḥammad Ibn Sīrīn (d. 110/728), best known for his work on dream interpretation, was also a legal scholar in Basra.

88. Thābit al-Bunānī (d. 127/744) was a Follower associated with a group of ascetics known as the Weepers.

89. An allusion to the imagery of 24:35, the Verse of Light, which likens God's light to a niche in which there is a lamp.

90. ʿUthmān ibn ʿAffān was the fourth Caliph (r. 23/644–35/656) and married two daughters of Muḥammad, most famous as the one who promulgated the first "official" written version of the Qur'ān.

91. Those about whom Muḥammad had said that they would enter Paradise: Muḥammad, Abū Bakr, ʿUmar, ʿUthmān, ʿAlī, Ṭalḥa ibn ʿUbayd Allāh (d. 36/656), Zubayr ibn al-ʿAwwām (d. 36/656), Saʿd ibn Abī Waqqāṣ, ʿAbd ar-Raḥmān ibn ʿAwf (d. 32/652), and Saʿīd ibn Zayd (d. 51/671).

92. I.e., that the good would always be waiting to be done.

93. According to GQ 1:479, Ḥudhayfa knew the names of the twelve people Muḥammad had considered hypocrites among his Companions.

94. Yazīd ar-Raqāshī (d.c. 115/733) of Basra was a student of Ḥasan, a magistrate and specialist in Ḥadīth.

95. Sulaymān ibn Mihrān al-Aʿmash (d. 147/764) was a Kufan-trained exegete and traditionist who was very influential in establishing the reading of Qur'ānic text.

96. Either to mark the end of Ramaḍān (ʿĪd al-fiṭr) or in observance of the day of sacrifice (ʿĪd al-aḍḥā) performed as part of the major pilgrimage (Ḥajj) to Mecca.

97. Probably Abū ʿAbd Allāh al-Hudhalī (d.c. 192/807).

98. "Scale" *(mīzān)* refers to the eschatological symbol of accountability for one's deeds. "Punishment of the grave" refers to the belief that the dead experience the terror and discomfort of confinement and must undergo interrogation in the grave by two angels, Munkar and Nakīr, sent to test the deceased on his or her beliefs.

99. Helpers: the *anṣār,* those citizens of Medina who have a special place in Islamic tradition because of the way they came to the Prophet's aid.

100. I.e., (Abū Sālim) Wābiṣa (ibn Maʿbad al-Asadī), a Companion who became a Muslim in 9/630, the man to whom Muḥammad was speaking.

101. Or, possibly: "who attests to the permanence of his witness/witnessing." This obscure expression may be an allusion to Q 50:37, "A reminder for anyone who has a heart and gives ear and witnesses."

102. Maʿrūf al-Karkhī (d.c. 200/815) was a major early Baghdadi mystic, possibly a convert from Christianity, who taught both Sarī and Ibn Ḥanbal, whose son is quoted here.

103. Manṣūr ibn ʿAmmār (d. 225/839) of Khurasan was credited with bringing popular preaching to Baghdad.

104. GQ renders this very enigmatic saying: "Leave us! the produce of a thornbush is not bitter, so it has burdened us with you so that we will be incinerated."

Other possibilities: "Leave us now! A palace guard (bearing spikes or arms) will pass by and, finding you with us, we will all be incinerated." Or, calling for a reading not attested in Gramlich's sources: "No load of thorns has passed by, so (God) has tossed you at us so that we would get scratched!" (reading the root of the final verb as *kharaqa,* "scratch/puncture," rather than *ḥaraqa,* "burn").
105. Here Makkī is glossing the various meanings of the verb *qaṣṣa,* which include "to pursue or track down" as well as "to narrate."
106. Qāsim ibn Muḥammad (d. 106/724) was a grandson of Abū Bakr, the first Caliph.
107. This would, of course, be the pinnacle of miserliness, to refuse to share with someone in need what one clearly had no personal need or use for.
108. Ibrāhīm at-Taymī (d. 92/710) was a Ḥadīth scholar, ascetic, and popular preacher of Kufa, who may have died in prison after Ḥajjāj confined him.
109. Ibrāhīm an-Nakhaʿī (d. 96/714), a Kufan traditionist associated with Ḥasan al-Baṣrī and the jurist Abū Ḥanīfa.
110. Sufyān ibn ʿUyayna (d.c. 198/813) was yet another traditionist of Kufa and a student of Ibn Shihāb az-Zuhrī.
111. I.e., by default, for he had outlived all the other authorities on Ḥadīth.
112. I am unable to locate texts similar to the first two in the canonical gospels; for the last saying, see Matthew 7:6 and 13:45.
113. Abū Bakr al-Kattānī (d. 322/934) was an early member of the Baghdad school of Sufism.
114. Rābiʿa al-ʿAdawīya (d. 185/801), who spent many years in Basra, is often called a pivotal figure in the transition from asceticism to genuine mysticism, and her poetry is some of the earliest extant Sufi verse.
115. GQ 1:499 provides the following variation from manuscript versions: (Sufyān) ath-Thawrī had said before him, "The temptation of the Ḥadīth is more intense than the temptation of woman, money, and children." And Rābiʿa al-ʿAdawīya said, "What a fine man Sufyān would have been had he not been so attached to the Ḥadīth!" And she once said, "If only he had not been attached to this world."
116. Ismāʿīl ibn Isḥāq al-Qāḍī (d. 282/896) was a magistrate *(qāḍī)* in charge of eastern Baghdad under the Caliph Mutawakkil from 860 to 861, and, eventually, the chief *qāḍī* of Baghdad.
117. Here GQ inserts the sayings marked by an asterisk below, according to manuscript evidence.
118. GQ 1:505 says this Abū 'l-Qāsim Ḥammād ibn Abī Laylā of Kufa (d. 772/73) was noted for his transmission of early Arabic poetry.
119. ʿAṭā' ibn Abī Rabāḥ (d.c. 114/732) was a Meccan legal scholar who specialized in matters pertaining to pilgrimage.
120. Early tradition ranked Companions using such criteria as date of conversion to Islam, making the Hijra in 1/622, participating in the Battle of Badr in 2/623,

being among those who prayed in both directions (i.e., were Muslims before the *qibla* changed from Jerusalem to Mecca, c. 3/624), and being present at the treaty of Ḥudaybīya in 11/628 (for greater detail, see M. Muranyi, "Ṣaḥāba," EI[2] 8:827–29).

121. Makkī may be alluding here to a text in Surat Luqman in which the sage reminds his son that "the most annoying of voices is that of the jackass" (Q 31:19).

122. Zayd ibn Thābit (d. 45/665) was a Companion associated with particular diligence in preserving Qur'ānic utterances in writing.

123. Philosophically speaking, that is, a property that can inhere in a substance.

124. Referring to Q 2:106, and to discussion as to what precise reading was correct.

125. I.e., reading the text in such a way that it does not mean "or situate it later or postpone it." The verse continues: "then We substitute for it something better or equivalent."

126. There follows a series of traditions belonging to the category of *aḥādīth al-fitan,* Ḥadīths about the coming trials that will be signs of an imminent end of history.

127. GQ 1:513 notes that, as indicated in Q 5:3, the flesh of an animal that has died as a result of being rammed is ritually impure and thus cannot be eaten; hence, Makkī appears to be referring to a person who will be shunned.

128. GQ 1:516 notes that ʿImwās (or ʿAmawās) was a district near Jerusalem believed to have been the place where a major plague began during the caliphate of ʿUmar (13–23/634–44 C.E.).

129. Aḥmad ibn Abī 'l-Ḥawārī (d.c. 230/844) was a Syrian member of the ascetical school of Basra and follower of Sulaymān ad-Dārānī.

130. The verse begins: "If you find no one at home, do not enter unless you receive permission."

131. Assimilated consonants, called "sun letters," are those that are in effect doubled when preceded by the definite article, "al-," so for example: Abū 'd-Dardā', rather than Abū al-Dardā'. The non-assimilated consonants, called "moon letters," are not doubled when preceded by the definite article, so for example: Ḥasan al-Baṣrī.

132. The Khawārij, plural of Khārij, meaning "those who secede," were originally a faction among ʿAlī's army that broke away when ʿAlī fought to a stalemate with Muʿāwiya at Ṣiffīn in 36/656. The Khawārij insisted that ʿAlī had too quickly acquiesced in mere human arbitration rather than relying on the judgment of God's word.

133. Referring to the full range of language studies, from correct grammar and pronunciation to embellishment for the sake of eloquence.

134. The *minbar* was a staircase usually situated to the right of the *miḥrāb,* sometimes with a small cupola atop the steps, from which the imām delivered his Friday or feast-day sermon.

135. GQ 1:529 cites an account that identifies this Abū ʿAbd Allāh as a chief judge of the Muʿtazila called Ibn Abī Du'ād (d. 240/854), who had been involved in the case against Aḥmad ibn Ḥanbal.
136. Following the order GQ noted in the manuscript versions; printed versions place this paragraph after the paragraph on the sayings of Ibn Mahdī and Mālik ibn Anas below.
137. GQ 1:531 notes that Ibn Ḥanbal's relationship to Muḥāsibī was ambivalent, for he respected Muḥāsibī as an individual but had serious reservations about his teachings, tainted as they were by contact with the speculative theologians.
138. Following the order of sayings that GQ 1:531 indicates occurs in the manuscripts. Printed versions given Mālik's saying before that of Ibn Mahdī.
139. Shurayḥ ibn al-Ḥārith (d.c. 76/695) was a storied judge of Kufa.
140. Manṣūr ibn ʿAmmār (d. 225/839) was a "preacher" *(wāʿiẓ)* and Ibn as-Sammāk (d. 183/799) was a "reminder" *(mudhakkir).*
141. The *maqṣūra,* an alcove or elevated platform reserved for the ruler and his family, often accessible through a separate entrance so that the sultan, for example, could bypass the gathered crowd if he wished.
142. As in 28:38: "Hāmān, make me a kiln for clay bricks so that you can build me a palace and I can ascend to the God of Moses."
143. Bishr ibn Marwān ibn al-Ḥākam (d. 75/694) was a member of the Umayyad family, which many early pietists faulted for its sinful penchant for regal splendor.
144. From a term that can also refer both to camel saddles and the wrapping of a turban.
145. A "measure" varying regionally from about a "forearm" in length to two feet.
146. Ḥajjāj ibn Yūsuf (d. 95/714) was a major administrator for the Umayyad Caliph ʿAbd al-Mālik (r. 73/692–87/705), son of counter-caliph Marwān. Shaʿbī's point is that such a turn of events would signal a dramatic deterioration of religious values, because Ḥajjāj became notorious for introducing countless innovations, as Makkī is about to detail.
147. Or "points," visual devices introduced to (1) make sure that certain consonants that might not otherwise have been easily distinguished from similar letters would be read correctly; and (2) indicate correct vocalization by means of red marks above and below the line to specify the vowels not otherwise included in most Arabic texts. Although Ḥajjāj was popularly believed to have introduced these additions, it is not certain who did.
148. But you are not allowed to profit by selling a text that you have embellished.
149. Majnūn, meaning "possessed by a jinn," or "madman," was the nickname of a fictional Bedouin character named Qays ibn al-Mulawwah, who went mad for love of the coy Laylā.

150. In other words, Makkī further interprets Anas's sarcastic comment that their apparent similarity to the Prophet's Companions is superficial and a coverup for a serious underlying problem.
151. GQ 1:538 translates the last clause, "These people have no share," and glosses by saying they have no share in the good things of the next world, referring to 2:102, 200, and 3:77.
152. "Young gentleman" and "rogue" and "gentlemanly demeanor" are all from the root *fatā,* which can carry the connotation of being a rascal or ne'er-do-well, member of a *futūwa* chivalric organization, or a noble youth.
153. GQ 1:540 notes that this was a saying of Muḥammad transmitted by Abū Hurayra.
154. Here two versions insert the saying from above: One of the ancestors in faith said, "A little humility suffices for a lot of action, and a little spiritual reticence suffices for a lot of knowledge."
155. The kinship name, or *nisba,* indicates one's tribal lineage. "Al-Quraẓī" indicates that the man belonged to the Banu Qurayẓa, one of the Jewish tribes of Medina, and ʿUmar suggests that, instead, the man say he was one of the "Helpers" or Anṣār, so-called because they supported Muḥammad's efforts in Medina.
156. Makkī refers to the subtle, insidious temptation to believe that one is making more progress than one actually has made. The divine ruse or stratagem *(makr)* is a classic Islamic theological concept designed to impress on the believer not that God lies in ambush or any such cruel device, but that one must be ever on guard against the temptation of thinking one knows the mind of God. The only safe course is to be ever vigilant and ready for surprises.
157. Using a derivative of the root *jahada,* often associated with the scholarly exertion required in interpreting matters of law, *ijtihād.*
158. GQ 1:544: This tradition appears here in manuscripts, but after the next one in printed versions.
159. GQ 1:544–45 supplies here the text of a Ḥadīth from ʿĀ'isha about three *"dīwāns"* or registers of which God keeps track, composed, respectively, of things God does not worry about, things God does not disregard, and things God does not forgive. The first includes faults such as failing to fast or pray; the last refers to polytheism; and the second, relevant here, includes injustices people perpetrate against each other.
160. The following text, translated here from GQ 1:547, para. 225, appears in only one of his manuscripts and not in printed versions: People have introduced as innovations also the refutation of innovators using speculative and rational science, for that too qualifies an an innovation. Anyone who employs such argumentation is an innovator. But in our time, this has become a science and the ignorant have regarded the dialecticians as learned people. It was the method of the ancestors in faith, however, to refute innovators using only sacred Ḥadīths and traditions, and never rational theology, analogical reasoning, speculation, and dis-

putation. Someone said to ʿAbd ar-Raḥmān ibn Mahdī, "So-and-so has produced a book in which he refutes the innovators." "How?" he asked, "With the scripture and tradition?" Came the response, "No, with rational science and speculation." So he responded, "He has disregarded sacred tradition and has refuted one innovation with another."

161. Makkī here reflects the longstanding controversy as to the importance of reproducing the precise wording as opposed to communicating the general sense of the tradition.

162. Using the technical term *marāsīl* (pl. of *mursal*), indicating that the chain of transmission lacks the name of a Companion, only beginning with the second generation.

163. Makkī actually uses the dual form here, but he then goes on to enumerate five issues explicitly, and follows those with an ongoing list of others uncounted.

164. Literally, "the tribes" *(al-asbāṭ)*, but here referring to Joseph's brothers specifically.

165. These are actually words that, according the Qur'ānic account, Joseph's brother Judah instructed his brothers to say to Jacob, as they tried to decide how to respond to the charge that their younger brother Benjamin had stolen Joseph's drinking cup.

166. As in 39:23, "At which your skin and your heart will become supple."

167. GQ 1:554 notes that these sayings occur in different order in the manuscripts.

4. ʿAlī ibn ʿUthmān Hujwīrī

1. Text translated from V. A. Zhukovskij, ed. *Kashf al-maḥjūb* (Leningrad: Dār al-ʿulūm, 1926).

2. I.e., of conditions under which observance of religious law might be deleterious to one's health or that might otherwise exempt one from religious obligation.

3. Literally, "of the menstrual period," the termination of which must be determined before a woman would be allowed to remarry after divorce.

4. It might still be spiritually worthwhile personal, non-required prayer, but it would not fulfill the ritual stipulations of required or "liturgical" prayer performed five times daily.

5. Ḥātim al-Aṣamm (d. 237/851) was from the present-day Afghan city of Balkh and was famous for his sage aphorisms.

6. The term *waqt* refers to the individual's spiritual condition at any given instant, so that a person who is fully in touch with that condition is called a "son of the moment."

7. Hujwīrī, like his fellow Sufi theorists, was ever aware of the need to emphasize the interdependence of outward, apparent and inward, hidden dimensions of all religious matters.

8. Literally, "roots" and "branches," terms referring to legal principles and their implications for action.

9. Muḥammad ibn al-Faḍl al-Balkhī (d. 319/931) is associated with a further development of Muḥāsibī's and Kharrāz's levels of knowledge into: knowledge *of* *(maʿrifa bi-)* God's attributes; knowledge *from* God concerning outward and inward meanings of God's law; and knowledge *with* God consisting of fear and hope, desire, and love. He carried on important correspondence with Tirmidhi. *KT* 178, note 1.

10. Alluding here to the rituals Muslims should reserve for pilgrimage to the Kaʿba, to the architectural feature in every mosque (*miḥrāb,* niche) that indicates the Mecca-ward direction of ritual prayer that is called the *qibla.*

11. Reading "Qur'ān reciters," as Nicholson did, rather than "mendicants," as Zhukovskij's text reads, would have the precedent of other traditional sayings in its favor.

12. Abū Jahl was actually ʿAmr ibn Hishām (d. 2/624), an enemy of Muḥammad whose opposition won him the nickname Father of Ignorance.

13. *Dil-gushā,* possibly an indirect reference to the Qur'ānic notion that God expanded the center of Muḥammad's being (94:1), an experience that Sufi theorists adapted as an essential aspect of spiritual experience along the Path.

14. Hujwīrī is punning here, suggesting that cause and means by themselves are *rāhbur* (highway robber, road interrupter) rather than *rāhbar* (one who shows the road, guide), as they might be with the help of God's grace or favor.

15. Abū Ṭālib (d. 619) was Muḥammad's uncle; he took care of the orphaned boy after the child's grandfather died but never converted to Islam.

16. Mainstream Muslim theology held that the only acceptable position meant balancing precariously between the affirmative approach of interpreting the anthropomorphisms of the Qur'ān entirely as metaphors, thereby putting at risk divine unity by effectively making God's attributes separate from the deity; and the negative approach of denying altogether that God possesses attributes, thereby compromising the divine connection with creation.

17. The term *ḍarūrī* has also been translated "intuitive." However, in the following paragraphs I have alternately used "necessary"—the opposite of contingent in the philosophical sense—and "innate" in order to capture something of the subtlety of the idea.

18. Abū ʿAlī ad-Daqqāq (d. 405/1015) was father-in-law and important teacher of Qushayrī (see J. Chabbi, "Abū ʿAlī Daqqāq," *EIr* 1:255–57).

19. Balʿam, Son of Bāʿūr (the biblical Baalam in Numbers 22—24) was a figure of ancient times whom some blamed for Israelite sexual dalliance with Moabite and Midianite women. Thus many Muslim mystics regard Balʿam as the "prototype of the spiritual man led astray by lust and pride" (G. Vajda, "Balʿam," EI^2 1:984).

20. Barṣīṣā was a quasi-legendary recluse whose story is associated with tales of Saint Anthony the desert father, in that Barsisa fell victim to the diabolical temptation to deny God (A. Abel, "Barṣīṣā," EI^2 1:1055).

21. Hujwīrī alludes, apparently, to Abraham, who repudiated the idols his father carved for a livelihood and learned from the setting of the heavenly lights that they were other than God (see 6:76ff.).

5. Abū 'l-Qāsim al-Qushayrī

1. For a translation, see *EIM* 97–150. For a translation of the material described below, see Barbara R. von Schlegell, trans., *Principles of Sufism* (Berkeley, Calif.: Mizan, 1990).

2. Translated from *Ar-risāla al-qushayrīya* (Beirut: Dār al-kutub al-ʿilmīya, 1998), 342–47.

3. Attributed in GR 429 to Abū ʿUbayda Maʿmar ibn al-Muthannā (d. 210/825 or later).

4. After an *isnād* including ʿAbd ar-Raḥmān ibn Muḥammad ibn ʿAbd Allāh al-ʿAdl, Muḥammad ibn al-Qāsim al-ʿAtakī, Sulaymān ibn ʿĪsā ash-Shajarī (Gramlich gives variant of as-Sijzī), ʿAbbād ibn Kathīr, Ḥanẓala ibn Abī Sufyān (d. 151/768–69), al-Qāsim ibn Muḥammad (ibn Abī Bakr aṣ-Ṣiddīq Abū Muḥammad (d. 106/724–25)—one of seven legal specialists in Medina—and (Muḥammad's wife) ʿĀ'isha (d. 58/678).

5. As reported by Shaykh Abū ʿAbd ar-Raḥmān as-Sulamī and Aḥmad ibn Muḥammad ibn Zayd.

6. As reported by Abū ʿAlī ad-Daqqāq and Muḥammad ibn Muḥammad ibn ʿAbd al-Wahhāb.

7. As reported by Sulamī's father, whom Gramlich identifies as Ḥusayn ibn Muḥammad ibn Mūsā ibn Khālid ibn Sālim al-Azdī (d. 348/959); Sulamī himself; and Abū 'l-ʿAbbās ad-Dīnawarī (d.c. 340/951), who was a Central Asian preacher and associate of Abū Saʿīd al-Kharrāz.

8. Hujwīrī cites the same two sayings together [355]. GR 431 notes that these words occur in a Ḥadīth reported by ʿĀ'isha, in which Muḥammad said these words during prostration in prayer in the middle of the night.

9. As reported by Muḥammad ibn al-Ḥusayn; Abū Jaʿfar Muḥammad ibn Aḥmad ibn Saʿīd ar-Rāzī; ʿAyyāsh (Gramlich reads ʿAbbās) ibn Ḥamza (d. 288/901); and Aḥmad ibn Abī 'l-Ḥawārī (d.c. 230/844), who studied with Abū Sulaymān ad-Dārānī in Syria.

10. Ruwaym ibn Aḥmad of Baghdad (d. 303/915) was an associate of Junayd and was a moderate mystic who put little stress on maintaining the appearance of asceticism.

11. As reported by Muḥammad ibn al-Ḥusayn, Muḥammad ibn Aḥmad ibn Saʿīd, Muḥammad ibn Aḥmad ibn Sahl (aṣ-Ṣayrafī, d. 347/958), and Saʿīd ibn ʿUthmān (d. 294/906–7).

12. As reported by Muḥammad ibn al-Ḥusayn, Abū Bakr ar-Rāzī (d. 376/986), and Abū ʿUmar al-Anṭākī.

13. As reported by Abū ʿAbd ar-Raḥmān as-Sulamī (d. 412/1021) and Abū 'l-Ḥusayn al-Fārisī.

14. Also as reported by Abū ʿAbd ar-Raḥmān as-Sulamī and Abū 'l-Ḥusayn al-Fārisī.

15. As reported by Sulamī, Muḥammad ibn ʿAbd Allāh ibn Shādhān (d. 376/986), and Yūsuf ibn al-Ḥusayn (d. 304/916–17).

16. As reported by Abū Ḥātim as-Sijistānī; Abū Naṣr as-Sarrāj; Wajīhī; and Abū ʿAlī ar-Rūdhbārī (d.c. 322/933), who was an Iraqi associate of Junayd and Nūrī.

17. As reported by Muḥammad ibn al-Ḥusayn and ʿAbd Allāh ibn Muḥammad ad-Dimashqī.

18. After an *isnād* including Muḥammad ibn al-Ḥusayn, ʿAlī ibn Bundār aṣ-Ṣayrafī and Jurayrī.

19. Abū ʿUthmān al-Maghribī (d. 373/983) was a Tunisian Sufi who traveled widely in the central Middle East.

20. After an *isnād* including Muḥammad ibn al-Ḥusayn, Muḥammad ibn ʿAbd Allāh (possibly ibn Shādhān), and Jaʿfar (al-Khuldī, d. 348/959–60, a prominent Baghdadi Sufi in the circle of Junayd).

21. Probably Muḥammad ibn al-Faḍl as-Samarqandī, after an *isnād* including Junayd and ʿAbd Allāh ar-Rāzī (d. 353/964).

22. After an *isnād* including Aḥmad ibn ʿAlī ibn Jaʿfar and (Abū Bakr) al-Kattānī (d. 322/934).

6. ʿAbd Allāh Anṣārī

1. S. de Beaurecueil, "*Le Kitāb-e ṣad maydān* de ʿAbdallāh Anṣārī," *Mélanges Islamologiques* 2 (1954), 1–90; Persian texts, 45–46. Khiḍr is the name attached to the enigmatic figure of Sūra 18 who functions as Moses' guide.

2. My translation of text in Ravān Farhādī, ed. and trans. (Persian), *Manāzil as-sā'irīn* (Tehran: Intishārāt-i Mawlā, 1361/1982), 130–32.

3. Beaurecueil, "*Le Kitāb-e ṣad maydān* de ʿAbdallāh Anṣārī," text on 42–43.

4. Farhādi, *Manāzil,* 212–14.

5. Ibid., 216.

7. Abū Ḥāmid Muḥammad al-Ghazālī

1. Richard McCarthy, S.J., published a translation of Sections 1–5, and 8, as Appendix 5 in his *Freedom and Fulfillment* (Boston: Twayne, 1981), 363–82. Sections translated here are based on the text of the Beirut: Dār al-kutub al-ʿilmīya edition, n.d., 3:14–29.

2. Continuing: "and those who are heedless of Our signs, (8) will dwell in the Fire because of what they have earned."

3. McCarthy, *Freedom and Fulfillment,* 378–81.

4. I.e., the heart's knowing by the two means of either inspiration or instruction.

5. The bracketed section does not appear in standard versions of the Qur'ān; the verse continues: "but that if he conceived a desire, Satan meddled in his desire."

6. According to a Ḥadīth recorded in *Mishkāt al-maṣābīḥ,* trans. James Robson (2:1302), ʿUmar became miraculously aware of the approach of the enemy at the scene of an impending battle and shouted out a warning while addressing the Muslim community. A messenger came later and reported to ʿUmar that the enemy was gaining the upper hand when someone shouted, "Sāriya, keep near the mountain!" and the tide turned in favor of the Muslim forces.

8. Ibn al-ʿArīf

1. Using the text in Miguel Asin Palacios, *Ibn al-ʿArīf: Maḥāsin al-majālis—Texte Arabe, Traduction, et Commentaire* (Paris: Librairie Orientaliste Paul Geuthner, 1933), 75–76, 101, 103–5 [these are the numbers in brackets]; supplemented by that in Ibn al-ʿArīf, Aḥmad ibn Muḥammad, *Maḥāsin al-majālis: The Attractions of Mystical Sessions,* trans. William Elliott and Adnan K. Abdulla (U.K.: Avebury Publishing, 1980), 20–25, 109–15.

2. Translating *ʿilla* as "instruction" following Asin Palacios (29 n. 8) that this is how Ibn ʿArabī defined the term from a mystical perspective.

3. The standard Arabic text of the Qur'ān reads "it has been revealed" *(uḥiyā),* but this text (as well as the ms. reproduced in the Avebury publication) reads "We have revealed" *(awḥaynā).*

9. Abū Ḥafṣ ʿUmar as-Suhrawardī

1. Translated from *ʿAwarīf al-maʿārif,* in Abū Ḥāmid al-Ghazālī, *Iḥyāʾ ʿulūm ad-dīn* (Beirut: Dār al-kutub al-ʿilmīya, n.d.), 5:55–74.

2. After an *isnād* including Sharīf Nūr al-Hudā Abū Ṭālib al-Ḥusayn ibn Muḥammad az-Zaynabī, Karīma bint Aḥmad ibn Muḥammad al-Marwazīya al-Makkī, Abū al-Haytham Muḥammad ibn (al-)Makkī al-Kushamayhanī, Abū ʿAbd Allāh Muḥammad ibn Yūsuf al-Firabrī, Abū ʿAbd Allāh Muḥammad ibn Ismāʿīl al-Bukhārī, Abū Kurayb, Abū Usāma (d. 201/817), Burayd, Abū Burda (ibn Abī Mūsā, d.c. 103/721), and Abū Mūsā al-Ashʿarī (d.c. 42/662).

3. Masrūq ibn al Ajdaʿ (d.c. 62/681) was a traditionist associated with many Ḥadīths from ʿĀ'isha.

4. After an *isnād* that includes Abū 'l-Khayr Aḥmad ibn Ismāʿīl al-Qazwīnī, Abū Saʿīd Muḥammad al-Khalīlī, Abū Saʿīd Muḥammad al-Farrukhzādhī, Abū Isḥāq Aḥmad ibn Muḥammad ath-Thaʿālibī, Ibn Fanjūya (variant: Fatḥūya), Ibn Ḥayyān (variant: Ḥabbān), Isḥāq ibn Muḥammad and his father, Ibrāhīm ibn ʿĪsā, ʿAlī ibn ʿAlī, and Abū Ḥamza ath-Thumālī.

5. Muḥammad, like Abraham, was a *ḥanīf,* a seeker after the one God.

6. After an *isnād* including Abū Ṭālib az-Zaynabī, Karīma bint Aḥmad ibn Muḥammad al-Marwazīya, Abū 'l-Haytham, al-Firabrī, al-Bukhārī, Sa'īd ibn Ḥafṣ, Ibn Wahb, Yūnus, Ibn Shihāb, and 'Abd al-Ḥumayd ibn 'Abd ar-Raḥmān.

7. The Arab traditionally identified as the addressee here is (according to GA 30 n. 66) either Ṣa'ṣa'a ibn Mu'āwiya or Ṣa'ṣa' ibn Nājīya, the latter of whom was the grandfather of the renowned Umayyad era poet Farazdaq.

8. That is, the heavenly counterpart or prototype of the Ka'ba, a spiritual structure called the *al-bayt al-ma'mur,* "the established house."

9. Underlying the comment is a pun on "he rubbed" *(masaḥa)* and "surveying" *(misāha).*

10. Following an *isnād* that includes Abū Manṣūr al-Muqri', the Imām and Ḥāfiz Abū Bakr al-Khaṭīb, Abū 'Amr al-Hāshimī, Abū 'Alī al-Lu'lu'ī, Abū Dāwūd as-Sijistānī, Musaddad, Yaḥyā, Shu'ba, 'Umar ibn Sulaymān (a disciple of 'Umar ibn al-Khaṭṭāb), 'Abd ar-Raḥmān ibn Abān and his father, Zayd ibn Thābit (d.c. 45/656).

11. *An-nafs al-ammāra bi 's-sū',* one of the four ways in which the Qur'ān says the *nafs* functions.

12. Ibn Sam'ūn Abū 'l-Ḥusayn ibn Aḥmad ibn Ismā'īl (d. 387/997) was a Ḥanbalī favorable to Sufism and a Baghdādī preacher legendary for his power to stir emotions.

13. The Parable of the Sower occurs in the Greek Testament in the Synoptic Gospels (Matt. 13:3–9; Mark 4:3–9; and Luke 8:5–15).

14. After an *isnād* including Ra'īs Abū 'Alī ibn Nabhān, Ḥasan ibn Shādhān, Da'laj ibn Aḥmad, Abū 'l-Ḥasan ibn 'Abd Allāh al-'Azīz al-Baghawī, Abū 'Ubayd (ibn) al-Qāsim ibn Sallām, Ḥajjāj, Ḥammād ibn Salama, 'Alī ibn Zayd, and Ḥasan (whom one text glosses as al-Baṣrī).

15. Or: "limit/endpoint"—*ḥadd,* also meaning possibly semantic field at one level, but more likely referring to the prescriptive or ethical sense of a text; GA 39 translates as "sphere of meaning."

16. *Maṭla'/muṭṭala',* "point of arising," possibly a reference to the spiritual or symbolic meaning of a text. Qāshānī defined this "Point of Departure" as "the stage in which the speaker actually experiences the verses of the Qur'ān which he is reciting. His speech is illuminated by the quality which is the source of that particular verse" ('Abd al-Razzāq al-Qāshānī, comp., *Glossary of Sufi Technical Terms,* trans. Nabil Safwat [London: Octagon, 1991], 47–48). GA 39 opts for "point of transcendence."

17. After an *isnād* that includes Ḥajjāj, Shu'ba, and 'Amr ibn Murra, Murra.

18. Ja'far aṣ-Ṣādiq (d. 148/765) was the sixth Shī'ī imām, after whose death dissenting views as to who was his legitimate successor eventuated in the divergence of two groups that have come to be called Sevener Shī'īs, or Ismā'īlīs, and Twelvers, or Imāmīs. Ja'far is widely acknowledged as a pioneer in sophisticated Qur'ānic exegesis (see, e.g., Paul Nwyia, *Exégèse Coranique* [1970], 156–208).

19. ʿAbd ar-Razzāq al-Qāshānī's *Glossary of Sufi Technical Terms,* 47–48, quotes the above saying of Jaʿfar, and Qāshānī then notes Suhrawardī's comment that Jaʿfar's tongue became like the Burning Bush and further specifies the meaning of the term: "It is the stage of witnessing the Truth in everything that is irradiated by its qualities—of which qualities that thing is an outward manifestation. But because it was said in a tradition of the Prophet: 'There is no verse of the Qur'ān without an outward and an inward meaning; for every letter there is an end point, and for every end point a point of departure,' the meaning has become restricted to this sense." L. Massignon, *EO* 82, calls *muṭṭalaʿ* the "anagogic sense" of a text, "which is a divine call. Then a dialogue begins between the humble, meditating soul and the transcendent Divine Wisdom. For the soul, words take on the fullness specific to their momentary reality in which God is heard to speak; the soul reforms its vocabulary in the image of the divine speech."

20. As GA 41 n. 90 observes, the author plays off the divine realm, with its power, its hiddenness, and its light, against the created realm, characterized by ordered wisdom, visibility, and unfolding phases.

21. *Istikhāra* refers to the practice of praying two prostration cycles of the ritual prayer before going to bed and asking God for a response, to be rendered perhaps in a dream or some other manifestation (see Cyril Glassé, *The Concise Encyclopedia of Islam* [New York: Harper & Row, 1989], 201).

22. After an *isnād* that includes Abū ʿAbd ar-Raḥmān aṣ-Ṣūfī, ʿAbd ar-Raḥmān ibn Muḥammad, Abū Muḥammad ʿAbd Allāh ibn Aḥmad as-Sarakhsī (or as-Sijzī according to 3 variants), Abū ʿImrān as-Samarqandī, Abū Muḥammad ʿAbd Allāh ibn ʿAbd ar-Raḥmān ad-Dārimī, Nuʿaym ibn Ḥammād, Baqīya, al-Aḥwaṣ ibn Ḥakīm, and his father.

23. Through an *isnād* including Ḥāfiz Abū 'l-Qāsim al-Mustamlī, Abū 'l-Qāsim ʿAbd al-Karīm ibn Ḥawāzin al-Qushayrī, Abū Muḥammad ʿAbd Allāh ibn Yūsuf al-Iṣfāhānī, Abū Saʿīd ibn al-Aʿrābī, Jaʿfar ibn ʿĀmir al-ʿAskarī, Ḥasan ibn ʿAṭīya, and Anas ibn Mālik.

24. Inattentiveness *(ghafla),* while obviously not desirable as such on the spiritual path, is nevertheless a gift of God in that it allows one to pursue certain goals in life.

25. After the following *isnād*: Abū 'l-Fatḥ Muḥammad ibn ʿAbd al-Bāqī, Abū 'l-Faḍl Ḥamd ibn Aḥmad, Ḥāfīz Abū Nuʿaym al-Iṣfāhānī, Muḥammad ibn Aḥmad ibn Muḥammad, ʿAbbās ibn Aḥmad ash-Shāshī, and [70] Abū ʿAqīl al-Waṣṣāfī.

26. In other words, the heart is two-sided and "rotates" (the root from which the word "heart" comes can mean "to turn around") between attentiveness to the promptings of the spirit, on one side, and the importunities of the ego-soul on the other. GA 54 n. 61 indicates that a gloss on one ms. explains that one side or "face" of the heart closest to the spirit is oriented toward the station of contemplation so long as it is inclined toward the spirit. The other side of the heart that

faces the soul, however, is capable of receiving knowledge. The marginal gloss concludes, "In short, the basis for the mutual affinity between knowledge and the heart rests on the fact that knowledge is distinct from the being (of God) even as it is joined with the Preserved Tablet, while heart is separated from the spirit and joined with the soul."

27. See Deuteronomy 30:11–14, in which the subject is not knowledge but the divine commandment.

28. After an *isnād* including the following names, the first two "with *ijāza*": Abū Manṣūr ibn Khayrūn, Abū Muḥammad al-Ḥasan ibn ʿAlī al-Jawharī, Abū ʿUmar Muḥammad ibn al-ʿAbbās, Abū Muḥammad [72] Yaḥyā ibn Ṣāʿīd, Ḥusayn ibn al-Ḥasan al-Marwazī, ʿAbd Allāh ibn al-Mubārak, Awzāʿi, Ḥassān ibn ʿAṭīya.

29. According to Fakhr ad-Dīn ʿIrāqī, this reads, "Satan often steals from you (or deprives you of) your knowledge," except in Sufi texts. Thanks to Aron Zysow for this information.

30. I.e., God would not have been able to enjoy Suhayb's worship in the ordinary course of things, since he would have circumvented all the things "ordinary" servants must perform?

31. Here Suhrawardī proceeds to gloss the next three verses (92:8–10), which read: "But as for the one who is stingy and believes he is not in need, and who lies about what is best, We will surely smooth his way to hardship."

Selected Bibliography

Primary Sources

ʿAbd al-Kader, Amir. *The Spiritual Writings of Amir ʿAbd al-Kader.* Trans. Michel Chodkiewicz. Albany, N.Y.: SUNY, 1995.

Anṣārī, Khwāja ʿAbd Allāh. *Kitab-i Ṣad Maydān.* S. de Beaurecueil. Mélanges *Islamologiques* 2 (1954): 1–90.

———. *Manāzil as-ṣā'irīn.* Edited and translated by S. de Beaurecueil. Cairo: Institut Français d'Archaeologie Orientale, 1962.

———. *Kitāb Ṣad Maydān* and other short works and selections in S. de Beaurecueil, author, editor, and translator, *Khwāja ʿAbdullāh Anṣārī: Mystique Hanbalite.* Beirut: Imprimerie Catholique, 1965.

———. *The Book of Wisdom.* Translated by Victor Danner. Mahwah, N.J.: Paulist Press, 1978.

———. *Abdullāh Anṣārī of Herat (1006–1089): An Early Sufi Master.* Translated by A. G. Ravan Farhadi. Surrey: Curzon Press, 1994.

ʿAṭṭār, Farīd ad-Dīn. *Tadhkirat al-Awliyā'.* Edited by R. A. Nicholson. 2 vols. London: Luzac, reprint 1959. Excerpts translated by A. J. Arberry in *Muslim Saints and Mystics.* London: Routledge & Kegan Paul, 1966.

Baghawī, Abū Muḥammad ibn al-Ḥusayn, al-. *Mishkāt al-maṣābīḥ.* Translated by James Robson. 2 vols. Lahore: Sh. Muḥammad Ashraf, 1975.

Bukhārī, Abū ʿAbd Allāh Muḥammad. *Kitāb al-jāmiʿ aṣ-ṣaḥīḥ.* Edited by L. Krehl and T. W. Juynboll. 4 vols. Leiden, 1862–1908.

Fanṣūrī, Ḥamzah. *The Poems of Ḥamzah Fanṣūrī.* Edited and translated by G. W. Drewes and L. F. Brakel. Dordrecht, Netherlands: Foris Publications, 1986.

Ghazālī, Abū Ḥāmid al-. *Worship in Islam.* Translated by E. W. Calverley. London: Allen and Unwin, 1957.

———. *The Book of Knowledge.* Translated by Nabih Amin Faris. 2d rev. ed. Lahore: Sh. Muḥammad Ashraf, 1962.

———. *Book XX of the Iḥyā'.* Translated by Leon Zolondek. Leiden: Brill, 1963.

———. *Al-Ghazālī's Book of Fear and Hope.* Translated by W. McKane. Leiden: Brill, 1965.

———. *Ghazālī on Prayer.* Translated by Kojiro Nakamura. Tokyo: University of Tokyo, 1973.

———. *Inner Dimensions of Islamic Worship*. Translated by Mukhtar Holland. Leicester: Islamic Foundation, 1983.

———. *The Remembrance of Death and the Afterlife*. Translated by T. J. Winter. Cambridge: Islamic Texts Society, 1989.

———. *The Ninety-Nine Beautiful Names of God*. Translated by David Burrell and Nazih Daher. Cambridge: Islamic Texts Society, 1992.

———. *On Disciplining the Soul*. Translated by T. J. Winter. Cambridge: Islamic Texts Society, 1995.

———. *Disciplining the Soul and Breaking the Two Desires*. Translated by T. J. Winter. Cambridge: Islamic Texts Society, 1995.

———. *Iḥyā' ʿulūm ad-dīn*. 4 vols. Beirut: Dār al-Kutub al-ʿilmīya, n.d. Translation of Book I by Nabih Amin Faris as *The Book of Knowledge*. 2d ed. Lahore: Sh. Muḥammad Ashraf, 1966. Translation of Book 21 by W. J. Skellie as *The Wonders of the Heart*. Cambridge: Islamic Texts Society, forthcoming.

(Ghazālī, Abū Ḥāmid al-.) *Freedom and Fulfillment*. Translated by Richard McCarthy (of *Al-Munqidh min aḍ-ḍalāl* and selections of five other works). Boston: Twayne, 1980.

Ḥallāj. *Kitāb at-Ṭawāsīn*. Edited by Paul Nwyia. *Mélanges de l'Université Saint-Joseph* 47 (1972) 183–237. Also edited by Louis Massignon. Paris: Paul Geuthner, 1913.

Hujwīrī, ʿAlī ibn ʿUthmān al-. *Kashf al-maḥjūb*. Edited by V. A. Zhukovskij. Leningrad: Dār al-ʿulūm, 1926. Translated by R. A. Nicholson as *Revelation of the Mystery*. London: Pir Publications, 1999.

Ibn ʿAjība, Aḥmad. "L'Autobiographie *(Fahrasa)* du Soufi Marocain Aḥmad ibn ʿAjība." Edited by and trans. Jean-Louis Michon. Parts 1–4 in *Arabica* 15 (1968) 225–69; 16 (1969) 25–64, 113–54, 225–68.

———. *Le Soufi Marocain Aḥmad Ibn ʿAjība (1746-1809) et son Miʿrāj*. Translated by Jean-Louis Michon. Paris: J. Vrin, 1973.

Ibn ʿAbbād of Ronda. *Ar-rasā'il aṣ-ṣughrā': Lettres de Direction Spirituelle*. Edited by Paul Nwyia. Beirut: Imprimerie Catholique, 1957. Translated by John Renard as *Letters on the Sufi Path*. Mahwah, N.J.: Paulist Press, 1986.

Ibn ʿArabī. *The Bezels of Wisdom*. Translated by R. W. J. Austin. Mahwah, N.J.: Paulist Press, 1980.

———. *The Sufi Path of Knowledge: Ibn al-ʿArabī's Metaphysics of Imagination*. Translated by William C. Chittick. Albany, N.Y.: SUNY, 1989.

Ibn al-ʿArīf. *Maḥāsin al-majālis*, Critical edition of Arabic text with translation by Miguel Asin Palacios (in French translation of his Spanish). Paris: Librairie Orientaliste Paul Geuthner, 1933. Arabic ms. text and English translation by William Elliott and Adnan K. Abdulla. London: Avebury Publishing Co., 1980.

BIBLIOGRAPHY

Ibn ʿAṭāʾ Allāh al-Iskandarī. *The Key to Salvation: A Sufi Manual of Invocation.* Translated by Mary Ann Donner. Cambridge: Islamic Texts Society, 1996.

Ibn al-Fāriḍ, ʿUmar. *ʿUmar Ibn al-Fāriḍ: Sufi Verse, Saintly Life.* Translated by Th. Emil Homerin. Mahwah, N.J.: Paulist Press, 2000.

Ibn al-Jawzī. *Kitāb al-quṣṣāṣ wa'l-midhakkirīn.* Critical edition. Translated by Merlin L. Swartz. Beirut: Dār el-Machreq, 1986.

Ibn Mājah. *Sunan Ibn Mājah.* 4 vols. Beirut: Dār al-Maʿrifa, 1996.

Ibn as-Sabbāgh. *The Mystical Teachings of al-Shadhili.* Translation of *Durrat al-asrār wa tuḥfat al-abrār* by Elmer H. Douglas. Albany, N.Y.: SUNY, 1993.

ʿIrāqī, Fakhr ad-Dīn. *Divine Flashes.* Translated by William C. Chittick and Peter L. Wilson. Mahwah, N.J.: Paulist Press, 1982.

Junayd. *The Life, Personality and Writings of al-Junayd.* Translated by A. H. Abdel Kader. London: Luzac, 1976.

Kalābādhī, Abū Bakr al-. *At-taʿarruf li-madhhab ahl at-taṣawwuf.* Edited by Mahmud Amin an-Nawawi. Cairo: Maktabat al-Kulliyat al-Azhariya, 1969. Translated by A. J. Arberry as *The Doctrine of the Sufis.* Cambridge: Cambridge University Press, 1935, reprinted 1978.

Kharrāz, Abū Saʿīd al-. *The Book of Truthfulness (Kitab aṣ-ṣidq).* Edited (Arabic text) and translated by A. J. Arberry. Oxford: Oxford University Press, 1937.

Makkī, Abū Ṭālib al-. *Qūt al-qulūb fi muʿāmalāt al-maḥbūb.* 2 vols. Beirut: Dār al-Kutub al-ʿIlmīya, 1997. Translated by Richard Gramlich as *Die Nahrung der Herzen,* 4 vols. Stuttgart: Franz Steiner Verlag, 1992–95.

Manerī, Sharaf ad-Dīn. *The Hundred Letters.* Translated by Paul Jackson. Mahwah, N.J.: Paulist Press, 1980.

Muḥāsibī, al-Ḥārith al-. *Kitāb ar-riʿāya li ḥuqūq Allāh.* Edited by ʿAbd al-Qādir Aḥmad ʿAṭāʾ. Cairo: Dār al-Kutub al-Ḥadītha, 1970.

Muslim. *Ṣaḥīḥ Muslim.* 5 vols. Beirut: Dār Ibn Ḥazm, 1995.

Niffarī, Muḥammad ibn ʿAbd al-Jabbār an-. *The Mawāqif and Mukhāṭabāt.* Translated by A. J. Arberry. London: Luzac, 1935.

Niẓām ad-Dīn Awliyāʾ. *Morals for the Heart.* Translated by Bruce B. Lawrence. Mahwah, N.J.: Paulist Press, 1992.

Qāshānī, ʿAbd ar-Razzāq al-. *A Glossary of Sufi Technical Terms.* Translated by Nabil Safwat. London: Octagon Press, 1991.

Qushayrī, ʿAbd al-Karīm al-. *Risāla fi 't-taṣawwuf.* Beirut: Dār al-Kutub al-ʿIlmīyya 1998. Translated by Richard Gramlich as *Das Sendschreiben al-Qushayris über das Sufitum.* Wiesbaden: Franz Steiner Verlag, 1989. Translated by (partial) B. R. von Schlegell as *Principles of Sufism.* Berkeley, Calif.: Mizan Press, 1990. Radtke, Bernd, ed. *Kitāb abab al-mulūk.* Stuttgart: Steiner Verlag, 1991.

Radtke, Bernd, ed. *Kitāb adab al-mūlūk.* Stuttgart: Steiner Verlag, 1991.

Rūmī, Jalāl ad-Dīn. *The Mathnawi of Jalal uddin Rūmī (Spiritual Couplets).* Translated by R. A. Nicholson. 8 vols. London: Luzac, 1925–40.

———. *Signs of the Unseen: Discourses of Jalaluddin Rūmī.* Translated by W. M. Thackston Jr. Putney, Vt.: Threshold Books, 1994.

Rundī, ibn ʿAbbād ar-. *Ibn ʿAbbād of Ronda: Letters on the Sufi Path.* Translated by John Renard. New York: Paulist Press, 1986.

Rūzbihān Baqlī. *Commentaire sur les Paradoxes des Soufis.* Edited by Henry Corbin. Paris: Adrien-Maisonneuve, 1966.

Sarrāj, Abū Naṣr as-. *Kitāb al-lumaʿ fi 't-taṣawwuf.* Edited by R. A. Nicholson. Gibb Memorial Series, no. 22. London: Luzac, 1914. Translated by Richard Gramlich as *Schlaglichter über das Sufitum.* Stuttgart: Franz Steiner Verlag, 1990.

Sells, Michael, trans. *Early Islamic Mysticism* (Selections of Sufi Texts). Mahwah, N.J.: Paulist Press, 1996.

Suhrawardī, Abū Ḥafṣ ʿUmar as-. *ʿAwārif al-maʿārif.* Beirut: Dār al-Kitāb al- ʿArabī, 1983. Translated by Richard Gramlich as *Die Gaben der Erkenntnisse.* Wiesbaden: Franz Steiner Verlag, 1978.

Sulamī, ʿAbd ar-Raḥmān. *Ṭabaqāt aṣ-ṣufīya.* Edited by J. Pedersen. Leiden: Brill, 1960.

Secondary Sources

Addas, Claude. "Andalūsī Mysticism and the Rise of Ibn ʿArabī." *In The Legacy of Muslim Spain,* edited by Salma K. Jayyusi, 909–33. Leiden: Brill, 1994.

Ali, M. Athar. "Hujwīrī, al-." *ER* 6:498–99.

Anonymous. "Al-Ḥasan al-Baṣrī." *EI*[1] 3:272; *SEI* 136.

Arberry, A. J. "Al-Djunaid." *SEI* 92-93.

———. "Al-Niffarī." *SEI* 446.

———. "Al-Sulamī." *SEI* 551.

———. "Ḳabḍ." *SEI* 198.

Attas, Sayyid N. al- *The Mysticism of Ḥamza Fanṣūrī.* Kuala Lumpur: Dewan Bahasa dan Pustaka, 1970.

Attas, Syed Naguib al-. *Ranīrī and the Wujūdiyya of Seventeenth Century Acheh.* Singapore: Malaysian Branch of the Royal Asiatic Society, 1966.

———. *Some Aspects of Sufism as Understood and Practiced Among the Malays.* Singapore: Malaysian Sociological Research Institute, 1963.

Awn, Peter. *Satan's Tragedy and Redemption: Iblīs in Sufi Psychology.* Leiden: Brill, 1983.

Bauer, H. "Ḳabḍ." *EI*[1] 4:592.

Beaurecueil, S. de Laugier de. "ʿAbdallāh al-Anṣārī." *EIr* 1:187–90.

Bel, A. "Abū Madyan." *EI*[1] 1:98.

Ben Cheneb, Moh. "Al-Herewī, ʿAbd Allāh Anṣārī." *EI*[1] 3:299–300.

———. "Ibn ʿAbbād...al-Rundī." *EI*[1] 3:352.

BIBLIOGRAPHY

Berkey, Jonathan. *Popular Preaching and Religious Authority in the Medieval Islamic Near East.* Seattle: University of Washington Press, 2001.

Böwering, Gerhard. *The Mystical Vision of Existence in Classical Islam: The Qur'ānic Hermeneutics of the Sufi Sahl at-Tustarī.* Berlin: Walter de Gruyter, 1980.

———. "Abū ʿAbd al-Raḥmān al-Sulamī." *EI*[2] 7:811–12.

———. "Abū Saʿīd b. Abī 'l-Khayr." *EIr* 1:377–80.

———. "ʿAlī Hamadānī." *EIr* 1:862–64.

———. "ʿAyn-al-Qozāt Hamadānī." *EIr* 3:140–43.

———. "Besṭāmī, Bayazīd." *EIr* 4:183–86.

———. "Dhū 'l-Nūn Mesrī." *EIr* 7:572–73.

———. "ʿErfān." *EIr* 8:551–54.

———. "Ghazzālī, Abū Ḥamed Moḥammad." *EIr* 10:358–63.

———. "Kalābādhī, al-." *ER* 8:230–31.

———. "Shabistarī, al-." *ER* 13:194–95.

Brockelmann, Carl. "Ibn ʿAṭā' Allāh…al-Iskandarī" *EI*[1] 3:364; *SEI* 147.

Burrell, David B. "The Unknowability of God in al-Ghazālī." *Religious Studies* 23 (1987), 171–82.

Burton, John. *An Introduction to the Ḥadīth.* Edinburgh: Edinburgh University Press, 1994.

Cameron, Archibald J. *Abū Dharr al-Ghifārī: An Examination of His Image in the Hagiography of Islam.* London: Luzac, 1973.

Carra de Vaux, B. "Dhū 'l-Nūn al-Miṣrī." *EI*[1] 2:963–64.

Chabbi, J. "Abdāl." *EIr* 1:173–74.

———. "Abū ʿAlī Daqqāq." *EIr* 1:255–57.

———. "Abū Ḥafṣ Ḥaddād." *EIr* 1:293–94.

Chittick, William C. *The Self-Disclosure of God: Principle's of Ibn ʿArabi's Cosmology.* Albany, N.Y.: SUNY, 1998.

———. "Ibn ʿArabi and His School." In *Islamic Spirituality: Manifestations,* edited by S. H. Nasr, 49–79. New York: Crossroad, 1991.

———. "Rūmī and the Mawlawiyyah." In *Islamic Spirituality: Manifestations,* edited by S. H. Nasr, 105–26. New York: Crossroad, 1991.

Cooperson, Michael. "Ibn Ḥanbal and Bishr al-Ḥāfī: A Case Study in Biographical Traditions." *Studia Islamica* 86:2 (1997): 71–101.

———. "The Renunciant Bishr al-Ḥāfī," in his *Classical Arabic Biography,* 154–87. Cambridge: Cambridge University Press, 2000.

Corbin, H. "ʿAbhār al-ʿĀsheqīn (of Rūzbehān Baqlī)." *EIr* 1:214–15.

Cornell, Vincent J. "ʿAbd al-Qādir." *OEMIW* 1:3–4.

Cour, A. "Al-Shādhilī." *EI*[1] 7:246–47.

Danner, Victor. "Ibn ʿAṭā' Allāh." *ER* 13:194–95.

———. "The Shadhiliyyah and North African Sufism." *In Islamic Spirituality II: Manifestations,* ed. S. H. Nasr, 26–48. New York: Crossroad, 1991.

Eliade, Mircea et al., eds. *The Encyclopedia of Religion.* 16 vols. New York: Macmillan, 1987.

Ernst, Carl W. "Mystical Language and the Teaching Context in the Early Lexicons of Sufism." *In Mysticism and Language,* edited by Steven T. Katz, 181–201. Oxford: Oxford University Press, 1992.

———. *Rūzbihān Baqlī: Mystical Experience and the Rhetoric of Sainthood in Persian Sufism.* Surrey: Curzon Press, 1996.

Ess, Josef van. *Die Gedankenwelt des Ḥārith al-Muḥāsibī.* Bonn: Selbstverlag des Orientalischen Seminars der Universität Bonn, 1961.

Esteʿlami, M. "The Concept of Knowledge in Rūmī's *Mathnawi.*" In *Classical Persian Sufism: From Its Origins to Rūmī,* edited by Leonard Lewisohn, 401–8. London: Khaniqahi Nimatullahi Publications, 1993.

Farhadi, A. G. Ravan. "The *Hundred Grounds* of ʿAbdullāh Anṣārī of Herat (d. 448/1056): The Earliest Mnemonic Sufi Manual in Persian." *HS1* 381–400.

Fierro, Maribel. "Opposition to Sufism in al-Andalus." In *Islamic Mysticism Contested,* edited by F. De Jong and Bernd Radtke, 174–206. Leiden: Brill, 1999.

———. "The polemic about the *karāmāt al-awliyā'* and the Development of Sufism in al-Andalus (4th–10th/5th–11th Centuries)." *Bulletin of the School of Oriental and African Studies* 55 (1992): 236–49.

Gardet, Louis. "Dhikr." *EI*[2] 2:223–27.

Goldziher, Ignaz. "Awtād." *SEI* 49.

———. "Abdāl." *EI*[2] 1:94–95.

———. "Asceticism and Sufism." *In Introduction to Islamic Theology and Law,* translated by Andras Hamori and Ruth Hamori, 116–34. Princeton, N.J.: Princeton University Press, 1981.

Gramlich, Richard. "Majdhūb." *EI*[2] 5:1029.

Gribetz, A. "The Samāʿ Controversy: Sufi vs. Legalist." *Studia Islamica* 74 (1991): 43–62.

Hirtenstein, S. and Tiernan, M, eds. *Muḥyiddīn Ibn ʿArabī: A Commemorative Volume.* Shaftesbury, U.K.: Element Books, 1993.

Horovitz, Josef. "Miʿrādj." *EI*[1] 5:505–8; *SEI* 381–84.

Huart, Cl. "Djunaid." *EI*[1] 2:1063.

———. "Ḥikma." *EI*[1] 3:305-6.

Hurvitz, Nimrod. "Biographies and Mild Asceticism: A Study of the Islamic Moral Imagination." *Studia Islamica* 85:1 (1997): 41–65.

Hussaini, S. Sh. Kh. "Abū ʿAbd-al-Raḥmān Solamī." *EIr* 1:249–50.

Izutsu, Toshihiko. "Ibn al-ʿArabi." *ER* 6:552–57.

Jabre, Farīd. *La Notion de la Maʿrifa chez Ghazālī.* Beirut: Imprimerie Catholique, 1958.

———. *La Notion de Certitude chez Ghazālī.* Paris: J. Vrin, 1958.

Johns, A. H. "Aspects of Sufi Thought in India and Indonesia in the First Half of the Seventeenth Century." *Journal of the Malaysian Branch of the Royal Asiatic Society* 27 (1955): 70–77.
———. "Malay Sufism." *Journal of the the Malaysian Branch of the Royal Asiatic Society* 30 (1957): 1–108.
Kinberg, Leah. "What Is Meant by *Zuhd*?" *Studia Islamica* 61 (1985): 27–44.
Kohlberg, E. "ʿAlī bī Abi Ṭāleb." *EIr* 1:846–47 (Section "Among Sufis").
Landolt, H. "Abū'l-Ḥasan Kharaqānī." *EIr* 1:305–6.
Lawrence, Bruce B. "ʿAbd-al-Qāder Jīlānī." *EIr* 1:132–33.
Levi Della Vida, G. "Salmān al-Fārisī." *EI*[1] 7:116–17; *SEI* 500–501.
Macdonald, D. B. "*Ḥaḳīḳa*." *EI*[1] 3:223–24; SEI 126.
———. "Ḥāl." *EI*[1] 3:227; *SEI* 127.
———. "Ilhām." *EI*[1] 3:467–68; *SEI* 163.
———. "ʿIlm." *EI*[1] 3:469–70; *SEI* 163–64.
———. "Kashf." *EI*[1] 4:786–87; *SEI* 227.
Madelung, W. "Abū Bakr Kalābādhī." *EIr* 1:262–63.
Madigan, Daniel. *The Qur'ān's Self-Image: Writing and Authority in Islam's Scripture*. Princeton, N.J.: Princeton University Press, 2001.
Makdisi, George. "The Ḥanbalī School and Sufism." *Boletin de la Asociacion Espagnola de Orientalistas* 15 (1979): 115–26.
Malamud, Margaret. "Gender and Spiritual Self-Fashioning: The Master-Disciple Relationship in Classical Sufism." *Journal of the American Academy of Religion* 64:1 (1996): 89–117.
Massignon, Louis. *The Passion of al-Ḥallāj: Mystic and Martyr of Islam.* Translated by Herbert Mason. 4 vols. Princeton, N.J.: Princeton University Press, 1982.
———. "Salmān Pāk and the Spiritual Beginnings of Iranian Sufism." In *Testimonies and Reflections,* edited and translated by H. Mason, 93–110. Notre Dame, Ind.: University of Notre Dame Press, 1989.
———. *Essai sur les Origines du Lexique Technique de la Mystique Musulmane.* Paris: Librairie Paul Geuthner, 1922. 2d ed. Paris: J. Vrin, 1954. Translated by Benjamin Clark as *Essay on the Origins of the Technical Language of Islamic Mysticism.* Notre Dame, Ind.: University of Notre Dame Press, 1994.
———. "Abū Ṭālib al-Makkī." *EI*[2] 1:153.
———. "Muḥāsibī." *EI*[1] 6:699-700; *SEI* 410.
———. "Sahl at-Tustarī." *EI*[1] 7:63; *SEI* 488–89.
———. "Al-Tirmidhī, Ḥakīm." *EI*[1] 8:797.
———. "Al-Ḳushairī." *SEI* 287.
———. "Shaṭḥ." *EI*[1] 7:335–36; *SEI* 533.
———. "Wird." *EI*[1] 8:1139; *SEI* 634.
———. "Zuhd." *EI*[1] 8:1239; *SEI* 661.
Meier, Fritz. "Qushayrī's *Tartīb al-sulūk*." *EIPM* 93–134.

———. "A Book of Etiquette for Sufis." *EIPM* 49–92.

Mir, Mustansir. "Ghazālī, Abū Ḥāmid al-." *OEMIW* 2:61–63.

Moayyad, Heshmat. "'Aṭṭār, Farīd al-Dīn." *ER* 1:500–501.

Murad, Ḥasan Qasim. "Ḥasan al-Baṣrī." *ER* 6:202–3.

Netton, Ian Richard. *Seek Knowledge: Thought and Travel in the House of Islam.* Surrey: Curzon Press, 1994.

———. "The Breath of Felicity: *Adab, Aḥwāl, Maqāmāt* and Abū 'l-Najib al-Suhrawardī." *HS1* 457–82.

Nwyia, Paul. *Exégèse Coranique et Langage Mystique.* Beirut: Dār al-Machreq, 1970.

O'Kane, John, and Bernd Radtke, trans. and eds. *Essays on Islamic Piety and Mysticism by Fritz Meier.* Leiden: Brill, 1999.

Rabb, Muḥammad Abdur. "Bisṭāmī, Abū Yazīd al-." *ER* 2:223–34.

———. "Junayd, Abū al-Qāsim al-." *ER* 8:209–10.

Radtke, Bernd. "Tirmidhiana Minora." *Oriens* 34 (1994): 248–60.

———. *Al-Ḥakīm at-Tirmidhī.* Freiburg: Klaus Schwarz, 1980.

Radtke, Bernd, and John O'Kane. *The Concept of Sainthood in Early Islamic Mysticism.* Surrey: Curzon Press, 1996.

Renard, John. *All the Kings Falcons: Rūmī on Prophets and Revelation.* Albany, N.Y.: SUNY, 1994.

Rosenthal, Franz. *Knowledge Triumphant: The Concept of Knowledge in Medieval Islam.* Leiden: Brill, 1970.

Schimmel, Annemarie. "Abū 'l-Ḥusayn al-Nūrī: Qibla of the Lights." *HS1* 59–64.

———. "Ḥallāj, al-Ḥusayn ibn Manṣūr al-." *ER* 6:173–76.

Sells, Michael. "Bewildered Tongue: The Semantics of Mystical Union in Islam." In *Mystical Union and Monotheistic Faith: An Ecumenical Dialogue,* edited by M. Idel and B. McGinn, 87–124, 163–74. New York: Macmillan, 1989.

———. "Heart-Secret, Intimacy and Awe in Formative Sufism." In *The Shaping of an American Islamic Discourse,* edited by Earle Waugh and Frederick Denny, 165–88. Atlanta, Ga.: Scholars Press, 1998.

Smith, Margaret. *Al-Muḥāsibī: An Early Mystic of Baghdad.* Reprint Amsterdam: Philo Press, 1974.

Stillman, Yedida K., Norman A. Stillman, and T. Majda. "Libās." *EI*[2] 5:732–53.

Tayob, Abdulkader I. "Abū Dharr al-Ghifārī." *OEMIW* 1:19.

Van Arendonk, C. "Ibrāhīm B. Adham." *EI*[1] 3:432–35.

Van den Bergh, S. "Suhrawardī, Abū Ḥafṣ." *EI*[1] 7:506.

———. "Suhrawardī Maktūl." *EI*[1] 7:506–7.

Waley, Muḥammad Isā. "Contemplative Disciplines in Early Persian Sufism." *HS1* 497-548.

Watt, W. Montgomery. "Ghazālī, Abū Ḥāmid." *ER* 2:541–44.

Index of Qur'ānic Citations

Brackets [ ] indicate a reference to the sūra and verse number only, without actual citation of the text. Parentheses ( ) indicate the number of times a reference appears on that page.

3:187	122, 158
3:199	158, 164
4:43	119
4:69	157, 199
4:78	[14]
4:82	92, 102
4:83	83, 93
4:91	245
4:114	123
4:122	250
4:131	141
4:162	137, 365
4:176	198
5:3	66, [394n127]
5:44	199
5:54	252
5:63	155
5:67	80, 97
5:83	110
5:86	14, 295, 296
5:108	140, 141
6:20	14
6:26	[13]
6:28	275
6:59	183
6:65	[14]
6:70	253
6:73	268
6:75	310
6:75–79	[32]
6:76	101, 281, [399n21]
6:91	54, 150 (2), 273, 286
6:93	250
6:98	[14, 15]
6:105	247
6:111	275
6:112	229
6:122	274, 276, 343, 368
6:125	171, 305
6:144	250
6:148	119
7:7–8	144

INDEX OF QUR'ĀNIC CITATIONS

INDEX OF QUR'ĀNIC CITATIONS

General Index

GENERAL INDEX

Sufyān ath-Thawrī, 126, 131, 135, 141, 146, 180, 197, 202, 206, 232, 237, 242, 245, 257; exoteric knowledge, 131; Ḥadīith, 197, 257; innovation, 180; learned persons, 146, 153; recitation of Qur'ān, 242
Sufyān ibn ʿUyayna, 193, 352, 354
Suhayb ibn Sinān, 371
Suhrawardī, Abū Ḥafṣ ʿUmar as-, 29, 30, 51, 57–60; texts, 332–74
Suhrawardī, Abū 'n-Najīb Diyā ad-Dīn ʿAbd al-Qāhir ibn ʿAbd Allāh as-, 58
Sulamī, Abū ʿAbd ar-Raḥmān as-, 41, 59
Sunna, 25, 35, 69, 230, 234, 241
Sunni Muslims, 35, 275, 279–80
Sūsī, Abū Yaʿqūb as-, 290
Sustenance of Hearts, The (Makkī), 33, 35, 37; text, 114–263

Taʿarruf (divine self-disclosure), 32
Tafakkur (reflection), 21
Tafsīr (exegesis), 16, 17–18, 19, 59, 349–50
Ṭanafīsī, 364
Taʿrīf (divine instruction), 32–33
Taʿwīl (symbolic interpretation), 59, 349–50
Taymī, Ibrāhīm at-, 193
Tayyāḥ, Abū 't-, 173–74
Thābit, Ḥabīb ibn Abī, 181
Thawbān ibn Ibrāhīm. *See* Dhū 'n-Nūn al-Miṣrī
Thomas Aquinas, 11
Tīnātī, Abū 'l-Khayr at-, 323–24
Tirmidhī, Muḥammad ibn Alī al-Ḥakīm at-, 24–25, 27, 36, 95, 101, 102–3
Traditionists, 67–68, 68–70, 72, 179–80
Treatise Explaining the Experiential Knowledge of God (Ghazālī), 50
Treatise of al-Qushayrī on Sufism, The (Qushayrī), 42–43, 61, 286; text, 286–93
Treatise on (Knowledge) from God (Ghazālī), 50
Truth *(haqq-al)*, 31, 84
Tustarī, ʿAbd Allāh Sahl at-, 25, 29, 192, 193, 196, 197–98, 202, 231, 253–54, 255, 362; ignorance, 255; learned persons, 147–48,

Other Volumes in This Series

Abraham Isaac Kook • THE LIGHTS OF PENITENCE, LIGHTS OF HOLINESS, THE MORAL PRINCIPLES, ESSAYS, LETTERS, AND POEMS
Abraham Miguel Cardozo • SELECTED WRITINGS
Albert and Thomas • SELECTED WRITINGS
Alphonsus de Liguori • SELECTED WRITINGS
Anchoritic Spirituality •ANCRENE WISSE AND ASSOCIATED WORKS
Angela of Foligno • COMPLETE WORKS
Angelic Spirituality • MEDIEVAL PERSPECTIVES ON THE WAYS OF ANGELS
Angelus Silesius • THE CHERUBINIC WANDERER
Anglo-Saxon Spirituality • SELECTED WRITINGS
Apocalyptic Spirituality • TREATISES AND LETTERS OF LACTANTIUS, ADSO OF MONTIER-EN-DER, JOACHIM OF FIORE, THE FRANCISCAN SPIRITUALS, SAVONAROLA
Athanasius • THE LIFE OF ANTONY, AND THE LETTER TO MARCELLINUS
Augustine of Hippo • SELECTED WRITINGS
Bernard of Clairvaux • SELECTED WORKS
Bérulle and the French School • SELECTED WRITINGS
Birgitta of Sweden • LIFE AND SELECTED REVELATIONS
Bonaventure • THE SOUL'S JOURNEY INTO GOD, THE TREE OF LIFE, THE LIFE OF ST. FRANCIS
Carthusian Spirituality • THE WRITINGS OF HUGH OF BALMA AND GUIGO DE PONTE
Catherine of Genoa • PURGATION AND PURGATORY, THE SPIRITUAL DIALOGUE
Catherine of Siena • THE DIALOGUE
Celtic Spirituality •
Classic Midrash, The • TANNAITIC COMMENTARIES ON THE BIBLE
Cloud of Unknowing, The •
Devotio Moderna • BASIC WRITINGS
Early Anabaptist Spirituality • SELECTED WRITINGS
Early Dominicans • SELECTED WRITINGS
Early Islamic Mysticism • SUFI, QUR'AN, MI'RAJ, POETIC AND THEOLOGICAL WRITINGS
Early Kabbalah, The •
Elijah Benamozegh • ISRAEL AND HUMANITY
Elisabeth of Schönau • THE COMPLETE WORKS
Emanuel Swedenborg • THE UNIVERSAL HUMAN AND SOUL-BODY INTERACTION
Ephrem the Syrian • HYMNS
Fakhruddin 'Iraqi • DIVINE FLASHES

Other Volumes in This Series

Francis and Clare • THE COMPLETE WORKS
Francis de Sales, Jane de Chantal • LETTERS OF SPIRITUAL DIRECTION
Francisco de Osuna • THE THIRD SPIRITUAL ALPHABET
George Herbert • THE COUNTRY PARSON, THE TEMPLE
Gertrude of Helfta • THE HERALD OF DIVINE LOVE
Gregory of Nyssa • THE LIFE OF MOSES
Gregory Palamas • THE TRIADS
Hadewijch • THE COMPLETE WORKS
Henry Suso • THE EXEMPLAR, WITH TWO GERMAN SERMONS
Hildegard of Bingen • SCIVIAS
Ibn 'Abbād of Ronda • LETTERS ON THE ṢŪFĪ PATH
Ibn Al'-Arabī • THE BEZELS OF WISDOM
Ibn 'Ata' Illah • THE BOOK OF WISDOM AND KWAJA ABDULLAH ANSARI: INTIMATE CONVERSATIONS
Ignatius of Loyola • SPIRITUAL EXERCISES AND SELECTED WORKS
Isaiah Horowitz • THE GENERATIONS OF ADAM
Jacob Boehme • THE WAY TO CHRIST
Jacopone da Todi • THE LAUDS
Jean Gerson • EARLY WORKS
Jeremy Taylor • SELECTED WORKS
Jewish Mystical Autobiographies • BOOK OF VISIONS AND BOOK OF SECRETS
Johann Arndt • TRUE CHRISTIANITY
Johannes Tauler • SERMONS
John Baptist de la Salle • THE SPIRITUALITY OF CHRISTIAN EDUCATION
John Calvin • WRITINGS ON PASTORAL PIETY
John Cassian • CONFERENCES
John and Charles Wesley • SELECTED WRITINGS AND HYMNS
John Climacus • THE LADDER OF DIVINE ASCENT
John Comenius • THE LABYRINTH OF THE WORLD AND THE PARADISE OF THE HEART
John of the Cross • SELECTED WRITINGS
John Donne • SELECTIONS FROM DIVINE POEMS, SERMONS, DEVOTIONS AND PRAYERS
John Henry Newman • SELECTED SERMONS
John Ruusbroec • THE SPIRITUAL ESPOUSALS AND OTHER WORKS
Julian of Norwich • SHOWINGS
Luis de León • THE NAMES OF CHRIST
Margaret Ebner • MAJOR WORKS
Marguerite Porete • THE MIRROR OF SIMPLE SOULS

Other Volumes in This Series

Maria Maddalena de' Pazzi • SELECTED REVELATIONS
Martin Luther • THEOLOGIA GERMANICA
Maximus Confessor • SELECTED WRITINGS
Mechthild of Magdeburg • THE FLOWING LIGHT OF THE GODHEAD
Meister Eckhart • THE ESSENTIAL SERMONS, COMMENTARIES, TREATISES AND DEFENSE
Meister Eckhart • TEACHER AND PREACHER
Menahem Nahum of Chernobyl • UPRIGHT PRACTICES, THE LIGHT OF THE EYES
Nahman of Bratslav • THE TALES
Native Mesoamerican Spirituality • ANCIENT MYTHS, DISCOURSES, STORIES, DOCTRINES, HYMNS, POEMS FROM THE AZTEC, YUCATEC, QUICHE-MAYA AND OTHER SACRED TRADITIONS
Native North American Spirituality of the Eastern Woodlands • SACRED MYTHS, DREAMS, VISIONS, SPEECHES, HEALING FORMULAS, RITUALS AND CEREMONIALS
Nicholas of Cusa • SELECTED SPIRITUAL WRITINGS
Nicodemos of the Holy Mountain • A HANDBOOK OF SPIRITUAL COUNSEL
Nil Sorsky • THE COMPLETE WRITINGS
Nizam ad-din Awliya • MORALS FOR THE HEART
Origen • AN EXHORTATION TO MARTYRDOM, PRAYER AND SELECTED WORKS
Philo of Alexandria • THE CONTEMPLATIVE LIFE, THE GIANTS, AND SELECTIONS
Pietists • SELECTED WRITINGS
Pilgrim's Tale, The •
Pseudo-Dionysius • THE COMPLETE WORKS
Pseudo-Macarius • THE FIFTY SPIRITUAL HOMILIES AND THE GREAT LETTER
Pursuit of Wisdom, The • AND OTHER WORKS BY THE AUTHOR OF THE CLOUD OF UNKNOWING
Quaker Spirituality • SELECTED WRITINGS
Rabbinic Stories •
Richard Rolle • THE ENGLISH WRITINGS
Richard of St. Victor • THE TWELVE PATRIARCHS, THE MYSTICAL ARK, BOOK THREE OF THE TRINITY
Robert Bellarmine • SPIRITUAL WRITINGS
Safed Spirituality • RULES OF MYSTICAL PIETY, THE BEGINNING OF WISDOM

Other Volumes in This Series

Shakers, The • TWO CENTURIES OF SPIRITUAL REFLECTION
Sharafuddin Maneri • THE HUNDRED LETTERS
Spirituality of the German Awakening, The •
Symeon the New Theologian • THE DISCOURSES
Talmud, The • SELECTED WRITINGS
Teresa of Avila • THE INTERIOR CASTLE
Theatine Spirituality • SELECTED WRITINGS
'Umar Ibn al-Fāriḍ • SUFI VERSE, SAINTLY LIFE
Valentin Weigel • SELECTED SPIRITUAL WRITINGS
Vincent de Paul and Louise de Marillac • RULES, CONFERENCES, AND WRITINGS
Walter Hilton • THE SCALE OF PERFECTION
William Law • A SERIOUS CALL TO A DEVOUT AND HOLY LIFE, THE SPIRIT OF LOVE
Zohar • THE BOOK OF ENLIGHTENMENT

The Classics of Western Spirituality is a ground-breaking collection of the original writings of more than 100 universally acknowledged teachers within the Catholic, Protestant, Eastern Orthodox, Jewish, Islamic, and Native American Indian traditions.